THE IMPERIAL WAR MUSEUM BOOK OF

THE WAR IN BURMA

Julian Thompson joined the Royal Marines a month after his eighteenth birthday and served for thirty-four years, retiring as Major General. His service, mainly in the Royal Marines Commandos, took him to seven continents. He commanded 3rd Commando Brigade, which carried out the initial landings to repossess the Falkland Islands in 1982 and fought most of the subsequent land battles.

He is now Visiting Professor in the Department of War Studies, King's College, London. He has presented a series of short Second World War commemorative films on BBC1. As well as writing books on military strategy, the Commandos and the Parachute Regiment, Julian Thompson has also written *The Imperial War Museum Book of Victory in Europe*, *The Imperial War Museum Book of War Behind Enemy Lines*, *The Imperial War Museum Book of the War at Sea* and *The Royal Marines*, and edited *The Imperial War Museum Book of Modern Warfare*.

THE IMPERIAL WAR MUSEUM BOOK OF

THE WAR IN BURMA

1942–45

A VITAL CONTRIBUTION TO VICTORY IN THE FAR EAST

Julian Thompson

PAN BOOKS

in association with

The Imperial War Museum

First published 2002 by Sidgwick & Jackson

This edition published 2003 by Pan Books
an imprint of Pan Macmillan Ltd
Pan Macmillan, 20 New Wharf Road, London N1 9RR
Basingstoke and Oxford
Associated companies throughout the world
www.panmacmillan.com

ISBN 0 330 48065 0

3 5 7 9 8 6 4 2

A CIP catalogue record for this book is available from
the British Library.

Typeset by SetSystems Ltd, Saffron Walden, Essex
Printed and bound in Great Britain by
Mackays of Chatham plc, Chatham, Kent

All Pan Macmillan titles are available from
www.panmacmillan.com
or from Bookpost by telephoning 01624 677237

Preface

This book is not a campaign study of the war in Burma. But, using the archive material in the Imperial War Museum, it aims to give the general reader some idea of what it was like to fight there both on the ground and in the air. As will become apparent, the Allied forces serving in Burma were among the most multiracial in the history of warfare. But the accounts I have included are overwhelmingly from the British, rather than the Indians, Gurkhas, Africans, Australians, Canadians, New Zealanders, Rhodesians, South Africans, Americans, Chinese and the host of others who fought in Burma, and who vastly outnumbered the British. This is because there are few accounts in the Imperial War Museum from other participants. Many of the Indian and African soldiers were illiterate, or, like the Chinese, can no longer be contacted. But fortunately the British served not only in all-British units, but also in the far greater number of Indian ones, as well as in the African divisions, so the accounts range widely across the experience of many non-British units; and the regard for their soldiers and pride in what their units achieved shine forth. Nearly as many Africans served in Burma as British soldiers. I hope what I have included in narratives by British officers in the two West African divisions, and one East African division, goes some way towards long-overdue recognition of the achievements of these soldiers, fighting someone else's war, in a strange land, against a formidable enemy, a very long way from home.

With the exception of one and a half chapters on the Chindits, and one other isolated story, I have concentrated entirely on the efforts of the main force army formations, which for my purposes includes the Commando Brigade because it was operating in a main force role. Contrary to the belief held to this day by many people, the war in Burma was won by 'standard' units and formations of many races, not by special forces, behind-the-lines operations, or even the Chindits. It was won in some of the bitterest fighting experienced by the Allies in the Second World War, against the toughest enemy they encountered. It was the longest and by far the biggest ground war fought by the British and Americans against the Japanese.

The war in Burma would not have been sustained, let alone won, without the efforts of the Allied navies, and the Royal Navy in particular, and of course by the Merchant Navy, which carried supplies thousands of miles across the Atlantic and Indian Oceans despite grave losses to U-boats. Space does not permit any accounts of the maritime war, which in the Indian Ocean alone deserves a book of its own. The air war was equally important, but I have compressed this into one chapter, because I wanted to give pride of place to the men who bore the brunt of the fighting, as they usually do, and without whom no campaign can be won: the soldiers of all races.

Quotations

The text contains many direct quotations from written documentary material and interview tapes. These are reproduced verbatim wherever possible, but obvious errors have been corrected and minor confusions clarified. It has not been thought necessary to indicate where quotations have been abridged.

Photographs

All the illustrations in this book have come from the Imperial War Museum Photographic Archive, and have been listed with their accession number in the list of illustrations.

Acknowledgements

As with my previous books in association with the Imperial War Museum it would not have been possible to write this one without the letters, diaries, accounts and taped interviews of the people I have quoted. My first acknowledgement must be to them. Their names are listed in the Index of Contributors, as are the names of copyright holders.

Next I must thank the senior members of the staff of the Imperial War Museum. Christopher Dowling, Head of the Department of Museum Services, who was encouraging throughout the project. Roderick Suddaby, Keeper of the Department of Documents, as always gave me much wise advice, and directed me to many interesting collections. I am also grateful to Margaret Brooks (Keeper of the Sound Archive), Brad King (Keeper of the Photographic Archive), and Richard Golland (Printed Books). I must also thank Peter Hart of the Sound Archive for allowing me to use extracts from his transcipts of interviews with members of the 2nd Battalion The Royal Norfolk Regiment describing their experiences in the Kohima battle. Richard McDonough provided much help and encouragement by directing me to recent acquisitions in the Sound Archive. Hilary Roberts, David Parry and the staff of the Photographic Archive were as ever a source of much sound advice and unfailingly willing help. Simon Robins, Steve Walton and everyone in the Department of Documents were tolerant and patient, and allowed me to join their 'coffee boat'; a source of welcome rest and refreshment.

I am grateful to the following publishers/authors/copyright holders for permission to quote from the published works listed below:

W. J. P. Aggett, *The Bloody Eleventh: History of the Devonshire Regiment*, Vol. III, *1915–1969* (The Devonshire and Dorset Regiment, 1995).

The Regimental Secretary, The Devonshire and Dorset Regiment, O. G. W. White, *Straight on to Tokyo: The War History of the 2nd Battalion The Dorsetshire Regiment (54th Foot)* (Gale & Polden, Aldershot, 1948).

HarperCollins, George Macdonald Fraser, *Quartered Safe out Here: A Recollection of the War in Burma*, HarperCollins 1992, copyright © George Macdonald Fraser 1992.

Regimental Association, 2nd (King Edward VII's Own) Ghoorka Rifles, G. R. Stevens, *History of the 2nd King Edward VII's Own Goorkha Rifles*, Vol II., *1921–1948* (Gale & Polden, Aldershot, 1952).

The Rt Hon. The Viscount Slim, Field Marshal the Viscount Slim, *Defeat into Victory* (Cassell & Company, 1956).

William Armstrong of Pan Macmillan has been most encouraging and supportive throughout. I am also grateful for the patient and wise advice I received from Ingrid Connell my editor and meticulous comment from Nicholas Blake, senior desk editor at Pan Macmillan; their work on my behalf is much appreciated, as in the expertise of Wilf Dickie the designer.

Without Jane Thompson's careful research, her eye for detail, ability to spot error, and editorial comment this book would never have been completed, let alone met the deadline.

Contents

List of Illustrations

All illustrations are courtesy of the Imperial War Museum.

1. Japanese troops enter Rangoon railway station, 7 March 1942. [HU 2773]
2. American air crew of Chennault's American Volunteer Air Group (AVG) with a Tomahawk aircraft taken in early 1942. [CF 27]
3. The message 'Plane Land Here Now' spelt out with parachutes. First Chindit expedition. [HU 88979]
4. A group of Chindits after being flown back to India from China or Fort Hertz at the end of the First Chindit Expedition. [HU 88978]
5. Elephants pass a Hurricane on a forward airstrip. [IND 3359]
6. One of the tunnels on the Maungdaw–Buthidaung Road in the Arakan. [HU 6258]
7. Sergeant of the 81st West African Division with his machet. [IND 3098]
8. A warning to jeep drivers. Picture taken in 1944, somewhere on the Assam–Burma frontier during the advance from Imphal. [IND 3131]
9. Naik Nand Singh of the 1st/11th Sikhs, greeted by his mother on return to his village after being awarded the Victoria Cross. [IND 3574]
10. Terrain in the Shenam Pass, 'Scraggy', after capture. [HU 88977]
11. Naik Agansing Rai VC of the 2nd/5th Royal Gurkha Rifles. [IND 4157]
12. Rifleman Manparsad Pun, of 3rd/2nd Gurkha Rifles, 25th Indian Division in the Arakan. [IND 4194]
13. Troops of 9th Royal Sussex, 72nd Infantry Brigade, British 36th Infantry Division during an advance along a jungle track. [SE 2152]
14. The 1st Queen's Own Cameron Highlanders bath in half oil drums. [SE 2115]
15. At 10.30 a.m. on 20 June 1944, the road to Imphal from Kohima is opened. Stuart Tanks of 33rd Corps meet the 1st/7th Dogra and Carabiniers, and the advance guard of 4th Corps. [HU 88980]
16. Ground crew arming a Hurribomber on a forward airstrip. [CF 196]
17. Two bombs fall away from a Hurribomber attacking a bridge on the Tiddim Road. [CF 176]
18. Brigadier Mike Calvert (centre), with two Chindits. [MH 7824]
19. Soldiers of the 11th East African Division enter Kalewa on the River Chindwin, in December 1944. [SE 1884]

List of Maps

Glossary

AP – Armour piercing (ammunition).

Bangalore Torpedo – A length of piping filled with explosive, used for blowing a gap in barbed-wire entanglements.

Beaufighter Mk VI – A British long-range fighter with crew of two. Armed with four 20mm cannon and six .303 in machine guns, and eight rockets.

Bren – The British light machine-gun of the Second World War and until the late 1950s. Fired a standard .303 in round from a 30-round magazine (usually loaded with 28 rounds).

Brigade Major (BM) – The senior operations officer of a brigade, de facto chief of staff.

Chagul – A canvas water bag. Keeps water marvellously cool in hot weather through condensation.

Chaung – Burmese for watercourse or minor river, could be as narrow as a ditch, or wide enough for small craft, particularly near the coast.

Commando – Refers to either the individual commando soldier or marine, or to the unit.

Corps – A formation of at least two divisions commanded by a lieutenant general.

CRA – Commander Royal Artillery.

CSM – Company sergeant major.

DCM – Distinguished Conduct Medal. Instituted in 1854 as the equivalent of the DSO for warrant officers, NCOs and soldiers of the army (and Royal Marines when under army command). Awarded for gallantry in action. Now discontinued.

DF – Defensive fire – mortar, artillery, or machine-gun fire by troops in defensive positions against attacking troops or patrols. Usually pre-registered on a number of key places, and numbered, so a particular DF can be called down quickly by reference to its number. Guns and mortars will be laid on the DF SOS when not engaged on other tasks. As its name implies, the DF SOS is the target deemed to be the most dangerous to the defenders.

direct fire – Weapons that have to be aimed directly at the target as opposed to indirect fire weapons such as mortars and artillery.

DSO – Distinguished Service Order. Instituted in 1886. Until the awards system was changed in 1994, it was a dual-role decoration, recognizing gallantry at a level just below that qualifying for the VC by junior officers, and exceptional leadership in battle by senior officers. Officers of all three services were and are eligible. Since 1994, it is far less prestigious, and awarded for successful command and leadership in 'operational' circumstances. What constitutes 'operations' is open to question, since DSOs appear to 'come up with the rations' after so-called operations when hardly a shot has been fired in anger.

DZ – dropping zone, the area chosen for landing by parachute troops, or on which supplies are to be dropped.

Flak – Slang for anti-aircraft fire, from the German for anti-aircraft gun, *fliegerabwehrkanone*.

FOB – Forward Observer Bombardment, a Royal Artillery officer who spotted for naval guns bombarding shore targets. His party consisted of Royal Naval telegraphists (the RN name for a radio operator), to communicate with the supporting ships.

FOO – Forward Observation Officer, an artillery officer who directs artillery fire. Normally one with each forward rifle company and provided by artillery battery supporting the infantry battalion.

Grant – See Lee-Grant.

GSO – General Staff Officer, a staff officer who dealt with General (G) Staff matters (operations, intelligence, planning, and staff duties), as opposed to personnel (A, short for Adjutant General's Staff), or logistic matters (Q, short for Quartermaster General's Staff). The grades were GSO 1 (Lieutenant Colonel), GSO 2 (Major), and GSO 3 (Captain).

Havildar, Havildar Major – See ranks.

HE – High explosive.

Howitzer 3.7in – A mountain gun, designed for operating in country impassable for wheeled vehicles, primarily the North-West Frontier of India. Dismantled into nine parts, breech, chase, cradle, split trail, carriage and two hard-rimmed wheels, it could be carried by eight mules. It could also be modified to be towed by a jeep, by fitting pneumatic tyres and a smaller shield. The shell weighed 20lb, and the gun had a maximum range of 7,000 yards. (A 25pdr's maximum range was 12,500 yards with a 25lb shell.)

Hurribomber – There were two fighter-bomber versions of the Hurricane Mk II, both with a 1,000lb bomb load; the Mk II C had four 20mm cannon, and the tank-buster Mk II D had two 40mm cannon.

Hurricane Mk II – A British single-engine monoplane, of Battle of Britain fame. Originally equipped with eight .303in machine-guns. Below 10,000 feet it was less manoeuvrable than the Japanese Zero, but above 20,000 feet proved superior. Also developed as a highly successful fighter bomber (see Hurribomber).

INA – Indian National Army, formed from Indian soldiers who were persuaded to fight for the Japanese. See Chapter 5 for a detailed explanation.

Jemedar – See ranks.

lantana – A particularly thick scrub resembling raspberry canes. It is impossible to advance through without cutting, and offers good concealment to the defender. The Japanese made skilful use of it.

Lance Naik – See ranks.

LCA – Landing Craft Assault, maximum load an infantry platoon, designed to be carried at a ship's lifeboat davits, and to land infantry in a beach assault. It was armoured to give its passengers some protection against small arms fire and shrapnel, but not air-burst.

Lee-Grant – American-built M3 tank named after two American Civil War generals, the Confederate General Lee and the Union General Grant, and sometimes called Lee in the USA and Grant in the British army. Had a 37mm gun in the turret, and a 75mm (main armament) gun in a sponson in the hull. This unusual arrangement meant that to engage a target using the main armament the tank had to expose its hull, and as the sponson gun had a very limited traverse the whole tank had to be swivelled to engage targets outside this arc.

Liberator Mk II – American B-24 four-engined heavy bomber, with a crew of eight.

Lightning P.38 – American twin-engine fighter, with a crew of one, and four .50 in and one 20mm cannon. A very effective low-level attack aircraft.

LZ – Landing Zone, originally an area chosen for glider landings.

MC – Military Cross. Instituted in 1914, it was awarded to army officers of the rank of major and below, and warrant officers, for gallantry in action. Now all ranks are eligible.

Mitchell – An American B-25 twin-engined medium bomber, with a crew of five. Good at attacking ground targets in support of ground troops.

MM – Military Medal. Instituted in 1916, it was awarded to army NCOs and soldiers for gallantry in action. Now discontinued; see MC.

Mohawk – An American single-engine fighter, an earlier version of the Tomahawk, with six .303in guns. It was obsolete by 1941, but retained by the RAF for use in India and Burma.

Mosquito Mk IV – Twin-engine light bomber, or high-level reconnaissance aircraft, with a crew of two. Almost as fast as a Spitfire, and much faster than any other aircraft, Allied or enemy.

MTB – Motor Torpedo Boat, a small, fast vessel mainly armed with torpedoes.

Naik – See ranks.

NCO – Non-commissioned officer; from lance-corporal to colour or staff sergeant. See also warrant officer.

OP – Observation post.

PIAT – Projector Infantry Anti-Tank. The hand-held anti-tank weapon of the British Second World War infantryman from about mid-1942 on, it consisted of a powerful spring, mounted in a tube which threw a hollow-charge projectile, effective up to 100 yards.

Ranks – Indian Army ranks below second lieutenant were:

Indian Army	Typical job	British army equivalent
Subedar Major	Senior VCO (see VCO)	None
Subedar	Company 2ic or platoon commander	None
Jemedar	Platoon commander	None
Havildar Major	Company Sergeant Major (CSM)	CSM
Havildar	Platoon Sergeant	Sergeant
Naik	Section commander	Corporal
Lance Naik	Section 2ic	Lance Corporal
Sepoy/Rifleman		Private

The word sepoy is an eighteenth-century British misspelling of the Persian word *sipāhī* from the Persian word *sipāh* meaning army.

RAP – Regimental Aid Post, the place where the Medical Officer (MO) of a battalion, or equivalent-size unit, set up his aid post. Usually the requirement here was to administer 'sophisticated first aid' to stabilize the casualty sufficiently to enable him to survive the next stage of evacuation; in 'conventional' warfare, this was usually within hours.

Regiment – Originally a regiment was of horse, dragoons (mounted infantry) or foot, and raised by command of King, and later Parliament, and named after its colonel, originally a royal appointee. The regiment has become the basic organization of the British army and Indian Army, for armour, artillery, engineers, signals, army air corps, and logistic units equivalent to battalions of those arms in other armies. In the case of the infantry, the British or Indian Army battalion belongs to a regiment, of which there may be one or more battalions.

The Indian Army reorganization of 1922 formed infantry regiments of up to six battalions each. There were several regiments with the same title, depending on the origin of their soldiers, and these were numbered. Hence the 5th/9th Jat Regiment is the 5th Battalion of the 9th Jat Regiment, whose soldiers are Jats, and the 1/2nd Goorkha Rifles is the 1st Battalion of the 2nd Goorkha Rifles, whose soldiers are Gurkhas (spelt Goorkha by this regiment).

In 1923 many British cavalry regiments were amalgamated, retaining both their old numbers; hence the 9th/12th Lancers is the combination of the 9th and the 12th Lancers, *not* the 9th battalion of the 12th Lancers.

Sapper – The equivalent of private in the Royal Engineers; also a name for all engineers.

SEAC – South East Asia Command. The Supreme Allied Commander SEAC, Admiral Mountbatten, was responsible directly to the British Chiefs of Staff in London, and through them to the Combined British and US Chiefs of Staff for all operations by land, sea, and air in Burma, Malaya, and Sumatra, and for clandestine operations in Siam and French Indo-China.

Sepoy – See ranks.

Sherman – A US-built tank with the same chassis as the Lee-Grant, but with the main armament 75mm gun on top of the hull in the conventional way. It also carried a co-axial machine-gun in the turret and a machine-gun in a ball mounting in the front glacis (sloping) plate of the hull.

Spitfire Mk VIII – The single-engine fighter of Battle of Britain fame. Proved superior to Japanese Zero and Oscar fighters.

Start Line – A line in the ground, usually a natural feature, stream, bank, or fence, preferably at ninety degrees to the axis of advance, which marks the start line for the attack and is crossed at H-Hour in attack formation. Can be marked by tape if there is no natural feature which lends itself to being used as a start line.

Sten gun – A cheap, mass-produced sub-machine-gun of British design. It fired 9mm ammunition, and had a 32-round magazine. Ineffective except at close quarters; it was inaccurate and the round had poor penetrating power. Because of its propensity to fire by mistake, it was sometimes more dangerous to its owner and those standing around than to the enemy.

Subedar, Subedar Major – See ranks.

Tac HQ – Tactical Headquarters, a small group including the CO, or brigade commander forward of the main HQ.

Vickers Medium Machine-gun – A First World War vintage belt-fed, water-cooled machine-gun, rate of fire 500 rounds per minute. Maximum range with Mark VIIIZ ammunition, 4,500 yards.

VC – Victoria Cross, the highest British award for bravery in the face of the enemy. To date, in the 145 years since its inception by Queen Victoria for conspicuous bravery during the Crimean War of 1854–56, only 1,354 VCs have been awarded, including a handful of double VCs, five civilians under military command, and the one presented to the American Unknown Warrior at Arlington. This figure includes the many awarded to Imperial, Commonwealth, and Dominion servicemen.

VCO – Viceroy's Commissioned Officer. There were three kinds of commissioned officer in the Indian Army of the time: British officers and Indian officers with the King's Commission who, in peacetime, or when not in battle or on operations, lived in the Officer's Mess, and Viceroy's Commissioned Officers. VCOs were commissioned from the ranks of the regiment or battalion, had a Viceroy's Commission, and were junior to all King's Commissioned officers of any rank. Their nearest equivalent in the British army was warrant officer, but VCOs had much higher status, commanded platoons, were second-in-command of companies, and lived in their own mess. They were addressed as Subedar Sahib, or Jemedar Sahib by all ranks including by King's Commissioned officers. The subedar major was the senior VCO in an Indian Army battalion, and had probably joined as a young sepoy or rifleman at about the same time as the CO joined as a subaltern. He was the CO's right-hand man and adviser on all regimental matters such as customs, promotions, recruiting, how well, or otherwise, the British officers (especially the younger ones) were relating to their Indian soldiers, and religion.

Vengeance – A single-engined light bomber of US design, with a crew of two, and six .303 in machine-guns. The bomb load was 1,500 lb.

Warrant Officer – Since 1913 there have been two classes of Warrant Officer in the British army: WOII, typically a company/squadron sergeant major, and WOI, usually regimental sergeant major, of which there is generally only one in each battalion, regiment, or commando. Just before the Second World War a WOIII, or platoon sergeant major grade, was created to command platoons or troops, but it was not a success and was allowed to lapse.

A WO has a warrant signed by a government minister or representative of the Army Council, unlike a commissioned officer (of the rank of second lieutenant and above), who has a King's or Queen's commission. Those junior to WOIs and WOIIs in rank address them as sir and Mr (Surname); those superior to them formally refer to them as Mr (Surname) but often address and refer to them as Sergeant Major or RSM. Unlike VCOs, they are not saluted by those junior to them, and live in the WOs' and Sergeants' Mess.

Chronology of Events

The chronology of the war in Burma is given in outline below, as well as some of the major events in other theatres in order to assist the reader in placing what was happening in Burma in context.

1941

7 December	Japanese air strikes on Pearl Harbor, Hawaii
8 December	Japanese land in Malaya
14 December	Japanese capture Victoria Point on southern tip of Burma
18–19 December	Japanese attack Hong Kong Island from mainland
25 December	Hong Kong falls

1942

15 January	Japanese *Fifteenth Army* invades Burma from Siam
31 January	Japanese capture Moulmein
15 February	Singapore surrenders
23 February	Sittang Bridge blown
5 March	General Sir Harold Alexander becomes GOC Burma
7 March	Rangoon falls to Japanese, the British retreat to the north and eventually to India begins
6–7 March	Battle at Pegu
16 March	Lieutenant General Slim arrives in Burma and forms BURCORPS made up of 17th Indian Division, 1st Burma Division, and 7th Armoured Brigade
29–31 March	Battle at Shwedaung
17–19 April	Battle at Yenangyaung and destruction of oil fields by British engineers
29 April	Japanese occupy and cut Burma Road
30 April	British withdraw beyond Irrawaddy River
1 May	Japanese capture Mandalay
10 May	Battle at Shwegyin, British pull back across the Chindwin, and back into India

| 23 October to 4 November | North Africa – Battle of Alamein turns the tide against the Germans in the West |
| mid December | First Arakan campaign begins |

1943

14 February	Wingate's First Chindit Expedition crosses the Chindwin River into Burma
17 March	Japanese counterattack on Arakan Front
5 April	Lieutenant General Slim's 15th Corps takes command of Arakan campaign
18 April	Chindits cross the Irrawaddy River
11 May	Failure of First Arakan campaign ending with the British withdrawal from Maungdaw
21 May	General Irwin replaced by General Giffard as Commander-in-Chief Eastern Command
18 June	General Sir Archibald Wavell appointed Viceroy of India, and General Sir Claude Auchinleck takes over as Commander-in-Chief India
25 August	Lord Louis Mountbatten appointed Supreme Allied Commander South East Asia, followed by reorganization including: General Giffard appointed Commander-in-Chief 11th Army Group Lieutenant General Slim appointed GOC Fourteenth Army Lieutenant General Christison takes over 15th Corps from Slim
30 November	Second Arakan offensive begins

1944

9 January	British capture Maungdaw in the Arakan
9 February	Japanese offensive in Arakan begins
5 February	Wingate's Second Chindit Expedition begins with Brigadier Fergusson's 16th Brigade starting the long march towards Indaw from the Ledo Road
13–25 February	Battle of the Admin Box in the Arakan. British clear the Ngakyedauk Pass
1 March	Fergusson's 16th Brigade crosses the Chindwin River
5 March	Calvert's 77th Brigade flown into Broadway
15 March	Japanese advance to seize Imphal and Kohima
24 March	Wingate killed in aircraft crash
29 March	Siege of Imphal begins
4 April	Japanese assault on Kohima starts
14 April	British 2nd Division breaks through to defenders of Kohima
3 May	Key ground overlooking Maungdaw–Buthidaung road in the Arakan taken by 15th Corps

16 May	Last Japanese troops cleared from Kohima Ridge
6 June	In Europe – Allied landings in Normandy
22 June	Road from Kohima to Imphal opened
26 June	Calvert's 77th Brigade captures Mogaung
30 July	Masters's 111th Brigade flown out of Burma
August	15th Corps renews its attack in the Arakan
25 August	In Europe – Paris liberated by Allies
27 August	Last Chindits flown out of Burma
17 September	In Europe – start of Operation MARKET GARDEN including Battle of Arnhem in Holland
2 December	Fourteenth Army, having advanced from Imphal, takes Kalewa on the Chindwin River, and proceeds to cross
19 December	Fourteenth Army begins the advance to the Irrawaddy

1945

3 January	15th Corps occupy Akyab in the Arakan
10 January	Fourteenth Army takes Shwebo
12 January	15th Corps attacks at Myebon in the Arakan
22 January	Landings at Kangaw in the Arakan and subsequent battle
12 February	Fourteenth Army begins Irrawaddy crossings
20 February	Fourteenth Army begins to advance to Mandalay
4 March	Meiktila captured by Fourteenth Army
9 March	Fourteenth Army enters Mandalay
15 March	Japanese counterattack at Meiktila
21 March	Fourteenth Army clears Mandalay
23 March	In Europe – Montgomery's 21st Army Group crosses the Rhine
26 April	Toungoo captured
2 May	In Europe – British 6th Airborne Division meets Russians at Wismar on the Baltic
2 May	Seaborne assault on Rangoon
	Fourteenth Army reaches Pegu
4 May	In Europe – enemy forces in north-west Germany surrender to Montgomery
7 May	In Europe – all German forces surrender to Allies
June	Mopping up Burma
July/August	Japanese break-out operations in Burma – attempting to reach Thailand
6 August	First atomic bomb dropped, on Hiroshima
9 August	Second atomic bomb dropped, on Nagasaki
14 August	Japanese surrender

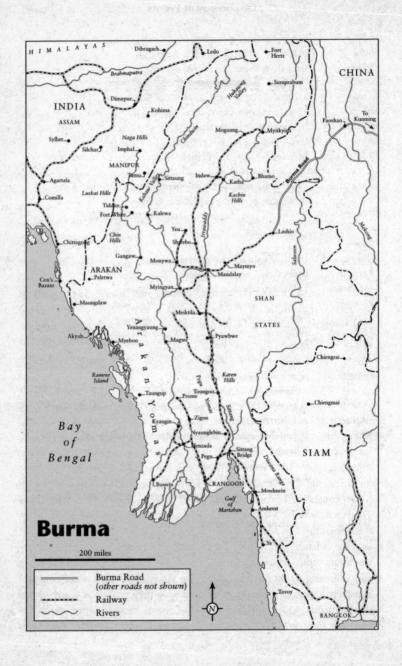

Burma

200 miles

| | Burma Road
(*other roads not shown*) |
| --- | --- |
| | Railway |
| | Rivers |

N

1

The Longest Retreat

At 0530 in the morning, as the first pallid hint of dawn appeared in the eastern sky, it happened – from the direction of the river, from Pagoda Hill, there came the reverberating roar of three enormous explosions and on the instant we realised that the bridge over the Sittang River had been blown up and our life-line cut.

Captain Kinloch, the adjutant of the 1st Battalion 3rd Gurkha Rifles, and his battalion were now cut off on the enemy side of a swiftly flowing river, 550 yards wide at the bridge, opening out to over 1,000 yards to the north and south of it. The premature demolition of the Sittang Bridge was a devastating blow, not only to the majority of the fighting troops in the 17th Indian Infantry Division, which included 1st/3rd Gurkhas, but also to any hope of holding Rangoon and southern Burma.

The events leading up to Captain Kinloch's predicament began on 14 December 1941, when the Japanese captured Victoria Point on the southern tip of Burma. By this time the Japanese had invested Hong Kong and invaded Malaya. A month before the fall of Singapore, the Japanese had seized airfields from which to support operations in Burma, at Mergui, Victoria Point, and Tavoy in Tenasserim, the strip of Burma in the Kra Isthmus. Following this, the Japanese *Fifteenth Army*, consisting of the *33rd* and *55th Divisions*, deployed in Siam (now Thailand), waiting for the moment to advance to seize Rangoon, when their operations in Malaya were nearing completion.

The defenders of Hong Kong held out honourably against overwhelming odds until Christmas Day 1941, suffering 4,000 casualties and inflicting 3,000 on the enemy. In Malaya the Allies were comprehensively trounced in a series of battles as they withdrew south down the peninsula. On 15 February 1942, General Percival surrendered the allegedly impregnable fortress of Singapore to the Japanese. The Allies lost 130,000 prisoners, far more than the total number of Japanese in the campaign.

The entry of Japan into the Second World War found the defence of Burma woefully unprepared. On 12 December 1941, five days after the Japanese attack on Pearl Harbor, General Sir Archibald Wavell, Commander-in-Chief India, finally persuaded Winston Churchill that Burma should be part of his bailiwick. Since August 1940, Burma had been under command of the Commander-in-Chief Far East. As the Far East was, in the British government's planning, well down the priority list for all manner of warfighting equipment, Burma, as an appendage to that theatre, was so near the bottom as to be almost out of sight. Until 1941 the garrison of Burma consisted of two British battalions, four locally recruited battalions of Burma Rifles, and six battalions of the Burma Frontier Force (originally the Burma Military Police); the first priority of all these troops was internal security.

'Peacetime soldiering in Burma was a lot of fun', wrote Lieutenant (later Lieutenant Colonel) Scott, attached to the Burma Frontier Force stationed at Pyawbwe, 250 miles north of Rangoon.

> We lived well at Pyawbwe. The Colonel [Lieutenant Colonel 'Hughie' Childers] had a lovely bungalow, and in fact all Pyawbwe belonged to him. Using his men as labourers he excavated a lake, indeed a series of lakes, which filled up with water during the monsoon, and remained full throughout the long dry season.
>
> Hughie and Gladys [the Colonel's wife] dressed for dinner every night, even when dining on their own.

No invasion threat from the east was foreseen; the terrain, jungle and mountains, was thought to be too difficult for any invader to traverse. Although strategically Burma was an outpost for the defence of India, no railways and only one underdeveloped road connected the two countries; the section from Imphal to Kalewa, some 185 miles, was a mixture of cart track and bridleway. Within the country the main arteries, of which there were few, generally ran north–south. Waterways were the main form of transport. The railway ran up the centre of Burma from Rangoon to Mandalay, where it branched off to Lashio, Myitkyina (pronounced Mishinaa) and Ye-U. A motor road connected Rangoon with Lashio, and northwards to join the Burma Road. This was the line of communication used by the Americans to supply the

Chinese, who had been fighting the Japanese since 1937. From Mandalay an all-weather road led to Myitkyina, and unmetalled roads to Sumprabum and Mogaung.

Burma is a large country, and if imposed on a map of Europe, Fort Hertz in the extreme north would be in the middle of the North Sea, Mandalay near Paris, Rangoon where the Pyrenees meet the Mediterranean, and Moulmein on Marseilles. Victoria Point at the southern end of the long finger of Tenasserim would be three-quarters of the way across the Mediterranean. The country is surrounded on three sides by mountain ranges covered in thick jungle. Four great rivers flow south into the Bay of Bengal. The Irrawaddy, and its major tributary the Chindwin, rise in the Himalayas to the north; to the east flow the Sittang and the Salween. All have numerous tributaries, most of which were a serious obstacle to movement. The valleys in central Burma open out into thickly wooded plains, dotted with low hills. In the flatter areas Burmese peasants cultivated rice in paddy fields. In the Irrawaddy valley there are large stretches of open paddy, millet and groundnut fields, and clumps of toddy palm trees. South of Mandalay and Shwebo the country is arid, with sparse vegetation. Between the Irrawaddy and Sittang Rivers lie the jungle hills of the Pegu Yomas. The Arakan Yomas range, rising to 3,000 feet, separates Burma from its west coast region, the Arakan. Here, as elsewhere in Burma, the flat river valleys are intersected by *chaungs* (streams) and rice paddy. The valleys are passable to vehicles in dry weather if the banks round the paddy are flattened. But in the heavy monsoon rains the muddy fields are impassable to wheels or tracks, and the chaungs flood, overflowing their banks. Near the coast they are fringed with mangrove swamps, so ferrying men and stores in craft is the only practicable way of crossing. In the Arakan the steep razor-backed hills are covered in dense forest. South Burma, Tenasserim, from the lower Salween to Victoria Point on the Kra Isthmus, is tropical rainforest.

In the cold weather, from mid-October to March, the climate is perfect, but temperatures rise in April and May and the heat strikes like an open oven with high humidity. The monsoon arrives in mid-May and lasts until about mid-September, enveloping the whole of Burma and Assam, except for the dry zone around Mandalay and Meiktila (pronounced Miketiller). During the monsoon malaria and dysentery flourish; the rivers swell; valleys and flat areas flood; thick cloud, thunderstorms, and turbulence make flying hazardous. In one year, 1943–44, British and other Allied troops recorded 250,000 cases of malaria and dysentery.

The Burmans, the indigenous Burmese, lived mainly in the central part of the country between Mandalay and the sea. James Lunt, who as a young officer was seconded (on loan) from the British army to the Burma Rifles, described them:

> They were a curious mixture of kindliness and savagery, usually docile but easily roused to a frenzy. Brave as individuals, they disliked discipline and saw no shame in running away to fight another day . . . With few exceptions their political leaders were venal, self-seeking and corrupt. If it was difficult to dislike the average Burmese, it was just as difficult to trust him. He was completely his own man.[1]

The Burmese deeply resented British rule, and detested the thousands of Indians brought in by the British as labourers on the railways and other public works. Many Indians and Chinese had cornered sections of the economy, including the rice trade, and made fortunes for themselves in the process. Before the arrival of the British, the Burmese had persecuted the Karens, Shans, Kachins, and Chins who lived in the hills and mountains to the east, north, and west of Central Burma, and, since independence in 1947, have continued to do so.

During 1941, the troop level in Burma was increased by raising more battalions of Burma Rifles, forming the 1st Burma Division, and sending in two Indian infantry brigades. Among the preparations for war made by the government of Burma was the formation of reconnaissance battalions from the Burma Frontier Force (BFF). Lieutenant Scott was tasked with the infantry training of the newly formed reconnaissance battalion of Frontier Force 4 (FF 4). The BFF had always been composed largely of Indians and Gurkhas who were domiciled in Burma, mostly the descendants of Indian soldiers who had formed the majority of the force with which the British had conquered the country, or of men who had served in the Burma Military Police, the forerunner of the BFF. These, with Punjabis, Sikhs, Kachins, and Karens, were recruited for the expanded force. The Burma Rifles had consisted exclusively of Karens, Kachins, and Chins, with British officers; the Burmans were considered unsuitable for military service, as being neither loyal nor martial enough. Although under political pressure some were recruited when the Burma

Rifles were expanded, most proved unreliable and even treacherous when put to the test of battle.

The role of FF 4 was to provide a screen to report on enemy movement near the border with Siam. Scott, now a captain, was positioned on a ridge overlooking the Salween River: 'It was at the RIDGE that we heard the fateful news that the Japanese had entered the war, and it was not until I heard this news that I fully realised just how far we were from help if anything happened.'

Following the Japanese invasion of Malaya on 8 December 1941, two more Indian infantry brigades were sent to Burma, and two Indian Divisional Headquarters, the 14th (not due to arrive until April) and the 17th, which had originally been destined for Malaya. The Japanese invasion found Burma defended by 1st Burma Division and 17th Indian Division, under the overall command of Lieutenant General T. J. Hutton. He deployed 1st Burma Division in central Burma to cover the routes in from the east from the Mekong Valley where it flows along the Burma–Indo-China border. The 17th Indian Division was ordered to hold the line of the Salween River and cover Rangoon. The soldiers in 17th Indian Division were of better quality than those in the Burma Division, but were not well trained for the conditions in which they found themselves. The principal cause was the 'milking' of battalions of experienced officers and NCOs to provide replacements in Indian units in the Middle East, and in training centres to train the hugely expanded Indian Army.[2] (The old Indian Army of pre-independence days was 'a thing apart' and the reader unfamiliar with it may find the experiences of John Randle, a young officer with the 7th Battalion 10th Baluch Regiment, which he relates in Appendix A, both interesting and informative.)

The problems faced by many Indian Army units are vividly illustrated by Philip Mason in his book *A Matter of Honour*:

The 1st/11th Sikh Regiment had been on the north-west frontier of India for the first two years of the War and had been drained of their best officers, NCOs, and men for battalions overseas. It was not until December 23rd 1941 that they were ordered to Jhansi for training with the 63rd Brigade which was going overseas. Hardly anyone, officer or man, had seen a three-inch or two-inch mortar, a bren gun or anti-tank rifle, a radio set or armoured carrier; there was not enough of such equipment for troops on the frontier. Six days before the move they had to send away another draft; one British officer, two Viceroy's Commissioned Officers and a hundred men. On arrival at Jhansi, they were told that they would have six months to train, but within a few days were suddenly ordered to mobilise on February 1st. They were made up to full strength by a draft of 400 recruits, mostly with only five months service; they had to form specialised groups – an anti-tank platoon, an anti-aircraft platoon, a pioneer platoon – to supply drivers for Brigade and Battalion Headquarters; above all to provide signallers. Their rifle companies were left with inexperienced officers, untried NCOs and recruits. There were not more than 20 trained men to a company. Within a fortnight they were on their way to Burma; they unpacked their new weapons in the ship and fired them over the stern as their only practice. They were soon in action; they were bombed and shelled, had to retreat again and again without any opportunity for rests, and were under great strain and badly shaken when they were ordered to charge the Japanese with the bayonet. This they did successfully, driving them off their ground, but were too inexperienced to maintain cohesion after the charge. Only B Company managed to retain any organised control.

Others were mixed up and did not know what they were supposed to do. The Battalion had marched and fought and fought again with practically no food or sleep for four days. Now they snatched three days in which they could rest, clean up, re-organise and do some training. The men soon recovered and their wonderful spirit gradually returned. They were all firmly determined that the chaos of the past would not be repeated and it never was.

It has to be recorded that in those first terrible days two VCOs and 24 men surrendered and deserted.[3]

This account, which probably errs on the side of understatement, particularly when describing the state of morale in the battalion, should be remembered when the exploits of the battalion are described in later chapters. As Lieutenant General Hutton wrote some years later:

For those who do not know the Indian Army, it should be realised that it was recruited from almost illiterate peasants. Its efficiency depended on long training, complete confidence in its British and Indian officers, and expertise in the use of weapons and equipment.

Given these conditions it was magnificent, but lacking them was no match for the Japanese or indeed any other trained army.

Although yeomen rather than peasants is probably a more accurate description of the class of men recruited by the Indian Army, Hutton rightly emphasizes training as the key to success. No army of any race, even composed of the most literate and intelligent men in the world, can stand for long against a trained army, unless it is itself trained properly, and has that difficult to define attribute, cohesion.

Japanese divisions were commanded by a lieutenant general, with the infantry group commanded by a major general. The latter could command a part of the division as a separate task force when it was deemed tactically necessary to operate the formation in two parts, which the Japanese frequently did. A division consisted of three regiments, each commanded by a colonel, and so corresponded to a British brigade, but at around 4,000 strong was larger than the British infantry brigade of the time. A regiment had three battalions, each of four companies; this was about one and a half times the size of the British equivalent. Following the practice in the British Official Histories, Japanese units and formations in this book are numbered in italics.

As well as the guns in the divisional artillery regiment, the infantry had their own regimental and battalion guns, often used in the direct fire role, notably at roadblocks. The Japanese were trained to fight with their fifteen-inch bayonet fixed to the .256in calibre rifle at all times in order to instil fear into their enemy. On the whole they were not particularly good shots, and shooting with a fixed bayonet does nothing for one's marksmanship. They were equipped with a very efficient grenade discharger which threw a 1lb 12oz shell out to around 700 yards, accurately and effectively. They had efficient medical units sited well forward so that sick and wounded could be returned to battle as quickly as possible.

The Japanese had not suffered the ghastly conditions of life on the Western Front in the First World War, and held simple beliefs in the glory of war. Their infantry especially was recruited from the rural population, whose tough farmers made excellent soldiers. It would be erroneous to imagine them as uneducated peasants, for the standard of schooling in Japan was high. They were indoctrinated to believe that they were the toughest race in the world, and that death was to be expected not feared. Unlike in many armies, the best men went into the infantry, recognizing that an infantryman's job demands not only more fortitude than any other, but more intelligence as well – many tasks undertaken by gunners, tank crews and the like are mechanistic and can be learned by rote. Every infantryman is an individual, and has to master an extensive range of skills – something that most Western armies fail to recognize.

Contrary to what was believed at the time, and by some people ever since, the Japanese had neither trained for, nor fought in, the jungle before the invasion of Malaya. They had, however, conducted extensive clandestine reconnaissance for years, and had made thorough preparations in the form of maps, terrain reports, and even a pamphlet issued to all troops to warn them what to expect. The key to the Japanese success was the high standard of training and hardihood of all their soldiers. Long marches and gruelling field exercises had turned them into superb light infantry, able to cover long distances on foot over rough terrain, carrying heavy loads. Their transport for the opening phases of the campaign was restricted to pack animals, and for much of the rest of the time in Burma, animals played a major part in their army; consequently, the Japanese were able to operate off roads, along jungle paths. Hardy, frugal, and ruthless, they were a formidable enemy. Surrender was unthinkable. Death either at the hands of the enemy or by one's own was the only honourable exit from the fight. Prisoners were regarded with contempt and as expendable, and treated accordingly. Lieutenant General Sir Ian Hamilton, a very experienced soldier, wrote about the Japanese soldiers after accompanying the Japanese army as the British observer in the Russo-Japanese War: '. . . . brave as lions, their constant ruling is to do their duty by their ancestors and their Emperor'.[4] His report had been long forgotten by the time the British encountered the Japanese in battle, and their preconceived notions of the enemy as inferior suffered a severe shock. They found that man for man the Japanese were better soldiers than the Germans.

Orders in the face of impending disaster in Burma to British and Indian troops to 'fight to the last man and last round' were obeyed more in the breach than in the observance. There were isolated cases where British soldiers, and in particular Gurkhas, sold their lives dearly rather than surrender. But more often troops were defeated psychologically long before they ran out of ammunition, and in some cases when they even outnumbered the enemy. With the Japanese it was very different. John Masters, who fought in Burma, wrote of them:

It is the fashion to dismiss their courage as fanaticism but this only begs the question. They believed in something and were willing to die for it, for any smallest detail that would help to achieve it. What else is bravery? They pressed home their attacks when no other troops in the world would have done so, when all hope of success was gone; except that it never really is, for who can know what the enemy has suffered, what is his state of mind? The Japanese simply came on, using all their skill and rage, until they were stopped by death. In defence they held their ground with a furious tenacity that never faltered. They had to be killed, company by company, squad by squad, man by man to the last.

By 1944 [the period he was writing about] many scores of thousands of Allied soldiers had fallen unwounded into enemy hands as prisoners, because our philosophy and history have taught us to accept the idea of surrender. By 1944 the number of Japanese captured unwounded in all theatres of war, probably did not total one hundred. On the Burma front it was about six.

For the rest, they wrote beautiful little poems in their diaries, and practised bayonet work on their prisoners. Frugal and bestial, barbarous and brave, artistic and brutal, they were the *dushman* [enemy], and we now set about, in all seriousness, the task of killing every one of them.[5]

By the end of the campaign in Burma in August 1945, about 185,000 Japanese had been killed, and some 1,700 taken prisoner, of whom only 400 were physically fit – the remainder were wounded or desperately ill. No regular officers surrendered. The few officers that did were not regulars and were all majors or below. Once captured, for the first week every prisoner tried to commit suicide, using whatever means they had to hand. Captain White saw a 'Japanese prisoner who had cut his own throat with the jagged edge of a bully-beef tin lid. He was a soldier, not an officer.' If prisoners survived, they cooperated with their interrogators, not through cowardice, but because no one had ever instructed them what to do in these circumstances, since it had never occurred to their senior commanders that any Japanese soldier would allow himself to be taken alive.[6]

*

The series of fateful events leading up to the disastrous Sittang battle, with which we started, were caused by attempting to hold too far forward and underestimating the enemy. The 17th Indian Division, comprising the 16th, 46th, and 48th Indian Infantry Brigades, with sapper and gunner support, commanded by Major General 'Jackie' Smyth VC, had been committed to the defence of southern Burma. With the exception of the 2nd Battalions of the King's Own Yorkshire Light Infantry (KOYLI) and Duke of Wellington's Regiment (Dukes), all the infantry, artillery, and engineers in the division were Gurkha or Indian. The Japanese entered southern Burma from Siam, and after savage fighting their *55th Division*, in a series of fast outflanking moves, nearly enveloped 17th Division holding a long front along the Salween. Second Lieutenant John Randle's battalion, 7th/10th Baluch, saw its first action here:

> We arrived in middle of an air raid at Rangoon, and moved by train to lower Burma in the general area east of the Sittang and west of the Salween. The part we went to was rubber not jungle, and we were used to the vast open plains of our training area in India. I like trees, but in rubber plantations, with no horizon, it is a bit depressing and confining.
>
> The Japs had barely started their offensive, we guarded bridges, then deployed on the West Bank of the Salween, before pulling back to Kuzeik on the River Salween opposite Pa-an. The Salween is broader [800 yards] than the Rhine at this point. The Brigade was dispersed. Our role was to hold the water front at Kuzeik, and we established company patrol bases to try to identify if and when the Japanese crossed the river. At which point the brigade reserve battalion would come up from Thaton and drive the Japanese back into the Salween. The positions had been dug by 1st/7th Gurkhas, concentrating on holding the river front and hadn't been developed as a perimeter to face an attack from the west. Because we had two companies out in bases, and one holding the front, the perimeter facing west was practically non-existant. Because the perimeter was so shallow our own mortars and the two mountain guns in support could not fire on our own front.

The 1/7th Gurkhas had already given the *215th Regiment* a bloody nose at Pa-an, before being relieved by 7th/10th Baluch, but this did not deter this very battle-experienced Japanese regiment, who were experts in night attacks. Randle:

A Company were in a patrol base at Myainggale 7 miles south of the battalion position. I was told to take over from A Company, and my Subedar Mehr Khan went off with one platoon as advance party. During the night the Japanese attacked and, as we learned subsequently, wiped out my platoon with Subedar Mehr Khan, and a platoon of A Company, the remainder of the company having already left. As I was moving to Myainggale with my remaining two platoons, I ran into the middle of *215 Regiment* just getting across and taking up positions on the west bank of the Salween. I had a hairy old night, lost a few chaps, but managed to get my two platoons out back to the main position. The visibility was quite good, in banana plantations, and, with the full moon you could see about 50 yards, it was so light you threw a moon shadow. The CO had not laid down routes for my company and A company to move on, in order to avoid a clash, and I was worried about having a shoot out with them. [A Company were to move leaving one platoon under Subedar Mehr Khan of B Company as soon as he arrived.] We were in single file one platoon leading, followed by Company HQ, and the other platoon, when a man charged in to our column. I thought it was one of my soldiers running away, and shouted at him. It was a Jap who ran off into the bush. A couple of Japs were shot by my men, the first dead Jap I had seen. There was quite a lot of firing, and I realised there were quite a lot of Japs about. I tried to get through on my radio, which didn't work. So I sent my runner, the company bugler, back with a message, to my CO to tell him there were a lot of Japs about. They cut in behind us and we could hear the runner screaming as they killed him with swords and bayonets. This was followed by an enormous lot of firing a couple of miles away from the base we were going to relieve. The Japs were running about, in a fair state of confusion too, having just come across the river. We had no idea what tactics we should adopt. I just formed a circle which looking back was the best thing to do: river on one side, Japs on two sides. It was pure luck not cleverness. It was clear to me there were a considerable number of Japs to the south of me, so I decided to return to the battalion position. I only lost a couple of chaps. Luckily I picked a route where there were no Japs and got back OK.

The next day they dive-bombed us. We weren't far from a major airfield at Chiengmai across the Thai border. Slit trenches saved us losing many chaps although we had no overhead cover. Later in the war, I used to lie back in my slit trench and fire up at aircraft with a Bren, that was fun. Morale was OK, and the chaps were not too upset.

That night at about midnight, we were attacked by *215 Regiment* and pinned against the Salween. The CO had sent one of my platoons and a platoon from another company out on a patrol, God knows what for, so I was down to one platoon, and a section of [two Vickers] MMGs. At about 12 o'clock (midnight) the Japs came in and we had hand-to-hand fighting. They overran us and C Company, whose commander [Captain Korla, an Indian officer, who was captured but escaped] got an immediate DSO.

The Japs came in with no artillery support in what started as a silent night attack [a Japanese speciality]. When they got close, they screamed *banzai* and came charging in shoulder-to-shoulder. The Vickers fired across my front and caused heavy casualties to the Japs. They surged into Company HQ, I killed the chap coming for me. I was standing up firing my revolver, and missed first time. My CSM was grappling with a Jap. My batman was killed by a grenade. Just before dawn realising if we stayed, we would get taken prisoner, we charged out and then lay up about 150 yards away, and after first light heard a second assault going in, on Battalion HQ. Then we had a pause, then at about 7 o'clock the next morning they finished us off. We lost 289 killed, and 229 taken prisoner in our first engagement.

I had fever and a temperature of 102. It took me two days to get back to our lines. I had two soldiers with me. We had no map, no compass. A whole Jap battalion, the *111/215* passed me as I lay up. We got back to the Donthami river, where I heard a shout, and thought oh Christ after all this. They were waving it was the 1st/7th Gurkhas and they sent a boat over.

I rejoined the Battalion. We were staked out there like a goat for the Jap tiger and sacrificed for no reason. The CO was killed and we lost over 60% of our officers. Only about fifty of the Battalion got away, but we had quite a big B Echelon [who were not involved] and the two platoons sent out on patrol got away. With the exception of one officer the Japs butchered all our wounded. News of this got back to us and this conditioned mine and the whole Battalion's attitude towards the Japs. We were not merciful to them for the rest of the war. We didn't take any prisoners. By then I commanded a coy of Pathans pretty hard men. The Japs fought with great ferocity and courage. We were arrogant about the Japs we regarded them as coolies. We thought of them as third rate. My goodness me we soon changed our tune. We had no idea about jungle fighting, no pamphlets, doctrine etc. Not only were we raw troops, we were doing something entirely new. In the early days we used to hack our way through the jungle, until we realised that this was useless, you made so much noise and it was so exhausting.

General Smyth withdrew to the Bilin River. Again marching fast, the Japanese started arriving at the Bilin before some of the units allocated to defend it. By outflanking and cutting in behind the British, they threatened the withdrawal route to the Sittang Bridge. Too late, Smyth was authorized to withdraw behind the Sittang. Once more the Japanese, using jungle paths and tracks, outmarched the British, moving along a narrow road clogged with transport. The Japanese knew that the British were withdrawing because orders to this effect were passed in clear over the radios by some units. The enemy were thus handed on a plate information for which they would normally have to fight. They did not waste time following up, but headed to cut off the British. The error was compounded by lack of drive on Smyth's part in allowing some British units to stop and rest instead of forcing on, and failing to send one of his brigades along the railway line on foot to relieve congestion on the road. One company of 1st/4th Gurkhas nearly got left behind in the confusion. Lieutenant Day:

History says that 1/4 GR cleverly withdrew in darkness and when the Japs attacked they found us gone. This is nonsense. I never received orders to withdraw. The Japs attacked in the morning, and we held out till midday, although surrounded. At which point a Lance-Naik from the Signal Platoon arrived with orders to withdraw. I was amazed to see him and couldn't understand how he made it. How I was going to get away I just couldn't see. The Japs had machine-guns at each end of the bund [embankment] on which we were pinned down. It never occurred to me to take the opportunity to move when the belt was being changed on these guns. The Gurkha said 'we wait and then we all go together and run'. That's what happened. I didn't think of it, it was entirely due to this young Lance-Naik.

We moved off to try to catch the battalion who were well ahead of us, and had stopped in the bend in a rubber estate near a place called Kyaikto when I heard a lot of noise coming through the jungle. We had very little ammo. All we could do was to hide in the jungle and hope to get away with scuppering the enemy and make a break. When they arrived, I thought we had had it. Round the bend came Peter Stewart with remnants of a company of 4/12 Frontier Force Regiment who I hadn't seen for years, one of my best friends. We went on different routes. Eventually we met a mountain battery who carried some of my men on their mules. Without the help of the mountain battery we wouldn't have made it.

After about 12 hours rest, the men made a wonderful recovery, and we set off on a dreadful march along trace cut by sappers through jungle to Sittang Bridge. It was very dry, water was short, and we marched in clouds of very fine dust. It was hard going, and we were hammered all way back by Jap air force and sadly by the AVG [American Volunteer Group] and RAF. The RAF had been told the Japs were coming along the jungle trace and we along the coast road. Pilots came back and queried the targets saying they looked like British vehicles, to be told that it was captured British transport. We had heavy casualties from our own aircraft. We fired at them and hit British aircraft. Many of the problems were caused by poor communications. The radios were useless. Civil telephone or within the battalion, runner, were the only reliable means of communicating.

Seen with the advantage of hindsight, perhaps Smyth's most fatal move was not following Brigadier Ekin's strongly expressed request that his whole 46th Brigade should move quickly back to the Sittang to secure the area for the remainder of the division to withdraw through. Smyth had already fatally weakened the bridge garrison by detaching the 2nd Dukes,* a fresh, full-strength, well-equipped battalion, which had just arrived in Burma, to join 46th Brigade at Kyaikto south of the bridge, leaving just one company at Sittang.

Lieutenant Firth of the 2nd Dukes recalled the chaotic state of the road jammed with transport as his battalion moved to join 46th Brigade: 'It was nearly dark. I asked this officer in the front of a 15 cwt truck if

---

* The 2nd Battalion The Duke of Wellington's Regiment.

I was now near the front line, and his tired answer was, "My dear chap this convoy is the front line", and drove on towards Mokpalin.'

The situation was not improved by RAF Hurricanes and AVG Tomahawks strafing their own troops on the road to Mokpalin. It was not only an unwelcome jolt to the morale of troops, but the attacks destroyed most of the radio sets, with dire consequences. Firth:

My baptism of fire in World War Two was from the front end of a Wellington [sic] about 200 feet above me coming straight at me with guns blazing. We were in the open in a rubber plantation. I could not get a clear view of the fighter aircraft through the trees.*

The remnants of the 7th/10th Baluch were among those at the Sittang Bridge. Randle:

We assembled pretty demoralised after an appalling baptism of fire, then moved east of the Sittang River and got involved in the early stages of the Sittang bridge debacle. All the Punjabi Mussalmans were put into one company of two platoons, which I commanded. We were at Mokpalin on the day of the opening part of the Sittang Battle and ordered to move up the railway line and cross the bridge to the west side. The Battalion was formed into two companies. The 2ic was in command. He was an Anglo-Indian [Eurasian] officer called Pat Dunn. As we were moving to the bridge still on the east side, my company was the first to come under fire from Pagoda Hill, from Jap MMG, and took casualties. One of my platoons panicked and ran back and joined the rest of battalion. I arrived at the bridge and reported to the CO of the 4th/12th Frontier Force Regiment who were holding the bridge. He told me to go up and give Sam Manekshaw of C Company a hand. The Adjutant of 4th/12th Frontier Force Regt was 'Turk' Roman a Muslim, a very fine officer. Sam was an Indian. (Thirty five years later in the war between Pakistan and India, Turk was commanding the Pakistan force and Sam was commanding the Indians.)

Meanwhile the 17th Division, led by the 48th Brigade, carried out an exhausting forced march, under repeated low-level air attacks, in a race with the Japanese *33rd Division* to reach the Sittang Bridge. Kinloch:

---

* In fact there were no Wellington bombers in Burma at the time, only Blenheims. Other accounts mention the devastating effect of the eight-gun Hurricanes.

Early in the morning of 22nd February, with little rest and no food, the weary troops of 48 Brigade finally reached Mokpalin, a fishing village of scattered bamboo huts on the banks of the Sittang River. Brigade HQ and the 1/4th Gurkha Rifles, who were in the van, gained and crossed the bridge, but then the advance was halted by a lorry which crashed on the bridge itself, blocking it completely, and by the time that the 1/3rd and 2/5th Gurkha Rifles entered the outskirts of Mokpalin, forward elements of the Japanese 33rd Division had reached the village in strength and put down their inevitable road block between 48 Brigade HQ, plus 1/4th Gurkha Rifles, and the rest of 17 Division. With the almost total lack of wireless communications, resulting from the previous day's air attacks, the scenario for the Sittang disaster was then complete.

As the 1st/3rd Gurkhas reached the outskirts of the village they heard heavy small-arms fire ahead as 2nd/5th Royal Gurkha Rifles cleared out the enemy, while they themselves came under fire from Japanese in the surrounding jungle. Having swept the enemy away from their route, 1st/3rd Gurkhas arrived at their rendezvous at Mokpalin railway station to find that the adjutant had been wounded, so the CO, Lieutenant Colonel Ballinger, appointed Kinloch, the third occupant of the job in three weeks. 'I wondered', remembered Kinloch, 'if it would be a case of third time lucky. I was soon to be put to the test'.

The final approach to the bridge was dominated by a double hill feature covered with dense jungle. The hill nearest the river was crowned by a pagoda, and the other by a large statue of Buddha – instantly dubbed 'Pagoda Hill' and 'Buddha Hill'. The railway line and road ran north more or less parallel to the river, between 600 and 700 yards in from the bank. While the road continued north over a feature which became known as OP Hill, curved slightly east, and ran behind Pagoda and Buddha Hills, before running down to a cutting at the eastern edge of the bridge, the railway curved to the east to cross the Sittang Bridge. Engineers had been toiling to bolt down sleepers on each side of the railway lines on the bridge to allow the passage of road transport, but it could only take traffic in a single line, and was not ready to accept vehicles until nightfall on 21 February. Smyth had very little time to get his whole division including a mass of transport over the bridge. The truck alluded to by Kinloch had veered off the sleepers during the night, and jammed itself across the bridge,

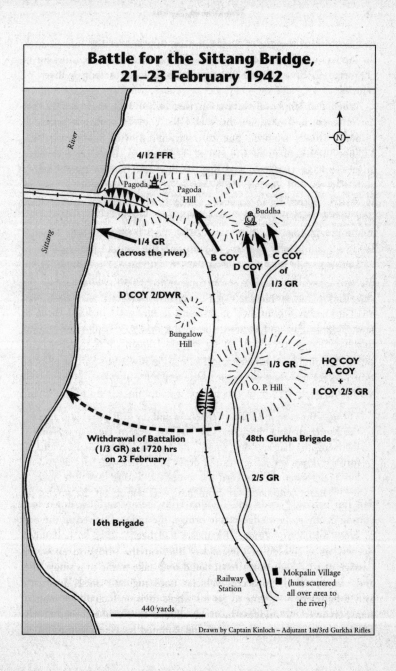

Battle for the Sittang Bridge, 21–23 February 1942

N

River

4/12 FFR

Pagoda

Pagoda Hill

Buddha

Sittang

1/4 GR
(across the river)

B COY

D COY

C COY
of
1/3 GR

D COY 2/DWR

Bungalow Hill

1/3 GR

HQ COY
A COY
+
1 COY 2/5 GR

O. P. Hill

Withdrawal of Battalion
(1/3 GR) at 1720 hrs
on 23 February

48th Gurkha Brigade

2/5 GR

16th Brigade

Railway Station

Mokpalin Village
(huts scattered
all over area to
the river)

440 yards

Drawn by Captain Kinloch – Adjutant 1st/3rd Gurkha Rifles

and because of the girders could not be tipped over the side. It took the sappers two hours under the personal supervision of the Chief Royal Engineer (CRE) to clear the obstruction, causing a long tailback of vehicles.

When 2nd/5th Royal Gurkhas arrived on OP Hill, they realized that the Japanese had occupied Buddha Hill. They immediately attacked, without artillery support, but were driven off with heavy casualties. Ballinger and Lieutenant Colonel R. T. Cameron, the CO of 2nd/5th Royal Gurkhas, conferred and they decided that 1st/3rd should attack both Pagoda and Buddha Hills, while 2nd/5th held a firm base in Mokpalin. According to Kinloch, standing with Ballinger on OP Hill, 'The attack started at 1130 hours with a 25 minute concentration by the mountain guns, the 19lb [sic – 20lb] shells from these little 3.7 inch howitzers falling with supreme accuracy on the two hill features.'

Unfortunately they also fell on the 4th Battalion 12th Frontier Force Regiment and HQ 48 Brigade, who, unbeknown to Ballinger, were on Pagoda Hill. The commander of 48 Brigade, Brigadier Hugh-Jones, who was responsible for the bridge garrison, immediately ordered them to leave Pagoda Hill and withdraw over the bridge. B Company 1st/3rd Gurkhas then succeeded in taking Pagoda Hill from the Japanese who had moved in, blocking them from advancing to capture the eastern end of the bridge. Meanwhile C and D Companies attacked Buddha Hill. Kinloch:

> Through the roar and crash of the shells and the drifting smoke came the stutter of light machine guns and the yells of our Gurkhas as following the barrage they found the Japs in slit trenches on the forward slopes and killed them or drove them back with bayonet and kukri. But when they reached the top of the feature they were held up by heavy automatic fire from Japs well dug in on the reverse slope.

Thanks to thick jungle, Ballinger and Kinloch could hear, but not see, the battle, and without radios had no means of knowing how it was progressing. Kinloch heard what had transpired some three hours later when Lieutenant Fay, C Company commander, came back to have a light wound dressed, by which time Ballinger was dead. With his subedar major (senior Gurkha officer), he had gone forward to see for himself. He joined one of his own platoons engaging the Japanese, who stood up to surrender. As the Gurkhas advanced to take them prisoner, the Japanese flung themselves down, and light machine-guns hidden behind them opened up, killing Ballinger and many with him. Only the subedar major and a small number of Gurkhas escaped.

Major Bradford took command of 1st/3rd Gurkhas, but was out of touch with his forward companies, B on Pagoda Hill, and C and D south of Buddha Hill, because by now the Japanese had infiltrated between OP Hill and Buddha and Pagoda Hills. He set off in a Bren-gun carrier to Mokpalin station to try to find a senior officer to get assistance. The road was jammed with transport under artillery fire, vehicles were in flames, and the Japanese were attacking. He encountered Brigadier J. K. Jones, commanding the 16th Brigade (not to be confused with Brigadier Hugh-Jones, his own Brigade Commander still by the bridge). J. K. Jones, who had assumed command of all troops in the Mokpalin area, said he had no troops to spare, and ordered Bradford to withdraw to OP Hill and go firm there. 1st/3rd Gurkhas consolidated just in time, because as darkness fell the Japanese launched a series of attacks.

At this stage it would have been possible for the troops in the Mokpalin area to make for the bridge on foot along the river bank, because the bridgehead was still in friendly hands, but with inadequate communications, J. K. Jones had no way of knowing this. The third brigade of 17th Division, 46th Brigade, at the tail of the division on the move to the Sittang Bridge, had been ambushed, and only remnants were coming in to the Mokpalin area. The road from Mokpalin to the bridge was jammed with double-banked transport. Meanwhile J. K. Jones planned an attack on Buddha and Pagoda Hills for soon after first light the next morning, supported by most of the divisional artillery (three mountain batteries), still on the east bank.

At the bridge, Brigadier Hugh-Jones was increasingly concerned about his ability to hold the bridge, which was already prepared for demolition. The intensity of Japanese probing attacks towards the bridge increased. At 0500, believing that all who could reach the bridge had crossed, and desperately worried that the Japanese might take it intact, thus opening their route to Rangoon, Hugh-Jones, having obtained permission from Major General Smyth, withdrew the bridge garrison and ordered the sappers to blow the bridge. Two spans fell into the river, and a third was damaged. Kinloch:

As the echoes of the explosions died away they were followed by utter silence. All firing had ceased abruptly and every living thing seemed to be holding its breath. For a few moments an eerie stillness descended on the battle-field, then suddenly the Japanese, sounding like a troop of excited monkeys, broke into shrill chattering. On OP Hill, dog-tired with incessant fighting and lack of sleep, food and water, and believing that we had been abandoned to our fate by the other troops who (we thought) had crossed the bridge and blown it behind them, we were filled with mounting anger.

Soon after the bridge was blown, Hugh-Jones, standing on the bank, received a message, carried by a subedar who had crossed the bridge just before the explosion. It was from J. K. Jones saying that he was going to withdraw to the river bank and fight his way north to the bridge on foot abandoning transport. Hugh-Jones collapsed and fell down the bank on which he was standing.

As the Japanese moved in to wipe them out, the men marooned on the east bank of the Sittang made desperate efforts to cross by swimming and building rafts out of anything that would conceivably float. One of the later ones to cross was Lieutenant Firth, commanding the Signals Platoon in the by now severely depleted 2nd Dukes:

At about 4.00 pm with a Lance Corporal in the KOYLI called Burns, I walked down to the river about 600 yards away, carrying a KOYLI private soldier with his knee smashed by a mortar [bomb]. We loaded him on a banana [tree] trunk raft, where he lay comfortably enough and secure. Burns and I stripped off except for my .45 Webley [revolver] round my neck [by its lanyard], and swam gently across in warm sunshine for 800 yards pushing the raft along. At this point there was no one else in sight. On the other side about 600 yards away we discovered a bullock cart and a group of KOYLI. It was carrying their CO or second-in-command. Our wounded man was made room for. Corporal Burns and I walked still only in our pants and vests, in the direction of a general 'hubbub' which turned out to be Waw Railway Station by which time it was getting dark. I was hauled into a carriage in which was the CO of the Jats, shivering with fever and wrapped in a blanket, with one or two of his VCOs [Viceroy's Commissioned Officers – see glossary]. These included a Jemedar, who the CO said, was the chap who had found the body of our murdered CO in a village downstream, and extracted due vengeance!* The train took us to Pegu where I found the remnants of the battalion had arrived and were re-forming.

Firth was lucky and was not attacked by Japanese aircraft, which buzzed the river machine-gunning the swimmers. Some 3,500 of the division made it across, mostly by swimming. Together with those already across the Sittang, the division was reduced to 41 per cent of its strength, with only 1,420 rifles. All the artillery and most of the transport with much other equipment was abandoned. Smyth was relieved of command. A brave, talented, and much-admired officer, he should have reported sick; he had to cope not only with the desperately inadequate state of the defence of Burma, but also an extremely painful anal fistula, so was not at his best.

Kinloch was one of the last to make it across the Sittang. The remnants of his battalion managed to stay hidden until nightfall, when he and two other officers volunteered to cross the river pushing a small bamboo raft. There they found all friendly troops gone, but discovered a large sampan, which they paddled back. Having ferried five loads across, at daylight Kinloch agreed with Bradford that he would cross to the west bank once more to try to organize more boats to lift the remainder of the battalion that night. From the far bank, he saw

Japanese troops swarm out of the jungle, and then a number of Gurkha soldiers swimming the river under fire. Some of the men were shot or drowned. The survivors told their sad story.

After a brief fire-fight the Battalion had been surrounded, they said, and to save what by then had become a pointless loss of life, Major Bradford had agreed to surrender; but it was not part of the soldier's code of Subedar-Major Gagan Sing Thapa, a veteran of several wars, to surrender to anyone, let alone a Japanese, so, as a Jap officer approached, the Subedar-Major drew his revolver and fired at him – and then shot himself through the heart. The Jap officer who had received Bradford's pistol, then shot the Major, whereupon a Gurkha Naik [Corporal] shot the Jap officer through the head, Eventually all firing ceased and the remainder of the Battalion was rounded up and marched off.

---

* The CO of 2nd Dukes, Lieutenant Colonel Owen, had been treacherously murdered by Burmese in a village where he was resting after swimming across the Irrawaddy.

Eventually Kinloch with a small party of Gurkhas ran into a patrol from 1st Battalion The Cameronians. He was awarded a richly deserved Military Cross (MC).

Donald Day of 1st/4th Gurkhas believes that the situation was almost saved, but lost for lack of a bugle. Perhaps he is right, stranger things have happened in war:

> We sent two coys back with the Dukes to secure the other side. I nearly linked up with the 1st/3rd Gurkhas on the other side. Every time we made progress, we squeezed the Japs out to a flank, but were fired on by the 1st/3rd Gurkhas. I believe that if my bugler had had his bugle, I could have blown the Ceasefire, I think they might have stopped firing long enough for us to link up.
>
> We were out of ammunition, so the remnants came across the bridge to join the Battalion at about 0445 in the morning and the bridge was blown about half an hour after we disentangled from the other side, my party was certainly still on the near end [west bank] of the bridge when the two spans went up.

The arrangements, or lack of them, for the proper conduct of the close bridge garrison at the Sittang used to be studied at the British Army Staff College at Camberley, at least in the author's day, as an example of how it should *not* be done. Communications were difficult because of the lack of serviceable radios, but the ambiguous command arrangements and responsibility, as well as lack of control and drive, combined to create the situation described. Randle is rightly scathing on the subject: 'when I was with Sam Manekshaw I had seen the Dukes moving up across the bridge very cheerfully going in to battle. Now some of them were swimming back':

> Jackie Smyth took no proper steps to defend the bridge. There was no close bridge garrison, no proper fire plan, no proper defence. This bridge was the jugular of the Division. The Japs were just probing at the first stage. They used to take a commanding bit of ground and sit to see what we would do about it. We would attack and take heavy casualties. By holding Pagoda Hill they had a key feature overlooking the bridge and approaches to it. Smyth lacked moral courage, he should have pushed 1st/4th Gurkhas across* and dug in

---

* Even better the Dukes, a fresh battalion.

a proper position in depth. I didn't know all this at the time. I didn't know what the hell was going on in my own little world.

The tragedy was heightened by the simple fact that the Japanese, with their all-animal transport organization, did not need the bridge in order to cross the Sittang; they marched upstream and crossed without difficulty. The British, with their mass of transport, and Indian units almost wholly composed of non-swimmers relied on it totally. This was caused by Smyth's order to destroy not only the power vehicle ferries provided by Hutton to meet the contingency of damage to the bridge, but also other local craft, for fear that they might fall into enemy hands. There were sufficient troops on the east bank to hold off the Japanese, or even push them back in order to allow most of the division to withdraw over the bridge. It was blown unnecessarily early.

Rangoon, now at great risk, was the only port through which desperately needed British reinforcements could come. On 27 February the battle-experienced 7th Armoured Brigade, consisting of the 7th Hussars and 2nd Royal Tank Regiment (2 RTR) in Stuart light tanks (Honeys), 414 Battery Royal Horse Artillery (RHA), and A Battery 95th Anti-Tank Regiment RA, disembarked in Rangoon.

Gunner Tutt, of 414 Battery RHA, as a battery of 104 Regiment (Essex Yeomanry) RHA, had fought in the Western Desert, including the siege of Tobruk. He remembers the arrival of 7th Armoured Brigade, among chaos and rumours:

Our arrival was largely unsung. The smell of disaster was everywhere. There were no dock gangs to take our hawsers and to help us berth. There were no stevedores to help us unload, no crane operators, no one. We understood now why some of the ships that we had passed going the other way and packed with civilians had saluted us on their sirens and the passengers cheered. We must have seemed to be sailing right into the arms of the Japanese. Over the city there was a dense pall of smoke, the sound of demolitions and rifle fire. Our Infantry friends had disembarked before us and were taking up positions to cover us while we unloaded the precious armour and artillery.

By osmosis we learnt of the dilemma which faced our Brigade commander. The Japanese were advancing on Rangoon very quickly. The civilian population had all departed, Europeans by boat and the Asians in anything which would carry them northwards en route to

India. With them had gone all the technicians and skilled dock
workers needed to unload us. If we stayed we would have to unload
for ourselves and hope that we got enough of it off to defend
ourselves if the Japanese turned up half way through the proceedings.
We also heard that our troops were failing to measure up to the
enemy, that we had lost over half a Division at the Sittang River. To
us the answer seemed simple, leave with all possible speed. Someone
decreed otherwise, we were soon carrying our kit down the gang
plank and cursing the humid heat. We thought that we had been
used to high temperatures in the Desert, but it had been a dry heat.
In Burma it was so damp that we were soon dripping with perspira-
tion and struggling for breath.

By the third day all our stuff was ashore and we were under
orders to move. But the trucks were sent back into Rangoon with
permission to liberate from the docks any stores which might be of
use to us in the future. Charges were being placed on all the oil
installations and it was pretty clear that anything that we didn't take
would be blown up or set on fire to prevent it falling into the hands
of the enemy. The kites had moved in on the dead and rose with
slow, laborious wing flaps from them as we passed. They were so
sated that they could hardly get off the ground, and as they moved
off, the dogs came in.

With the departure of the established administration the place
had rapidly slipped into anarchy. The Burmans started to settle old
scores with the wealthy Indians and Chinese who had grown rich in
their country. Later on roles were reversed slightly, the Burmans were
attacked by the Karens and other northern tribes who saw the turmoil
as an opportunity to emphasise their claims for independence.

We were given tacit permission to help ourselves from the
warehouses to anything that might be useful to us in the field. There
was everything for the taking, from big American cars to paper clips.
After a few goes at charging along the quay sides on looted Harley
Davidsons we really concentrated on supplies of food and tinned
milk.

We were not without company as we drifted through the miles of
sheds, opening a crate here and there. Some of the visitors were
official; a party of Royal Engineers were wiring up as much as they
could for demolition. The authorities when they left had freed all
the prisoners in the jail, had liberated the inhabitants of the lunatic

asylum and had allowed the lepers to leave the lazarette. The bulk of the prisoners had been Dacoits, professional killers and they were rather a murderous lot. I found myself disputing possession of a leather case containing two matched shot guns with one of them. One look at the determination in his eyes and the razor sharp parang on a cord from his wrist, and I thought to myself, 'Who the hell needs a pair of shot guns anyway.'

To my eternal shame I could not bring myself to even show a little compassion for the lepers. Some of them were in the last stages of the disease and were featureless wrecks of men and women. Even so the poor devils had no wish to be left to the tender mercies of the Japanese. As our trucks left the dock area they crowded around begging for lifts out of the city. God forgive me. I could not look at their fingerless stumps of hands and ravaged faces. I do not think that they were an embarrassment to the Japanese for very long. They had a way of dealing with such problems with a bullet in the back of the head and, maybe, in this instance, they showed the lepers a greater kindness than did we.

We continued to stock up for the months ahead. Our experience in the Desert had taught us that the things which we would find the most useful were tea, sugar, tinned milk; and tobacco or cigarettes. After this, food of any kind, not luxury, space wasting comestibles but good, solid tins of meat or fish. Some of the less knowledgeable drivers, who had joined us at Sarafand, were intoxicated with all the largess for the taking and brought back such wildly unsuitable things as cases of talcum powder or hair shampoo. But, new as they were, they were beginning to develop a sense of survival and the gee gaws and the irrelevant were dumped among the rubber trees and replaced by more sensible loot.

Our Battery Commander, Major Tom Pereira, really came into his own in Burma. As a completely detached battery there was no Regimental Headquarters to say him 'Yeah or Nay.' He was in complete charge of our destiny, and often of that of other formations as well. He had a good team of officers in the main, a judicious mixture of yeomen,* for their experience, with a rejuvenating shot in

---

* Members of the Yeomanry, the volunteer cavalry force first embodied in 1794 and subsumed into the Territorial Army on its creation in 1908. Some regiments retained Yeomanry in their name.

the arm of some keen young lieutenants straight from O.C.T.U. In
conditions, completely alien to our experience and training he used
the Battery efficiently and one of the happy memories I have of the
war in Burma is the warmth with which both the 7th Hussars and
the 2nd Tanks spoke of our work as their supporting Artillery. They
had never been served better, they reported, and this from two of the
best armoured units in the famed 7th Armoured Division, was praise
indeed. But he was not an easy man to serve under and he never let
up on us for a moment. I believe it was his uncompromising attitude
that brought us out of Burma still well disciplined and as a cohesive
group, where some others had degenerated into a rabble.

By now Major General Cowan had relieved Smyth as commander
17th Indian Division, and on 5 March Lieutenant General the Hon. Sir
Harold Alexander had replaced Hutton as Army Commander. Alexander,
a gallant Irish Guardsman, with a brilliant fighting record in the First
World War, had commanded an Indian brigade on the North-West
Frontier between the wars, unusual for a Guardsman. A talented linguist,
he had learned Urdu, so was able to talk to the Indian soldiers in their
own language. In France in 1940 he had proved to be a most successful divisional commander. Throughout that disastrous campaign, and
especially during the evacuation at Dunkirk, where he was promoted
to command the rearguard corps, he remained calm in the face of
the utmost danger. Now he had been handed a poisoned chalice at the
express wish of Churchill, who admired him unreservedly.

The day after taking command, Alexander ordered the evacuation
of Rangoon, which was already in a state of chaos, as observed by Tutt.
The army got away by a whisker; as it marched and motored north,
the Japanese *33rd Division* was already across the route. Fortunately a
roadblock established to protect the flank of the division as it marched
towards Rangoon was lifted before the British needed to put in an attack
to clear it.

Southern Burma was lost. The Japanese had a port through which
they could reinforce and resupply. Until now a small Japanese force had
been supported overland from Siam. Had the equally small British force,
with all the logistic advantages of a port, rail, and road system, been
properly trained and equipped, and most important deployed in a
tactically sensible manner, they could have defeated the Japanese. Now

the boot was on the other foot. The Japanese shipped in two more divisions, the *18th* and *56th*, with heavy equipment, including heavy artillery and tanks, and advanced up the Sittang and Irrawaddy valleys. From the day of abandoning Rangoon, the loss of the whole of Burma was merely a matter of time. The British were faced with a logistic nightmare. An army always tries to withdraw along its main supply route, and usually its supply problems lessen as it gets closer to its logistic base, while the enemy, moving away from his, finds life more difficult. The British had no logistic base, and had to take most of their supplies with them. Fortunately Hutton had stockpiled some supplies in Central Burma, so at least as far north as Mandalay, the army could count on replenishment of some of the essentials.

Alexander hoped to hold the Japanese on the line Prome (on the Irrawaddy) to Toungoo (on the Sittang); loss of either would result in being outflanked. He was given authority to coordinate the activities of two Chinese armies under the command of the American Lieutenant General Stilwell, and made him responsible for the Sittang axis of withdrawal, including Toungoo and the Shan States. He ordered 1st Burma Division and 17th Indian Division, with 7th Armoured Brigade, onto the Irrawaddy axis. Now he was responsible for all Burma, Alexander asked for a corps commander to take charge of what for ease of reference we will call the British formations (albeit they consisted mostly of Indians, Gurkhas, Karens, Shans, Chins, and Burmese). He was given Lieutenant General W. J. Slim, to command what became known as BURCORPS. It was, as events would show, an inspired choice.

By the end of March, 17th Indian Division was firm at Prome and Allanmyo to the north. Wavell now called for a counteroffensive, south down both axes back towards Rangoon: the British south from Prome and the Chinese at Toungoo. Accordingly a strike force commanded by Brigadier Anstice of 7th Armoured Brigade, consisting of 7th Hussars, 414 Battery RHA, the 2nd Dukes and the 1st Battalion The Gloucestershire Regiment (Glosters), one company of The West Yorkshire Regiment, and 24 Field Company Bombay Sappers and Miners, was ordered to seize first Paungde followed by Okpo, an advance of some forty miles. The Japanese *33rd Division* was also advancing, in the opposite direction, on three axes as was their wont. Anstice's strike force was about to run into the most experienced division in Burma. Just after they cleared the village of Shwedaung, on the east bank of the Irrawaddy some eight

miles south of Prome, the Japanese slid a battalion in behind them and
set up a block in the centre of the village on the bridge over the Kala
Chaung, which flowed into the Irrawaddy, and dug in around the village.
With them were some 1,200 men of the Burma Independence Army
(BIA), the anti-British Burmese movement, one of whose leaders was
Aung San.[7]

Anstice's force encountered and fought a brisk battle with the
Japanese as they pushed north through Paungde. However, Cowan, who
by now had heard of the enemy block at Shwedaung, countermanded
any further attempts to advance south, and ordered Anstice back to
Prome. Cowan also ordered an attack on Shwedaung from the north,
and 48th Brigade to advance to counter the Japanese thrust up the
railway from Paungde.

4th/12th Frontier Force Regiment attacked a small village just north
of Shwedaung, where they encountered the BIA and utterly routed them.
The BIA had 60 killed, 70 taken prisoner, and 300 wounded; 350
deserted, while the rest withdrew. Never again would the BIA engage in
a formal battle, contenting themselves with terrorizing villagers, following like jackals on the heels of weaker forces, and torturing and
murdering prisoners. The 4th/12th Frontier Force Regiment pressed on
but could make no further progress beyond the outskirts of Shwedaung.
They dug in for the night.

The first attempt by Anstice's force to break through the block at
Shwedaung failed, except for one troop of 7th Hussars. A second attack
during the night also failed. A further attack was ordered for first light
on 30 March. Major Hemelryk was commanding A Battery 95th Anti-
tank Regiment Royal Artillery:

> Lieutenant Kildair 'Husky' Patteson was captured [in the initial
> attack] and his tank put of out of action. He and his crew were
> marched off to the Japanese Colonel, who ordered that the crew be
> shot and 'Husky' tied to a tree. He led 'the fun' by hitting 'Husky' in
> the face and then letting the other Jap officers have a go. Knowing
> that we should bring down artillery fire on to the block at dawn, they
> tied him to the tree trunks forming the block. Among others my own
> battery was there and we could all see him. Owing to the close
> proximity of so many of our troops, D Troop of 414 Battery RHA
> led by Major Pereira, opened fire beyond the block, and reduced

range by creeping [i.e. 'walking the fire back' on to the target].
During this process one of the trees forming the block must have got
dislodged, because 'Husky' found he could slip the ropes that held
him, and with his hands still tied, was able to run back to our lines.

The British were, as usual, hampered by a large column of soft-
skinned vehicles jamming the road, double-banked and nose-to-tail,
for about a mile. The British Stuart tanks, although light and soon to
become outmoded for use in war against European armies, were more
than a match for Japanese armour. Their frontal armour could not be
penetrated by any of the Japanese anti-tank guns, and only Japanese
75mm and heavier artillery in a direct fire role could deal with them.
The Stuarts had no high-explosive ammunition, and were restricted to
firing armour-piercing solid shot from their 37mm main armament, a
disadvantage when fighting infantry, and their only other weapons were
two medium machine-guns. They were vulnerable to anti-tank mines
and petrol bombs, so close support by infantry was essential, especially
in built-up areas and forested country. Used to fighting in the open
desert, these conditions were new to 7th Armoured Brigade, and all the
infantry in Burma were ill-trained in all phases of war, not least infantry/
tank cooperation.

Lieutenant Collister commanded a platoon in C Company, 1st
Glosters:

At about five in the morning, shivering with cold in our shorts and
open-necked shirts, the order was given to attack the village, but
there was a delay, and we did not start moving until the sun was up.
Suddenly a whole line of men stood up and began moving at an
ordinary walking pace across the stubbly [paddy] fields. Holding
my .38 pistol warily in front, with a Burmese Dah at my side, still
wearing my solar topee, I remember thinking how absurdly similar it
was to Hollywood.

As we approached the copse in which the village was embedded,
disorder set in, partly because of the unevenness of the ground,
accentuated by ditches and nullahs crossing our front. As we closed
the wood, with a great din from 25-pounders and 3-inch mortar
shells screeching over us, I looked behind to see a host of unfamiliar
faces in a throng of men bunched out behind, no longer in recognisable units. I and about half a platoon, had become enmeshed in a

company of West Yorks. At the edge of the wood, the Japanese
opened fire, at first with rifles and machine guns, then with mortars,
whose swishing noise was the most petrifying of all, followed by a
scrunching explosion. As we began to double up the road towards
where we presumed the road block to be (in fact there were several),
I was hurled back by the blast from a mortar bomb. I was pretty
shaken as I picked myself up, conscious of blood streaming down my
right cheek and neck. A sergeant major of the West Yorks shook me
roughly as I stood still and slightly shocked, and yanked a jagged
piece of shrapnel out of my cheek. I yelped with pain, but it was
the right treatment. I instinctively began running forward, as he
yelled over the din, 'come on Sir, it's nothing much'. By this time
our momentum had exhausted itself and we found ourselves – a
hotch-potch of Gloucesters, West Yorks, Duke of Wellingtons, and
Cameronians aimlessly massed in the centre of the village with no
one obviously in command.

The Japanese cut in behind, and attacked the massed vehicles. They
had already attacked the gun position of 414 Battery before it limbered
up to move. Tutt:

> At first light we began firing, almost immediately the gun position
> came under fire from some low scrub about three hundred yards to
> our flank. We spotted movement and happily assumed it was our
> infantry moving in to clear the area. Someone shouted, 'look out
> they're Japs!'
>   Every spare man grabbed a rifle and took pot shots at them.
> Artillerymen are not much use with a rifle, but we held them off
> until a couple of spare tanks came up and drove them back into
> cover. Some infantrymen went up to clear the wood, but we noticed
> they didn't go in very far.*
>   While this was going on, the guns, with the minimum of gunners
> to serve them, went on firing consistently as though they were on the
> ranges at Trawsfynyd.

Attacks north of Shwedaung by 4th/12th Frontier Force Regiment
and 2nd Battalion the 13th Frontier Force Rifles, supported by armour,

---

* Tutt is very critical of the British infantry at this time. Although one must make
  allowances for inter-arm rivalry, he judged those he encountered as poor quality
  compared with those he had met in the desert.

failed to break the Japanese defences, but allowed a number of trapped troops and vehicles from Anstice's force to break out. In the late afternoon 4th/12th Frontier Force Regiment and 2nd/13th Frontier Force Rifles were ordered to break off the battle and withdraw to the north.

At this point, the tanks of A and B Squadrons 7th Hussars battered their way through the village, and crossed the chaung, bypassing the bridge, followed by Anstice's HQ tanks. The fighting was fierce and by the time the armour emerged on the other side of the enemy positions, the tanks were out of ammunition. But the determination and skill of the two squadron leaders had allowed a number of infantry and soft-skinned vehicles to escape. However, C Squadron, with the gunners, sappers, infantry, and masses of transport, were still on the wrong side of the block. The commanding officers of the four infantry battalions decided that break out they would, so C Squadron smashed through the houses, and led some of the soft-skinned vehicles through. Tutt:

> It was decided to run the gauntlet at speed. We were almost out of ammunition as were the tanks. The tanks led off, blasting in every direction with everything they had. We followed and immediately most of the enemy fire was directed at the soft-skinned vehicles. We copped everything, bullets, mortar bombs and grenades. For the first time we saw the Japanese using their version of Molotov Cocktails to set tanks on fire. One of our 25-pounders received a direct hit and was blown off the road. The headlong rush slowed and stopped. We were under heavy machine gun fire from a house at the very edge of the road. Lieutenant Simcox took over one of the sub-sections, they unhooked the gun from the quad [gun tower], and he fired over open sights at the house with about our last round, and blew it and the machine-gunner to smithereens.

At one stage, while the progress of the column through the village was held up, many of Tutt's battery took cover in the monsoon ditches that line every road in Burma.

> We all had our heads well down, when Battery Sergeant Major Ward came down the road on his motor cycle, ignoring the bullets. He was as calm as if he were going for a Sunday afternoon ride at home. He wound his way between burning and abandoned vehicles, working his way to the head of the column. I think he was demonstrating to us that it was possible to move about and to carry on fighting, even

though things looked so bad. If it wasn't his intention, perhaps he was just seeking another way through. But this was the last that we were to see of him.

Desperately thirsty, and without food for over forty-eight hours, the situation looked bleak indeed for men still on the wrong side of the block. It was decided to try the road again. Tutt:

Led by Captain Shorten of Don Troop in a tank we would intersperse our vehicles and guns in groups of two or three between tanks. They would blast off with all the ammunition they had left. When they reached the blocked bridge, they would leave the road, and it was up to us to follow. If our trucks were hit or stopped, they had to be manhandled out of the way so that they did not block the escape route for others.

The tank commander looked back to see that his chicks were safely moving, gave us a thumbs up and battened down his hatches. Almost immediately he was fired at by an anti-tank gun, but it was silenced by machine gun fire from the tank. He went off at a hell of a lick, and for a moment I thought he was abandoning us, but he was getting up speed to shunt an empty truck out of our way. He stopped just short of the bridge and fired with everything into the area where he thought most of the enemy fire was coming from.

Tutt's vehicle, loaded with infantry who he refers to as 'unwanted cuckoos', drove off the road to avoid the blocked bridge, and smashed into the monsoon ditch, 'a spine shattering five feet' drop. They drove along the monsoon ditch in low gear, and must have already crossed the chaung, although Tutt does not mention it in his account.

The enemy on the far side of the road could not depress their weapons low enough, their bullets danced on the road and tore the canvass of our truck to shreds, but did no harm. There was the unpleasant crack of mortar [bombs] close at hand, but they were going after 'our' tank, which was busy turning in the road to go back for another vehicle. Suddenly Joe [driving] spotted a place where we could get back on the road. He shot up it at an angle, and for one moment I thought the truck was going to go over on top of me. Then it settled on four wheels and we were away down the road like mad.

They made contact with Indian troops after a few moments, and were clear. Collister of the Glosters was wounded again, in the leg. He was helped back to an ambulance and was

heaved in to join half a dozen others. I think I must have passed out for a bit, as my next recollection was of hearing a voice somewhere down the road calling out 'this is Colonel Faithfull of the Duke of Wellingtons. I am ordering all men who can do so to make their way out of this and rejoin their units which will try to reform on the other side of the village if possible'. He then lifted up the flap of the ambulance and said, 'Sorry chaps, but if any of you can manage to walk, do your best to save yourselves'. One or two of us levered ourselves out and bidding good luck to those left in the vehicle, we limped off as best we could.

Collister collected up all the men he could see and made his way to the bank of the River Irrawaddy. Eventually, after crossing the mouth of the chaung where it met the Irrawaddy, he and his party managed to reach the outskirts of Prome, and was given a lift by a British officer in the Burma Military Police. After dropping off two of his companions at the casualty clearing station, he 'prevailed upon the Major to take me to the GLOSTERS before going back to the casualty clearing station. When I saw the familiar Regimental sign it was like coming home again.' After seven weeks travelling north by ambulance and river steamer, Collister was eventually flown out of Burma from Myitkyina, some 500 miles north of Rangoon.

British casualties would have been even greater than 400, if it had not been for the gallant work by the 7th Hussars. Ten tanks were lost, as well as two 25pdrs and over 200 vehicles. It was, as the Hussars' War Diary says, 'a useless venture'. The Chinese attack never materialized, in fact they abandoned Toungoo on the day of the Shwedaung battle.

The Japanese, following up and constantly outflanking the Chinese, threatened Mandalay, and the British withdrawal route to the north-west and India, as well as the Shan States in eastern Burma. Two more Japanese divisions now appeared on the scene: the *18th Division*, veterans of three years' fighting in China and the capture of Malaya and Singapore, and the *56th Division*, many of whose conscripts had seen service in China.

By mid-April the 1st Burma Division had been severely mauled at the disastrous battle at Yenangyaung on the east bank of the Irrawaddy. Despite being given a bloody nose by 48th Gurkha Brigade and 7th Armoured Brigade at Kokkagwa, south of Yenangyaung, the Japanese *33rd Division* outflanked and cut off 1st Burma Division's escape route to the north across the Pin Chaung, a tributary of the Irrawaddy. The division eventually evaded the clutches of the Japanese, and found a route across the Pin Chaung, largely thanks to the efforts of 2 RTR. Only tracked vehicles, animals, and men on foot could cross. Some of the wounded were transferred from ambulances to the tanks, but most were abandoned. A gunner officer who had bravely volunteered to go back for them after dark found that every man had been bayoneted to death or had his throat cut.

> That our situation should have fallen to such a level that we had to abandon our wounded to the attentions of an enemy notorious for his savagery and brutality, must mark that last day of the Yenangyaung battle as one of the blackest in the long history of British arms.[8]

On 25 April, Alexander ordered the British to withdraw across the Irrawaddy. The rearguard, 48th Gurkha Brigade, crossed on the night of 30 April, and the great Ava bridge at Mandalay was destroyed. The Japanese advance to the Irrawaddy had been severely delayed by the actions of the 48th Gurkha Brigade, which had struck the Japanese *18th Division* a stunning blow, inflicting over 500 casualties for the loss of only ten. The Gurkhas rated this vaunted division, which had spearheaded the advance in Malaya, as far less formidable than their old adversary the *33rd Division*, which was reorganizing after the Yenangyaung battle. The British gained themselves some breathing space, but from now on there would be no more coordination with the Chinese.

The British route to India led across the Chindwin River from Shwegyin to Kalewa on the west bank. Once again the Japanese raced to cut them off. The Japanese *33rd Division* seized Monywa just ahead of the 1st Burma Division, who might have regained the town after a hard battle, but were called off in a signal whose origins are unclear to this day. This gave the Japanese the freedom to use the Chindwin River as a follow-up route, while the British were forced to move overland to Shwegyin and ferry across the Chindwin. Before the British withdrawal from Shwegyin was complete the Japanese arrived and seized key ground overlooking the ferry site. The Chindwin River at this point was 600 yards wide, and flowed at about three to four knots. But the end of the track on the eastern side of the Chindwin at Shwegyin was six miles downstream of Kalewa on the western bank, so the turnaround distance for craft ferrying across was twelve miles not 1,200 yards, and half of this journey was against the current. Only five river steamers were available to the British, and loading was painfully slow, not helped by all but one of the Chittagong crews refusing to work by day for fear of air attack. The sole route to Shwegyin was a very difficult track which generally followed the tortuous course of the dry bed of the Shwegyin Chaung, a tributary of the Chindwin. Hemelryk:

> All around us was jungle which encroached on the track and the sides of the hills were so steep that deep cuttings had been made in order to make it possible to get up and down them. Here and there were vehicles which had gone over the edge or been left behind because they were too big to negotiate the bends. We had to cross and recross chaungs with cliffs of several hundred feet towering above us with roads cut into their faces. At times it was a perilous task. At one corner a portee [gun-towing vehicle] ditched itself by getting one wheel over the precipice. As we were holding up the column, I feared we might have to ditch it by throwing it right over. However, by means of a block and tackle attached to a large tree, the fitters managed to lift the back of the vehicle and tow it back on to the track.

This track finally led to the jetty through an area known as 'The Basin', a level hollow of dry paddy fields with, at the rim, steep cliffs, 200–300 feet high, covered in jungle. 'The Basin' was some 800 yards long and 400 yards wide. The track in the Shwegyin Chaung for ten miles to the east was crammed with troops, animals, guns, tanks, and vehicles waiting to be called to the jetty. The Japanese air force were not slow to take advantage of such a juicy target, but although they caused surprisingly little material damage, their appearance did not help the morale of the retreating army. The Japanese *33rd Division* approaching from the south were well positioned to attack and cut the track which ran south-west and lay across their axis.

Fortunately the troops responsible for defending the embarkation point were the best available, the 48th Brigade, Gurkhas and Jats.

Lieutenant Colonel Thornton had been flown out to take over command of 1st/3rd Gurkhas after Ballinger was killed at the Sittang. He wrote later to friends about his Gurkhas:

> I always thought they were pretty good, but now I am convinced that they are the finest soldiers in the world. At the end of the show their morale and their discipline was every bit as good as when the war started. After about 900 miles of retirement [retreat], the Gurkha Bde (helped by the British Armoured Regiment thank God), had to stand and fight to gain time for the others to get away. Honestly I don't think the Gurkha knows what fear is. Every one of the survivors are convinced that given equality all round in numbers etc. 'they will beat hell out of the little yellow bellied—*'.

Donald Day of 1st/4th Gurkhas echoes the above sentiments:

> The Gurkhas were a bit bewildered. We keep lambasting the Jap and then had to retire. They did not understand this constant retreat. Every time they met the Jap they beat them, and then had to retire.
>
> Gurkhas prefer the kukri to the bayonet, they can cut a man in half with it. A standard blow is cross-cut to the shoulder. They cut off heads. It is a terrifying weapon, and used in the hand of the Gurkha is lethal. I have used the kukri in anger only once. I was using it to sharpen a pencil by a haystack, and a Jap suddenly appeared round the corner, and I had to hit him with my kukri as I had nothing else to attack him with. My orderly was so convulsed with laughter at my ineptness, he failed to despatch the chap quickly. The Gurkhas have a strange sense of humour. I made a mess of him, and my orderly finished him off.

The action to which Thornton refers is that at Shwegyin, and as well as 1st/3rd Gurkhas, involved the 1st/4th Gurkhas, 2nd/5th Royal Gurkhas, 1st/7th Gurkhas, and the 1st Battalion 9th Royal Jat Regiment, as well as tanks from the 7th Hussars, 25pdrs of the 1st Indian Field Regiment, and four Bofors guns of the 3rd Indian Light Anti-aircraft Battery. Lieutenant Colonel Godley commanding the Jats had arrived at 'The Basin' first and been made responsible for its defence, so as each unit of the rearguard came up, it was agreed that he would continue to direct operations. The four Bofors were used both in the anti-aircraft

---

* The word after 'yellow bellied' was deleted before the letter reached the museum.

and ground role, the latter notably when 1st/9th Royal Jats and a company of 1st/7th Gurkhas were sent to clear the enemy off East Ridge, one of the features overlooking 'The Basin'. Major MacFetridge, commanding 3rd Indian Light Anti-aircraft Battery:

In order to distinguish friend from foe on the jungle clad cliffs, some of the advancing Gurkhas wore on their backs yellow screens as on the North-West Frontier [made from the saffron robes of a Buddhist priest]. Because of the accuracy of the Bofors and skill of the layers in the gun detachments, it was possible for some of this covering fire to be put down at right-angles to the line of advance.* The numbers 1 of the guns [the gun aimers] were faced at one time with engaging the enemy ground troops over open sights, or enemy reconnaissance aircraft, and chose to engage the latter which fled homewards, swerving violently from side to side. This possibility was not envisaged in the drill book!

By this time, most of Hemelryk's guns had been ferried across the Chindwin, with some of his vehicles. While he was overseeing the recovery of one of his two remaining guns:

Suddenly I was shot at. I saw, not 200 yards from me, a Jap taking a second aim. He missed me by a yard. It just shows what rotten shots the Japs are. I was so pleased at having at last seen something to shoot at – the first Jap I had actually seen during all the time in Burma – that I let him have a full magazine from my Tommy gun. I thought I saw movement in a bush near him, so I changed magazines and let go with a short burst, but I can't be sure that I hit anything the second time.

The 'empty battlefield' where one rarely sees the enemy in person would have been no surprise to Hemelryk after his time fighting in the desert. By now most soldiers in Burma were aware that one of the otherwise well-trained enemy soldiers' few weaknesses was poor marksmanship, possibly a result of a Japanese emphasis on silent attacks with the bayonet, for psychological reasons.

On the afternoon of 10 May, a message was received by HQ 17th Indian Division, who with 48th Brigade were part of the rearguard, that

---

* Always preferable to overhead fire because it can be brought down closer to own troops at less risk of inflicting casualties to one's own side.

only one more steamer would come in that night, because the remaining
crews refused to take the risk. This steamer was used to take off over
100 wounded, the sick and some civilian refugees. The remainder of
the rearguard would have to march out along a rough track to the north
to a spot opposite Kalewa, from where the ferry crews were prepared to
operate. Tanks, vehicles, and guns would be abandoned. MacFetridge:

> The withdrawal started at 7.55 pm and was a very close-run thing.
> A barrage lasting 20 minutes from three Bofors guns completely
> silenced the enemy and enabled the 1/9 Jats and 7 GR to withdraw
> with only one casualty and in good order; it is a tribute to their
> discipline that not one man withdrew before time.
>
> At 8.15 the guns ceased fire and five minutes later we received the
> order to go. As we left 'The Basin', enormous fires were getting hold
> on dumps of stores, ammunition, tanks and lorries. From the
> Japanese there wasn't a sound.
>
> I led a party of about twenty-five out of 'The Basin', and was very
> thankful to be met by Cameron, commanding 2/5 GR and acting as
> brigade commander, who guided my party to the footpath leading
> north.

MacFetridge quotes Lentaigne describing the scene. He was commanding 1st/4th Gurkhas, whose battalion guarded the entrance to the
pathway, and was the last battalion out.

> 'I found 4,000 troops of sorts concentrated in the Nala bed patiently
> waiting for the track to clear in front of them. I put out stops and
> prayed hard that the Jap did not follow up; he did not, and we stayed
> there until 0400 hours. One Jap with a tommy gun could have
> killed thousands. The block was caused by a mountain battery and
> line of communications troops with their mules heavily overloaded
> and unable to see where they were going. All night we were almost
> deafened by ammunition and lit up brilliantly by blazing lorries, but
> up the deep jungle-covered side nala [nullah – dried watercourse]
> where the goat track twisted its tortuous way, it was pitch dark.
> When we eventually moved off, we found the track littered with kit
> and a mule over the khud [hillside] every ten yards. We did ten miles
> of this beating along the stragglers from the Armoured Brigade who
> had to march for the first time in months, and then got to a place on
> the river bank where the steamers could lift us off.'

My party was just ahead of Lentaigne's battalion and the embarkation with them on the steamer was wonderfully orderly.

Hemelryk's battery, hitherto vehicle-borne, took part in this march. Laden with two haversacks containing a mass of kit, including an album of photographs, he soon discovered what every infantryman knows; do not carry any more weight than you have to.

The first hour of our march was up and down such steep gradients that everyone was exhausted. So steep were these slopes that you had to wait for the man in front of you to scramble up before you could follow. Sometimes there was a path to follow, sometimes two paths, and at other times no path at all. I was never so hot or exhausted. I had to throw away my bed roll and some of the heavier tins of food from my haversack. Never take a tin of cheese for a long walk – it weighs more than bully beef. Soon I had no water in my water bottle and we all had a killing thirst. It was an extremely hot night.

Eventually we struck a good sized stream and marched down the middle of it. It smelt a bit, but some people drank from it and filled their water bottles. I felt it too much of a risk. At all costs I had to keep going and get my men out of this nightmare and not get ill.

We were fortunate in having no-one [from the Battery] killed on these precipitous climbs. A number of mules lost their footing and were killed, and our mule-driver, an Indian, failed to turn up, in fact neither he nor our remaining mules were ever seen again.

The Japanese did not follow up. By mid-afternoon on 11 May the whole of BURCORPS, except 1st Burma Brigade moving on a separate axis to the north, were across the Chindwin. The Japanese had suffered a bloody nose, the *33rd Division* taking more casualties in the Shwegyin battle than any other in the campaign, one company being down to twelve men. Hemelryk:

The crossing of the Chindwin was a pleasant change after all our marching. Soon after eleven am everyone was accounted for much to my relief. It was hard to believe that it was still only the 11th of May – we had done so much during the past twenty-four hours; but the day was not finished yet. We were told we would have to march, and would start when it was dark – the thought of another long night march was somewhat daunting.

48th Brigade were sent up the River Chindwin to Sittaung in five river steamers, where they disembarked and marched to Tamu. At Sittaung the steamers were scuttled by the Royal Marines of Force Viper, which had steamed on BURCORPS' left flank all the way from Rangoon. Lieutenant Firth and 2nd Dukes were with 48th Brigade at Sittaung:

> Here two officers of the Gurkhas sneaked off to have a look at the Mawlaik Club and came back with two or three fantastic volumes of bird books by Audubon, now worth a fortune. While at Sittaung we were visited by a platoon of elephants presumably to collect heavy baggage (I hope somehow those bird books were sneaked on board the elephants). .

The Japanese did not follow BURCORPS across the Chindwin. The enemy was now the impending monsoon, in steep, mountainous, jungle-covered country that boasts the highest rainfall in the world. The march from the Chindwin to Imphal has been covered in detail elsewhere, and the rigours have sometimes been exaggerated. As long as the monsoon held off, marching conditions were not too bad, but the men in BURCORPS were undernourished, weary, and mentally played out. Alexander decreed that the priority for transport should be given to civilian refugees, most of them women and children and many of them sick. However, most troops covered some of the distance in transport, which ferried parties forward before returning to pick up the next load.

At Tamu the marching conditions deteriorated. There were hundreds of dead refugees, as well as streams fouled by the excreta of the thousands of civilians who had passed by. The 48th and 63rd Brigades took it in turns to be rearguard, and when the monsoon began on the evening of 18 May, both brigades still had three nights of bivouacking in the open in the drenching downpour. Sickness rates among Indian and Gurkha troops, which had been low in Burma throughout the campaign, rocketed, especially malaria. Nevertheless, almost all the British and Indian units of the two divisions marched into India with their personal weapons, and to the surprise of those who met them their morale was high. The laurels for the formations with the best fighting record in the campaign must go to the 7th Armoured and 48th Gurkha Brigades. Firth:

The monsoon broke as we crossed the Indian [Assam] Frontier. The screw guns of 12th [Indian] Mountain Battery were in action positions to cover us as we crossed. They had marched about one thousand miles with their screw guns from south of Moulmein. As we marched up to Palel, General Slim was there to see us. John Williams' company still carried one of their Boyes anti-tank rifles, a four-man load. We had all our own weapons.

'They might look like scarecrows, but they looked like soldiers too', wrote Slim.[9] Lieutenant Firth

had to remain in Imphal commanding the last 90 all ranks of the remaining fit men, including our padre, our MO, John Williams, Jackie Wardle and Horsfall. Our MO was 'Doc' O'Hara who got an MC for his performance between Kaikyto and the Sittang Bridge and divisional counter attack at Paungde/Shwedaung.

All but two of the Burma Rifles battalions came apart; many of the soldiers deserted, fearing for their families' safety at the mercy of the Japanese, and worse, the detested Burmese. The most steadfast soldiers in the Burma Rifles were the Sikhs, Punjabis, and Gurkhas. But some 500 Karens, Chins, and Kachins also remained loyal, and after retraining many were to take part in Wingate's two Chindit expeditions. He was to write of them after his first expedition: 'I have never had under my command in the Field as good a body of men as the 2nd Burma Rifles.'[10]

The Burma Army had carried out the longest withdrawal in the history of the British army, 1,100 miles under the most testing conditions. Outnumbered, lacking air superiority, and with the majority of soldiers badly trained, they had learned and learned fast. They had hit the Japanese hard at times, and inflicted more casualties than they suffered. They now knew they could beat the Japanese. There was a great deal more to learn and put into practice, and the fact that they had so much leeway to make up when the campaign started was not their fault. The blame lay with politicians who in peace had failed to provide the necessary funding for a battle-ready army. The bill was met with the lives of soldiers, British, but mostly Indian, and Gurkhas.

2

Striking back: the Arakan and the First Chindit Expedition

The first Burma campaign ended with both sides at the end of their respective logistic tethers. The Japanese had no plans for an immediate advance into Assam and the conquest of India was not on their strategic agenda. Even if they had entertained such ideas, a great deal of logistic preparation would have been required before an advance in force across the Chindwin could be possible. In mid-July 1942, General Terauchi, commanding the Japanese Southern Area, based in Singapore, was ordered by Imperial General Headquarters (GHQ) in Tokyo to reconnoitre and prepare for an offensive to seize an area bounded by the line Imphal in Assam to Akyab in the Arakan, followed by exploiting to the River Brahmaputra. This was seen not as a preliminary to the invasion of India as a whole, but as an attempt to deny British and American use of the airfields in Assam and eastern India, thereby choking off supplies to China by air; the only other route, the Burma Road from Rangoon to well inside the Chinese border, was in Japanese hands.

The British also fostered plans for a comeback in South-East Asia, which included a thrust from Imphal into northern Burma. This required the establishment of a huge base organization, and much work on lines of communications to provide logistic support for the formations taking part in the offensive; the beans, bullets, and fuel without which war can not be fought. Strategic communications in India were designed with campaigning on the North-West Frontier in mind, the obsession of British India for over 100 years. It had never occurred to anyone that there would ever be a threat on the North-East Frontier. Now a great deal of work was needed to improve the inadequate communications with Assam, which ran from Calcutta, the main port and railhead, roughly round three sides of a square including crossing the Ganges and the even larger Brahmaputra River; the latter by ferry only. In a straight line, Calcutta and the Imphal plain are roughly as far apart as Rome and Belgrade. Troops and supplies using the rail and road system joining Calcutta to Imphal completed a journey equivalent to travelling from Rome to Belgrade via Venice, southern Austria, Slovenia and Croatia, changing rail gauges at least once on the way, and ferrying complete trains across a major river, followed by transferring loads on to trucks for the final 100 miles. The alternative was to use rafts and barges on the Brahmaputra River, which involved a journey of 1,136 miles to Dibrugarh (roughly equivalent to a trip up the Danube from the Black Sea to Vienna). The Arakan front could be supplied by water, but to begin with there was a shortage of craft, as many of the river steamers and flat-boats had been sent to Iraq to work on the Euphrates, and were not released until 1943.

It was to take both sides until early 1944 before major operations in Assam were possible. By then the British had established air superiority, and tactical lessons learned in 1942 and 1943 had been digested and applied.

Meanwhile GHQ India ordered a limited offensive in the Arakan to clear the Japanese out of the Mayu Peninsula and seize Akyab Island, which controlled the mouths of the two major rivers in the Arakan, the Kaladan and the Mayu. The main purpose of the offensive was psychological; following on the heels of defeat, it was intended to raise morale, and show that the British were beginning the comeback. It was also important not to allow the Japanese to seize the initiative in this area. A glance at the map will show that whereas the capture of Akyab would certainly not open the way back to Rangoon and the reconquest of Burma for the British, the Arakan was a possible Japanese invasion route to India.

Captain Rissik was then the second-in-command of the special service company of the 2nd Battalion The Durham Light Infantry (2 DLI). The company had been formed for special tasks in connection with amphibious operations planned for the British 6th Infantry Brigade, of which 2 DLI was one of the four battalions, the others being 1st Battalion The Royal Scots, 1st Battalion The Royal Welch Fusiliers, and 1st Battalion The Royal Berkshires. According to Rissik:

The Arakan theatre of operations – that is to say the area south of Chittagong and north of Akyab – was a mixture of coastal plain and jungle covered hills. The width of the coastal plain varied between some twenty or thirty miles just south of Chittagong and a few hundred yards at Foul Point. The greater part of the plain consisted of paddy fields intersected by innumerable streams or chaungs. Occasional hillocks rose from the paddy fields and the whole landscape was dotted with villages set among trees and bamboo clumps. The chaungs were tidal and many were several hundred feet wide. Not a few were fringed with mud banks and mangrove swamp. The coastline itself was partially mangrove, partially stretches of sandy, surf ridden beach. The grain of the country ran from north to south dividing the area into two combat zones. The first of these – and the one we would be concerned with – was the Mayu peninsula, bounded by the Naf River valley and the coastal plain on the west and by the Mayu River on the east. This latter valley was topographically similar to the coastal plain. Down the centre of the peninsula ran the Mayu range consisting of numerous steep ridges covered by dense jungle. The average height of the peaks was 1,500 feet, but owing to their steepness the hills were deeply cut by numerous water courses which in the rains became raging torrents, and in the dry season provided possible pathways across the range. The second zone was that of the Kaladan Valley. It could only be reached overland by coolie tracks or by water down the Sangu River valley. It was similar to the Mayu Range, but higher and more difficult to cross. Above the village of Kaladan itself there was practically no cultivation as the valley narrowed to a gorge. There was little fighting in this area although a force of approximately battalion strength advanced down the Kaladan valley when the offensive began. Apart from the two river valleys and the coastal plain, the rest of the area consisted of precipitous jungle covered hill tracts inhabited by primitive tribes – some of the more remote of whom were reputed still to be head-hunters, and much of it was completely inaccessible except by jungle paths.

Foul Point at the tip of the Mayu peninsula is only five miles from Akyab and guns situated there could dominate the northern part of the island. Hence the capture of Foul Point was an important precursor to the amphibious operation to take Akyab, assigned to the 6th British Infantry Brigade.

The Japanese held the Arakan with only one regiment of the *55th*

Division, so Major General W. L. Lloyd's 14th Infantry Division which was assigned to the task would have a comfortable numerical superiority. Slim was originally responsible for the offensive, but as he was now commanding 15th Corps, Eastern Army under Lieutenant General N. M. Irwin assumed direct control before the operation began.

For a number of reasons, logistical, lack of suitable craft, and adverse weather, Lloyd did not start his advance along both sides of the Mayu Range until mid-December 1942, in the course of which he seized the small port of Maungdaw, and the town of Buthidaung. These were linked by the only west–east road on the peninsula, which passed through tunnels under the Mayu range. By January 1943, patrols in Bren-gun carriers had penetrated as far as Foul Point. But delays in following up allowed the Japanese to reinforce the area and establish strong positions in Donbaik on the seaward side of the peninsula, and Rathedaung on the east side of the Mayu valley, respectively about ten and fifteen miles north of Foul Point.

A series of disjointed, uncoordinated, and piecemeal attacks failed to take either. Here the Japanese defensive bunker positions were encountered for the first time. These were well sited, in mutual support so that attackers assaulting one bunker came under flanking fire from at least one other. Roofed with logs and about five feet of earth they were impervious to field artillery shells and all too often even to medium bombs. Well camouflaged, they were only spotted with difficulty, even from as close as fifty yards or less. Each would be held by five to thirty men manning medium and light machine-guns. Attacking troops arriving on top of the bunkers would be treated to a heavy enemy bombardment brought down on themselves by the Japanese, secure in their own inviolability, and in any case not caring overmuch if they inflicted casualties on their own troops. Every single occupant of each bunker had to be killed before the position could be deemed secure.

Major Landon was appointed to command the 8th Mountain Battery Royal Indian Artillery, and arrived after the first attacks.

It was a really splendid Battery of Jat Sikhs and Punjabi Mussalmans with four King's Commissioned Officers, three British and one Indian (a Hindu a splendid young officer). The battery had recently come from the North West Frontier (where there was no opposing air force), and was used to Frontier drills. So, just before I arrived it had been caught in the open (guns not dug in and mules formed up behind the guns), by a Jap bomber and had some casualties to men and mules. The then OC left, and when I arrived my first job was to teach the men the rudiments of camouflage; gunpits camouflaged first, then dug, slit trenches for gunners, move the guns in next; mule line deep in a chaung in the jungle; the Jap Air Force never found us. At night we would move a couple of guns to the old position and carry out a harassing fire programme before moving back to our new gun position. Occasionally Jap parties landed from the sea to attack our old gun position, but were easily beaten off.

When I arrived I was told that a Royal Indian Army Service Corps (RIASC) truck had lost its way and driven down the beach to Donbaik. The few Japs had hurriedly left, leaving an uneaten meal, which the RIASC people ate, after which they had driven back to brigade. If only brigade had acted quickly, they could have advanced down the peninsula and taken Donbaik without any trouble. But they waited a day and then started to advance slowly, expecting to reach Donbaik without any trouble.

But the Japs had had their warning, and they quickly reinforced Donbaik and dug themselves in one and a half miles to the north in a deep chaung which stretched from the sea right into the jungle; in advance of this chaung they dug a strong bunker with [several] machine guns. When the Brigade [47th Indian Infantry Brigade] reached the Jap defensive position, the leading elements were held up.

Brigadier Blaker commanding the 47th Brigade estimated, correctly, that Donbaik was held by one company and ordered the 1st Battalion Inniskilling Fusiliers to move along the coastal strip and the 1/7th Rajput Regiment along the foothills supported by the 130th Field Regiment (less one battery), the 8th Mountain Regiment and a company of Jat machine-gunners. Both attacks failed with heavy losses, particularly in officers, so Blaker ordered them back to a defensive position between the sea and the foothills some 400 yards north of the FDL Chaung.*

More coordinated attacks on Donbaik were mounted, including attempts with tank support, but all failed. Landon:

---

* FDL was army shorthand for Forward Defensive Locality.

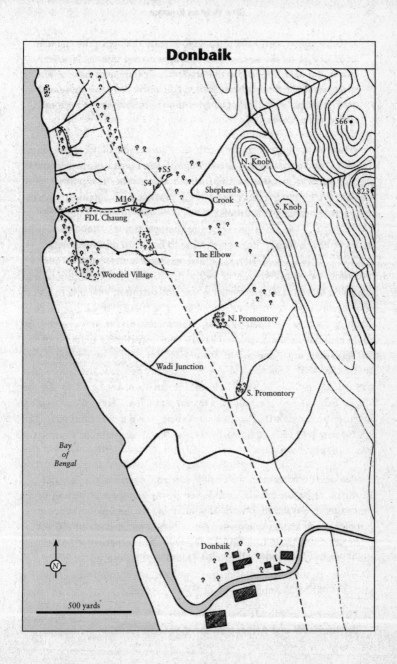

Donbaik

566

N. Knob

S. Knob

823

Shepherd's
Crook

S5
S4

M16

FDL Chaung

The Elbow

Wooded Village

N. Promontory

Wadi Junction

S. Promontory

Bay
of
Bengal

Donbaik

N

500 yards

Artillery support consisted of a rolling barrage in front of the infantry attack and/or smoke screens – everything was tried. But the Japs were always too well dug in for the artillery preparation to have much effect, and the infantry always started late and so kept too far behind the barrage giving the Japs plenty of time to man their fire positions and repel the attack.

When tanks were sent forward, they were not all from the same squadron, and therefore not used to fighting as a team, as Slim, who had been ordered to provide them, protested at the time. The tanks arrived too late for a proper reconnaissance or practice with infantry unaccustomed to working with armour. After a month of attacks here and at Rathedaung, 14th Division were no nearer taking Foul Point. The Japanese had, however, been given time to bring up reinforcements.

After further failed attacks, Lloyd realized that there was now no possibility of assaulting Akyab before the onset of the monsoon, and suggested that he adopt a defensive role and abandon attempts to secure Foul Point. Irwin agreed and told him to prepare layback positions in depth in the area bounded by Indin, Buthidaung on the Mayu peninsula, and Kyauktaw in the Kaladan. Wavell, who consistently underestimated the Japanese, now chipped in from GHQ at Delhi, overruling Irwin, saying that a decisive success was required to persuade the troops that they could beat the Japanese. He told Irwin to order Lloyd to use the 6th British Infantry Brigade in concert with the 71st Indian Infantry Brigade to overcome Donbaik by sheer weight of numbers. The 6th Brigade had been standing by for the Akyab amphibious landing for over a month. Rissik:

> The months of training the brigade had put in were not, at any rate, as yet, to be completely wasted. For it was decided that instead of assaulting Akyab, the brigade should be landed behind the Japanese defences at Donbaik and so secure Foul Point in that way. What purpose the capture of Foul Point would serve once the attack on Akyab had been called off was left in obscurity.

This attack too was cancelled. Rissik:

> The next piece of news was that the brigade was to be committed to the command and tender mercies of the 14th Division for employ-

ment on the Mayu peninsula in an effort to succeed at Donbaik where everyone else had failed.

Having been ferried across the Naf River from Teknaf to Maungdaw, the brigade marched south to take up positions in the Donbaik area by 9 March 1943. The DLI and the Royal Scots were in the line while the Royal Welch and the Royal Berkshires were about a mile in the rear. The 55th Indian Brigade, one of the original brigades of 14th Division, had handed over the position to the 6th Brigade, before moving to Rathedaung. The 55th Brigade were jumpy, and according to Rissik, 'on the nights before the hand over, they kept us on [under?] almost continuous small arms fire during darkness, firing presumably at shadows or noises. It was almost unbelievable.'

The Japanese defensive layout was based on a chaung about a mile north of Donbaik village (also known as FDL Chaung). There was water in the chaung only as far as the jungle-clad foothills, where it twisted in the shape of a crook, nicknamed 'the Shepherd's Crook'. Between the Shepherd's Crook and the beach was flat, open paddy nearly 1,000 yards wide. The chaung was a natural obstacle, which had been improved by the Japanese digging a system of mutually supporting weapon pits and bunkers. The two strongest of these, designated S 4 and S 5, were on a small tributary chaung leading north-east from the main chaung. S 5 was extremely strong, having been hollowed out in an existing mound; S 4 was if anything stronger, consisting of a series of bunkers dug into the banks of the chaung. The main positions were covered by subsidiary defences at chaung junctions and other likely approach routes. The whole of FDL Chaung was overlooked by two steep, densely wooded hills to the east of the Twin Knobs, or North and South Knob. Both hills held the Japanese mortars, artillery and machine-guns.

The positions occupied by the British were reminiscent of the Western Front of the First World War, in a jungle setting. Rissik:

Battalions held lines of trenches and between them and the Japanese posts in and around the the chaung was an area of no man's land – the playground of patrols. In some cases the trenches were already provided by nature in the form of dry chaung beds, and many of them were deep enough for a man to stand upright unseen by the enemy. But in others you had to dig or die; foxholes, weapon pits,

and occasionally sand-bagged revetments were the order of the day.
Down by the beach the field of fire from these trenches would be a
matter of hundreds of yards, but as they approached the foothills and
jungle, visibility was limited to a matter of feet.

The only ground gained by the various attacks so far was the Twin
Knobs. The previous attack by the 55th Brigade had succeeded in
securing the western end of FDL Chaung and the wooded village just to
the south of it. However fierce Japanese counterattacks had ejected the
British from this hard-won ground leaving abandoned equipment and
the rotting corpses of the Inniskilling Fusiliers who had borne the brunt
of the attack.

The attack on Donbaik on 18 March was to start with an artillery
and mortar bombardment at 0530 hours. A quarter of an hour later two
companies of Royal Welch, starting from concealed positions north and
east of S 4 and S 5, were to capture the eastern end of FDL Chaung
up to M 16. An hour later the DLI were to capture an area known as
'the Elbow' due south of the 'Shepherd's Crook'. At 0710 hours the 1st
Battalion The Lincolnshire (of 71st Brigade) would advance southwards
off the Twin Knobs and secure the North Promontory. Firmly ensconced
behind the FDL Chaung by attacks coming in from the flank, rather
than frontally as hitherto, exploitation south by the Royal Scots, the
Royal Berkshires and the 5th/8th Punjabis on loan from the 47th Brigade
would result in the seizure of Donbaik; at least that was the grand
conception. It was, to be fair, an imaginative plan, made by Brigadier
Cavendish, commander of the 6th Brigade. But his proposal that the
attack should not be preceded by an artillery and mortar bombardment
in order to catch the Japanese by surprise was overruled by Irwin, 'back-
seat driving'.

The attack was preceded by some deception including a simulated
dawn attack in the hope that the Japanese would open fire and reveal
their positions. A preliminary attack by a squadron of RAF Blenheims
planned for the FDL Chaung and S 4 and S 5 in particular was a failure,
as the aircraft dropped their bombs on Donbaik village. An ingenious
plan was hatched to destroy S 5 with a pole charge. A handcart packed
with explosive was to be pushed out on the end of sections of metal
tubing from a hidden position in the jungle. Sapper Raggatt's diary entry
for Saturday 13 March:

What a day. We are 40 yards from the Japs, shells, mortars, bombs, bullets. We fix our charge by six o'clock. At one o'clock on Sunday morning we go over and boom our charge to the Jap position. They throw grenades at us. The truck [handcart] sticks in hole 12 ft from Japs and we have to blow. All hell let loose for an hour.

The Japanese had dug slit trenches around the bunker, and it was one of these that frustrated the gallant attempt by the sappers. Another attempt was made on 15 March. Raggatt's diary:

We did not reach the strongpoint by 12 yards and we do it again [i.e. have another attempt]. This time 500 lbs explosive. A very hard day. Blow at 6.30 terrific – pipe bends and charge still 2 yards from target. Brigadier pleased but we are mad.

Tuesday 16th
Hampson the swine lost his nerve. We learn today that the position is not wrecked. We go and salvage a few pipes and return to base. Royal Artillery are blasting away all day. Good lads.

'Unfortunately', wrote Rissik, 'apart from shaking the garrison inside the bunker, the effect on the exterior was negligible'.
Raggatt:

Wednesday 17th
We load our mules and move up to final battle position half mile from Jap lines. No sleep. Very tired. I pray.

Company Sergeant Major (CSM) McClane of 2 DLI, aged twenty-eight, was an experienced soldier, a regular who had served in India before the war, and fought in France in 1940. Before the battle his company along with the remainder of the battalion had been issued with ammunition manufactured in the arsenal at Kirkee in India. His company formed up

in a dry nullah bed. There was a series of them every few yards. We were carrying an average of sixty pounds of kit. The artillery fire was going over, and everything was dusty in the early morning light. The company commander gave the order 'bayonets on, smoke if you want to'. The men dragged on their cigarettes, and were hanging on to them for grim death, because let's not be heroic, a man is only going to do a job if he's ordered to. He's going into an attack and the chance of him being killed is tremendous.

The order came, 'right, get ready, over the top'.

I had the signallers and company clerk with me. As we went over the top, I saw a Jap. I up with the Tommy Gun, and the bloody thing wouldn't fire. I was disgusted, here I was a professional soldier, and I couldn't hit him. He had been throwing grenades, but scarpered.

I never heard our brens firing, only desultory shots from rifles [which died away]. I had been in attacks in France and knew what it should sound like. All there was was Japanese firing, nothing of ours at all. The CO spoke to me on the set.* He asked what was happening.

I said, 'this is the funniest attack I've been in. I can't hear a Bren, I can't hear a rifle. There's nothing moving, all I can see is bodies.'

He said, 'do something about it then'

'What can I do?'

'Get the men in'

Well I only had Company HQ with me, the other two platoons were off on their own [one was detached]. I found the company commander wounded. He'd been wounded in France in the knee, and his same leg had been hit again. He was bleeding badly. I dragged him back through the nullah, found A Company Commander and put my company commander on a stretcher.

McClane returned to his own company HQ, spoke to the CO on the radio, and was ordered to get moving. He was leaning on the lip of a nullah when a shell burst nearby. A splinter hit the set. He found he could hear the CO, but could not transmit. He ordered his own company HQ to stay put while he went to find the two rifle platoons of his company. He passed a stretcher on which was Lieutenant Greenwall, one of the platoon commanders.

He was full of shrapnel from a Japanese plastic grenade, lying smoking a cigarette. He said, 'well Sergeant Major', stroking his 'old man', 'they didn't hit that'. He was newly married.

I found seven of his platoon lying down. I shouted, 'come on lads, bayonets'

---

* radio – the company rear link to battalion HQ, often with company rear HQ which usually includes the CSM.

A corporal said, 'wait, wait, Sergeant Major, these Brens and rifles won't fire'.

I didn't believe him and got down behind a Bren. One round fired and then the gun jammed solid. I went through all the drills, but nothing would work. I slung it aside in disgust.

'Give us your rifle'.

I fired it but the bolt stuck solid and I could not eject the round, except by putting the butt on the ground, and booting down the bolt with my foot.

McClane located the other platoon in a nullah bed, where they had been showered with Japanese grenades. The casualties included the platoon commander. All the officers were out of action. By now his signaller had got the set working again, and McClane arranged with the CO for mortar and artillery smoke and high explosive to cover his withdrawal. He told the platoon to stand by to move when the fire came down, to take the wounded and leave the dead. Some were very badly wounded.

They looked at me beseechingly. Although they call you what they like, the Sergeant Major is the king pin of the company, and the men depend on him for so much. I went back and picked up some more wounded, but our artillery started dropping short among us. But we were very lucky to have only two more casualties.

After reorganizing, the defective ammunition was all dumped in a chaung and replaced by serviceable rounds.

The attack by the Royal Welch Fusiliers failed, ending with one company cut off by the Japanese in the FDL Chaung. They had gallantly persisted again and again, but fire from other enemy positions including 75mm infantry guns and mortars mowed them down as they desperately searched for openings through which to throw grenades into the strongpoints. Sergeant Jones of 1st Royal Welch Fusiliers anti-aircraft platoon (Bren guns and usually working direct to battalion HQ):

At 0500 hours the attack began. All hell was let loose. Three-quarters of A Company got onto the bunker, but couldn't hold it. They got into some of the trenches on the outside which were empty. I came in from the right and lost half my men trying to attack similar bunkers. I was told over the radio to move up to A Company, and

take over [if necessary]. I wriggled forward and grabbed hold of the
first man I could see and asked what was going on. He pointed to an
officer doubled up down in a foxhole. He [the officer] said 'are you
taking over?'

'Yes', I said.

'Leave me here and get on with it'.

I then got a message to go back to the CO, who said 'D Company
are cut off. The Royal Scots are going to reinforce us and attack to
get D Company out. I'm coming back with you to A Company,
which he did.

The Lincolns had initially been successful, but the Japanese hooked
round and got across their rear and supply line, and the battalion
withdrew. A night attack was mounted by a company of the Royal Scots
aimed at extracting the Royal Welch company. Rissik, from the area of
the Shepherd's Crook (his special service company was not engaged):

The Royal Scots' attack went in at about two in the morning. I was
on watch at the time and heard the shouts as they charged across the
short distance separating them from their objectives. Why do men
shout when they want to gain surprise? One could hear the sounds
of Tommy Gun, grenade and mortar, but it only seemed a short
while before it all died away. Morning brought the news that this
attack had failed as dismally as that of the Royal Welch. We all began
to realise that the Brigade's attack had been as abortive as had all the
others.

Sergeant Jones, 1st Royal Welch:

The Japs were very astute, and shouted out in English, things like;
'British soldier why are you here? Your wives are waiting for you'.

The CO shouted in Welsh through a loudspeaker to D Company,
to hold on. This flummoxed the Japs.

A Company and the Royal Scots attempts to reach D Company
went well for the first fifteen minutes, but then came under Jap
bombardment. After two hours of fighting, we did get out about
forty men of D Company. There were no officers alive.

At midday on 19 March, the position opposite Donbaik was little
changed from that forty-eight hours previously. Raggatt:

Saturday 20th
The last few days have been hell on earth. I wonder how much longer
we are to stay here.

Although the British tried other stratagems, and patrolled, it seemed
that nothing could shift the Japanese. Rissik:

> Had we but known it, we might well have saved our energy; for on
> the other side of the Mayu range and in the Mayu valley beyond,
> events were taking place which were very shortly to have a profound
> effect upon our actions and were to make vain and worthless all the
> endeavours of the past few weeks.

By this time the Japanese had already mounted a counteroffensive.
Lieutenant General Takishi Koga now had his complete *55th Division* in
the Arakan. From Akyab he was well placed in a central position by
using the rivers to concentrate against the British, who were operating
piecemeal in three groups separated by the Kaladan and Mayu Rivers.
Having swept aside the British flank guard operating in the Kaladan
Valley, Koga ejected the British from the east bank of the Mayu River,
thus threatening formations on the Mayu Peninsula. Lloyd called off
further attempts to take Donbaik. The Japanese crossed the Mayu and
began their familiar tactic of cutting in behind brigades and battalions.
Lloyd had been ordered to go firm, but ordered a withdrawal. He was
relieved of command on 30 March by Irwin, who took personal control
of the battle pending the arrival of Major General C. E. N. Lomax with
his 26th Divisional Headquarters.

Meanwhile Wavell had again stepped in, ordering Irwin to regain
the initiative and inflict a severe defeat on the enemy. Unfortunately the
Japanese, retaining the initiative, were well on their way to achieving all
their objectives, and not content with having already thrashed a considerably superior British force, struck again. On 4 April 1943, Slim was
returning to Ranchi from leave in Simla, when he was summoned from
his night sleeper at four o'clock in the morning at the station at Gaya to
be told over the telephone in the station master's office that his Corps
HQ was required back in the Arakan. No sooner had he arrived in the
Arakan, finding Lomax newly in the saddle, than the Japanese attacked
the rear of the 6th British Infantry Brigade pulling back from Donbaik.

The first inkling of trouble had been reports of an attack in the early hours of 4 April, on troops guarding the bridge over a chaung a mile north of Indin where 6th Brigade Headquarters was sited. At this time Rissik's special service company formed part of an ad hoc force called Hopforce, after its commander Colonel Hopkins, composed of 1st Royal Berkshires, a company of 1st Royal Scots in Indin, and the dismounted carrier platoons of three of the 6th Brigade's battalions. Hopforce HQ was deployed with a field artillery battery in Kyaukpandu, a village three miles north of Indin. Rissik was sent to investigate with a platoon from the special service company and a section of carriers. They interrogated a couple of Indian soldiers from a mule company fleeing from the bridge and established that the Japanese were in about company strength. Rissik's force approached the bridge, but before arriving at the site

> found the remains of the mule company. There were fourteen bodies
> in all and about six dead mules. All had at least half a dozen bayonet
> wounds, and some were badly slashed with sword cuts. Only one
> man was still alive, and though we dressed his wounds as best we
> could he was dead before we could get an ambulance or stretcher.

There was no sign of the Japanese in the area of the bridge. This did not surprise Rissik: once dug in, the highly disciplined and well-trained Japanese soldiers were rarely seen in daylight, and did not usually open fire unless it was absolutely essential. He set up a position to control the road north of the bridge approaches.

> We did not have long to wait before something happened. We had
> just completed digging slit trenches, when about twenty men topped
> the small rise some six hundred yards east of us. They were walking
> in single file and appeared very tired. They seemed to be carrying
> heavy packs and were wearing khaki similar to our own. At first we
> thought they were Indian troops. It was not until they were within
> four hundred yards, that it was possible to see they were wearing
> knee breeches, long puttees and the cloth caps which were normally
> part of Japanese equipment. They were Japs all right, they had not
> seen us, and were making for the bridge. I told John to let them get
> a bit nearer before his platoon opened fire. It looked as if we should
> have them exactly where we wanted them. But it was not to be. Just
> at that moment, a lorry trundled up the road from Kyaukpandu. As
> soon as they saw it, the Japs went to ground with remarkable rapidity,

and although we shot at whoever we could see, the ground was very broken and there were a number of paddy bunds [banks].

No dead Japanese were found when the ground was subsequently searched. An attack by the whole of 1st Royal Scots to dislodge the Japanese on and around the bridge failed. The Japanese blew the bridge. A subsequent brigade-strength attack cleared the enemy from the bridge, and secured half of Point 251, which the Japanese had previously seized. Hopes were high; the withdrawal road to the north was open, by using the beach to bypass the bridge. However the Japanese, at regimental strength (three strong battalions), had some surprises up their sleeves. By now the DLI complete with the Royal Welch were north of the bridge, the Royal Scots were in Indin, with the brigade echelons and transport, and the 130th Field Regiment (25pdrs) were south of Indin in Kwason. The Royal Berkshires were around Ywathit in the foothills to the east of Kyaukpandu.

That night the Japanese struck at Indin. Rissik:

The still moonlit night re-echoed with the rattle of small arms fire, the grunt of bursting mortar bombs and grenades, and with the cries of attacker and attacked. The Japs streamed into the camp shouting in English, 'Royal Scots don't shoot.'

They were greeted with a blaze of fire, showers of grenades, and the bayonet. Brigade Headquarters had been foolishly located south of the Royal Scots and outside any defensive perimeter other than that provided by its weak defence platoon. The Japanese overwhelmed it, captured Brigadier Cavendish and his brigade major, and killed three of the staff officers. The remainder of the staff escaped down to the beach and made their way to Hopforce at Kyaukpandu. Before Brigade Headquarters was overrun, Cavendish had ordered 2nd DLI and 1st Royal Welch to attack southwards to relieve the pressure on the Royal Scots in the morning.

At dawn the CO of the Royal Scots emerged from his command post, to find the ground littered with the bodies of his 'Jocks' and the Japanese right up to the entrance. But the dogged resistance of the Royal Scots had paid off, the boot was now on the other foot. Having suffered heavily during the night, daylight revealed the Japanese, mostly in the open plain, attempting to find cover among bamboo clumps and scattered huts. British mortars and artillery were turned on them. Rissik:

The result was a glorious slaughter of Japanese who ran screaming from their coverts only to be shot down in scores by light automatics, rifles and mortars positioned round them like a rat hunt. If they remained under the cover of the trees they were blown to pieces by the 25 pounders, for they had not had sufficient time to dig themselves in adequately – and if they came out into the open, as very many of them did, they fell easy prey to the murderous fire of numerous small arms now so conveniently placed to effect their destruction.

During the day, plans were made by Hopkins to withdraw the brigade back to Kyaukpandu that afternoon along the beach, starting at 1300 hours, and the necessary orders were passed by radio. Rissik:

> Meanwhile the slaughter of the Japanese in the Indin area continued throughout the morning; and it was so effective that he was powerless to intervene. The trucks trundled down the beach and the long columns of troops marched along practically unhindered by the fire of any Japanese weapons. Alastair [his company commander] and I watched the extraordinary spectacle of the beach black with marching men making their way to safety, like a column of ants moving house after a shower of rain. The guns kept up a continuous and prolonged fire; and so it was the brigade passed safely by, beneath the very noses of the Japanese, with the loss of hardly a man or vehicle. By three o'clock the operation was successfully completed.

The 1st Royal Berkshires, cut off by the Japanese infiltration of Indin, had a message dropped to them from an aircraft telling them to withdraw to Kyaukpandu, which they did during the night of 6/7 April without difficulty. The 47th Indian Infantry Brigade was also cut off, and unable to use the tracks blocked by the enemy. The brigade commander ordered his men to break out across country, abandoning all equipment that could not be carried. Eventually the brigade broke into small parties, and between 8 and 14 April managed to marry up with the 6th Brigade. The 47th Brigade ceased to exist as a fighting formation and was sent back to India to re-form.

In one of the brighter moments of the Arakan campaign, the Japanese had been satisfactorily thrashed in the Indin area by the 6th Brigade. Documents, including a diary, captured later by the Royal Welch

Fusiliers disclosed the measure of the Japanese losses, with all battalions badly mauled, and one of them reduced to a total of eighty riflemen. Morale in the 6th Brigade was high, despite the loss of their brigade commander. Rissik concluded: 'In a straight conflict the British soldier had shown himself to be the master of the Japanese'. It must be said that although the Japanese had been seen off by 6th Brigade, overall Koga had good reason to be pleased with himself, since in one month he had inflicted a severe defeat on a British force of nine brigades.

According to Japanese reports, Cavendish and his brigade major were killed by British artillery fire. This is likely, as before his headquarters was overrun, Cavendish, speaking in whispers over the telephone, had ordered his artillery to shell the area as it was henceforth to be treated as enemy territory. During the British counter-attack, fire was brought down, badly wounding the Japanese commander, Colonel Tanahashi, and killing or wounding several of his staff. A Japanese medical officer sent to deal with these casualties found Tanahashi, and later, together they examined the body of Brigadier Cavendish lying nearby. The shelling was so fierce that the Japanese were pinned down and unable to attack the British and Indian troops as they made their get away. The brigadier had deliberately risked his own life, in the hope that his own soldiers would escape the trap. Tanahashi later told his son that he considered Cavendish the bravest man he had ever met.

Despite these setbacks, Lomax remained cool, and regrouped to cover the vital Maungdaw–Buthidaung Road (see map p. 88). However, in subsequent fighting the Japanese seized Point 551, which overlooked the road, and clearly the prospects of holding this position were dim. The arrival of Slim was soon felt among the troops in the Arakan: according to Rissik, 'with a marked change in the direction of affairs and a more realistic touch – the result of the new headquarters closer proximity to the battle area'. It became clear to Slim that a clean break was required. He wrote:

If we hold the Cox's Bazaar Area firmly the Japanese will find it extremely difficult to maintain large forces over so long an L of C [Line of Communication] through hill country. Let him. Pursuing this policy we give the Japanese all the dirty work. If he comes on he must do so in small bodies – we then kill them. If he goes back we send mobile columns after him to harry him. If he turns round and snarls we withdraw . . . once more . . .

The surest way of quick success in Burma is, not to hammer our way with small forces through the jungle where the Japanese has every advantage, but to make him occupy as much area as possible, string himself out until he is weak, and then, when we have got him stretched, come in at him from the sea and air. By luring him northwards into the Chittagong and Cox's Bazaar districts we get a better chance to get in behind his forward troops. His L of C runs along the coast and is vulnerable throughout its length. It gives us an opportunity of striking anywhere from Teknaf to Moulmein, a long coastline whereon we are almost bound to find an undefended beach. A block by a division landed astride this L of C, and kept there, would finally ensure the putting of all troops northwards into the bag or at least force them to adopt a difficult getaway across the hills.[1]

By pulling back he could protect the vital airfields at Chittagong, Cox's Bazaar, and Ramu, whereas all the possible blocking positions between Maungdaw–Buthidaung and Tumbru at the head of the Naf River could be outflanked and infiltrated by the Japanese moving through thick jungle country, and allowing them to lever out the defenders as they had so often demonstrated. The Cox's Bazaar–Ramu–Ukhia area consisted of open ground, giving Slim the opportunity to use his tanks and artillery, in which he was considerably superior to the Japanese. In advocating this plan, Slim was following one of the enduring principles of war: that a general should attempt to take advantage of *his strengths* and the *enemy's weaknesses*, while negating his own weaknesses and the enemy's strengths.

Irwin, the army commander in Delhi, reluctantly agreed to Slim's plan, and on 11 May 1943 he pulled back to where the British had started in October 1942. A great deal of equipment had been lost, and the 2,500 battle casualties were far outnumbered by the sick, mainly from malaria, but the biggest damage caused in the Arakan campaign was to morale. Major Gebhard rejoined his battalion, the 5/16th Punjabis, at Bawli Bazaar about sixteen miles north of Maungdaw on 13 May 1943:

Morale was low. In addition to the killed and wounded, there were a number of sepoys reported missing and unaccounted for. At one point some wounded had been left lying as the battalion had withdrawn, and this was preying on everybody's minds. The knowledge had already been circulated that wounded soldiers who fell into Japanese hands were quickly liquidated.*

Surprisingly few British officers seemed to be about. Many of them had gone sick, and the Colonel was showing distinct signs of strain. He clearly considered that his battalion had not come out of its first battle well, and was going round telling people that there would have to be a court of enquiry.

As always mail had a considerable effect on morale, for good or bad, and was eagerly awaited. Sapper Raggatt's diary for Sunday 11 April includes the entry: 'Mail at last, Phyllis and Doris. Doris [his fiancée] is married. That makes me a bachelor for life.'

In the well-led units, however, morale remained high. Raggatt recorded on 17 April:

Jap patrol through lines. Royal Scots move up. We stand to all day and night. Rather awkward.

The Gurkhas allowed the Japs to pass and were going to kill at leisure. Royal Scots therefore apologise and return. Gurkhas very annoyed indeed.

The rebuilding of the army's morale was to be Slim's main concern over the monsoon season when campaigning petered out, for in mid-October 1943 he was appointed to command the newly formed Fourteenth Army. By then Irwin had been replaced by General Sir George Giffard, who was the Land Commander-in-Chief and commander 11th Army Group, and became Slim's immediate superior. A newly created appointment was filled by Admiral Lord Louis Mountbatten, as Supreme Allied Commander South East Asia Command (SEAC), responsible for all Allied forces in Burma, Ceylon, Malaya, the Dutch East Indies, Siam and Indo-China. General Sir Claude Auchinleck had succeeded Wavell as Commander-in-Chief India, and the latter was elevated to Viceroy. Lieutenant General Sir Philip Christison replaced Slim at 15th Corps.

Giffard's arrival and subsequent actions were to have a profound and lasting effect on morale, but more immediate and dramatic were the exploits of Orde Wingate. Much has been written about this extraordinary

---

* Or not so quickly if the enemy wanted some bayonet practice.

man and his deeds.[2] He was a man of mercurial moods, and fiery temperament. He could be outrageously offensive – especially to his seniors and their staffs. The unswerving loyalty he demanded from his subordinates he conspicuously withheld from his superiors, thinking nothing of going over their heads, lying, plotting, and lobbying to get his own way. He was either hated or loved, there was no middle ground with Wingate. Much of what he preached strategically, operationally, and tactically was flawed, and some of it was downright nonsense. But all who met him, even those who found him extremely trying, including Slim, agreed that you could not ignore him. He could inspire men to achieve things that they had thought impossible. In character he was one of Sir Walter Raleigh's 'black swans' who, he said, 'behold death without dread and the grave without fear, set apart from the generality of men'.[3]

Following the British retreat from Burma, Wingate persuaded Wavell, then still C-in-C India, that the Japanese lines of communication would be an ideal target for what he called a 'long range penetration (LRP) force'. Wavell had met Wingate when he was C-in-C Middle East, in Palestine before the Second World War, where Wingate raised and commanded clandestine Jewish units against the Arabs, and again in Abyssinia in 1941, where he had commanded partisans as an adjunct to the successful campaign to oust the Italians, and now authorized the raising of 77th Indian Infantry Brigade to carry out Wingate's ideas. He originally intended to use Wingate's brigade ahead of an attack across the Chindwin by the 4th Corps from Assam, timed to coincide with offensives by the Chinese mounted from Yunnan, and the American General Stilwell's Chinese–American force south from Ledo. Wingate was to cross into Burma in mid-February 1943, and cut the railway between Shwebo and Myitkyina, which supplied the Japanese facing Stilwell. Having harassed the Japanese here, he was then if possible to cross the Irrawaddy to cut the enemy communications with the Salween front, where the Japanese confronted the Chinese in Yunnan.

The administrative difficulties in 1943 described at the beginning of this chapter made any offensives other than in the Arakan impossible, but Wingate pressed Wavell to allow his expedition to continue. He gave six reasons: his theories needed testing; delay would be bad for morale in his brigade; he could see whether the Burmese would cooperate in the liberation of their country; he would prevent a Japanese offensive on Fort Hertz, the last British toehold in Burma; he would stop Japanese infiltration across the Chindwin; and finally, he could interrupt any Japanese offensive against Assam.[4] Wavell agreed that he should go ahead, leaving Imphal on 8 February 1943. He also ordered the formation of another LRP brigade, the 111th Indian Infantry Brigade, which would go into Burma when 77th Brigade came out.

Wingate chose as his brigade formation sign the chinthe, a mythical beast which stands guard outside the temples and monasteries of Burma. It became mispronounced as 'chindit', and the name stuck. He organized his brigade into eight 'columns', each consisting of about 400 men, based on an infantry company. (No. 6 was broken up to replace casualties, sickness, fall-outs etc. incurred in training among the other columns.) A small headquarters, a reconnaissance platoon of Burma Rifles, two mortars and two Vickers machine-guns, a mule transport platoon, an air-liaison detachment of one RAF officer and radio operators to communicate with the air base for resupply, a doctor and two orderlies, and a radio detachment to communicate with Brigade Headquarters completed each column. Wingate's concept was that columns should march independently, be self-supporting for a week, and be supplied by air. In theory the column was mobile and secure. By having neither wheeled transport nor lines of communication it could go where it wished, and the enemy would have difficulty in finding it in the jungles and teak forests of northern Burma. Using the radio, Wingate would concentrate the columns for specific tasks.

Columns also trained to disperse if they encountered the enemy in strength. This worked well in the relatively calm atmosphere of exercises, but more often than not resulted in chaos when columns dispersed in the middle of a real 'shoot-out', when it proved impossible to brief everyone on the rendezvous (RV) to which every man should head. This dispersion drill was so ingrained that on at least one occasion a column encountered a small enemy patrol, which it should have easily 'rolled up' following correct jungle-contact drills, and instead dashed off in all directions. In battle the column often proved to be unwieldy, inflexible, and uneconomic in its teeth-to-tail ratio; 300 men supported one infantry company and a few sabotage squads. To produce these columns, infantry battalions were broken up, and much of their training wasted. Wingate was a gunner, and had never commanded as much as a platoon in a conventional battle. In his after-action report he made frequent comments on the low standard of training of most of the officers and men in his brigade. For example, training in river crossing before his first expedition proved inadequate when put to the test; a curious error since his mission would take him over two major rivers, the Chindwin and the Irrawaddy, as well as several smaller ones. Major Scott commanding Number 8 Column commented subsequently about the crossing of the Chindwin that 'it took all night. Lots of chaps couldn't swim'. That this should be so, after Wingate had six months to prepare his men, is an indictment of him as a brigade commander and his training methods.

The material he had to work with was of mixed quality, and very few soldiers were volunteers. The 13th Battalion The King's Regiment (Liverpool), consisting mainly of overage men (average thirty-three years), had been sent to India for internal security duties. The 3rd/2nd Gurkha Rifles were formed largely of underage recruits with inexperienced officers and NCOs, because of the 'milking' of the Indian Army mentioned earlier. The understrength 2nd Battalion Burma Rifles were seasoned troops, and, as well as forming their own column, supplied reconnaissance platoons for all other columns. The Sabotage Group (142 Commando Company) were mainly volunteers, well-trained and picked men. Some of them were also distributed among the columns. Many of the mule leaders were found by an extra company of young and ill-trained recruits from the 2nd Goorkhas led by the twenty-one-year-old Lieutenant Dominic 'Nicky' Neill of the same regiment: 'I and my Gurkha muleteers received no tactical training whatsoever until I came face-to-face with the Japanese. We were badly trained, badly led, and the plans were over-optimistic'.

Many Chindits, especially the younger and more impressionable, thought the world of Wingate, and were, and remain, uncritical of his training methods. Neill's verdict on the state of training of Wingate's brigade deserves more attention than the opinions of most of his fellow Chindits, because he subsequently fought in the Arakan with the 3rd/2nd Goorkhas, after the Second World War in Borneo and Malaya with the 2nd/2nd Goorkhas, and instructed at the Jungle Warfare School in Malaya. In this time he saw, and helped train, the British and Gurkha soldier in his transformation from a mediocre jungle fighter to surpassing the Japanese by 1944, and, by 1960, among the best in the world. By these standards Wingate's brigade *was* poorly trained in every aspect of jungle operations, as well as escape, evasion, and survival skills. Wingate had never operated in the jungle in his life, so was hardly fitted to shape the training to cope with the reality of what lay ahead. As events would show, many of his men would pay for the many shortcomings in their preparation.

Lieutenant Wilding was in his early thirties, but his enthusiasm was typical of the younger element in the Chindits. He had been posted to the 6th Gurkha Rifles on arrival in India, and, after some leave during which he amused himself riding a well-trained polo pony called San Toy, found himself detailed for a cipher course. This did not please him, so he

> obtained an interview with the Chief Instructor and informed him that I had not joined the Army to spend the rest of the War in Delhi or some other static HQ mucking around with ciphers. He could have told me that I joined the Army to do as I was told and he would have been quite right to do so. Instead he said, 'Well there is a posting to a Brigade where you will be expected to be able to ride and swim backwards – if you do well, you could go there'. I could swim pretty well, and I thought my outings with San Toy constituted an ability to ride so I gratefully accepted.

On his arrival near the Seonee, the scene of Kipling's *Jungle Books*, he found

> a camp fire in the middle of some jungle with some rather scruffy officers sitting around it. Everyone was most welcoming, and I was handed a soft drink. I later found out that Brigadier Wingate preferred us not to drink.
>
> When bed time was upon us, the BM indicated a bush, and said, 'Under that if you like'. So I slept, not at all disturbed by the information that this was splendid tiger country. As if I didn't know. Shere Khan had roamed this jungle.

Wilding was an unreserved admirer of Wingate's powers of leadership, intelligence, and guts, about which no one, including his worst enemies, has ever expressed any doubts. Wingate was also ruthless, which all commanders must be at times. Wilding:

> He [Wingate] never threw a life away, but you always felt that he realised that his life and the life of each of us was expendable if it was necessary.
>
> When things were very bad, I was sitting under a bush with my

sergeant trying to decipher a more than usually corrupt signal and hearing him ask the MO, 'How long can Wilding last?' The MO replied, 'About a week I think'. The Brigadier replied, 'I only want him for another two days'. Of course neither of them knew I was within earshot, and were taken aback by my not very respectful interjection, 'After that I suppose you will have me shot like the bloody mules.'

Some of the staff officers in Wingate's Brigade HQ rode horses to enable them to move around more quickly. Wilding was issued with a flea-bitten grey called Freckles. Thinking the colour bad camouflage, Wilding sought out a major, a supposed expert on the subject, who advised potassium permanganate.

I tried it out on Freckles's off-fore. The result was pink, I went no further and contented myself by lending my charger to people I didn't like. None of them came to any harm. We ate poor Freckles in the end.

Wilding's perceptive and amusing comments on his fellows in brigade HQ include Flight Lieutenant Tooth RAF, posted in as an assistant RAF Liaison Officer, saying 'mournfully':

'Twenty four hours ago I was drinking gin in New Delhi and now I find myself an infantryman, and your brigadier has put me in charge of those elephants. And they'll die. And the army will stop their value out of my pay.' He needn't have bothered. We took them only as far as the Chindwin and they all survived. Anyway he was no more in charge of them than I was – the elephants made it quite clear that they only took orders from their oozies (mahouts) and the oozies were an independent lot.

The Chindits crossed the Chindwin in two groups. The Northern Group, five columns and Wingate's HQ, crossed at Tonhe heading for the Shwebo–Myitkyina railway, and thereafter for the Irrawaddy. The Southern Group, the two remaining columns, crossed the Chindwin thirty-five miles south of the Northern Group, cut the railway, and again headed for the Irrawaddy.

Private Hyner of the 13th King's Liverpool was in Number 7 Column commanded by Major Gilkes and with Wingate:

This afternoon we arrived at the Chindwin. Orders were given to cut down bamboo canes to make rafts ready for a dawn crossing. The Column Commander, Major Gilkes, read to us the order of the day. 'Today we stand on the threshold of battle'. Anxiety was with us as we did not know what to expect on the other side of the river, as we knew the Japs occupied the territory. It was still dark when I was told to get on to the raft with about 20 others. On moving off from the bank the raft immediately sank. We managed to scramble back to the shore. Luckily enough, the water on my side of the raft wasn't too deep, so I only got half wet. Officers, which included Brigadier Wingate and Gilkes decided that other means had to be found to cross the river. Canoes were found and we were ordered to board them. Seven of us which formed the Bren Gun Squad went into the first canoe and we began to cross the river. It was still dark.

Wilding commented: 'I will draw a veil over the crossing. . . . resembling a boat race between Colney Hatch and Bedlam [two famous London lunatic asylums] – but we got away with it. Sadly one of the British muleteers was drowned – our first casualty'.

Both groups crossed the Chindwin without encountering the enemy. The Southern Group split into its two columns to attack the railway at separate points. Number 1 Column destroyed a bridge, but Number 2 Column walked along a branch line in daylight because it was easier. They compounded the error by bivouacking within 200 yards of the line. The Japanese ambushed the column as it was leaving the bivouac, so the group commander, Colonel Alexander, ordered a bayonet assault to clear the ambush; instead the column dispersed. The column commander added to the confusion by changing the RV in the middle of the firefight, and consequently the column was spread to the four winds. Most made it back over the Chindwin, and others, with Colonel Alexander, found Number 1 Column, and eventually crossed the Irrawaddy.

The Northern Group cut the railway in several places and continued towards the Irrawaddy. By now a month had elapsed since 77th Brigade had crossed the Chindwin, and while Wingate pondered his next move, he heard over the radio that the Southern Group had crossed the Irrawaddy, and that Columns 3 and 5 (Majors Calvert and Fergusson) were seeking permission to cross, as at present they were unopposed. He told them to cross, and followed with the remainder of his brigade. It is difficult to fathom why Wingate chose to do this, unless he was spurred

on by the realization that his brigade's achievements to date had been
modest. According to Wilding (and as cipher officer he was privy to
most of what went on), there was talk in Wingate's HQ at the time of
operating in Kachin territory. Certainly Wingate had sent Captain
Herring ahead with a platoon of Burma Rifles into the Kachin Hills. If
this was in Wingate's mind, he had not thought it through sufficiently.
If he had discussed it with the RAF before setting out, they would have
told him that they could not supply him so far to the east.

Wingate's brigade, 2,000 men and 1,000 mules, crossed without
much difficulty in commandeered country boats, no mean feat; the
Irrawaddy was between 500 and 1,600 yards wide with a rapid current.
It was however a foolhardy move, and showed Wingate's limitations as
a brigade commander when faced with a tactical problem. The Japanese
knew exactly where he had crossed, and now proceeded to 'fix' him. The
country between the Irrawaddy and the Shweli is hot, largely waterless,
and crisscrossed with tracks on which enemy vehicles could operate. On
24 March he was ordered to withdraw by 4th Corps commander, who
added that operations further east would be difficult to supply by air.
Wingate ordered all his columns, except Calvert's, to whom he gave an
independent mission, to rendezvous east of the Irrawaddy and cross at
Inywa. Wilding:

> At this time we were about 40 miles from where we had crossed the
> Irrawaddy. We marched those 40 miles in 24 hours and arrived in
> the vicinity of Inywa early in the morning. We were very hungry and
> very tired, but we had jettisoned a great deal of our kit, and our
> mules had been decimated by Anthrax. Our packs were lighter as we
> carried no food.

Wilding was ordered to take his ciphers, cipher sergeant, and trans-
mitter across the river to be ready to send a message to the RAF for help
if the crossing was interrupted. He decided to take an RAF inflatable
dinghy, which had been carried all the way into Burma on the back of a
mule, and tow it across by a canoe he found. As they crossed:

> To my horror we were fired on from the west bank. I much regretted
> the dinghy which was bright yellow. It is a very odd feeling when you
> are fired at for the first time. Also the noise made by bullets
> ricocheting off the water is a bit intimidating.

The paddlers, who were locals, knew that the Japs would kill them, but were pretty sure that in spite of my lurid threats, I would not, so they turned back and we regained the east bank. Very sadly Sergeant Crawford of the Royal Signals was killed. It was rotten bad luck – he was hit by a bullet which ricocheted off the water and hit him in the throat killing him instantly.

I reported to the Brigadier, who fortunately had seen it all.

Others making the crossing also came under attack. Wingate told his column commanders to split up and fan out to cross the Irrawaddy at as many places as possible. The argument about whether Wingate was right to split up or fight his way across and back to India as a brigade continue to this day. Small parties had more chance of evading the Japanese, but less chance of fighting their way out if caught, and certainly those groups who were without radios to call for air supply suffered.

Brigade HQ was split into five parties, each between thirty and forty strong. Wilding:

We (that is Party 5) were instructed to go North, cross the Shweli, swing west and go home [about 200 miles].

First we had to get some food for Brigade HQ and the three nearby columns. Punctual to the dot the RAF delivered an enormous drop. This included some rum, and I believe this was a gift from the RAF station, bless them, some chocolate bars specially produced by Firpos.*

We had 10 days rations each. We were much cheered by the rum and the chocolate and especially grateful because, when I opened up my rations [the issue pack], I found every bar of chocolate and every cigarette had been stolen, presumably by the packers.

Our group withdrew for a few miles and just at nightfall we had the grisly job of killing our remaining mule. Because of the proximity of the Japs we were forbidden to shoot him, and had to cut his throat, a difficult and literally bloody job. I suppose we could have eaten him, but the mule had been with us for many miles and we were fond of him.

Most of Calvert's column, well briefed, and commanded by one of the greatest fighting soldiers of the Second World War, recrossed the

* The smartest restaurant in Calcutta.

Chindwin in five groups weeks before the others. Calvert destroyed part of the railway en route. Gilkes took most of his column into China, from where, with part of Fergusson's column, they were flown back to India by the Americans. Others marched to Fort Hertz, from where they too were flown out. Others, mainly because of inadequate training, were not so lucky. Wilding:

31st March. We organised our group like an over officered platoon – 3 Officers, 3 Burma Riflemen (Jemedar Jameson Rfmn Tunnion and Orlando). Sgts Napier and Mills and three sections commanded by L/ Cpl Purdie, L/ Cpl Willis and L/Cpl Coffin. We were about 30 strong. Then we marched North towards the Shweli River.

We had endured a very hard march two days before and had experienced a dreadful disappointment when we failed to cross the Irrawaddy and although we were mentally and physically exhausted, our packs were full and heavy. We only managed 8 miles or so and we found a reddish stream, but it was flowing, so we bivouacked within 100 yards of it.

1st April. Quite early we arrived at the South bank of the Shweli. I told my Sgt to arrange 4 parties of 7 each and to be prepared to swim the river. It was only about 200 yards wide and not very swift flowing. I was sure that any competent swimmer could manage it. I was alarmed when the Sgt came back with the news that only about 8 men could swim, and that included the Officers. This was a blow.

We decided to make rough rafts and, using the swimmers as propellants, get across. The only material available was dead bamboo and this is very noisy to work. After moonset, we launched the first raft we were greeted by heavy fire from the North bank. We were exhausted and seemed unable to formulate a plan, so we withdrew.

I wonder if this rather supine behaviour was not the product of slinking about behind enemy lines for six weeks and, perhaps, very inadequate rations. We had become furtive and had lost our aggression. Had it been possible to arrange a reasonably bloodless (on our part) battle early on, it might have helped.

We had two choices. The swimmers could cross that night and the rest could make their own arrangements or we could stick together. It is arguable that the proper course was to get the swimmers over and back to India, but I suggest this may win battles, but will not win wars. The men had a right to leadership. We decided to stick together.

2nd April. We disengaged and marched back towards Inywa [on the east bank of the Irrawaddy from where they had started]. We knew we could get water in a partly dried up river bed called the Nalo Chaung and water we had to have. It was a thoroughly nasty march of, perhaps, 10 to 12 miles.

3rd April. We thought that, just possibly, the Japs had abandoned Inywa believing that we had gone elsewhere. So we decided on a double bluff and try there again. We got within a couple of miles and the Burmese went off to make a recce. We waited all that day and the next. We only had the water in our water bottles and that was not nearly enough in that heat. As a precaution, I took over all the water bottles and rationed it out.

4th April. The Burmese returned late in the day without Jemedar Jameson who, they reported, had been wounded and captured. We just had to have water so early on the 5th we set off back to our beloved Nalo Chaung – we just managed it, some of the men were almost insane with thirst. Clearly elephants had been there before us but we didn't care!

6th April. Rations were getting a bit short and we still had a long way to go so it was a worry. 2/Lt Pat Gordon took a party off to the site of our last drop in the hope of finding something. He came back with an amazing 15 days rations per man. As we still had a couple of days rations left this made 17 days rations and, in our condition we just couldn't manage to carry this load. So we stayed where we were for the 7th and 8th intending to set out on the 9th April. We planned to make South east, make individual rafts (just enough to carry rifle, boots and pack) and try to cross the Irrawaddy supported by them. At least, so long as he hung on no one would drown.

9th April. A party set out for the Nalo Chaung to fill water bottles (it was foolish to bivouac on top of water, because (a) the enemy needs water too, and (b) mosquitoes). They returned without one of the party. A Pte Simons. We could only assume that he had got lost and would be captured. We did not think that the Japs were particularly nice chaps and were pretty sure that he would be made to talk, and who should blame him. We decided that we could afford to wait three days and then put our plan into action. We did not think that the Japs would hold an ambush for three days. It would, we feared, be rough on Simons.

So on the 9th, 10th and 11th we stayed put and very nice too. We ate rather more than a day's ration each day so that we could reduce our load to 10 days rations.

12th April. We set off very stiff for the first 2 or 3 miles. It was an uneventful march, we covered, perhaps 10 miles and found a stream – a real running stream far superior to the muddy pools in the Nalo Chaung. We were tempted to bivouac near there. We had barely settled down when to our horror we heard the sound of a motor vehicle, and we found we had bivouacked within 50 yards of a motorable track much used by the Japs. it was a stupid thing to do. I should have checked all round. I was tired, but that is no excuse.

13th April. We started early to get over the road before the traffic started, marched to a place well clear of the road, lay up, and continued by night. That night we had a ludicrous adventure. We heard a teak bell. These are usually round the necks of elephants and, as a general rule where there were elephants there were Japs. So we laid an ambush. The bells, there seemed to be two of them, came very slowly towards us. We checked and re-checked our weapons and then, at last from the jungle emerged two water buffaloes all by themselves, clearly let out into the jungle to graze. We felt a lot of chumps.

Wilding's party marched in a generally south-easterly direction for the next seven days. They attempted a crossing opposite Tigyaing village, where the bulk of Wingate's brigade had crossed the month before heading east. However, thanks to poor reconnaissance, they found they were unable to carry the bamboo rafts they had constructed through swampy country on the approaches to the river bank. They decided to head east and cross the Shweli into Kachin country, and take refuge in one of the Burma riflemen's village. On 21 April, before they set off, they went into a village to buy food, where the headman promised to ferry them over the Irrawaddy, so abandoning the plan to go east, they agreed to pay 'the very considerable consideration' he demanded.

That night, and we were not exactly sure where we were – we embarked, paddled round one Island and disembarked, handed over nearly all of our money and set out for the hills to the West. Alas we found a wide stretch of water between us and the hills. I saw the tracks of a bullock cart going into the river and deduced a ford. As was my duty I led the party into the water. It got deeper and deeper until I was swept off my feet. It was the main river; we had literally been sold up the river.

The island on which they had been marooned by the treacherous headman was about a mile long and half a mile wide, and contained one small village. During the next seven days, desperately weak from hunger, they managed to buy one cooked meal from the village, and on the eighth, found a boat.

29th April. It was decided that Pat Gordon, L/Cpl Purdie and Signalman Belcher with Orlando and Tunnion as paddlers should make the first trip. On landing Pat would decide what could be done. Ideally he should pinch some boats and come back for us but it was for him to decide. They set out and reached the other side. We could hear Pat rallying his men and a good deal of firing and then silence. Orlando and Tunnion survived but the others were all killed.

I arranged that small parties should hide in the elephant grass (there was lots of it) for 3 days and that we would rendezvous at the old bivouac at sunset on the third day.

30th April to 2nd May. Those three days were the worst that I can remember. I was very weak, tired and hungry. Apart from the meal we had bought from the villagers we had had nothing since the 23rd, six days ago. During those three days I thought of dozens of plans each more impracticable that the last; finally coming to the conclusion that there were only two choices – to fight or to surrender. I did manage to steal a water melon one night but though I suppose the sweetness gave some energy it was not nourishing.

The 2nd May was a bit trying. The Japs, or possibly the Burmese Police, decided that my particular bit of elephant grass should be searched. As they were not game to go into it, they set fire to it. The flames came very close indeed but I was not burnt. I must say that the sun seemed to take its time about setting but, at last, it did and we rendezvoused.

I was confident that if I gave the order the men would have fought but only one rifle was serviceable, the one belonging to L/Cpl Willis. The others – well, you could hardly move the bolts. This was an administrative fault and no blame attaches to the men. In the butt of each rifle is an oil bottle, a pull-through and some 4 x 2 [cloth]. But in the 11 or 12 weeks since leaving Imphal the oil had been used up and nobody had thought of having more dropped. Why then was one working? L/Cpl Willis had used mosquito cream, not exactly according to 'cocker' [according to the rules], but it worked.

I would ask the reader if he would order his men to attack a well armed enemy when they (the attackers) had rifles which would not fire, more than one shot (if that). We didn't even have bayonets. And so, alone and very frightened, I went into the village – and that was that.

The Japs were away searching for us and the Burmese tied my wrists, rather cruelly tight with a sort of bark string. In spite of this discomfort, when the men arrived I curled up and slept for hours.

It is a frightful thing to be a POW. You have failed. You have lost your liberty and you have a nagging feeling that you should have done better. What pulled me together was one of the very few undisciplined soldiers saying 'We are all equal now.' I replied, 'Are we hell, I am in command and you'd better not forget it – our only hope of survival is to keep our discipline and it is for me to make sure that we do so.'

When the Japs returned to the village they were really quite decent.* They released me from the very tight bonds on my wrists and let me sleep for, I think, 24 hours.

We proceeded to Tigyaing where we lived in what must have been the school house and were given three meals of curried chicken and rice each day. This was the only time we were adequately fed during our captivity.

Out of the thirty-strong party, twenty-four eventually arrived in Rangoon jail where they spent the remainder of the war. Seven survived.

The experiences of Scott's Number 8 Column headquarters, a larger party, with more determined leadership, and above all a radio, were different. He moved in smaller parties, only concentrating at major

* Unusually so.

obstacles, or to take supply drops. He headed north, so had to cross both the Shweli and the Irrawaddy. Scott:

I asked the RAF to drop a 'floating' rope.* Having swum this across the Shweli, we pulled ourselves across in small parties in an RAF rescue dinghy which had also been dropped to us. The dinghy was attached to the floating rope by a loop. After about forty men had crossed, the loop tangled in the floating rope, a sergeant in the dinghy panicked, tried to cut the loop, but succeeded in cutting the floating rope instead. The dinghy was taken down-stream by the current and the sergeant and his party were captured. The RAF dropped another rope and more dinghies the following night.

Most of the party that crossed the second night, were subsequently captured en route to India. I had my CO with me [CO of 13th Liverpool Regiment] who was very sick with malaria and dysentery. After the Shweli we headed for the area of the Irrawaddy where we had not been before, about 20 miles downstream from Bhamo. We tried making bamboo rafts, but the current was so swift they were useless. There were no village boats, because the Japs had taken them all. We were in quite a narrow gorge and noticed that the Burmese boats had a hard time rowing up stream, and kept close to the bank.

One came within fifteen yards of us, so some of us jumped into the shallows, and scrambled aboard, capturing the boat. We crossed the Irrawaddy in this boat, with our one remaining mule and wireless set. I paid the boatmen well.

Once across I sent a signal to the RAF telling them where we would be in five days time, and requesting a drop of 14 day's rations. I gave them another DZ seven day's on from there, and a further one as well.

When I saw the first DZ, I saw it was such a big clearing that I thought that we could use it to fly out the wounded, the sick and the CO. By now the wireless batteries were dead, and I could not talk to the aircraft. So I laid out parachutes from the first loads to form the agreed sign, 'plane land here now – wounded'. The plane tried but couldn't make it. He dropped a streamer with a message telling me to hold on there. Two days later we got another supply drop, so we now had 12 day's rations. The plane dropped a streamer telling me to mark out a strip with parachutes. He tried once, lifted and went

* Probably grass.

round again, the second time he landed and took out the CO and fourteen sick and wounded. Within two hours they were in hospital in Imphal.

I received another wireless set and a signal telling me to wait, and the whole lot of us would be lifted out. But I felt we had been there too long now, and the Japanese garrison at Indaw might react, and the sooner I moved on the better. We walked on, eventually crossed the Chindwin, and arrived back in India. The strip eventually became the one called 'Piccadilly' for the second Wingate expedition.

Of some 3,000 men who had marched into Burma in February, 2,182 had returned four months later. Of around 1,000 missing, about 450 were battle casualties. Of the 210 Chindits (including Wilding's party) who arrived in Rangoon as prisoners, 168 died or were deliberately killed, a survival rate of about 20 per cent. About 120 Kachins and Shans remained in their tribal area with Wingate's permission. Very few of the men who returned were ever fit for operations again; sickness, mainly malaria, and gross undernourishment had taken its toll. Major Scott commanding Number 8 Column was one of the few exceptions: 'I didn't even lose weight'.

The daily ration, designed to sustain paratroops in an emergency for two to three days, consisted of: 12oz of Shakapura biscuits, like large dog biscuits; 2oz of cheese; 1oz of milk powder; 9oz of compressed almonds and raisins; 1oz of acid drops or chocolate; ¾oz of tea; 4oz of sugar; ½oz of salt; two packets of ten cigarettes; a box of matches; and for Gurkhas and Burmese, rice if available. There was no meat in the ration, and far too little other protein. The ration produced a daily intake of 3,000 calories. Wingate planned that another 1,000 calories would be supplied by local purchase and shooting game. Even 4,000 calories is inadequate for marching troops, carrying big loads, and was hardly ever achieved. It was pure fantasy on Wingate's part to imagine that sufficient game to feed 3,000 men a day could be shot or trapped. Apart from the delays in progress caused by the time needed to track and find game, and the noise of shots endangering security, very few Chindits possessed the necessary level of bushcraft and hunting skills. Buying from villagers was risky, and obtaining sufficient stocks could not be relied upon. It was this fantastical aspect of Wingate's make-up that his detractors have with some justification seized on.

His attitude to preventative medicine was irresponsible, preaching that sickness was unnecessary provided one had sufficient willpower.[5] He did not learn from his first expedition, and sickness and starvation were hallmarks of his second.

What did the first expedition achieve? In tangible terms very little, whether set against Wingate's six reasons for the expedition given earlier, or any other benchmark. Postwar interrogation of senior Japanese officers bears this out. Even Scott, a loyal Wingate supporter, expressed the view that the achievements of the first expedition were confined to 'making Wingate's name and proving that the Japanese were not invincible'. His column, well led though it was, inflicted no damage on the enemy whatsoever.

But, as Slim, no fan of Wingate or his ideas, wrote:

Whilst, like the Arakan offensive it [the Chindit expedition] was a failure, there was a dramatic quality about this raid, which, with the undoubted fact that it had penetrated far behind the Japanese lines and returned, lent itself to presentation as a triumph of British jungle fighting over the Japanese. Skilfully handled, the press of the Allied world took up the tale, and everywhere the story ran that we had beaten the Japanese at their own game. This not only distracted attention from the failure in the Arakan, but was important in itself for our own people at home, for our allies, and above all for our troops on the Burma front. Whatever the actual facts, to the troops in Burma it seemed the first ripple showing the turning of the tide. For this reason alone, Wingate's raid was worth all the hardship and sacrifice his men endured, and by every means in our power we exploited its propaganda value to the full.[6]

Looking back from the distance of over fifty years, and aware of the eventual smashing victory over the Japanese, it is easy to forget the depths to which morale in British and Indian units had sunk after the disastrous first Arakan campaign following so soon after the retreat from Burma. Wingate's exploits played a major part in restoring morale and spreading the message that the Japanese were not invincible.

There was another outcome of Wingate's expedition, unforeseen in 1943, but on which Slim capitalized in the fullness of time. Hitherto the Japanese had been wary of attacking Assam across the grain of the inhospitable country astride Chindwin. They now took note that, contrary to their earlier belief, it was possible to cross it with large bodies of troops, and set about polishing up plans to do just this in 1944.

3

The Arakan: Both Sides Take the Offensive

> Now we are going into battle and you will conquer and overrun the British as you have always done. You will smash them and drive them into the sea. Now the sea will run red with your blood as well as theirs and you must take pride in it.
>
> Colonel Tanahashi, CO *112th Regiment*, Japanese *55th Division*

On 23 September 1943, Lieutenant Colonel Macdonald, the CO of the 4th/5th Royal Gurkha Rifles, was standing with his adjutant Captain Birch and Subedar Major Manraj Gurung at Taung Bazaar on the east bank of the Kalapanzin River waiting to greet a party of reinforcements under the command of Second Lieutenant Marshall, a young officer recently commissioned into the 5th Royal Gurkhas.

While at school an Indian army brigadier came to speak to us. The Bursar of Radley was a retired Gurkha officer and I learnt about the Gurkhas and basic Urdu from him. On leaving Radley in 1942 I volunteered for the Indian Army and was interviewed at the Great Central Hotel Marylebone with a large group of other public school-boys. Two hundred and fifty of us were made Officer Cadets, and within three weeks embarked for India. We did the six months course at Bangalore.

Eventually, after more training at the 5th Royal Gurkha Regimental Centre at Abbottabad in the North-West Frontier Province of India (now part of Pakistan), Marshall, with Second Lieutenant Malone, was posted to the 4th Battalion in the Arakan, in charge of two Gurkha officers and 150 Gurkha other ranks.

We went by train to Madras and by steamer to Chittagong; from there to Dohazari by train, and from there marched for five days to Tumbru Ghat. From Tumbru Ghat we were taken by river steamer to Bawli Bazaar. From there we marched on a mule track over the Goppe Pass to Goppe Bazaar; it poured with rain all the time. I met the Quarter Master of the 4th/5th before starting the march. I was wearing the trench coat I had brought with me from London. He said abruptly, 'We don't wear raincoats in the Arakan, we get wet.' I took the point and never wore one again. At Goppe Bazaar we were taken in sampans down the Kalapanzin River to Taung Bazaar. The entire journey from Abbottabad took 28 days.

The Commanding Officer had been commissioned in 1916 and served in the Dardanelles, so had the Subedar Major. As the Battalion had suffered some casualties the previous week, and the numbers of sick had increased, they were delighted to see how many reinforcements we had brought. The monsoon had only recently finished, and this part of Arakan consisted of a series of hillocks surrounded by water. The paddy fields were about a foot deep in water. The four companies were spaced out on hillocks wherever there was dry ground. All the rivers were flooded. We were permanently damp. Our positions were about six to seven miles from the Jap forward posts. Colonel Mac, as he was known, posted me to B Company, whose commander had been drowned four days earlier. He had been demonstrating to his men how to swim the Kalapanzin River in full battle order. He was a strong swimmer, and it was thought his legs had become entangled with weeds. There were no other British officers in B Company. In October 1943 I became a full Lieutenant at the age of 19 years and 4 months.

The Battalion's task was active patrolling. Each company took turns to send out fighting or standing patrols for three or four days at a time. As I was totally inexperienced I was sent out to learn what I ought to be doing. This was not easy as I had a limited knowledge of Urdu and my knowledge of Gurkhali was not much better. On one patrol I had 10 men, plus a very experienced Subedar. He always spoke to me in Gurkhali, and if I didn't understand that, in Urdu. It was only back at base when I heard him talking on the inter-company telephone system to the CO in perfectly good English that I realised that he had no intention of making my life easy; I would only learn Gurkhali by speaking nothing else.

One of the 4th/5th Royal Gurkha's tasks was to keep watch on the area of Awlinbyn village, which overlooked the Ngakyedauk Chaung, so a standing patrol was established on a ridge from which the area could be kept under observation. Standing patrols are usually instructed to open fire only if attacked, or to fight their way out of trouble. Marshall led one of these patrols

with a Jemedar from my own company and about six men, going out at night, through paddy the whole way. At about 2 o'clock in the morning we were shot at while crossing open paddy. We all got down into the water and stayed for about half an hour. We had probably been heard by a small Jap patrol who had fired but did not stay to investigate. When we moved on, most of us had forty to fifty leeches hanging off us, and we spent a good half hour removing them when got to a bund. So penetrative are some leeches they can go through lace holes in boots.

We eventually reached the patrol position and on the second morning the Jemedar said that through his binoculars he had spotted a small sampan with a Japanese officer with a soldier and two villagers coming down the Ngakyedauk Chaung, about 1200 yards away. They must have come from Japanese positions on the ridge in front and and be heading for Awlinbyn Village. My instructions on leaving the Battalion position were to take evading action only, unless absolutely necessary; my main task was observation. As the sampan got closer, I felt that we ought to do something about it. When it reached 700 yards away, the Jemedar agreed, and opened fire with the LMG. The occupants of sampan disappeared. Later we were told that a senior Japanese officer and his orderly had been killed. Although not due to leave for a further four or five hours, I decided it prudent to do so, and we left for Taung Bazaar. The trip took us about twelve to fifteen hours. After we left, we heard mortar fire approximately on the position we had left, and a great deal of noise from Japanese positions.

When I reported to the CO his views were mixed.* However the following night a patrol from another company occupied almost the same position as I had been in; not very clever of them. During

* Not surprisingly.

the night the Japs sent in a patrol, and our patrol had one killed and one wounded.

The Regimental history of the 5th Royal Gurkha Rifles comments on this incident. 'This was the first time since the arrival of the Battalion that the enemy had taken the initiative . . . This incident marked the end of the hitherto rather negative Japanese attitude and from then on fighting increased in intensity'.[1] Both sides in the Arakan were beginning to stir.

The monsoon and the beginning of the dry season up to November 1943 had closed down major operations on all fronts in Burma. Patrolling and local probing attacks, like those described above, continued, but it was a time for planning, preparation, and training. The British and American planners were as one: Germany would be defeated first. Therefore, when resources were tight, the forthcoming Normandy invasion and operations in the Mediterranean would take priority over Burma. This was especially so in the case of landing craft, of which there were never enough until the defeat of Germany. On the matter of the strategy for Burma, however, there was a considerable divergence of opinion between the Allies.

Burma was strategically important to the Americans solely as their supply route to Chiang Kai-shek's Nationalist Chinese; by air for the present, but again by road once northern Burma was liberated. They had yet to learn that much of the materiel sent to Chiang Kai-shek would not be used against the Japanese, but was hoarded for the impending struggle against the Chinese Communists after the defeat of Japan. As seen at the time, there was a powerful reason for supporting Chiang Kai-shek; the hope that his armies would tie down considerable numbers of Japanese. Chinese troops, if used in overwhelming strength, and if well led (the latter, a big 'if'), could sometimes beat the Japanese. With hindsight the Allies were deluding themselves, but until they became aware of Chiang Kai-shek's chicanery, the Chinese dimension exerted an undue effect on strategy, and hence on operations. The Americans supported operations in northern Burma, but viewed suggestions for amphibious assaults to recapture southern Burma with indifference or hostility. They were not interested in backing British ambitions to regain part of their empire. American opinion mattered because not only were they the dominant partner in the war against Japan, they also supplied the bulk of the transport aircraft to the RAF and the USAAF supporting the British effort in Burma. 'He who pays the piper . . .'

Meanwhile the British planned to drive the Japanese out of Burma, and not being enamoured of slogging down through northern Burma, except perhaps as an ancillary operation, believed that amphibious operations should play the primary part in this strategy, and especially a major seaborne assault on Rangoon. The Americans eventually fell in with British plans, but only because engaging the Japanese in South-East Asia might draw off enemy forces from the Pacific, where massive American activity was gathering momentum. To begin with, Mountbatten, the supremo in South-East Asia, planned seven offensives including two sizeable amphibious operations. Ultimately, mainly for lack of landing craft and other resources, he was forced to be content with more modest schemes, abandoned what Slim later called 'the correct strategy of a landing in southern Burma', and opted for a 'four-pronged invasion'.[2] In northern Burma, a Chinese force led by the American Stilwell would advance south from Ledo, take Myitkyina, and thus connect Ledo with the upper end of the Burma Road. China could then be supplied by road again, instead of by the nerve-racking air route over the 'Hump', the nickname for the eastern end of the Himalayan range lying between the airbases in Assam and China. Transport aircraft of the time lacked the power to climb above the often appalling weather, and crashes were all too frequent. On the Chindwin front, 4th Corps was to mount a limited advance. To support these two operations, a greatly expanded LRP force of Chindits under Wingate was to be deployed to create mayhem on the lines of communication of the Japanese facing Stilwell and 4th Corps. Meanwhile 15th Corps was to have another crack at securing the Maungdaw–Buthidaung road in the Arakan.

By now two training divisions in India, staffed by battle-experienced officers and NCOs, were responsible for producing battle-worthy reinforcements for Fourteenth Army by putting them through a rigorous course in jungle training. Newly arrived divisions and brigades also trained in the jungles of central India before entering the operational area. The formations, such as the 23rd and 26th Divisions, who had been blooded after fighting the Japanese along the Chindwin and in the Arakan, had now assimilated the necessary skills.

Captain Wilson had fought with the 2nd Battalion The Argyll and Sutherland Highlanders in Malaya. With the CO, Lieutenant Colonel

Stewart, he had been ordered out of Singapore just before the surrender to the Japanese, in order to pass on his experiences of fighting the Japanese to the army in India. He ran the 2nd British Infantry Division's jungle battle school, and armed with his own experience and that of the British 6th Infantry Brigade, which had recently returned to the division after fighting in Arakan, inculcated the necessary skills required to fight in the environment encountered in Assam and Burma.

Most British people, many brought up in towns, have never really been in the dark, because there are always street lamps, or some sort of light. Few of our soldiers had ever been alone at night. We have lost our sense of hearing and smell. These are basic animal-like characteristics which are vital in the jungle. The Japs smelt different to us, and you could smell them in a defensive position, or if they had recently passed down a track. The Japs smelt rather like scented powder. Indians smelt differently to us too. Your smell depends on what you eat. At night you feel very much on your own and are susceptible to noises deliberately made by the enemy, and you shoot at these, and at shadows, which you mustn't do. Slim's adage was, 'the answer to noise is silence'. It was almost a crime to shoot without having a corpse to show for it in the morning. The antidote is endless training at night. We practised movement by night, the use of pole charges to attack bunkers, and bringing down supporting fire from mortars and guns very close to us. There was a very great deal to learn.

Radio communications were a problem in jungle and hills. You found an enormous number of 'blank areas' for communications; specially at night. You had to find the right spot for siting wireless sets by moving around.*

We learnt about the siting of defences and use of local materials (logs, parts of buildings etc) to build bunkers, which were shell-proof, and even [proof] against anti-tank guns, and marvelously well concealed. Their camouflage was superb. You seldom saw a Japanese move by day. They took pains to conceal their tracks because by 1944 we had superiority in the air and in artillery. They realised this and they trained to operate at night. Their positions were well sited to support each other. Like the Vietnamese did years later, they

---

* And not just sitting wringing one's hands when one could not communicate.

tunnelled and connected firing positions with covered ways. They could call down their own gun and mortar fire on their own positions. They cleared fields of fire, but not in such a way that it gave away the location of the bunker. What you could do was try to draw their fire at night. By shooting at them, moving about etc. They did it to us.

Additional battle-experienced divisions such as the 70th British and the 5th Indian were now arriving from the Middle East. The latter, the 'Ball of Fire' after its formation sign (or the 'flaming arsehole' to its rival divisions), came with a high reputation from the Western Desert. Its commander, Major General H. R. Briggs, made every member of his division learn his 'Five Commandments'. The second read: 'Be determined not to let the Jap frighten you with ruses and induce you to disclose your positions and waste ammunition. Ambush him and do unto him as he would unto you.'[3] The newly raised 7th Indian Division had not been in battle, but was commanded by Major General F. W. Messervy, with a dashing reputation from his days in the Western Desert.

By the end, the Burma campaign involved a colourful mix of races. As well as English, Scottish, Irish and Welsh soldiers, sailors, and airmen, there were in the RAF Newfoundlanders, Australians, Canadians, New Zealanders, and South Africans. There were considerable numbers of Americans, mainly aircrew, logistic troops, and engineers, with a handful of infantry. Eventually there were 90,000 West and East Africans in three divisions and two independent brigades. In an army that took a perverse pride in calling itself 'Forgotten', the Africans, and what they did, are truly forgotten today.

Slim's Fourteenth Army was one of the most multinational armies in history, but by far the greatest number of soldiers came from the Indian Army, the largest volunteer army the world has ever known.

There were men from every caste and race – Sikhs, Dogras, Pathans, Madrassis, Mahrattas, Rajputs, Assamese, Kumaonis, Punjabis, Garhwalis, Naga head-hunters, and from Nepal, the Gurkhas in all their tribes and sub-tribes of Limbu and Rai, Thakur and Chetri, Magar and Gurung . . . They worshipped God according to the rites of the Mahayana and Hinayana, of Sunni and of Shiah, of Rome and Canterbury and Geneva, of the Vedas and the sages and the

Mahabharatas of the ten Gurus, of the secret shrines of the jungle. There were meat-eaters and fish-eaters, and men who ate only rice, and men who ate only wheat; and men who had four wives, men who shared one wife with four brothers, and men who openly practised sodomy. There were men who had never seen snow, and men who seldom saw anything else. And Brahmins and Untouchables, both with rifle and Tommy Gun.[4]

The commander of this army was an officer of the Indian Army, in late 1943, Lieutenant General William Slim, 'Uncle Bill', to his soldiers, 'with that robber-baron face under his Gurkha hat, and his carbine slung, looking rather like a scruffy private with general's tabs'.[5] One of them described the effect he had on them:

The biggest boost to morale was the burly man who came to talk to the assembled battalion by the lake shore . . . Slim was like that: the only man I've ever seen who had a force come out of him, a strength of personality . . . His appearance was plain enough: large, heavily built, grim-faced with that hard mouth and bulldog chin . . . nor was he an orator . . . His delivery was blunt, matter-of-fact, without gestures or mannerisms, only a lack of them.

. . . British soldiers don't love their commanders, much less worship them; Fourteenth Army trusted Slim and thought of him as one of themselves, and perhaps his real secret was that the feeling was mutual.[6]

Slim *was* the Fourteenth Army, and one of the greatest soldiers since Wellington, another 'Sepoy General'. Slim had served in the First World War with the Royal Warwickshire Regiment, and was wounded at Gallipoli and in Mesopotamia where he was awarded the MC. After the First World War he transferred to the 6th Gurkhas in the Indian Army. He passed out top from the Staff College at Quetta, subsequently being selected to fill the only Indian Army post on the staff of the British Army Staff College at Camberley. He commanded a brigade in the conquest of Abyssinia, where he was wounded again, and the 10th Indian Division in the campaign against the Vichy French in Syria. He was plucked out of this theatre to command BURCORPS in March 1942.

Slim was responsible for the direction of all four offensives outlined earlier, even Stilwell's, for, in a fit of cantankerousness, the latter had announced that he would serve under Slim's command and no one else's. Stilwell was a prickly subordinate, who was prone to conducting himself entirely to his own satisfaction. But Slim could usually persuade him to cooperate in the end; unlike Slim's highly efficient boss, Giffard, whom, perversely, Stilwell disliked, and Mountbatten, whom he despised. Stilwell, although personally brave and a rugged soldier, harboured a visceral loathing of the British, which he rarely bothered to conceal. Although he fancied himself as a 'soldier's general', his treatment of men under his command, American as well as the hated British, belied this image. A fluent Chinese speaker after years of service in that country, he probably got on best with Chinese soldiers, whom he believed, correctly, would perform if well led. His nickname for his boss (actually one of his many bosses in the convoluted command structure), Chiang Kai-shek, was 'the peanut', but not to his face.

Lieutenant General A. F. P. Christison's 15th Corps kicked off the Arakan offensive on 30 November 1943, astride the Mayu Range, with Messervy's 7th Division to the east, and three weeks later, with Briggs's 5th Division to the west. This approach avoided the errors of the previous Arakan offensive, with its narrow frontal tactics. As the screen of patrols preceding the two divisions bumped up against the Maungdaw–Buthidaung road, the Japanese defensive layout became clearer. This was the only lateral road fit for wheeled traffic until one reached the Taungup–Prome road 200 miles to the south. The Japanese had a continuous string of defences in the steep jungle-covered hills along the length of the sixteen-mile-long road. In addition they had constructed three heavily fortified positions, in the two tunnels through which the road ran under the Mayu range, and on buttresses at Letwedet east of the road tunnels and at Razabil to the west. These defences had been tunnelled into the hills with dugouts up to thirty feet deep for troops and supplies. Around the main defences was a network of mutually supporting machine-gun nests, all linked with tunnels.

Christison ordered the two divisions to eliminate the enemy outposts in front of the main defences, followed by capturing the Letwedet and Razabil positions, before finally clearing the tunnels. The 5th Division was allocated Razabil, while the 7th Division was to take Buthidaung, before swinging in to take Letwedet from the south. Christison ordered his third division, the 81st West African, to advance down the Kaladan Valley, take Kyauktaw, and cut the Kanzauk–Htizwe road, which linked the Kaladan and Mayu Rivers and was the Japanese main

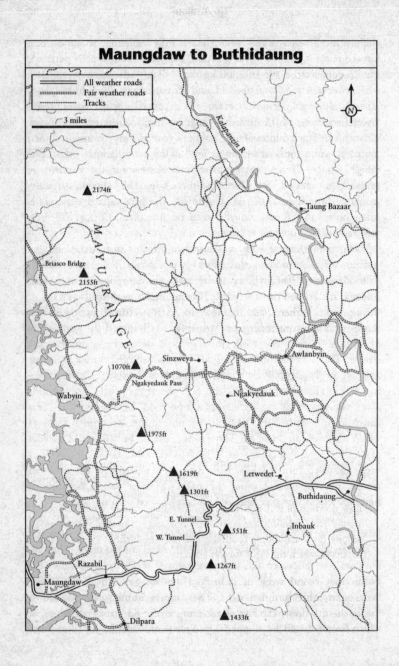

Maungdaw to Buthidaung

All weather roads
Fair weather roads
Tracks

3 miles

Kalapanzin R.

▲ 2174ft

● Taung Bazaar

M A Y U   R A N G E

Briasco Bridge
▲ 2155ft

1070ft ▲

Sinzweya ●

● Awlanbyin

Ngakyedauk Pass

Wabyin ●

● Ngakyedauk

▲ 1975ft

▲ 1619ft

Letwedet ●

▲ 1301ft

Buthidaung ●

E. Tunnel

W. Tunnel

▲ 551ft

Inbauk ●

Razabil ●

▲ 1267ft

Maungdaw ●

Dilpara ●

▲ 1433ft

supply route between the two valleys – thus inflicting Japanese tactics on them.

To support the 7th Division's attack on Buthidaung and ultimately on Letwedet, a road over the Mayu range capable of taking tanks, guns, and supply vehicles had to be found, or made. A footpath which crossed about five miles north of the Maungdaw–Buthidaung road seemed to offer possibilities, although the sappers had already pronounced it a hopeless route for a road. Brigadier Roberts, commanding the 114th Indian Infantry Brigade, at Messervy's behest, having cast about for an alternative, decided that the path offered the only solution. Roberts quickly moved part of his brigade to the key Ngakyedauk Pass, where the path wound its way over the crest of the range, and forestalled the Japanese. When they moved to seize the pass, they were beaten off after an all-night battle with part of the 4th/14th Punjab Regiment. Christison gave orders that the road must be made fit for use by tanks, and by the end of January 1944, although never surfaced, the road over the Ngakyedauk, nicknamed the 'Okeydoke' by the British, was just that. Captain Rissik of the Durham Light Infantry, now ADC to Christison, drove with his general to a conference with Messervy.

> The Ngakyedauk Pass was an impressive sight and a fine engineering feat. It was symbolic of the determination and ability to overcome difficulties which now pervaded the atmosphere in marked contrast to the muddle and incompetence of 1943. As a line of communication its chief disadvantage lay in the fact that it ran parallel to the fighting front – a disadvantage which made it extremely vulnerable to Japanese attack, and one which was shortly to become as real as it was apparent. But for the moment this new way, following its dusty course, carried a ceaseless line of jeeps, supply trucks, guns, ambulances and mules, twisting and turning along its leafy shade, now up, now down until it debouched from the range into an area occupied by the 7th Division's administrative 'box', which nestled, basinwise, among the surrounding foothills. This was the lifeline, the artery by means of which the 7th Division existed.

In the second week of January 1944, Briggs's 5th Division took Maungdaw after a tough fight. The sappers immediately worked to make the little port capable of receiving river and coastal steamers, so that supplies could be shipped in direct from Calcutta or Chittagong, avoiding the long journey by road. Briggs then set about taking Razabil. Everyone expected it to be a tough nut to crack, and it was the first time the British encountered a position which the Japanese had prepared with a view to holding it whatever the odds.

The British brought tanks to the Arakan, but kept their presence a surprise until the last moment. Rissik:

> Every precaution had been taken to keep their [the tanks'] presence unknown to the Japanese. They had been assembled in Calcutta and had been shipped by sea in tank landing craft to Cox's Bazaar. While in Calcutta and later until they actually went into action, the crews were forbidden to wear their berets so that they could not be identified. The tanks were landed on a deserted stretch of beach some miles south of Cox's Bazaar, laid up in harbour a short way inland and locals were forbidden the area. When they moved south into a concentration area before going into action, they moved by night, and the road was closed for their passing.

The Lee-Grant tanks were obsolete, and superseded by Shermans in armoured units in Italy and preparing to land in Normandy, but far outmatched any Japanese armour. Rissik

> accompanied the General to a suitable vantage point, situated on a convenient peak of the Mayu range to watch the whole course of the battle.
>
> At ten o'clock sharp the first wave of bombers [Liberator heavies and Mitchell mediums] appeared, to schedule, over the target area and dropped their bombs with what appeared to be effect upon the Japanese positions. They were followed by Vengeances whose accuracy, soon to become a byword, was all that could be desired. Then came another wave of Mitchells and here for the first and only time something went wrong. The pilot of one of the planes in the second flight must have misjudged the area in which his bombs were to fall and to our horror they were seen to burst well away to the west in the area where it was known that some tanks and troops of an Indian battalion were forming up for the attack. Fortunately only slight damage was done. The Subedar Major of the battalion was killed and one of the tanks received superficial damage; otherwise the only effect was to frighten a number of RAF officers who were in the area observing the operation. Not inappropriate it seemed! Once the

bombing was completed it was difficult from so remote a perch to follow developments, and although up to a point, the activities of the tanks could be seen, no really accurate impression could be obtained on the course of the battle. So it was not until returning to Corps Headquarters in the evening, that detailed reports were available of what had happened.

When the supporting artillery lifted, the tanks and infantry moved in. Slim had been told by the 'experts' that armour would never get to the scene of the battle, and if by some miracle it did, the tanks would not be able to climb the hills, and the trees would slow them so badly they would be sitting ducks for the enemy anti-tank guns. Following Slim's precept on the use of armour, 'the more you use, the fewer you lose', a mass of the 25th Dragoons' Grants swept over and crushed the anti-tank guns in their weapon pits. Then, as the infantry of the 161st Indian Infantry Brigade moved out ahead into the final assault, the tanks had to stop firing to avoid hitting their own soldiers. This allowed the defenders to man their weapon slits and pour fire on the attackers. During the next three days attacks were repeated with artillery and tank support, but although bunkers were apparently destroyed, they sprang into life as soon as the tanks lifted their fire. On 30 January, 161st and 123rd Brigades were ordered to go firm on the ground already taken.

The problem was eventually solved in the Arakan and copied elsewhere in Burma. Tanks cleared the foliage around bunkers by firing high-explosive (HE) shells, followed by delayed-action HE to smash the frontal slopes of the bunkers, and finally armour-piercing solid shot at the weapon slits. Because the solid shot did not burst, it could be fired close to friendly infantry, although they had to be well trained and cool to cope with shells whizzing past their ears.

By now part of the 7th Division were established on the east bank of the Kalapanzin River (north of Rathedaung, the Mayu becomes the Kalapanzin), but were under increasing attacks by the Japanese who were preparing an offensive of their own. West of the Kalapanzin, the 89th Brigade after a hard struggle lasting several days captured a feature nicknamed Able that overlooked the area of the eastern tunnel on the Maungdaw–Buthidaung road. Holding this ground was going to prove costly.

While 5th Division on the right drew breath, Christison sent all but one squadron of the 25th Dragoons across the Ngakyedauk Pass to join in 7th Division's attack on Buthidaung and Letwedet. Trooper McKnight, a tank driver in the 25th Dragoons, found driving over the pass somewhat hair-raising:

> Tank commanders and drivers were ferried over the pass in trucks during daylight to see what problems would be involved when we made the move in darkness. To gain height the track was constructed in a series of hairpin bends, some of which were quite horrific, and the track seemed to cling to the side of the mountain for dear life. Not giving the tank drivers much room for manoeuvre, and on nearing the crest, the drop over the edge was quite precipitous for hundreds of feet. There was thick jungle growth all around on the way up, and on the down side to the 7th Div area. Near the bottom, as well as sparse jungle, there was a forest of teak trees to pass through before reaching open ground in the administrative area. The drive over the pass was quite hazardous, no lights permitted, and it was pitch black. I had assistance from my tank commander who dismounted several times to guide me past the dodgy parts. Also from the 75 mm gunner who was outside the tank lying alongside the gun barrel, shouting instructions to [help me] negotiate the hairpin bends.
>
> We arrived at the 7th Div end of the pass just before dawn, and after topping up with fuel had a quick meal. We were then deployed about seven miles south to attack fortified hill positions which were straddling the route to Buthidaung.

Meanwhile Major General C. G. Woolner's 81st West African (WA) Division had begun to move down the Kaladan Valley. Shortly after setting out, the leading formation, 6th WA Brigade, captured two prisoners from the Japanese *1/213th Battalion*, a most unusual occurrence. Even more unusually they talked, and said that their battalion was leaving Kaladan for Buthidaung. This was one of several portents that the Japanese were up to something, and to find out what we must fast rewind.

Strategically the Japanese planned to stay on the defensive in Burma, but, reckoning the British would attack, they reasoned that the best way to keep them off balance and spoil their plans was to mount offensives first. Lieutenant General Renya Mutaguchi, commander of the Japanese *Fifteenth Army* responsible for upper Burma, planned to take Imphal and Kohima, the base for the British offensive in his area of operations. A further advance might follow. There was an additional bonus for the Japanese in taking Imphal and securing Assam, because here were situated the airfields from which supplies were flown over the 'hump' to the Chinese. The airlift would have to be abandoned, cutting the lifeline to Chiang Kai-shek. Lieutenant General Masakuzu Kawabe, commanding *Burma Area Army*, approved Mutaguchi's plans, and reinforced *Fifteenth Army* bringing it up to four Japanese divisions, and one Indian National Army (INA) Division formed from dissident prisoners of war. Mutaguchi was to start his Imphal offensive, codenamed U-GO, on 15 March 1944.

Twenty-eighth Army was formed for the Japanese Arakan offensive under Lieutenant General Shozo Sakurai, and consisted of the *54th Division* (some troops were already in Arakan or en route), the *55th Division* (already in Arakan and the Kaladan Valley), and the *2nd Division* from Siam. There was also an INA formation attached to Sakurai's army. He was to kick off his offensive, codenamed HA-GO, on 4 February. The assault was to be commanded by Major General Tokutaro Sakurai, the commander of the *55th Divisional Infantry Group* (not to be confused with the commander of *Twenty-eighth Army*). Major General Sakurai was allocated the *112th Regiment* (Colonel Tanahashi), two additional infantry battalions, the *2/143rd* and *1/213th*, and the *55th Engineer Regiment*. He was ordered by his Divisional Commander, Lieutenant General Hanaya, to pass through the British lines on the left bank of the Kalapanzin River, seize Taung Bazaar, cross the river, block the Ngakyedauk Pass, and swing down to attack the 7th Division between the crest of the Mayu Range and the river. At the same time Colonel Doi, the CO of *143rd Regiment*, was to attack 7th Division from the south. Meanwhile Kubo Force (1/213 Regiment) was to attack the Arakan Road.

The additional divisions for both armies were moved from Siam into Burma along the infamous death railway built by Allied prisoners of war and wretched conscripted local labour. The story of the Japanese offensive against Kohima and Imphal will be told in Chapters 5 and 6. The overall operational concept was to keep Slim's eyes fixed in the Arakan, while the main attack went in at Imphal. But if the operation in the Arakan went well, they would exploit forward, and even invade India.[7]

Although there had been indications that the Japanese were planning an offensive, Christison had no inkling of the scale of it. On 3 February he visited Messervy and found his HQ well forward. 'I remonstrated with him. He replied that he liked to keep well out of the way of superior officers and staff officers. It nearly brought about his end'. Messervy had twice been captured and escaped in the desert. On one occasion he had torn off his rank badges and posed as an officer's batman, before making a break for it.

One of the most valuable sources of intelligence was V-Force. Its origins go back to April 1942, well before the Japanese had pushed the British out of Burma completely. Wavell ordered that a guerrilla organization be formed to attack the Japanese line of communication should they invade Assam. V-Force, as it came to be called, was built around platoons loaned from the Assam Rifles, and augmented by some 1,000 hill tribesmen. The Assam Rifles were a force of five military police battalions maintained by the Assam government, and composed of Gurkhas commanded by British officers seconded from the Indian Army. Until 1944, for reasons given earlier, the Japanese did not follow up into Assam, so V-Force's role was changed to gathering intelligence and maintaining a line of outposts roughly along the line of the Chindwin as far south as Kalewa, and thence across to the northern Arakan.

One of the problems impeding gathering enough intelligence to build up an enemy 'picture' was identifying units. Christison had urged Messervy to try to put this right. From behind enemy lines a V-Force report came in of a pond where two Japanese officers sometimes fished. A Gurkha patrol was sent out. On their return two of them, carrying a wicker basket, demanded to see Messervy. According to Christison:

> they entered and with shining eyes saluted smartly, opened the basket and out fell two grisly human heads and a number of fish.
>
> 'Take those horrible heads away', shouted the General.
>
> The heads were replaced in the basket, but the two Gurkhas remained standing at attention.
>
> 'Well what are you waiting for?', demanded Frank.
>
> 'Please sir may we have the fish'?

During this period, the 114th Indian Infantry Brigade operated east of the Kalapanzin River, its main task being to work round the enemy's eastern flank, to cut his communications with Akyab, while the 81st West African Division moved down the Kaladan Valley much further to the east. In one of a number of brisk actions, Marshall's B Company was part of an attack on an enemy roadblock. In the jargon of the time, it was conducted as a 'blitz' attack; without artillery support, advancing with Brens and Tommy guns fired from the hip. Close-quarter fighting ensued which cost the 4th/5th Royal Gurkhas seven dead and twenty wounded. Marshall:

It was the first time I had heard Gurkhas actually shouting *Ayo Gurkhali* ['The Gurkhas are Coming'], a fearsome noise at close quarters, which undoubtedly scared the Japs. It was also the first time I had seen them using their kukris at close quarters. They mostly went for the throat. The Japs ran, they were not properly dug in otherwise they probably would not have run.

The next morning I was told to take two platoons back to this position to bury the dead. I instructed the Jemedar to carry on, and went off. I returned to find that instead of digging graves, the Gurkhas were using the foxholes dug by the Japs. The bodies had rigor mortis, and would not fit, so the Gurkhas were cutting them up and stuffing them into the holes. I stopped this, but they thought I was being pernickety. The Gurkha has all the nicest characteristics of the British soldier, he likes sport, drinking, women, and gambling. However, he has little feelings for the dead, either the enemy or his comrades. Once gone they'd gone and there were no feelings of sadness nor remorse. When killing the enemy he is elated, and Gurkhas' eyes become bloodshot when going into action at close quarters.

The Jap was a very courageous opponent and suffered enormously. But the Gurkhas were better. I was glad I was with them not against them. My Battalion took no prisoners until well into 1945 and none of our men were taken prisoner; neither side took prisoners. At this time in the war the Japs were thought to be invincible by some people, including many British troops. This was not the attitude of my Gurkhas.

Marshall's last action of the Arakan campaign took place on 4 February 1944. He was attacking

a known Jap position together with C Company. The two companies set off at 0630 hours in the typical early morning mist which hangs over paddy in the Arakan. We climbed up through jungle within some four or five hundred yards of what we thought was the Jap position and the attack went in. There was considerable Jap fire coming back. We used our 2 inch mortars and grenade dischargers. They did the same. Eventually the position was taken by us. We suffered one killed and 13 wounded one of whom being me. I was wounded together with my orderly by a Jap grenade falling behind me, being hit in the backside, back, and left arm. We all carried morphine syringes in our kit, and my orderly who was badly wounded in both legs, managed to extract the syringes and we injected each other. Luckily my haversack containing my binoculars, compass and two grenades, which were badly dented, took most of the blast. Without them I would probably have been killed.

I was taken back to C Company; unaware of what was happening. The Jap position was mopped up by my company. I was taken by stretcher to Battalion HQ. From then on strange events occurred.

The 'strange events' referred to by Marshall was the order to the battalion along with the rest of the 114th Brigade to withdraw immediately – for the Japanese offensive had begun. Marshall:

I was carried on a stretcher for two days back to the Admin Box [the 114th Brigade Admin Box at Oktaung in the vicinity of Kwazon]. I was put in a temporary hospital with other wounded. Limbs were being amputated without anaesthetic. My orderly had both legs amputated and he didn't survive. Although the surgeons wanted to amputate my arm which was infected, one of my fellow officers gave me some sulphonamide tablets which no one else had, and I did not have to go through with it. On 17 February a landing strip was built at Kwazon [to which the whole Brigade had moved], and I was lucky to be the first to be evacuated by L-5 light aircraft.

The Japanese struck while Christison was still regrouping his corps for the assault on Buthidaung. Rissik:

The skies normally quiet except for our own aircraft, were suddenly filled with an unusual number of Jap planes whose aggressive behaviour clearly indicated that they were out to conceal something. There were reports of a large number of Japs in the hills to the east of the Kalapanzin and the previous night a column of Japs and mules, which had apparently lost its way were reported among the positions of our own troops on the far side of the river. They were

identified as belonging to the very regiment which previous information had indicated was free for offensive action. Lastly, early on
the morning of February 4th, Taung Bazaar, a village on the river
well in rear of the 7th Divisions dispositions, was attacked by a
considerable number of Japs, and the village occupied. Events began
to move rapidly. At 9 am [on 2 February], I was told to meet the
Army Group Commander [Giffard, then visiting the Arakan front]
at the entrance to Corps Headquarters; he was apparently on his way
back over the Ngakyedauk Pass. When he arrived he told how a Jap
aircraft had bombed and machine-gunned a convoy in the Pass, and
had dropped a bomb not so very far from his own jeep. He seemed
highly amused. After a short conference with the Corps Commander,
he returned to [Slim's] Army Headquarters fully impressed with the
fact that things were far from quiet on the Arakan Front. This indeed
proved to be the case. On the afternoon [of 4 February] the 7th
Division reported that there were a thousand Japs in Taung Bazaar.
That evening a senior member of the Corps staff returned from 7th
Division Headquarters with the news that a large number of Japs
were approaching the Mayu Range, and were already in some places
well established in the foothills to the east of it. He gave it as his
opinion that they might well be over the range by the following
morning.

Sakurai's column had infiltrated the 114th Brigade's widely dispersed
forward posts in thick early morning mist, marching up the valley in
a dense column sixteen men abreast. Captain Gadsdon commanded
A Company of the 4th/14th Punjab Regiment in 114th Brigade, and had
mounted standing patrols out in the paddy fields in the valley that night:

> They heard troops coming and said, 'Halt who goes there?' Some
> Indians replied, 'Tikka bai ... it's all right ... don't bother ... no
> problem', and they walked straight past. The sentries came and
> reported this to us. There was a very thick mist and we could see
> absolutely nothing. This column appeared to have gone through our
> position. We took it to be just some of our own ration parties. In
> fact it was the Japs with INA pushing the sentries on one side.
>
> Our carrier platoon commander, Jemedar Pir Gul, a Pathan, sent
> a carrier out into the fog to investigate, and came back with a dead
> Japanese on the carrier.

The Japanese burst into Taung Bazaar at about 0800 on 4 February, and within an hour the leading battalion had crossed the Kalapanzin in boats captured from the 28th Inland Water Transport Company, whose HQ shared the village with a few baggage guards. Delayed by a clash with part of 89th Indian Brigade, at the rear of 7th Division, it took the Japanese until noon on 5 February before their column was across. Sakurai's next move was to send Kubo Force over the Mayu Range to Briasco Bridge to cut the Bawli Bazaar–Maungdaw road. Colonel Tanahashi (*112th Regiment*) was ordered to seize the Ngakyedauk Pass with one of his battalions, and with the rest of his regiment capture Point 315, thus blocking the route in and out of 7th Division's area. Sakurai with a battalion and the whole of *55th Engineer Regiment* was to attack into the rear of the 89th Brigade at Awlanbyin. Colonel Doi's column meanwhile slid past the 33rd Brigade's flank and headed north for the Ngakyedauk Pass.

The jaws of Tanahashi's pincer, and Doi's column, were about to close on Sinzweya, around which was disposed the 7th Division's Administrative Area. Shortly to become famous as the 'Admin Box', it lay in an amphitheatre about a mile long and half a mile wide, surrounded by jungle-covered hills. Here were massed the division's workshops, main dressing station, and a host of other administrative units, along with supply and ammunition dumps, the latter grouped round the jungle-covered 'Ammunition Hill' which jutted out into the amphitheatre. 7th Division HQ was sited about three to four miles north-east of Sinzweya. Messervy had ordered the 1st/11th Sikhs, the battalion assigned to defend the HQ, to help deal with the oncoming Japanese off to the east. Defence of the HQ devolved on to the HQ personnel themselves, especially the Divisional Signals under Lieutenant Colonel Hobson, and a company of Indian Engineers.

The Japanese were gambling on supplying themselves at the expense of the British, and their logistic arrangements were scanty to say the least; they even relied on captured transport to carry their supplies, and brought gunners without guns to man captured British pieces, augmenting their artillery. They calculated that the British would react to being cut off as they almost always had previously, by retreating, and the Japanese looked forward to carving them up as they scrambled frantically to claw their way out of the trap laid for them.

In the closing stages of the previous Arakan campaign, Slim had evolved a tactic which did not dance to the Japanese tune. Realizing that in the vast and thickly wooded terrain of Burma his defence positions could always be turned, his plans included well-stocked, strong anchor positions covering ground the enemy would be forced to attack if they wanted to clear their own line of communication. From these anchor positions, mobile forces would sortie to destroy the enemy. Slim preached that the aim was the destruction of the enemy, not seizing or holding ground as an end in itself. He told Fourteenth Army that when units and formations were cut off they were to hold firm unless ordered to withdraw, and they would be supplied by air. They would provide an anvil against which the enemy could be smashed by forces held in reserve for the purpose.

As the scale of the Japanese offensive in the Mayu Range area became clearer, Slim ordered Lomax's 26th Division to move forward and come under Christison's command, sending his 71st Brigade on ahead as quickly as possible. Slim watched the 26th Division move out, and, having ordered Major General F. W. Festing's 36th Indian Division to take over as army reserve, could be excused for feeling that all was going well. The next morning, 6 February, he learned that Tanahashi had overrun 7th Division's HQ and the whereabouts of Messervy was unknown. Initially the attackers had been ejected after fierce hand-to-hand fighting. But the signal centre was eventually overrun, and communications cut, so Messervy was unable to exercise command of his division. The story that Messervy led his men out of the HQ clad in his pyjamas was one of the many myths that were circulating at the time. He *was* in pyjamas when the attack on his HQ began, but after walking about in the confusion trying to find out what was going on for about an hour, walked back to his tent, dressed, grabbed his carbine, and it was only when he realized that nothing could save the Divisional HQ that he ordered all secret documents and radio sets destroyed and to make for the Admin Box in small parties. Most arrived there over the following twenty-four hours.

By now all the brigade commanders of 7th Division had agreed that HQ 33rd Brigade should take over command of the division until the situation clarified, and that everyone would stand fast. Meanwhile, Christison, assuming that Messervy was dead or a prisoner, ordered 5th Division to send Brigadier Evans, with whatever troops he could spare from his 9th Brigade, post haste to Sinzweya, to secure it and hold it to the last man. Slim told Christison that the Japanese could maintain a force of the size that had been identified for a short time only. Therefore it was essential that both 5th and 7th Divisions held firm, and the reserves he was sending forward would crush the enemy against the anvil of the two divisions. Christison now told Lomax that his task was to use his two remaining brigades to destroy the Japanese in the rear of 7th Division.

In the early afternoon Messervy turned up at Sinzweya. He told Evans to continue to command the garrison, and ordered a number of changes in the dispositions of his division over radio sets borrowed from the 25th Dragoons. The Admin Box was defended mainly by troops from the administrative units, supplemented by two companies of the 4th/8th Gurkhas, three companies of the 2nd West Yorkshires, two batteries of the 6th Medium Regiment, a section of four 3.7in guns of the 8th Heavy Anti-aircraft (AA) Regiment, and 25th Dragoons as a mobile reserve operating from two harbours held by a company of the 3rd/4th Bombay Grenadiers.

Lieutenant Colonel Cree, commanding the 2nd West Yorks:

Brigadier Evans told me to bring my whole battalion less one company into the 7th Division Admin Box. One company had to remain behind with the 3rd/14th Punjab Regiment still up in the hills next to our own Division, the 5th. He said I must keep two companies in mobile reserve for counter-attacking, and only one company for static defence. I got in touch right away with [Lieutenant] Colonel Cole the commanding officer of the 7th Division Light Ack Ack [anti-aircraft] Regiment, who had been in charge of the defences of the Admin Box up to that time, and discovered what he had done. As a result I put C Company into the static defence role, occupying a hill just above the eastern entrance to the Ngakyedauk Pass.

Colonel Cole had mustered every man he could find to defend the place, all the Indian followers [contractor wallahs], admin people and so on. They were all holding their positions and acting like soldiers. We found that by lending out our troops, putting one British soldier in a platoon of bakers and butchers etc. it lent moral support.

My battalion headquarters was in adjoining trenches to Brigade and Divisional HQs.

Tokyo 'Rose', who broadcast in English on Japanese radio, announced in her cajoling contralto tones:

> The march on Delhi has begun.
> Tanahashi, victor of Arakan, will be in Chittagong within a week.
> New British Fourteenth Army destroyed.
> Why not go home? It's all over in Burma.

'Actually,' wrote Slim later, 'it was just starting'.[8]

On the night of 7/8 February the Japanese attacked Sinzweya. On one side the 4/8th Gurkhas threw the enemy out after heavy fighting, but on the other side of the 'Box' the Japanese overran the main dressing station (MDS). Here they massacred the wounded, the doctors, and staff. Men who survived by shamming dead, or hiding, told the story to the troops who retook the position some thirty-six hours later.

Lieutenant Basu of the Indian Army Medical Corps (IAMC) was asleep on a stretcher in the medical inspection room. The Japanese rushed in and led him away at bayonet point to be interrogated by a senior Japanese officer. As more prisoners were brought in, including orderlies and British Other Ranks (BORs in the jargon of the time), they all had their hands tightly tied behind their backs. The five medical officers among the prisoners were taken to the dispensary and ordered to pack up certain medicines and drugs, for the Japanese, before being taken to a nullah with all the others. The Japanese ignored requests for water, and the bonds were very tight and painful, causing some of the prisoners to cry out. When a tank approached the area where the prisoners were being held, the Japanese immediately took shelter in slit trenches they had dug, and dragged the BORs in front so they would be hit first. Eight men were wounded in this way. The Japanese did nothing to help the wounded, and requests for a cigarette were answered with the burning end of one. About ten more prisoners were wounded by friendly mortar fire, and during the second night the worst wounded lay dying crying out for water. Friendly mortar and machine-gun fire killed and wounded more prisoners. Earlier the Indian officers and orderlies had their bonds taken off, but the BORs remained bound. A wounded man who asked for water was shot, and another bayoneted. In the evening before they pulled out, the Japanese starting shooting the BORs, and the Indians knew they would all be shot too. The Japanese shot everyone there, including those wearing Red Cross armbands, and

Lieutenant Basu and Captain Paul, who were quite clearly doctors, having stethoscopes. All were killed outright, except for Basu.

They shot me twice in my left ear. Just after the shot I was stunned. After some time I could feel I was not dead, but still in some doubt. I put my fingers in my ears, but could not feel any blood coming out. I felt that the facilities of sight and thinking were retained. Then just to befool the Japs, I stealthily took some blood from the wounds of my friends and applied it over my face, nose, ears and over my shirt, groaning all the time. There was a trench just beside me. With another groan I slipped into it and passed a horrible night there. In fact the Japs did not leave me at once. They formed two parties. The first consisted of the majority. In the second there were about five snipers, armed with machine guns and hiding themselves in the bushes. I could hear their footsteps just beside us and in the jungles. They cleared off from their defensive positions in trenches one by one. In the morning I saw two BORs coming towards us with tommy guns.

It was A Company of the West Yorkshires supported by B Squadron 25th Dragoons who cleared the Japanese out of the MDS. They found that the enemy had camouflaged their machine-gun posts with stretchers in the wards and theatres. The West Yorkshires found the bodies of thirty-one patients and four doctors, as well as seventy Japanese. All this had happened within a few hundred yards of B Squadron's night position in the Box. The squadron was totally unaware of what was going on, and had they been curious could not have left their positions, for to do so would have risked being shot by their own sentries.

Cree:

That night the Japs pulled out after our counter-attack and started trickling down a chaung that ran up into the main dressing station. Both sides of the chaung were held by our Brigade B Echelon personnel: muleteers, orderly room staff, sanitary men, quartermasters' storemen, chaps like that, nearly all old soldiers, including the Regimental Sergeant Major. They twigged what was happening, and let the Japs have it. They killed an enormous number of them in the chaung, which became known as Blood Nullah. These were chaps who had raided the dressing station, so we felt we'd avenged that one. They continued to come down this chaung, although it was a stupid thing to do. Perhaps they'd been ordered to some rendezvous.

Messervy ordered out strong fighting patrols from his division to attack the tracks along which Japanese porters and mules were carrying supplies to their units. Time was running out for the Japanese, it was in fact they who were cut off. The West African Division, in the Kaladan Valley, was already threatening the Japanese rear, while Lomax began pressing down from the north. Japanese supplies were running short, and whereas the British brigades could be supplied by air, Sakurai's lifeline lay round or through 7th Division, who squeezed down hard on it at every opportunity. He had suffered heavy losses, and no reinforcements were to hand: the Japanese, instead of doing the sensible thing and calling it a day, hurled themselves into the attack, and nowhere more fiercely than at the 'Admin Box'. Here, time and again, the reserve, consisting of two companies of the 2nd West Yorkshires supported by part of two squadrons of 25th Dragoons, had to turf out parties of Japanese who had infiltrated the perimeter. The fighting was savage and no quarter was sought or given.

A staff officer in HQ 7th Indian Division recalled life in the 'Box':

Although it [the Box] had already been divided into sectors for defence purposes and although weapon pits had been dug, a complete reorganisation of life in the 'box' became necessary, and men whose tasks had previously been solely administrative were made to 'stand to' at dawn and dusk and to fight off Jap attacks during the night.

February in the Arakan is a hot dry month and this one was no exception. The main source of water was the chaung in which there were water points for men and animals and washing points as well, but most people were too busy to wash much. One of the features of the Arakan is its sandy soil, even on the Mayu range itself it is difficult to find stones. After two days fine weather the roads were covered in dust and every vehicle left a cloud behind it as it passed. In the confined space of the 'box' it was impossible to get clear of the tracks with the result that everything had a covering of dust. Dust got into your hair, your eyes and clung to your sweating body. There was no escaping it.

More trying than the dust was the noise. Over thirty tanks in a small space made their presence felt. Engines had to be started every morning; and all through the day it seemed as it they were moving in or out on some mission so often did we hear the clanging of their tracks. I think the Heavy Anti-aircraft guns, firing at ground targets, were the worst offenders. Their sharp bark made us all jump every time they fired. But Medium artillery firing over our heads took a lot of beating; added to which our friends across the range and other 'boxes' used to fire shells towards us to help us, and, of course, Jap shells and mortar bombs landing in our midst did not improve our nerves or temper. It was always a joke to see someone duck at the sound of an approaching shell, only to find it was one of our own and to hear it go sailing gaily over our heads to crash on some Jap position outside our perimeter.

Whereas we had previously left our rifles behind during our daily routine now we carried them with us. Whether a man was collecting supplies or cleaning a lorry, his rifle was never far away. Every thicket might contain a Jap who had crept close up to our positions during the night; and quite a number did. Throughout the day the occasional rifle shot told that some Jap sniper was active.

At night conditions were very different. We were all manning dug positions; clerks, cooks, everyone, no matter what he had done during the day. There was no room for the non-combatant who relied on others to defend him. As the Japs attacked at nights they were met by fire which must have approximated to the idiomatic 'solid wall' as nearly as any yet. In the morning a count of dead Japs was made and it was seldom small. However, the nights' activities were, to say the least of it, most disturbing and we all went back to work the next morning heavy-eyed through lack of sleep.

After the MDS was overrun, the dressing stations and regimental aid posts were moved to the narrow beds of dry chaungs. There was no means of evacuating sick or wounded, and the facilities available had neither the staff nor equipment to hold patients.

It was a pitiful sight to see the wounded lying there with the battle going on all round them and they with the knowledge that if the Japs broke in they faced the alternative of slaughter or captivity at the enemy's pleasure.

Meanwhile the Japs were not idle. From their positions along the ridge they could overlook the whole area. With this observation went the power to put down shell fire whenever we exposed ourselves too much. Why they did not do so more often will always be a mystery. After all we were a sitting target, all bunched together as we were: but I can only suppose that our great air and artillery superiority made them shy. By night, however, they always attacked in some sector and were driven off with casualties. On two occasions they got astride the ridge overlooking the gaps through which the chaung flowed. If they had been allowed to stay there our position would indeed have been serious. But the tanks were put on to the job and literally blasted the Japs off these hills. The noise, dust and smoke were tremendous: trees as large as oaks were felled by shells and crashed down the hillside. two months later the same hills were quite brown: all vegetation had been destroyed. There were comic moments too, as when a Jap platoon tried to march into the position in fours, down the road.

The 'Box' was kept supplied with air drops, without which the siege would have soon been over. Sergeant Adrain was a clerk in B Squadron 25th Dragoons:

Even our Spitfire reconnaissance planes as they passed over the Box heaved out a bag of mail. The first time a mail bag was received in this manner occasioned a laugh against me. I joined the eager rush for news from home, but there was only one letter for me. It was from the Income Tax in England and read; 'In regard to your application, will you please send me a full statement of all earnings, both civil and military received by yourself and your wife from the day you joined HM Forces to the present date.' I got more laughs than sympathy.

A section of four 3.7in guns from 8th Heavy Anti-aircraft Regiment RA was sited in the box, initially to provide anti-aircraft protection. But they were used more often in the direct-fire role, unusual for the British; unlike the Germans, who often deployed their equivalent, the 88mm, against ground targets, armour especially. Both types of gun were accurate and fired very high velocity shells. In the 'Box' the guns were overlooked from high ground. Sergeant Adrain's diary:

8th morning: Being pounded by Jap 75 mm gun and mortars from hill at opposite end of valley. Men in good spirits. Received our first severe casualties two direct hits on gun site, first one in the morning about six were wounded but not severely. In afternoon it was a bad smash. Jack Thompson and about a dozen others were severely wounded. Bombardier Sherrard was killed instantly on J Dubois's gun, and Talbot on Bren Gun pit nearby. I brought vehicle on to park to take wounded to ADS [Advanced Dressing Station] about 100 yards away, we had a job getting them into the ADS as Jap gun fire was coming right over the lorry, and we had to take shelter.

Dive bombed.

By this stage the section had suffered eight dead and around twelve wounded, all from enemy artillery and mortars, which was extremely unusual for a heavy anti-aircraft unit.

9 February: Gun park shelled again and more casualties. The officers and men are sticking it extra well as defence posts are manned all night. Thomas and I only get an hour's sleep every other hour.

10 February: Received another direct hit on gun; very bad smash on gun park, more lorries ablaze, and exploding ammo and hand grenades. When I was able to leave dugout, found two dead on number 1 gun. Sergeant Dubois and all gun team injured. Military Police and West Yorks helped to take them to ADS.

Captain Reid was mad [angry] and also Mr Francis and it was decided to blast the hill. Sergeant Sharp was in charge of one gun and the scratch team for the other gun still in action was Number 1 Sergeant Arthurs, Dials Bombardier Pain and Gunner McGillavray. Lieutenant Bing, Lieutenant Francis, Sergeant McLloughlin and myself loaded, and we fired ten rounds each gun at the hill where the Jap gun was. The number 1 Gun was hit on the barrel and recuperator and is out of action.

Lord Louis [Mountbatten] message: 'hold on you are making history'.

In a 'normal' campaign, armoured units liked to pull back to a safe leaguer at night to replenish fuel and ammunition, and carry out maintenance relatively undisturbed; not so in the 'Box', where it was the other way round, as Trooper McKnight relates:

During the hours of darkness the tanks were spread out in a ring right round the perimeter, my tank being in the northern section, ahead of ammunition hill. We had to dig a weapons trench in front of the tank, man it with a Browning machine gun [from the tank] mounted on a tripod, plus hand grenades and a Tommy Gun. The other tanks in the Squadron were to the right and left of us, and had similar slit trenches and weapons. There would be 50 to 100 yards between tanks. Two crew-men manned the slit trenches, two hours on and four hours off. The four hours off was supposed to be spent under the tank wrapped in a blanket getting some sleep, but was not always possible. Sleep was a luxury that twenty-one days, you were lucky if you could get four hours out of the twenty-four. At dawn we backed away from the defence line, and made for ammunition hill, where we had a small base, where we could cook, do tank mainten-ance, etc. All our spare kit had to be off-loaded from the tank and left under a tarpaulin at our base when we went out on operations during daylight. The Japs put in attacks at all hours of the day and night, using their infantry on frontal assaults and their artillery and mortars to rake the area with HE.

When the Japs found ammunition hill with a salvo of HE, the ammo dug into the hill exploded setting off a chain reaction. The whole complex exploded setting light to everything, including all our spare kit. We had been parked at our base, and had to evacuate in a hurry. Small arms ammunition was going off like squibs on Guy Fawkes night, and huge chunks of shrapnel from exploding shells whizzed round our ears. We moved the tanks away from the cover of the hill, and into the open, good targets for the Jap gunners. There was nowhere to go, it was inside or under the tanks for shelter.

The tanks were used to shore up the perimeter when a break-in by the Japanese was threatened. Sometimes a troop of three tanks would go, sometimes a single tank was all that could be spared; again, unusual and against 'the book'. McKnight's tank was sent off to where

a party of Japs had pushed back the defenders from the perimeter, and occupied the position. Our task was to dislodge them, and reinstate our infantry back to the original position. I was told to advance along the track, ascend a steep incline, veer left when level ground was reached, and stop. We closed down all hatches, and set off. As soon as we stopped on the top of the incline we were met by a hail of small arms and machine gun fire, which just bounced off the hull. McDonald went into action with the turret guns and the Japs fell silent. I was studying the area through my periscope, and saw the Japs taking cover in a nullah about thirty to fifty yards ahead of our position. This was too close to get at them with the turret guns – even when fully depressed.*

Sergeant Branson [the tank commander] told 'Mac' to keep shooting at them to keep their heads down while he thought something up. I could see the Jap steel helmets scuttling back and forth between the bursts of Browning 'Mac' was giving them.

Sergeant Branson radioed to his squadron HQ and arranged for either a 3in mortar section (two mortars) or a platoon (four to six mortars), McKnight does not say which, to fire a ranging smoke bomb. From this first bomb, Branson was able to correct the fire (presumably relaying the message through squadron HQ), to land a smoke bomb in the nullah.

This caused panic among the Japs, they were rushing about trying to get out of the nullah, but 'Mac' kept their heads down with the Browning. Branson announced to the crew [on the intercom] that he had asked for a 'flight' of HE mortar bombs to be sent over next, and as we were so close to the target, we might get damaged, and to brace ourselves. I was observing through my periscope when the bombs arrived, mostly on target. The noise was deafening, and when the dust and smoke cleared away, there was no sign of life or movement in the nullah. Sergeant Branson called for the infantry to move forward, they crept past our tank in strength and occupied the nullah.

After dealing with an infantry casualty, Branson was ordered to move forward to check the track for half a mile or so to ensure it was clear of enemy. Having encountered and destroyed a Japanese mortar team with 37mm and Browning fire from the turret, they were ordered back to base.

This action lasted for six or seven hours, and when we got back it was late afternoon. We replenished fuel and ammo, had a meal of bully beef and K Rations, and got ready to spend another night on the 'night defence line'.

---

* Moving back to open up the range would have taken the tank down the incline and would have made the situation worse.

Sergeant Branson was an interesting character, who had been prominent in the British Communist movement, and fought with the International Brigade in the Spanish Civil War, ending as a prisoner of General Franco. His tank took part in the first attempt to force a route through the Ngakyedauk Pass, which was a combined effort with troops from the 5th Division attacking from the western end supported by the squadron of tanks from 25th Dragoons still over that side of the range, and infantry supported by tanks from B Squadron. By now Messervy had ordered the remainder of the 89th Brigade into the 'Box' to reinforce the garrison, who were beginning to show signs of strain.

The first attempt at a link-up with the 5th Division did not succeed, and with wounded infantry on the backs of the tanks, the force retraced its steps back into the 'Box'. The return was not without incident, as they had to clear a Japanese block consisting of felled trees which had been set up to catch them on their return, or delay reinforcement if they had succeeded in forcing on to the west. On regaining the 'Box' it was back to the familiar routine. McKnight:

> There was no place that could be termed 'safe', you were at risk at all times, trying to have a wash, visiting the latrines, or even trying to enjoy a hot meal. The 75 mm gunner, Ken Arnell, our tank cook, had a talent for acquiring rations out of thin air, and producing a hot meal from weird ingredients. His masterpiece being porridge oats boiled up with water and a full tin of syrup. Usually, when everything was on the boil, we would be under attack from artillery or mortars. Everybody would scatter and climb in or under the tank, leaving the cooking, to find when we emerged, that pots had been toppled by blast or the food contaminated by dust and grit. So we devised a Tee shaped slit trench, for the cook. The leg of the Tee was partly under the tank and the Tee cross piece out in the open. The fire and pots were in the Tee cross piece, and Ken occupied the leg, under cover.

The next attempt at a link-up with 5th Division also involved Branson and McKnight's tank. Driving round a tricky corner in the track, nicknamed Tattenham Corner, McKnight heard a loud clang, denoting a hit on the tank by an anti-tank gun firing solid shot. A few seconds later, after another loud clang followed by flying debris across McKnight's periscope,

My earphones seemed to leap from my head, Arthur Bears (the loader) yelled into his microphone as loud as he could, 'Branson is dead'. With my ears still ringing from the message, and concentrating on driving the tank through a very hostile situation, I couldn't comprehend what I had just heard. Branson had just been speaking to me.

It transpired that Branson's command periscope had taken a direct hit from a Japanese anti-tank gun, and had been blown into his head. He had fallen across McDonald to drop to the floor of the turret where he had to remain for the time being. Resisting the temptation to look round, McKnight concentrated on driving when

> a hand appeared in front of my face, and a voice in my earphones told me to drink the contents, it was neat rum, which I gulped down greedily. All the crew had a tot to help steady them. After a long hard, fast drive we reached our destination. We were given the sad task of extricating Sgt Branson from the turret, and laid him to rest in a temporary grave adjacent to the track, which was marked and recorded.

On the twenty-first day of the battle of the Admin Box, the link-up was achieved. Christison wrote:

> When I got through to Messervy's HQ in the BOX, I found it dug in well protected by a dead mule which stank to heaven, and the whole valley was pungent with the stale smell of rotting corpses in the sun.
>   On the 27th February I issued an order which began: 'No victory is complete without pursuit', and all Units moved forward driving the remnants of the' Japanese *54th* and *55th Divisions* well to the south. [sic]

The Battle of Ngakyedauk Pass, which included the siege of 'Admin Box', cost the British 3,506 casualties. As the Official History states,

> The battle which took place on a not very important part of the Burma front, was of far greater importance than might at first appear. It marked the turning point in the war in South-East Asia. It was the first time the Japanese met well-trained British/Indian formations in battle and the first time that their enveloping tactics, aimed at cutting their opponent's line of communication, failed to produce the results they expected.[9]

4

The Arakan: Kaladan Valley and Victory on the Maungdaw–Buthidaung Road

Since 18 January 1944, the 81st (WA) Division had been advancing down the Kaladan Valley, with the 6th Brigade moving on each side of the river, and the 5th (Gold Coast) Brigade moving along the line of hills to the west of the valley. The Division was short of its Nigerian brigade, the 3rd West African, which had been given to Wingate for his second LRP expedition. The East African Scouts from the 11th East African Division had been loaned to General Woolner to replace his own Reconnaissance Regiment, which being Bren-carrier borne could not be employed in the Kaladan Valley, and was deployed on the main Arakan front. The artillery support consisted of three batteries each with four 3.7in pack howitzers. The division's supplies, ammunition, and equipment, such as 3in mortars and the pack howitzers broken down into one-man loads, could be carried on the heads of unarmed soldiers, UAS for short: for example, a platoon would have some fourteen UAS head-loading the balance of its first-line ammunition not on the riflemen, spare radio batteries, and so forth. In addition, each brigade was supported by an Auxiliary Group of 660 UAS. The UAS were trained soldiers who could act as battle casualty replacements if required, and their use allowed the division to operate in areas inaccessible to wheeled transport. Captain Cookson of the 1st Gambia Regiment:

> Every African carried some kind of load on his head; it was a natural place to put a load and many of them grew a special tuft of hair to act as a cushion. It was a commonplace sight to observe an African with his pack, haversack, water bottle, pair of boots, Bren gun, and slouch hat, perched in a neat pyramid on his head. Considerable

weights were carried in this fashion; the charging engines for wireless sets weighed almost a hundredweight, and yet they were head-loaded up and down hills for day after day. Even the stretcher bearers used to carry their patients head-high.

Unlike the Indian Army, with few British officers and no British NCOs, African units had approximately the same number of British officers as in a British army unit. So an infantry battalion would have about thirty British officers, including all the platoon commanders. In addition there were British NCOs at all levels down to platoon. These British NCOs were 'shadowed' by African NCOs. Some of the British NCOs were not necessarily of the highest calibre – 'the RWAFF [Royal West African Frontier Force] suffered from NCOs being sent to the force by English Battalions in order to get rid of them', recorded Captain Theobald (of the 82nd WA Division), who had to charge at least one of them for drunkenness. One of the reasons given for such a high proportion of British NCOs was, according to Theobald, because

> Quite a number of African NCOs could not read or write. They did however have very good memories. I could give out a page of detail to English and African warrant officers together, and the white warrant officers would make copious notes and fail to carry out some of their instructions. The African warrant officers would just listen and every detail would be remembered.

Woolner decided that instead of head-loading the guns and ammunition in, or having them dropped or flown in, he would cut a jeep track through to Satpaung on the upper Kaladan. A seventy-three-mile-long track was constructed in four weeks by four infantry battalions and some of the Auxiliary Group across the grain of the country. The decision to tow the guns by Jeep released the gun-carrier UAS to take in additional 3in mortars, which proved invaluable.

The 81st (WA) Division established a Dakota strip at Medaung on 21 February, and 1st Gambia Regiment occupied Kyauktaw three days later. Before this the East African Scouts reached Pagoda Hill, 350 feet high, on the other side of the 400 yard wide tidal Kaladan River from Kyauktaw, and dominating the town. The Japanese, realizing that the West Africans posed a threat to *Twenty-eighth Army* communications, had reinforced Myohaung and formed *Koba force* (under Colonel

Tomotoki Koba) for the defence of the valley, consisting of the HQ and one battalion from the *111th Regiment*, a battalion of *143rd Regiment*, the *55th Division Reconnaissance Regiment*, and a composite unit under Captain Honjo formed from *144th Regiment* reinforcements. The *55th Division's Reconnaissance Regiment* had three mounted infantry companies, one MMG company, and one anti-tank company. They referred to themselves as cavalry, as did some of their opponents. The anti-tank gun company and part of the MMG company did not take part in the Kaladan campaign.

On 24 February, with the Ngakyedauk Pass battle won, Christison told Woolner that he was about to launch his corps into the offensive. Woolner was to direct his 81st (WA) Division's efforts towards the Mayu River to cut the Japanese line of communication between his main base at Akyab and Buthidaung. On 27 February the 6th Brigade, less 1st Gambia, and all divisional troops, had been ferried over the Kaladan to Kyauktaw, a total of in excess of 11,000 men, plus 180 jeeps and 15cwt trucks, all three light batteries, and a Bofors troop.

The next day an order arrived from 15th Corps telling Woolner that in addition to the tasks given earlier, it was vital that the Japanese did not establish themselves at Kyauktaw. This came as somewhat of a surprise to Woolner, because Christison had committed the military sin of giving him two missions: holding a wide front to protect the left flank of 15th Corps, and advancing at the same time; in a different direction. Furthermore the odds were not favourable to Woolner. He was up against five Japanese battalions with their excellent artillery. He had six lightly armed battalions, seven if one counts the even weaker EA Scouts, twelve light pack howitzers and four light anti-aircraft guns. It had taken more than three divisions, well supported by tanks, artillery, and aircraft, to see off one understrength Japanese division on the main front.

Koba was planning too. He aimed to capture Kyauktaw, and destroy the West African Division. He ordered Honjo and the *55th Reconnaissance Regiment* to hold up the 81st Division south of Kyauktaw, while he took two battalions and captured Thayettabin and Pagoda Hill overlooking the river, cutting Woolner's communications, and attacking him from the rear – standard Japanese form: pin the enemy in the front, while swinging round to kick him in the bottom.

Woolner underestimated the speed with which the Japanese could move when the mood took them, and ordered a two-brigade advance

with Htizwe, on the Mayu, as the objective, which was in line with
Christison's order to cut the Japanese line of communication. He covered
his left flank with the East African Scouts, whose task was to watch any
threat to Pagoda Hill and operate towards Myohaung. By 2 March the
leading battalion of the 6th Brigade was in Apaukwa, but now the East
African Scouts reported that they had been forced to retire to Thayettabin, and Pagoda Hill was threatened. Woolner ordered 1st Gambia to
send a company across to help the Scouts and secure Pagoda Hill, and
asked 15th Corps for permission to use 7th/16th Punjabis as a counter-
attack force. At 0730 the leading company of 1st Gambia crossed, and
the remainder of the battalion followed, as communication with the
East African Scouts was cut. Captain Cookson was company second-in-
command of D Company, 1st Gambia:

> A damp mist was drifting off the river and we shivered violently in
> our thin uniforms. Andy and his khisti [local boat] flotilla had begun
> work and groups of cold, dejected Africans were bunched together
> on the mud waiting their turn to cross.
>
> Presently Gordon [the company commander] returned looking
> grave. Between the Japs and the natural fortress of Pagoda Hill, the
> few askaris [EA Scouts] were fighting a delaying action until we could
> come to their assistance. With no more information than this we
> began to cross the Kaladan. The beach was alive with rumours, for
> the less the information the more the imagination.
>
> Pagoda Hill was on the edge of the Kaladan and one side dropped
> straight down to the water. Further inland was a belt of small ridges
> covered in stunted jungle, beyond the ridges was a tract of open
> paddy fields, and somewhere beyond was the enemy. The plan was
> to defend Pagoda Hill by occupying the ridges and shooting the Japs
> as they came across the open.

By the approach of twilight, Cookson's company was sited on a
'tactically hopeless position on the flank of the battalion, half a mile
from the nearest company'. Cookson with his orderly were on a
reconnaissance to find water for the company when

> I heard a faint thud far away over the paddy fields and then a screech
> as a heavy shell passed overhead. It was an excellent shot and burst
> at the foot of the Pagoda. This proved to be the forerunner of a brisk

bombardment and I had no difficulty in deciding that the time was unpropitious for water divining.

When he returned he found radio and telephone links with the battalion cut, but, thanks to orders received just before communications failed, most of the men were now out of the position on tasks ordered by battalion HQ. After an eventful night, during which only part of Cookson's company was engaged, with one section overrun, his company commander ordered a withdrawal as there was little they could do where they were. During the move back, the company encountered Japanese machine guns, and the leading platoon broke through. But Cookson, the next in the column, with forty unarmed soldiers, decided that an attack on machine guns was not in order, as only he and four others were armed:

> For the moment we were in the backwater of full-scale battle. On our right the Japs who had overwhelmed Paul [the detached platoon] during the night were commencing a reckless attack on Pagoda Hill; on our left another force of Japs was making noisy progress down the road.
>
> I was dependent entirely on my ears and intuition for my information and as the responsibility of the route was mine I had to be exceptionally wary in my movements. The route required three qualifications; it had to be unobtrusive and it had to be easy on account of the carriers and it had also to lead in the right direction. In the normal type of warfare skylines were avoided, but in the topsy-turvy conditions of the jungle they were welcomed, for on the crest of ridges the undergrowth was usually thinner than elsewhere and provided a practical line of advance. On this occasion I was delighted to find a ridge that led more or less in the direction I wanted. It was a narrow undulating ridge and I went along it with all the sensations of a tight-rope walker at his debut. In the valley on one side there was shouting and on the other side there was shooting. As though this was not enough, Gordon sent a message from the rear to ask if I would mind hurrying, since a party of Japs was following us. These Japs must have been singularly incompetent trackers, for they eventually lost trace of us and moved down to the paddy-fields where Gordon estimated their strength at over a hundred.
>
> The ridge ended at a small pimple above the road. The slopes that led down to the road were covered in the same kind of compact

shrubbery we had encountered before. I waited for Gordon to come forward and in the meantime sent a couple of men to find a way down to the road. The pimple was a fine viewpoint. To the right the road led straight across five hundred yards of open ground to where the shaggy slopes of Pagoda Hill rose above the Kaladan. The askaris on the hill were firing at the Japs on the river bank and the Japs were returning the fire. There was a continuous confused chatter of Brens and machine-guns of various timbres and rates of fire. Some of the Japs were using tracer bullets and their red sparks fanned up into the hillside. To the left the road plunged out of sight into a densely wooded valley towards the company we were trying to join. A violent battle was being fought in this direction. The Japs had a high-velocity gun – its distinctive Whizz-bangs could be clearly heard – and from time to time a cloud of dust and smoke was hurled into the air above the tree-tops with a resounding explosion. The one direction that was still peaceful was across the road in front of us.

Gordon was determined we should join our friends up the road to the left and to warn them of our arrival he scribbled out a message which he gave to his orderly to deliver. The men I had sent to find a route to the road had not returned – as it happened they never returned – so Gordon and I began to descend the slope to see for ourselves if there was a possible way down.

It took us a quarter of an hour's hard struggle to cover the hundred yards between the top of the pimple and the road. The bushes were not high, but they were thick, dark and bound together by creeping branches as tough and pliable as alpine ropes. The only way to make progress was to crawl on hands and knees and attempt to slip along between the lower branches and the ground; even so the roots and branches became entangled in our equipment in an exasperating manner. When we had squirmed to the edge of the bushes by the roadside, we paused to draw breath.

They had a close call: they heard troops approaching, and thinking they were friendly Cookson nearly jumped out to great them, but was restrained by his company commander:

He was wiser than I; our friends turned out to be a company or more of Japs who swaggered along, chattering among themselves and never glancing to left or right.

With fascinated interest I watched them pass. We were lying so close to them that I noticed one man had his bootlace dangling loose. They were broad, well-developed men whose steel helmets made them appear taller than they actually were. A detachment of the Imperial Guard was believed [incorrectly] to be in the Arakan and if these men did not belong to it they were at least physically worthy of it, in every way they presented a contrast to the squat bandy-legged members of the *55th Cavalry*. They tramped jauntily past our hiding place without seeing the pair of dishevelled British officers under the bush and halted further down the road where we could hear them crash about in the shrubbery.

Having seen a good deal more than we had bargained for, we wormed our way up the undergrowth tunnel to the top of the pimple. Once we had rejoined our own men, Gordon and I held a whispered discussion in which we strove to assess the situation in a calm, judicial manner. A quick survey showed that we had fifty men at our disposal and three quarters of them were unarmed soldiers who had been carrying loads. As a fighting force we no longer existed.

It took the remnants of the company three weeks to rejoin the battalion.

Before leaving the pimple, we dumped all unnecessary loads into the jungle, so that the carriers should have a chance to use their machetes in self-defence if it became imperative for them to do so. Among the dumped loads was the Company safe, a steel box weighing fifty pounds, which was full of the Army forms deemed indispensable even on a campaign as well as the balance of the Company account, amounting to seventy four rupees. If I had the vaguest inkling of the endless correspondence that was to ensue between the Paymaster and myself concerning the conditions under which this money was to be written off, I would have carried away that safe single-handed.

Unknown to Cookson, the Japanese had forced 1st Gambia off Pagoda Hill. Woolner, aware that 6th Brigade was split with 1st Sierra Leone east of the river, which made holding Kyauktaw, and any notions of continuing the advance, impossible, ordered his division to withdraw north across the Praing Chaung, a tributary of the Pi Chaung (itself a tributary of the Kaladan River). This was successfully accomplished despite the crossing place of the Praing Chaung being under the observation of the Japanese on Pagoda Hill.

On their way north the division concentrated in the area of the Kyingri loop of the Pi Chaung, and constructed an airstrip capable of taking Dakotas, to fly out casualties and bring in supplies. The Japanese made several unsuccessful attempts to cut off the division by wide hooks, and several times received a bloody nose for their pains. On one occasion, the Japanese *3/111th Battalion* was given a severe mauling by the 7th Gold Coast Regiment in the vicinity of the Kyingri loop. Captain Poore, second-in-command of C Company:

At about 2.00 am on 11th March 1944 firing started in A Company area and continued until dawn. When a message from Battalion Headquarters ordered C Company to prepare to make a counter attack. Bill was really sick and handed the Company over to me, I can remember the sad look in his eyes but there really was no other choice. Some Platoons of the 5 G.C.R. [5th Gold Coast Regiment] took over our position, and off we went to Battalion Headquarters, where most people were very much on edge. Two platoons of B Company had been rushed to A Company Headquarters to stop what seemed a determined push by a Japanese force. They had already overrun the Mortar observation post and cut off the two forward platoons of A Company. That was all the information available. I was given the support of the 3 inch mortar platoon which consisted of six mortars instead of the normal four.

The plan was to advance along the ridge and retake the mortar observation post with Lt. Paris's platoon. A Company Headquarters and reserve platoon were already in the bottom of the valley on the path engaging the Japanese. So my second platoon was to advance halfway up the slope and keeping contact with Lt Paris to drive a wedge between the observation post and the rest of the Japs, and maybe outflank any opposition Lt. Paris had. I had been lent another officer, Lt Sparey, he was an excellent man and I was delighted to have him. He took the 3rd platoon and stayed back a little in reserve, and became my 2nd in command should I get knocked over.

I followed the lower platoon with Company Headquarters. It soon came under heavy fire from a wide area; and stopped to return fire. As you see movement first, those that advance get shot at about 30–40 yards range, which should be deadly. This was a problem, so we used the 3 in mortars but the range was rather short about 200 yards and the mortars had a hard job to be accurate. One bomb burst just behind the platoon and I saw some anxious faces, so I yelled out 'That's okay, that's only one of ours' and they seemed reassured. I realised ours were much more dangerous than those of the Japs. The mortar officer managed to sort it out

While this was happening and I was trying to estimate the strength and position of the enemy, a cheeky Jap had a shot at me from 30 yards (I paced it later). The bullet struck just in front of my nose, close enough to throw dirt into both my eyes so that I could not see. This was very lucky for him as I had a sub-machine gun in my hands and I don't miss at 30 yards. I removed myself before he had time to reload, and wiped my eyes clear. Then I thought I might 'go him' but soon realised I had more important things to do. I then nipped up to Lt. Paris's platoon to see how things were going there. To my dismay there was Lt Paris with a horrid bleeding wound in his leg and to make matters worse the African Sergeant with a similar wound. It appeared they were held up by a Japanese machine gun and Lt Paris had gone forward to investigate, unfortunately he walked instead of crawling and the sergeant followed him as he always did on parade, and they both stopped the next burst in the legs. They were patched up and their orderly helped them limp back to the dressing station. I thought I would fix the bastard with the grenade discharger, just the job for this kind of thing, the grenadier came forward, and then explained that when we left all our heavier equipment such as packs and bedding behind, the special cartridges needed to fire the grenade were also left behind. Nobody had checked. I was getting cross; I sent him back to get them, but it was too late for this job. I crawled forward to the section concerned. We had taught our gunners only to fire at a target they could see and be sure to hit it This was to stop wasting ammunition and to make sure we did not shoot up our own people. The Japanese were not doing this, they were shooting at sound. The Bren gunner said 'Sar, I no fit see um how I go shoot. Japanee dey for over there small way'. The next moment there was a blast of bullets that almost parted my hair, but I heard and got a fix on the gun. I borrowed the Bren gun and put a new magazine on and let the Japs have it in five bursts in the pattern of the 5 of spades. We then had a rather violent shoot out, I being the last one to fire. Then I explained to the Africans what I had done and said they were to do the same when the need arose but to use their common sense.

There was a senior corporal, a steady man but not very bright. I could rely on him to hold the platoon together and defend to the end; but not lead an attack. All leadership had gone, and I could not expect too much. So I gave him orders to advance if he could, otherwise stay put and drive off any Japanese attack

With my orderly we ran down hill to A Company Headquarters to report progress and check on what else had happened. We went fast to make ourselves a difficult target, and cut the time of the journey down as there were quite a few stray bullets flying around plus Jap 50 mm mortar bombs. One pitched between me and my orderly, hit him in the foot but missed me although I heard bits whizz by. The stretcher bearers collected him, and he would not go until he had handed over the very [Very] light pistol and other odd things he was carrying. I was sorry to lose him we had grown to understand each other, he was a bright lad who could use his head and was a great help to me.

Captain Macdowell was commanding A Company and senior to me and therefore in charge. We had a discussion and he really did not know any more than I did, just what was going on the 'fog of war' was as thick as the bamboo. We decided to separate as there was so much high explosive and bullets flying around and it would be foolish for us both to get caught together. I had just seen a similar thing happen. Macdowell was going to try and get through to Jimmy Chapman on the left while I applied pressure on the right and centre. All this time we could hear fighting going on at the forward platoons, but could only guess what was happening, at least they were still there. We used the 3 in mortars wherever we could locate a target. This proved more effective than we realised at the time. We had a telephone line to the captured Mortar observation post, so I rang up, and was answered in Japanese. I don't know what he said, it certainly sounded very disrespectful. Apart from being rude he was very foolish as I obviously knew where the end of the phone was. So we gave the observation post ten rounds of rapid fire from six 3 inch mortars. There were no trial shots or warning of any sort. All sixty bombs were in the air before the first one landed. There was a sound like an earthquake for 20 seconds. Thunder rumble and earthquakes give a sudden roar and stop. I phoned again to enquire about their health but got no reply.

What seemed a moment later Captain Macdowell came by on a

1. Japanese troops enter Rangoon railway station, 7 March 1942.

2. American air crew of Chennault's American Volunteer Air Group (AVG) with a Tomahawk aircraft taken in early 1942. The man on the right could be an RAF ground crew.

3. The message 'Plane Land Here Now' spelt out with parachutes.
First Chindit expedition.

4. A group of Chindits after being flown back to India from China or Fort Hertz
at the end of the First Chindit Expedition.

5. Elephants pass a Hurricane on a forward airstrip.

6. One of the tunnels on the Maungdaw–Buthidaung Road in the Arakan.

7. Sergeant of the 81st West African Division with his machet.

8. No comment.

9. Naik Nand Singh of the 1st/11th Sikhs, greeted by his mother on return to his village after being awarded the Victoria Cross. In March 1944, although wounded six times, Naik Nand Singh accounted for seven Japanese and captured three enemy trenches single-handed in the fighting to break through to Buthidaung in the Arakan.

10. Terrain in the Shenam Pass,
'Scraggy', after capture.

11. Naik Agansing Rai of the
2nd/5th Royal Gurkha Rifles,
awarded the Victoria Cross for
his actions in the recapture of
Water Point and Mortar Bluff
on the Silchar Track in June 1944
during the Imphal battle.

12. Rifleman Manparsad Pun, of 3rd/2nd Gurkha Rifles, 25th Indian Division in the Arakan.

13. Troops of 9th Royal Sussex, 72nd Infantry Brigade, British 36th Infantry Division during an advance along a jungle track. The man one from the rear is carrying a folding stretcher, so this group could be part of a company headquarters. The rear man has grenades on his belt. They are all equipped with the Lee Enfield Rifle Mk 3 and the eighteen-inch bayonet.

14. The 1st Queen's Own Cameron Highlanders bath in half oil drums.
L–R back to camera: Captain David Murray, Captain Neil White MC (Cambridge
Rugby Blue), and Major Alan Roy (Scottish Rugby cap).

15. At 10.30 a.m. on 20 June 1944, the road to Imphal from Kohima is opened.
Stuart Tanks leading the advance guard of 33rd Corps consisting of the
2nd Durham Light Infantry and 149th Regiment Royal Armoured Corps meet
the 1st/17th Dogras and Carabiniers, the advance guard of 4th Corps.

stretcher and handed over command to me. He had not been able to make any progress on the left. The muddle was thickening and a deadlock was developing. I became very worried as I could hear a good deal of Japanese fire around Lt. Chapman's area, but not much return fire. This is usually a bad omen, suggesting that the defence has suffered heavily and there are not enough defenders left to reply with vigour. We had been out of touch with them for about 12 hours and I felt I had to do something to help them. Knowing that Lt Chapman's platoons were dug in and that any attacking Japanese would be standing up I took a desperate risk, and fired some 3 inch mortar bombs right on top of and also just beyond Chapman's position, hoping I would clear out the Japanese without killing too many of our own people.

Jimmy Chapman afterwards said it did indeed help a rather desperate situation, which was not quite so bad as I had feared and by sheer good luck we did not hurt any of our own people.

By this time the jungle floor was on fire, not a serious fire but the smoke just added to the nightmare of the situation. It would have been no surprise to see the Devil himself appear complete with horns and tail. The Japs were giving us a hard time with their 50mm Mortars and I was wondering what to do about it. I remembered that when I was a child at school about the age of 10 I had problems with a bully, and discovered that if you are engaged in a bashing match he who bashes hardest wins. I resolved to use those tactics now. Just then a patrol from the forward platoon came in. They had managed to get through the Japs at the base of a cliff on the extreme left. They said both platoons were intact but very short of ammunition. Jimmy's platoon had three rounds per man left and one magazine each for his three bren guns. The other platoon under Sergeant Jamieson had five rounds per man left and none for the brens. If anyone fired a shot they had to crawl back to platoon headquarters to get another round to replace it. I assume the platoon commanders had a few extra rounds in their pockets.

This was great news, it explained the lack of return fire; and it meant the Japs were stuck and in a worse muddle than we were. The two forward platoons had beaten off every attack mounted against them, and they were still intact. The Japanese had also shelled them with two little field guns at close range. I did not realise this. It would have told me we were up against a Japanese battalion and not the much smaller force we had imagined. Lt Chapman had just enough ammunition left to fight his way back but had decided not to do so and stay fighting. One more attack by the Japanese and his ammunition would have all gone. The Japanese at this stage were taking no prisoners except for live bayonet practise, so that was never an option. Encouraged by Jimmy's determined stand I saw a chance to give the Japs some of their own medicine. I would reinforce the forward platoons who were doing so well and showing such spirit and attack the observation post from the other side. I got a signaller and radio set, a couple of thousand rounds, some grenades and some canvas bags of water. [I took ?] The reserve platoon under Sergeant Reilly and the Company Order group (part of Coy HQ), Lt. Sparey was left in charge of A Company rear platoon and the two C Company platoons. He was to take over if I got hit. We followed the patrol back to the forward platoons. Once the ammunition had been delivered the situation changed dramatically.

Headquarters was demanding we obtain some identification of the enemy. The battle had been going for 12 hours or so and we still had not managed to get our hands on any information. Just in front of Jimmy's platoon lay several dead Japanese caught in the early morning gun fire, one was an officer, so I nipped out in front to rifle his pockets, taking care to put a bullet through his head first just in case. You could take no chances with Jap officers, but he was cold and stiff. I got just what was wanted, his identity disc, wallet and diary and quite a haul such as letters and a photo of his wife and two daughters aged about 5 and 7 all in their best kimonos. I could not help feeling sorry for this family and thinking what a rotten cruel thing war is. All this and his sword was sent by special patrol under the African Sergeant Major to Battalion Headquarters and was well received.

Jimmy Chapman explained where the Japanese were in front of his platoons and I tried to direct mortar fire onto them. I had never directed mortar fire before and did not know the correct method. The mortar platoon were puzzled and could not understand my directions. Sergeant Reilly who had been watching my efforts said, 'Give me the radio and I will direct the fire, I am an ex mortar man', with relief I handed it over to him and things began to happen. He obviously knew the ropes, so I swapped places with him and left him and Jimmy to get on with the job. I then took his platoon to assault the observation post. We advanced up the hill two sections forward and one back Everything was black from fire. As we drew near the top we came across two dead Japanese. The fire must have burnt over them and set off the rather primitive grenades the Japs carried on their belts. It had made a very messy job of disembowelling them and the fire singed what was left. The smell was sickening, I reached, but the adrenalin had shut down my digestive system for some time now and nothing was forthcoming. The thought that I could end up in the next minute or so in a similar heap of human garbage was a thought to be put aside quickly. We were almost there, and got ready to charge with the bayonet It is a very bad health risk leading a bayonet charge. It cannot be done from behind and you are between two lots of close range shooting if you are in front. What happens is you start the charge in line and end up in front, a prime target for the enemy.

Well charge we did. There were 20 Japs there all killed by mortar fire earlier. It was a pathetic sad sight which I could not regret. The rude man and his mate were by the telephone, and in one place eight were laid out like a star with a bomb crater in the middle. I sent a messenger (always a pair) to bring Lt. Paris's platoon forward and told the Corporal to dig-in on the mortar observation post and hold it to the last man, and to use the telephone. My platoon I sent with the African Sergeant to work back towards the rear platoons as we had now closed the net and hopefully turned the tables and trapped the Japanese. It appears they must have realised they were in a mess and managed to escape the net before it was in fact closed. I went back to Jimmy and when they had thrashed all the known places I, with Sergeant Reilly's expert help, 'went to town' on all the places I thought the Japs might be. Five rounds rapid onto a map reference target where the Japs could be forming up. Ten rounds rapid fire onto a dry stream junction which would be a likely place for their Head Quarters. The mortars were firing at the rate of 30 rounds per minute each, and again all 60 bombs were in the air before the first one landed. In 50 minutes we had used up all the Battalion's ammunition and half of the Brigade reserve, after which we did not get a 'peep' out of the Japanese. I asked my Commanding Officer if he would please come forward and assess the situation and issue fresh orders as I had now completed the task given to me. The problem was I was now commanding two companies and could not be in two places at once, so C Company stayed with me.

We had three officers left in the two companies and at Head Quarters there were the C.O., 2nd in Command, Adjutant, Intelligence Officer but no one would come forward and I dare not go back in case another attack was sprung on us. Finally the 2nd in Command came forward and I was able to show him our positions and what I thought of the enemy. I also learnt that the General had withheld any artillery support in an effort to 'make us fight'. Fortunately my C.O. had the good sense to refuse to pass that on. That is the sort of childish stab in the back we did not need. As it happened, I did not know the guns were available for support, and the mortars did a much better job in any case.

Major Bowen and Captain Olsewski (O'chefski) turned up with a company from 5 G.C.R. As we had the situation completely under control we did not need them and they returned. Had I been more experienced I would have tried to persuade them to attack in the morning with the guns in support on the left of the path while I did the same with the mortars on the right and we would have ripped the pants off the Japs.

It was two days before it became clear that we had in fact ruined the Japanese *IIIth Regiment* of about Battalion strength It appears the Japanese Colonel had called his company commander in; maybe to give them fresh orders, when one of our guesswork salvos landed on them and killed them all, totally wiping out the Headquarters and all their commanders. We got their War diary, codes and from then on they were a mob of lost sheep, and we let them get away.

It is a great credit to Lieutenant Chapman and Sergeant Jamieson that they stopped a Japanese Battalion and disorganised it by holding on even with very little ammunition left. It was this stubborn action that eventually made the destruction of the Japanese possible. I was given a Military Cross for this action; but really half of it belongs to Jimmy Chapman.

On 23 March Woolner visited Corps Headquarters and was surprised to learn that both there and in Army HQ there was a strong impression that his division was almost at the point of disintegration. Nothing could have been further from the truth, and the units had not suffered bad losses themselves and hit the Japanese hard on a number of occasions.

However, the Japanese offensive in Assam had by now opened, and 15th Corps had been reduced to two Indian and one West African divisions, so Christison decided to close down operations in the Kaladan Valley. He ordered the West Africans to the Kalapanzin, less 1st Gambia and 7th/16 Punjabi who would keep the Japanese in the Kaladan occupied until the monsoon. The jeeps and guns were driven up the jeep track, while the whole division marched to the Kalapanzin on a head-load basis.

Parts of the division were to remain in contact with the enemy until June 1944. Captain Hamilton who served with the 81st (WA) Division wrote of the African soldiers:

> they adapted well to the trying and arduous conditions of Arakan with patience, endurance, and seldom-failing good humour. They marched a very long way (General Woolner's estimate for the first campaign is 1,500 miles for the average infantryman) mostly over atrocious going, seldom on the level and almost always in full marching order. With hand tools only (picks, shovels and matchets) they constructed some 150 miles of Jeep track, built four Dakota strips, and twice that number of Moth [light aircraft] strips (the last requiring the clearance of over 3,000 trees in four and a half days). They followed their leaders in attack, and stayed with them in defence; they were more ready than most to engage in hand-to-hand combat, often resorting to their matchets. Even the unarmed soldiers very seldom panicked, though when under attack by a determined enemy with a 40 lb load on one's head and only a matchet and perhaps a grenade for defence, it takes a good man not to do so; their stamina was amazing and some of their feats of strength and balance under awkward loads over difficult going were almost beyond belief.

Not every British officer in the division was so enamoured of the concept of unarmed soldiers. Captain Poore certainly saw men from the Auxiliary Group rushing off in a panic, and said of an incident in which large numbers took off into the bush:

> it showed how foolish it was to bring unarmed men into close contact with an enemy like the Japanese. It was grossly unfair on the men and made our transport system very unreliable. Who could blame them. Looking back which is always easy, it would have been

better to have armed and trained them and carried less essentials. They were carrying about 50 lbs plus all their food and kit. A rifle would have cut it down to 40 lbs which is 20% drop but the gain in moral and the freeing up of guard troops would greatly increase the Division's fighting effectiveness even if it had less reserve ammunition.

Bill Duhan [his company commander] decided that we would arm and train all unarmed carriers and steward boys [to take their place in the company]. No one would be unarmed in C Company. This was achieved due to an administrative oversight. The wounded when evacuated by Tiger Moth could not take their rifles to hospital, so a pile of rifles developed that could not be moved or disposed of. The Medical department were overjoyed that some one would collect the embarrassing dump of rifles.

Having everyone armed meant we dumped some picks and shovels and reduced the reserve ammunition in order not to overload the carriers, and cause them to lag behind exhausted. We gained in morale, no longer were they in a state of panic every time a shot was fired.

But when all was said and done, the West Africans had proved themselves, and learned many useful lessons which they were to put into practice with good effect in the second Kaladan campaign.

On 15th Corps's main front, the Japanese resistance after the battle did not, as Christison hoped, merely consist of rearguards, and some very hard fighting was required to secure the Buthidaung–Letwedet area, to reduce the Razabil fortress and the tunnels, before taking Point 551. Captain David Gardiner, the adjutant of the 2nd/13th Frontier Force Rifles, wrote to his brother on 29 May 1944:

Dear Mike

I don't know whether this will interest you, but please could you keep it. There's a 1″ map with it too.

I may be a bit bitter at the end but think I have a right to be. During the time we had 3½ Company's [sic] across the road, Bn HQ still remained about 1½ miles away, – nobody came to see things after the attack of the 25th and the general character of senior commanders was not inspiring to say the least.

David

April opened with us probing across the road to a feature Pt 551, which you may have read something about. The 8/13th [sic] attacked it last year when the Japs came up and cut off 14 Div. They took it and were driven off. This year it fell to us. I mean the lot of taking it which we didn't accomplish and which is the cause of much bitterness. I may as well say here that 551 has been our undoing, but however, may in the end be our making.

On the 5th, after patrolling the feature [indistinguishable] approaches, A Coy put in a platoon after an artillery concentration. The platoon reached a point below the first crest. They suffered some thirty casualties and poor old Peter Plenty was killed when they started to mortar us. A Coy was by this time getting very depleted in good old stiffs [experienced soldiers, not bodies] and though we had had reinforcements, the new recruits aren't up to much. More preparation followed, more patrolling and more planning generally from right back in Brigade HQ from a map.

There was more to come; Captain Wallace was with 34 (Indian) Mountain Battery:

The big attack on the sinister point 551, the hill to the south of the road from Maungdaw to Buthidaung, was scheduled for the 15th April. The next two days were spent in registering targets and bringing up the ammunition. The observation post was established on the top of a jungle-clad hill looking down on the Japanese position across the road.

The attack was to be supported by a major artillery barrage. Deane of 32 Battery was to go forward as forward observation officer [FOO] with the attacking infantry and if he should become a casualty, Capt Downie of 33 Battery was to take over from him.

At dawn of the day of the attack the infantry were all lined up along the road waiting to assault this precipitous hill. Deane and Downie were waiting apprehensively with them; nor were their apprehensions groundless. At 5.30 am the guns opened fire, and for three-quarters of an hour the Japanese-occupied hill was pounded. Nothing could be seen of it; a heavy pall of smoke and dust hung over it.

After the gun-fire, the attack went in. A company of Frontier Force Rifles with Deane as artillery observer clawed their way up the precipitous hill-side. Almost at the summit they were met with a hail of grenades from the reverse slopes. Leaving their dead on the summit the company was forced to withdraw and on the way down a Japanese machine-gun, hitherto unnoticed, suddenly opened up on them. Deane rolled over riddled with bullets and killed instantly. The company returned to the bottom of the hill, and formed up again. They were ordered to rest awhile and to repeat the grim assault in the afternoon. Downie was informed of Deane's death and ordered to take his place. Downie was not in the highest spirits.

After some further artillery fire on this sinister hill, the company returned to the assault. Again they reached the summit, exhausted after their climb, and again were met by a hailstorm of grenades. Downie's worst fears were realised and he rolled over with half his face blown off by a grenade. His body was only recognised by the spectacles when it was recovered three weeks later on the final capture of the hill.

So the attack failed again and nothing had been won save some small features called 'Hump' and 'Goggles' to the east of the main Japanese position. On that day we lost two officers [out of four]. Our morale was not high.

Accounts of the same battle by different people can differ. This was Gardiner's view of the second attempt on Point 551:

On the 15th another attack was put in on the whole Brigade front. A terrific barrage of all available artillery went down and the Wiltshires on our left were supported by 25 Grant tanks, and we had a few firing from the tunnels area. A Coy was put in at the same place and on the left. The old man [CO] was convinced that they would just walk in and have the honour of taking the first ridge.

However there was no catch. Exactly the same thing happened as before. A Coy was caught by MMGs firing from the flank and suffered about 50 casualties and the two FOOs with them killed. C Coy got their objectives and the Wilts got some of their's after very close support from tanks. Then came snag one for the FF Rifles. A platoon of Dogras, B Coy was following up A Coy and were ordered to put in a second show on the same place. Usual bloody, bloody wicked things these fxxxxx . . . heads do [sic]. Christ, I could weep at times. Of course they didn't go in. They got half way up and the first men were killed. This mind you was on a one-man front with two MMGs firing across this only track up, a drop on either side of the path. Then they stopped. Of course the Corps Commander who was watching the battle from a far hill wanted to know why, why didn't they charge gallantly on so that we could have another thirty casualties?

On the night 16/17 April, C Coy was ordered to advance up the spur they were established on and dig in when they came under heavy fire. The orders were pretty clear but given over a telephone with no bloody idea of the ground. Ronnie Walker made a xxxx xx and the platoon was not dug in in the morning. Immediately he was ordered to send a platoon forward in daylight and they were to dig in when under heavy fire. Ronnie was never one to mince matters and flew off the handle and told everyone what was wrong. Result was, I found myself commanding a Coy in the middle of a show I didn't know anything about.*

By the time I got forward quite a little battle was raging, and Elsmie told us to go forward to the ... platoon of the Coy to see what was happening. I got up to find old Sheristan very worried indeed with his platoon pressing themselves into the ground. However, he soon brightened up when we got people digging and some water up as it was bloody hot. Elsmie then put D in on the right of us and the forward platoon got up onto the top of the feature on our right with the VCO [Viceroy's Commissioned Officer] Jemedar Moud Gafoor (who's now got an MC), and the six men left of his platoon. Narang went up with another platoon of mine with him and we put in a small feint from our side. It was hopeless from our point of view, the two blokes next to me were killed after we had gone five yards, and others wounded. We carried them back, and I saw Narang on the thing to our right. Of course the blokes were yelling their heads off. We then consolidated firmly where we were, and I went down to see Elsmie. He had just been informed to withdraw people on the hill to my right. God, I was furious. Then I learned that Narang had been wounded going up, and then got a burst in the face which killed him. This made me madder still. My platoon came back and the remainder of the platoon of D Coy and another platoon to dig in on a small knoll below the big feature.

We collected people and got fixed for the night. 3 inch mortar Arthur Bramwell was with me. Old Arthur put up some good DF

* He was sent forward by his CO to relieve Ronnie.

[defensive fire] that night and morning came and we'd got dug in further. The next few days were quiet.

Wallace:

The next day I was idling at the OP, when a message came I was to take over Deane's job in 32 Battery, that I was to step into a dead man's shoes. With few regrets I said goodbye to 34 Battery with the insane BC [Battery Commander] and illiterate signallers.

A further attack was put in on Point 551, to no avail. Wallace again:

Two days later I was ordered up 'Goggles'. The hill was an appendage of the ridge which was held by the Japanese and rather lower. The most forward infantry positions were within 25 yards of the Japanese. The infantry commander on 'Goggles' was a man called Gardiner, whom I discovered was an old Cliftonian [like him]. He appeared to face the war with astonishing sang-froid. 'The only thing to do', he said, 'is to lie back and roar with laughter when your best friend has his head blown off just beside you'. The other two officers on the hill had the same fatalistic attitude. Their chances of survival were not very high. Five times the same battalion had been thrown at this hill and five times repulsed.

Gardiner:

On the 25th we put in another attack; most of the show depending on B [Company], a platoon of mine to go round to the left and one to the right where it had gone in before. I need hardly say Coy comds didn't have much say in 'attacks'. It was . . . [sic] of planned from an air photo or a map. This time they concentrated 40 X 3in mortars and MMGs to fire at the thing. Wilts going in from the left. The mortar barrage was spectacular. My platoon went up and the other round to the left. I made the mistake of trying to control from my centre platoon and then chased across to my right platoon which couldn't reach the top and came off with ten blokes left.

Poor old 'Deli' was hit by a lump of splinter almost as soon as . . . [sic] started. However, they got their objective OVAL [its nick-name] and I went up and saw them in fine spirits and could see the Japs coming off in front of me. The whole curse of it then was no reserves. I was commanding 3 xxxxxx Coys, and people giving me instructions over two miles of line, together with a dose of fever, I was feeling pretty bloody minded. Finally B [Company] consolidated and A [Company] took over – this was a big mistake. A already half strength, one VCO [Viceroy's Commissioned Officer], one BO [British officer], and very few old NCOs. That night was OK but the next night the Japs counter-attacked heavily and they just ran – there's nothing more to it. I know Arthur Butterworth and I ... [sic] he came back. Of course poor bugger, he couldn't do much, one has no control at night whatsoever. It's your NCOs that hold the show together. Coupled with this, they hadn't got half enough ammo up, or rations or water. There was nothing to dig in and all day they were subjected to harassing MMG fire.

Wallace eventually found himself with the 13th Frontier Force Rifles as the FOO.

Precisely the same procedure was followed as before. An artillery concentration preceded an infantry assault. This time however after considerable casualties the infantry secured a foothold on the summit. Two of our officers had already died on the hill and there was considerable anxiety who was to be selected for forward-observation officer to go with this attack. The choice fell on Mackenzie who duly went up the hill with the infantry, passed the scene of Deane's death, passed the body of Downie which was still lying out on the hill, and established an OP on the summit of the hill called 'Wembley'. This foothold secured by the infantry was very precarious as the Japanese still held the dominant height and most of the ridge on which Wembley stood. Also they swept the South face of the hill with machine-gun fire so that the only route up was up the Western face. This route was literally precipitous and in several places ropes had to be fixed to allow the climber to obtain a hold. Ammunition had to be dragged up this 500 foot precipice as a first priority with the result that the supplies of food and water were very meagre.

The first night the Japanese threw in a counter attack but were beaten off with considerable losses. In the morning I received orders to relieve Mackenzie, and with some trepidation I set off on this climb. Though the distance was not more than 3 miles, it took me more than 3 hours to reach the summit. We were very heavily loaded with food water spades ammunition etc and the route took us up a high ridge then down on to the Maungdaw–Buthidaung road which had an unpleasant tendency to be shelled. From the road began the major climb onto the ridge. On arrival at the OP I immediately drank a whole water-bottle and still felt thirsty. In the middle of the day the temperature was well over 100 degrees.

The summit of the hill was not inviting. A sharp wind was blowing the sand all the time into your face. If you opened a tin of bully-beef it was filled with sand almost before you had had a single mouthful. The ridge was a razor-edge with very steep sides. If you put your head over the top your life was forfeit and so you had to cling to the reverse slope precariously aided by a few tree-roots which had escaped the obliteration of most of the vegetation. Several corpses were still lying about unburied.

So I took over from Mackenzie whose misery was not mitigated by putrid jungle-sores which were festering on both his arms. I was thankful to escape that foul and very prevalent complaint.

Supplies were very meagre and of course it was impossible to cook a hot meal or boil a cup of tea. By the evening the men had all had some sort of a meal and a small reserve of ammunition had been brought in. Rather miserable we settled down in our fox-holes to face the night. With darkness the wind which had been lashing sand into our faces all day dropped dead and the smell of dead bodies became almost suffocating without a breath of air to disperse it. I took off my boots and belt and curled up. Soon after midnight the Japanese attack started. They had effectively cut our telephone lines so that we had no communication except the wireless, which as so often at night refused to work. The attack was punctuated with wild yells which were intended not without good reason to dampen our already low spirits. This attack continued for about two hours during which time the Sikhs* had got rid of most of their ammunition. The noise was so great that our own artillery fire was inaudible. Occasionally the wounded would go sobbing and staggering past me.

At about 3.0 am when I was still fiddling with the wireless set in my fox-hole, a signaller suddenly jumped into the hole and said that the infantry were going. Remembering the appalling difficulties of ascent by daylight, it had not entered my head as a remote possibility that I might be asked to descend by night and I had made no preparation for evacuation whatsoever. However deeming discretion

* The Sikh company in the 2/13th Frontier Force Rifles – which like many Indian Army battalions had companies of Punjabi Muslims and Sikhs.

the better part of valour I gave the order to depart with all speed and I did not have time to look for my boots and belt in the dark before departure.

We descended the hill with great speed at times falling 20 or 30 feet, and scattering in confusion. I lost touch with most of my OP party but I met the company commander. Many wounded were climbing down with great difficulty. At one moment we came to a precipice down which it was quite impossible to climb. It was a vertical pitch without any handholds. However fortune was with us as the company was composed of Sikhs, and they unwound their puggarees [a long slip of muslin bound round the helmet] and knotted them together to make ropes down which everyone was able to slide.

Nearing the foot of the hill we heard movement in the dense undergrowth ahead of us and we suspected that it might be some of our own troops. Confusion was almost certain in the darkness if we went on, so we decided to halt in the ravine where we now lay. Mercifully the Japanese did not appear to be following us. For nearly two hours we sat dead-still not daring to talk. Gradually the day dawned and the long night ended. With daylight we endeavoured to sort out our various groups and I managed to collect my OP party together less three men. One man only had been slightly wounded in the head by a grenade. Otherwise they were all intact. Of the three missing men two had been seen on the way down the hill but had disappeared in the darkness. One had not been seen at all. Collecting what men I could I darted across the very exposed main road and climbed up the hill back to regimental HQ to report. Oddly enough I did not feel nervy or shaken at all, simply rather tired and looking forward to a good wash-down. I had an excellent breakfast before returning to my battery.

Of the 3 missing men 2 found their way back to the gun position – one in bare feet. The third was picked up by the infantry having been knocked out by a grenade and having fallen some way down the hill. He recovered and managed to crawl down the hill until he reached our lines.

So once again we were back in the same position as before with the Japanese in full possession of this amphitheatre. More of our men lay dead or wounded on the hill and it was obvious that the infantry had not the physical strength or morale to capture this

all-important feature. The Japanese were still able to control the road.
There followed a few quiet days, though we suspected the powers
that be were hatching some sinister plot. Sure enough two days later
we were surprised to see Gurkhas [1/8th Gurkha Rifles] in the area
and discovered that they were relieving the Sikhs. I had high hopes
that during the forthcoming attack I should not be the FOO as I felt
that I had had enough of that job for the time being. However I was
very soon disillusioned. I was ordered to report to the Gurkha HQ
where I would receive instructions. I spent a very pleasant day at the
HQ talking and drinking nimbu [whisky and water]. I discovered
that the coy commander who was to make the attack was an old
friend from Quetta days. To my intense relief I was told that the
attack was to be by night without artillery support and that therefore
no artillery observer was needed to go with the attacking infantry.
My duty was to go up 'Goggles' and hold myself there in readiness.
The morale of the Gurkha was infinitely superior to that of the Sikhs
and hopes ran high that this attack would be successful. All previous
assaults had been stereotyped affairs in daylight preceded by the
orthodox artillery concentration. A night attack was the obvious
answer.

In the evening I went up to the OP on 'Goggles', met the Gurkha
company commander there and settled down to await developments
during the night. The plan was briefly that the Gurkhas and [2/7th]
Rajputana Rifles should creep round the back of the hill and capture
it from the rear. The great danger lay on their being cut off. If
they failed to capture the ridge they would be without any lines of
communication at all.

That night there was a tense silence until about 2.00 am when
with the most blood-curdling yells the Raj-Rifs [Rajputana Rifles]
went in with the bayonet. It was impossible to make out what
was happening from our point of vantage but next morning found
the whole feature captured with the exception of 'Wembley' and the
ridge leading up to 'Goggles'. It was essential to capture this ridge if
we were to maintain any line of communication.

A company of Gurkhas had established themselves during the
night close beneath the crest of 'Wembley' and from 'Goggles' we
could see them crawling forward and we could also see the Japanese
kneeling behind the crest of the hill waiting for them. Slowly they got
closer and closer. We gave what assistance we could with Bren guns

and eventually the Gurkhas leaped to their feet and went in with the bayonet. The hill was captured with only a few casualties. There remained only the ridge running from 'Wembley' to 'Goggles'. A message came through for me that I was urgently needed by another company commander who was in difficulties round the back of the ridge and wanted artillery fire brought down on a bunker which was in his way.

There was nothing for it, so I loaded the OP party up with wireless set, batteries, food etc and set off with a guide. We hurried through a valley where Japanese medium shells had a habit of landing, and then plunged into almost impenetrable jungle. Fortunately the guide was intelligent and someone had put white pieces of paper on the trees along the route. Most of the way lay along the bed of a small stream which wound its precarious way through this labyrinth of foliage and creepers. How the Gurkhas contrived to negotiate this route during the night was almost a miracle. Eventually I discovered the company dug in on a subsidiary knife-edge ridge close beneath the main Japanese-held ridge. The company commander then pointed out the bunker which was holding him up. This bunker was rather less than 50 yards away and very difficult to see through the dense foliage. However I climbed up a tree and started to range onto it. It was almost impossible to hit as it was so close to our own troops and also the target was between our own troops and the guns. After a few rounds the Japanese objected with a sudden staccato of machine-gun fire followed by a sinister sausage-shaped bomb which rolled down the hill at us and went off with a loud explosion but doing no harm. I descended the tree with considerable speed and returned to the company commander.

It was decided that it would be sheer suicide to try to advance in the face of this bunker so I returned to my old station on 'Goggles'. The company was also withdrawn and all idea of an attack from the rear was abandoned. But the ridge had to be captured quickly so a very hurried plan for gunner support was made for the renewed attack on 'Wembley'. There was no adequate time to register the guns and in fact the artillery support was a ghastly fiasco.

With great difficulty a single gun had been dragged up to the top of a hill overlooking the Japanese position and was firing directly on the Japanese. Unfortunately the wireless communication with this gun, called a sniping gun, was by no means perfect and the officer who was in charge of it did not fully understand the plan of attack. Looking through his binoculars he thought he could see a Japanese machine-gun holding up the Gurkhas. On his own initiative therefore he opened fire on this supposed machine-gun, but in fact on the unfortunate Gurkhas. Two shells went crashing right in among the Gurkhas before any message could be got through to stop the gun. It was only good fortune that only one Gurkha had his head blown off. This did not make the Gurkhas exactly enamoured of the gunners.

The attack, however, apart from this slight contretemps was a brilliant success. The Gurkhas lined up and ran along the crest of the hill. Throughout they were in full view of all the surrounding hills. Caution was thrown to the winds and every vantage-point was crammed with troops yelling and shouting and throwing their caps in the air exactly as if one was watching a football match. This was the most exhilarating moment in the war that I ever experienced. Seldom if ever is an attack staged with the auditorium crammed with cheering spectators.

As soon as the ridge was secured I hurried forward and established my OP in the centre of it. For some six weeks the fighting for this ridge had continued and the scene was not pleasant to behold. At the end of the ridge a mere 25 yards had separated the Japanese positions from our own troops, and for week after week dead bodies had been lying out halfway between these positions. Neither side had been able to approach them in order to bury them, and the consequent smell had been quite literally nauseating. The leading troops had to be continually relieved and while they were in the leading fox-holes they had to to have field-dressings tied over their noses to prevent themselves from being physically sick. I may say it takes a considerable smell to make a Gurkha sick.

We cleared away these bodies and dug ourselves in on the summit of the ridge. There were several Japanese still lurking in the fox-holes dug in underneath the ridge, but it was as much as your life was worth to crawl into a fox-hole to see if there was a Japanese inside it. So they were left inside while we established ourselves on the top of them. During the night most of them tried to run out and the silence of the night was punctuated by the explosion of the hand-grenades thrown by the Gurkhas at the Japanese as they bolted. Several managed to escape in the darkness. The smell and the noise were not exactly conducive of sound sleep. However we were hardly bothered by that as we were feeling so elated that at long last this wretched amphitheatre had been captured.

Gardiner bitterly commented:

The ridge in front of my positions is called Gurkha Ridge and 551 is called Rajput Hill. We're just the 2/13 FF Rifles who've lost almost 350 men and several bloody fine officers in the 'soften us up' process.

We then moved to the Kalapanzin side [of the Corps front] which was restful – so ended April.

Slim rated the capture of Point 551 the toughest fighting of the whole tunnels battle. He expressed satisfaction that it had fallen to Lomax's 26th Division, for here his plans for the Maungdaw–Buthidaung road in 1943 had fallen apart. It was the first time that the British had won a battle on the same spot where they had previously lost one; 'later we were to do this again and again, and it always gave me an especial satisfaction. Revenge *is* sweet. 15 Corps had now achieved all the tasks I had set it'.[1]

Before the Arakan battle finished, the Japanese offensive began in Assam. As Slim had already committed his reserve, the 26th and 36th Divisions, he had to reconstitute a fresh reserve. So he withdrew the 5th Division to rest and refit in Chittagong, replacing it with the 25th Division. At the same time he warned Christison that the 7th Division would follow the 5th Division, and thereafter both divisions would transfer to the Assam front by air and rail.

With approach of the monsoon, Slim needed to guarantee maximum air supply for the Assam battle, and wanted 15th Corps to be deployed so that it could be supplied by road and water. Accordingly he ordered Christison to pull his corps back from Buthidaung which was difficult to hold, and, being low-lying, malarial.

Slim was delighted with the outcome of the second Arakan battle, deeming it the turning point of the Burma campaign. British and Indian soldiers, and he might have added African, had proved themselves capable of beating the best Japanese formations, as well as smashing the 'legend of Japanese invincibility in the jungle, so long fostered by so many who should have known better'.[2]

5

The Japanese Main
Assault: Kohima

... jungles vary so considerably, that it is difficult to give an apt
general description. Perhaps the best way is to compare the jungle
with a beautiful woman, the pin-up dream girl in full technicol-
our, cool, alluring, attractive to look at, but, once approached
and negotiated with, full of the greatest possibilities of danger and
death to the unwary. This simile is particularly apt because, like
the figure of the pin-up girl, the jungle is never flat.

Lieutenant Colonel O. G. W. White DSO
CO 2nd Battalion the Dorsetshire Regiment[1]

Early in February 1944, well before operations in the Arakan ended with
the decisive defeat of the Japanese, the indicators that Mutaguchi's
Fifteenth Army was about to strike Lieutenant General G. A. P. Scoones's
British 4th Corps on the Imphal front were becoming increasingly plain.
The first signs of the impending offensive were reports of large bodies of
enemy troops crossing the Chindwin, many of these seen by V-Force.

Although a steady stream of reports from V-Force, and other patrols,
gave pretty clear indications that a Japanese build-up was taking place,
both Slim and Scoones were taken by surprise by the speed of the
Japanese advance; and their superb camouflage and concealment meant
there were no follow-up sightings, so the patrol reports were initially
discounted. The picture was further muddled and information delayed
because some V-Force patrol posts and other positions were betrayed to
the Japanese by Kuki tribesmen who had decided to side with the enemy,
unlike the Nagas, who remained loyal throughout. But the V-Force
information was accurate despite the setbacks caused by Kuki treachery.

Lieutenant Colonel 'Tim' Betts, a coffee planter in civilian life who earlier in the war had seen service with the Indian Army in Abyssinia and in the Western Desert, was operating with V-Force in the area of Tamanthi on the Chindwin, directly in the path of the Japanese *31st Division*. He returned from patrol to find that his Kuki V-Force scouts had deserted to the enemy. Unable to contact base, he decided to take the men who had remained and make for Kohima. It was about eighty miles as the crow flies, but twice to three times that distance by the route he took, skirting villages occupied by the Japanese, and for the first ten days avoiding even the minor jungle paths.

Assam, and especially the Naga Hills, in which the action described in this chapter took place, is one of the wettest places on earth. Slim called them 'those hellish jungle mountains'. Men and animals are tormented by sand flies, ticks, mosquitoes, and leeches. The bite from some strains of mosquito produces huge septic sores. Pulling off a leech before it has sated itself on blood, and leaving its head in the skin, results in a Naga sore, a foul-stinking, five-inch-long blister which eats away flesh and can result in death. Dengue, scrub typhus, malaria, cholera, scabies, yaws, sprue, and dysentery are endemic. The monsoon from mid-May to early September turns streams into rivers and jungle paths into glutinous swamps. The Intelligence Officer of the 4th Infantry Brigade, Captain Howard, Royal Norfolks, wrote afterwards: 'the country is so large that it absorbs rapidly vast numbers of troops, it denies the deployment of large formations, operating in mass. Assam is a country where a platoon well dug in can hold up a division, and a company a corps'.

Betts's journey lay through this country, some of it left blank on maps and merely designated 'dense mixed jungle'. Later he wrote up a journal in his pocket diary while in hospital.

Under 25 March – actual date uncertain.

    I can't go on with this cross-country mountaineering. My only chance is the river and the main tracks, and that is the only way we will make progress. If the men won't come with me we shall soon have to part. I was for getting down to the river again where we should at least get fish and flat going and not this appalling side hill clambering along slipping precipices and across gulf-like nullahs.

After meeting some Nagas who gave them food, they pushed on:

Under 26th March

My mind made up. The only thing to do to go straight along valley to near Molhe and bypass it after dusk. We walked on along the river and before we knew it crossed the main Somra/Kuki track in full open, not seeing a soul. That finally determined me. I told the men what I intended and ordered them to follow me. Havildar A B now like a paralysed rabbit. Wouldn't go near the Japs. I gave the word and marched. After half a mile looked back and they were not coming. I

(continued under 27th March)

felt no compunction. They had a day's rice and knew where they were, and the only blanket and cooking-pot and kukris. I had a map and compass and a tin of bully [beef] and one of sardines and half a dozen K [ration] biscuits.

He pressed on, in darkness skirting a village full of Japanese which was a blaze of light and torches. He vainly tried to sleep on a ridge at about 8,000 feet covered only with grass for a blanket. In the morning he could see towards Jessami and heard sounds of fighting which indicated friendly troops and cheered him up. Here, unknown to him, the 1st Assam Regiment were putting up a heroic fight against overwhelming odds, crucially delaying the Japanese.

Betts missed the track, and struggling along a stony nullah bed shredded what was left of his shoes. After a nightmare day, he found a deserted hut stocked with wood, some rice and sweet potatoes, which he cooked, and was at least warm, but did not get much sleep. After six more days marching across appalling country, trying to skirt Jessami and the Japanese, living off rice found in abandoned huts, and on one occasion dynamiting fish, he struck a jeep track where he met men of the Assam Regiment who had just vacated Jessami. Some three days later he made it to Kohima in a truck, having marched all but the final twelve miles; and slept, 'Flat out with violent diarrhoea, feet like footballs and so weak I could hardly stand'. Betts was a tall, lean but strong man, whose normal weight was 11 stone 7lb. He now weighed 6 stone.

*

The 4th Corps was deployed with the 17th Light Division (Major General D. T. Cowan, in command since the Sittang Bridge disaster), in the south at Tiddim; Major General D. D. Gracey's 20th Division at Tamu and Sittaung; and Major General O. L. Roberts's 23rd Division to the north of Imphal, and also responsible for Kohima and Ukhrul. Slim had three options to counter Mutaguchi. He could mount a spoiling attack across the Chindwin and try to beat him to the punch; he could hold the enemy on the line of the corps's forward positions on the line of the Chindwin; or he could pull back the corps to the Imphal Plain and fight on ground of his own choosing. He chose the third option, a courageous move as withdrawal can be bad for morale, and withdrawals had been an all too familiar feature of British operations in Burma for the past two years. Also, a commander who withdraws, even for the best of operational reasons, lays himself open to criticism, especially from fire-eating politicians far from the scene of action.

Slim's reasoning was impeccable, and arrived at with the invaluable assistance of ULTRA, the codename for the reading of Japanese (and German) enciphered radio traffic, which he does not mention in his memoirs as the subject was still classified when he wrote them. The 4th Corps's lines of communications on this front ran through rugged, jungle-covered hills, whereas east of the Chindwin the Japanese had comparatively good supply lines. By withdrawing, 4th Corps would be falling back on well-stocked bases, shortening its line of communication, while the Japanese supply lines would be stretched to near breaking point through the same difficult country west of the Chindwin that the British had abandoned. If Slim could hold the Japanese for two months, the onset of the monsoon would make the Japanese supply routes almost impassable. Slim also hoped that Mutaguchi would find that his lines of communication well east of the Chindwin were becoming increasingly vulnerable thanks to the actions of Wingate's second LRP operation which had begun in mid-February, of which more later.

With the Japanese stalled on the Imphal Plan, Slim, reinforced with formations from India and the Arakan, could smash the *Fifteenth Army*. The final factor that persuaded him to adopt this course was air power. By now air supremacy had been wrested from the Japanese; and Mountbatten had prised transport aircraft away from Stilwell, enabling the 4th Corps to be supplied by air using the two good airfields at Imphal and several other smaller landing strips in the corps area, as well as air-dropping supplies to troops deployed forward or cut off by the enemy. Imphal was normally supplied by road from the railhead at Dimapur, and both were stocked with combat supplies essential to any advance into Burma by Slim; or to a Japanese advance in the opposite direction.

As outlined in Chapter 3, Mutaguchi's intention was to destroy the 4th Corps, and seize the Imphal Plain with its supply bases, his aims within the overall Japanese strategy being to deny the Imphal Plain to the British as a mounting base for an advance into Burma and to seize the airfields from which supplies were flown to the Chinese. The seizure of the British stocks was a key ingredient in his plan, indeed he gambled on capturing them in three weeks. Until he succeeded, his men would have to exist and fight with what they could carry on their backs, or on a small number of mules and horses, supplemented by meat on the hoof in the shape of cattle that accompanied their columns.

To this day there is disagreement on whether or not the Japanese intended to stop at Imphal. Mutaguchi was a fire-eater, who as a regimental commander was suspected of having engineered the Marco Polo Bridge incident which sparked off the 1937 Japanese war with China. Later, he commanded the *18th Division* for the capture of Malaya and Singapore. He argued for pressing on from Imphal into Assam and, with the assistance of uprisings by Indian Nationalists in India, ejecting the British from the subcontinent. Such a reverse, he believed, might persuade the British to abandon the war against Japan, and the Americans might follow suit: all highly speculative, and somewhat typical of Mutaguchi's 'off the cuff' approach to war which was to be his and his men's downfall. General Kawabe, commanding *Burma Area Army*, Mutaguchi's superior and friend, approved the capture of Imphal, but said that any further advance would have to be cleared with Imperial Headquarters in Tokyo.

It is possible that Mutaguchi fostered private hopes of pressing on into India if 4th Corps had been destroyed, because he agreed to the attachment of Indian National Army (INA) formations to *Fifteenth Army*, with Kawabe's support. The INA was worthless in battle so Mutaguchi would hardly have burdened himself with 7,000 useless mouths had he not intended to use them for propaganda on arrival in India. Although Kawabe and HQ in Tokyo may have vetoed advancing beyond Assam, they might have found it difficult to resist the temptation to press on if the British were utterly defeated in Assam. In that event they would have used the INA to spread mayhem ahead of them in India.

An enquiry conducted by the British in 1948, at which fourteen senior Japanese admirals and generals were present, noted that 'a search of all the available records failed to reveal any documents which would provide a conclusive answer to the question of whether or not the Japanese Government entertained concrete plans for an invasion of India by the Japanese Army.'

The man who the Japanese envisaged leading the revolt against British rule was Subhas Chandra Bose, President of the Indian National Congress in 1939, who saw the outbreak of the Second World War as an opportunity to throw off British rule. He escaped internment by the British authorities in India by fleeing to Afghanistan and thence to Germany where he became an admirer of Hitler in particular and fascism in general, aping Hitler by calling himself the *netaji* (leader, or in German, *führer*). In 1943 he was shipped by submarine to Japan via Singapore to lead the 'Free India' movement, and become a figurehead in the INA, the latter the brainchild of a Japanese officer, Major Fujiwara. The INA was formed at least a year before Bose's arrival in Singapore, from the 60,000 Indian soldiers taken prisoner in Malaya, Singapore, and Burma. There was no conscription in India, so one should not picture these soldiers as down-trodden conscripts pressed into serving the British against their will, and suddenly woken to a life of light and freedom by the rising sun of Japan. But most of those taken in 1942 were young, impressionable, under-trained, and indifferently led by inexperienced British officers because of the eight-fold increase in the strength of the Indian Army since 1939, and consequent dilution of seasoned leaders in battalions. Morale had been further undermined before the Japanese invaded, by the disgraceful racial discrimination to which Indian King's Commissioned officers were subjected by the civil authorities in Malaya.[2] If the GOC had possessed a spark of fire, he would have put these pompous functionaries in their place, by refusing to countenance such nonsense. Instead he wetly acquiesced.

Fujiwara persuaded his masters that an army of Indians would have immense propaganda value, and assisted by Captain Mohan Singh of the 14th Punjab Regiment persuaded some 5,000 young Indian soldiers to volunteer; eventually this number rose to 20,000. Those who refused were threatened with starvation and torture, threats that were carried out in the case of many gallant Indian officers and soldiers who rebuffed the traitorous advances of Captain Singh, such as Captain Hari Chand

Badhwar and Captain Dhargalkar of the 3rd Cavalry, who were locked in underground cages for eighty-eight days for refusing to cooperate with the Japanese, Lieutenant Colonel Mahmood Khan Durranani, awarded the George Cross for resisting torture, and Subedar Major Hari Sing Bohra of the 2nd/2nd Goorkhas who died in May 1944 of internal haemorrhages caused by beatings, and was blind from ill treatment. Very few Gurkhas joined. Those Indian soldiers who joined the INA fell into three categories: first, a small number of enthusiastic believers in the propaganda; second, those who swam with the tide, the majority; and a third group, including the handful of Gurkhas, who saw operations in Burma in contact with the British Army as a chance to escape at the first opportunity. Typical of the third type were Rifleman Dhanbahadur Rana and twenty-six of his fellow 2nd/2nd Goorkha soldiers who marched into British positions bearing with them a map showing the Japanese dispositions in the locality.[3]

On arrival in Tokyo, Bose declared himself head of the Indian government in exile, which was recognized by the Axis governments, and the Anglophobe Prime Minister of the Irish Republic, de Valera. Bose took to strutting around in jackboots and military style uniforms, despite never having been a soldier. Although the Japanese were happy to use the INA as a propaganda tool against British rule in India, they neither respected nor trusted them. The INA soldiers had already lost marks in Japanese eyes by surrendering in the first place. Following this by renouncing their oath of loyalty to their King Emperor (King George VI) was hardly likely to impress the Japanese who unhesitatingly died for theirs.

The inquiry in 1948 recorded that (in the opinion of the Japanese senior officers present):

> Subhas Chandra Bose was a remarkable man since, despite his lack of plans and the hare-brained nature of his schemes, his listeners could not fail to be influenced by him. Major General Sanada asserts that Subhas Chandra Bose's plans did not at any time affect the conclusions of the Japanese General Staff and yet it seems likely that the senior officers concerned did not escape his influence even if it was only to the extent of being bamboozled into wishful thinking.

The inquiry further established that:

The plan in outline was that units of the Indian National Army would follow up the Japanese advance and that after the Japanese troops had smashed the British forces barring their way, Subhas Chandra Bose would cross the frontier at the head of his troops, march into India and raise the standard of revolt against the British. It seems that Bose was most emphatic that Indian National Army troops should be the first to cross the Indian frontier. He maintained that the success of his plans depended on this, and that an advance by the Japanese would only cause an unfavourable reaction amongst the Indian populace.

In the Fourteenth Army soldiers of all races commonly referred to the INA as 'JIFs' or 'Jiffs', an acronym which has a contemptuous ring about it and stood for Japanese Indian Forces. The INA totally underestimated the extent to which the confidence and loyalty of the ordinary Indian soldier had been retained, or restored, despite the tribulations of 1942 and 1943. Retaining a sense of humour is often a good indicator of high morale. On one occasion some Indian troops were listening to a Japanese broadcast announcing that Bose and his army would be in Delhi in ten days' time. An Indian soldier who had just returned from leave, much of it spent on the less than perfect Indian railway system, got a big laugh by calling out, 'Not if they go by rail they won't.'

The INA had put up a poor show in the Arakan. When they advanced confidently on to positions held by Indian soldiers, calling on them to join in the 'march on Delhi', they were usually shot without compunction by their fellow-countrymen, who regarded them as traitors. The effect was shattering. They had dishonoured themselves, and now there was nothing left for which to fight. The INA's lacklustre record in battle led to the employment of many of them as rear area troops by the Japanese, where their conduct was characterized by brutality, especially when on prison guard duties. Before long Slim had to issue orders that JIFs who surrendered were not to be shot, but treated more kindly, if only for the intelligence that could usually be extracted from them with little difficulty.

Mutaguchi's attack was to be carried out by three divisions. The *33rd Division* was to attack Imphal from the south, advancing in four columns. One, under Major General Seiei Yamamoto, the second-in-command of the division, was to advance straight up the road from

Kalewa to Tamu, part of which would hive off to march west across the hills to cut the Tiddim Road. Another column was to swing wide round Tiddim, aiming to cut the road into Imphal from the south, before marching to attack Imphal. A regimental-size column was to march due west from the Chindwin, again to cut the Tiddim Road. The smallest column, consisting of only one rifle company but strong in artillery and engineers and with a company of light tanks, was to move straight up the Tiddim Road. These outflanking and cutting-off tactics were aimed at one thing, the destruction of the 17th Light Division, and they nearly succeeded. The *15th Division* was to cross the Chindwin in three columns to assist with the attack on Tamu and the destruction of 20th Indian Infantry Division, while other columns attacked Kohima from the north, and cut the road between Imphal and Kohima. The *31st Division* was also to cross the Chindwin in three columns, and seize Kohima having first eliminated the defences in the area of Ukhrul/Sangshak, and Jessami. With the exception of Yamamato, and the small central column, all Japanese troops would have to march along jungle tracks across high mountain ranges, carrying the three weeks' supplies on their backs or on mules.

A typically meticulous and detailed, probably V Force, report of the Chindwin crossings in the 17th Division written after the battle reads:

On night 15/16 [March], I was on the east bank [i.e. the enemy bank] opposite MYAINGTHA. A large fire was lit and there was much noise of hammering and boats being pushed together. There was shouting and waving of torches. I was forced to lie up to avoid Jap patrols, but at 0200 hrs I went down stream to where the noise came from. It seemed to be a stores area. I lay up all day and considerable quantities of stores were carried up from lorries to the top of the hill where I was. In the evening they were taken down to the river bank. At 1630 hrs 16 Mar[ch] men were seen going NORTH along the bank to collect boats which were spaced at about 20 yard intervals along the bank. The boats were approximately 8 ft long by 4 ft wide, with sharp prows, and appeared to have a mounting for an outboard motor. I saw two motors on the bank. After dark, six boats were collected, lashed with bamboos and then lengths of decking placed on top. Various lengths [collections of boats] were lashed together and one end was fixed to the bank. The other end was allowed to swing across the river until it hit the opposite bank

300 yards away. Immediately a number of men crossed the bridge with amn [ammunition] boxes and these were followed by bullocks, ponies and horses. The ponies might have been carrying a dismantled mtn [mountain] gun. Some 100 men with green and white boxes followed, and each made two journeys. Some bullocks seemed to be carrying collapsible carts. Loaded metal hand-carts drawn by four men, were also seen. At daylight, a motor boat dragged the far end of the bridge upstream back to the east bank, where it was dismantled and decking removed.*

The fighting that ensued when Mutaguchi attacked across the Chindwin was not one battle with the troops on both sides neatly drawn up as on a wargamer's table, but a myriad of engagements lasting five months spread out over some 12,000 square miles in the forested hills of Assam and the marshy, open paddy of the Imphal Plain. Bitter battles for key tracks and roads, and myriads of features with names such as 'Jail Hill', 'Scraggy', and 'Nippon Hill', swayed back and forth. The outcome sometimes rested on the efforts of small bodies of men, and even individuals. On the maps at headquarters, British or Japanese, the chinagraph pencilled arrows 'marched' effortlessly across the talc-covered maps, and swiftly drawn circles depicted defended positions. On the ground these arrows more often than not consisted of small groups of sweaty, stinking, hungry men weighed down with weapons and equipment, dragging their exhausted bodies up steep slippery slopes to take yet another position at the point of the bayonet. The neat circles would consist of an assortment of weapon pits, in which men ate, slept if they were lucky, and often died, enduring wounds, mortar, and artillery fire, and beating off attacks with showers of grenades, firing their weapons until the barrels were red hot.

At the start of the battle the most exposed British formation was the 17th Light Division, which had been re-organized after the 1942 retreat on an animal and jeep basis, hence its title. The headquarters was at Tiddim, 164 miles from Imphal, reached by a narrow road capable of taking three-ton trucks in only one direction at a time, and winding through the mountains, often with a sheer drop on one side; perfect for ambushes and roadblocks, easily blocked by landslides and washed away by rain. The two brigades, the 48th and 63rd Indian Infantry, were even

---

* To hide the boats from the prying eyes of the RAF.

further forward, and in contact with the Japanese. The 20th Indian Infantry Division, although nearer Imphal, was in contact with the enemy in the area of Sittaung on the Chindwin and Tamu. Both divisions had been steadily working their way forward to the general line of the Chindwin for months, had given a good account of themselves, were planning further offensives, and were consequently extremely disgruntled when they learned that Scoones's plan for his corps was to withdraw to the Imphal Plain and fight the Japanese there. This would involve giving up all the ground they had gained over the past six months, and destroying large quantities of supplies which there was neither the time nor transport to backload. Slim, aware of the possible adverse effect on morale, told Scoones that he was to order the withdrawal 'only when he was satisfied beyond all reasonable doubt that a major offensive had begun – a proviso that was to lead to the withdrawal of 17th Division being left until too late'.[4]

The delay in withdrawing the 17th Division allowed the Japanese to get in between them and Imphal. But whereas before such tactics had served to dishearten the British, this time they fought back ferociously, assisted by close-support aircraft of the RAF, and by the artillery. The division was fighting their old enemy, the Japanese *33rd Division* which had dealt them such a devastating blow at the Sittang Bridge two years before, and they had some scores to settle. In three brilliant battles the Division utterly defeated the *33rd Division*'s attempts to cut them off and destroy them, and withdrew safely to the Imphal Plain. It was, however, a close call. Because the withdrawal of 17th Division had been left too late, it was encircled, and Scoones had to commit his reserve to assist its escape from the trap, which left part of Imphal open to attack from the north. However, the Japanese *31st Division* (Lieutenant General Koyoku Sato) were distracted from seizing the opportunity to reinforce the attack on Imphal from the north because of the stand of the 50th Indian Parachute Brigade at Sangshak. The fly-in of the 5th Indian Infantry Division to Imphal was a key move in ensuring its successful defence. Supply from the air played a crucial part in the fighting, and without it, the British would have lost.

While the 17th Division was still fighting its way north, a potentially even graver crisis was developing. It was becoming apparent that the whole of the *31st Division* was driving for Kohima and Dimapur, instead of just one regimental group as had originally been expected. Kohima had a small garrison, but Dimapur none at all. If the Japanese invested Kohima, the road to Imphal would be cut, extremely dangerous but not disastrous, but Dimapur in enemy hands would spell the end of any hope of relieving Imphal, and threaten the whole Brahmaputra Valley with its airfields thus halting supply to Stilwell and to China. Slim therefore changed the plan for the fly-in of the 5th Division to Imphal, ordering that one of its brigades, the 161st Indian Infantry, be flown direct from the Arakan front to Dimapur instead. He also asked for Lieutenant General M. G. N. Stopford's 33rd Corps Headquarters and the 2nd British Infantry Division, both training in India, to be assigned to Fourteenth Army. Stopford was to take charge of operations to clear the road from Dimapur to Imphal, while Scoones and Fourth Corps dealt with the battle round Imphal. Slim ordered that Kohima was to be held and that Dimapur must not fall.

Although the fighting at Kohima and Imphal was carried out concurrently, it is convenient to deal with events at Kohima first, since this was the key to the success or otherwise of Slim's plan. Whole books have been written about Kohima, and the necessity to compress this account into one chapter means that the activities of all the units who participated in that legendary and complex battle cannot be covered; there is space for only sufficient detail to give the reader a flavour of what was arguably the most important engagement of the whole Burma war.

*

The ground over which the battle for Kohima was fought was difficult to imagine by those who had never seen it. Kohima was both the civil administrative centre of Nagaland and a military supply depot, hospital, and staging post about a third of the way between Dimapur and Imphal, and the names of the features that were to become so familiar to thousands of British, Gurkha, and Indian soldiers reflect their military or civilian use at the time. The road from Dimapur climbed in a curve round the 53rd Indian General Hospital (IGH) spur, and after passing the Deputy Commissioner's (DC's) Bungalow, it turned in a sharp hairpin to the south-west, whence another road ran east to the village of Kohima. From the DC's Bungalow the road ran south along the Kohima ridge past Garrison Hill, the Kuki Picket, Field Supply Depot (FSD) Hill, Daily Issue Store (DIS) Hill, Jail Hill (where civil prisoners were normally held), and General Purpose Transport (GPT) Ridge. The

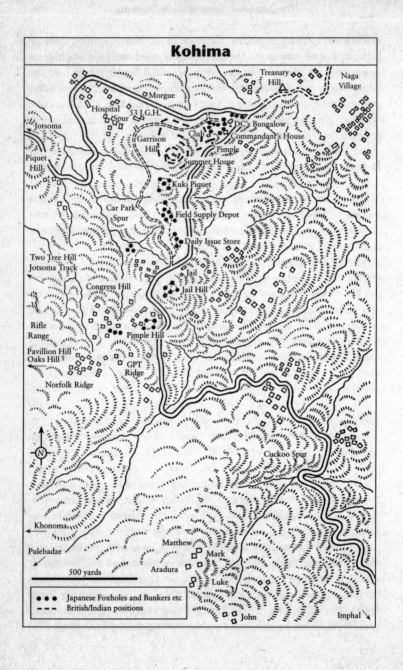

Kohima

Treasury Hill
Naga Village
Morgue
Hospital Spur
53 I.G.H.
Jotsoma
DC's Bungalow
Club
Commandant's House
Garrison Hill
Pimple
Piquet Hill
Summer House
Kuki Piquet
Car Park Spur
Field Supply Depot
Daily Issue Store
Two Tree Hill
Jotsoma Track
Jail
Congress Hill
Jail Hill
Rifle Range
Pimple Hill
Pavillion Hill
Oaks Hill
GPT Ridge
Norfolk Ridge
N
Cuckoo Spur
Aradura Spur
Khonoma
Pulebadze
Matthew
Mark
Aradura
Luke
John
Imphal

500 yards

● ● ●   Japanese Foxholes and Bunkers etc
- - -   British/Indian positions

complex included a field bakery, a transport company, and an ordnance store. There were few defensive positions prepared and no barbed wire. Most of the personnel at Kohima were administrative; the only fighting troops were the rear echelons of the Assam Regiment, whose rifle companies were at Jessami and Kharasom, some platoons of Assam Rifles, and a Manipur State Forces battalion of uncertain quality. Kohima lay open, ready for the taking.

Fortunately the Japanese advance on Kohima was delayed by the stubborn defence by the Assam Regiment at Jessami and Kharasom, and perhaps most of all by the 50th Indian Parachute Brigade at Sangshak. The epic defence of the 50th Brigade, which was to have an effect on the Japanese advance on both Kohima and Imphal, was rewarded by the sacking of its commander Brigadier Hope-Thomson amid totally unjustified recriminations that made him a scapegoat for the events that followed at Kohima and Imphal. His brigade was cut off, out on a limb, with minimal support and little understanding of their predicament by 33rd Corps under whose command they came. The conduct of the 50th Indian Parachute Brigade penned into a perimeter 400 by 800 yards was heroic; their eventual breakout equally so. Now, nearly sixty years later, this is an overworked word applied indiscriminately by a fatuous press to mostly self-regarding sportsfolk, or military achievements of the most trivial nature. One of Hope Thomson's parachute battalions had more than 350 men killed out of 700, with just two British officers and 90 other ranks remaining unwounded, a loss of 80 per cent. The other parachute battalion lost 35 per cent, with other units losing from a quarter to three-quarters of their strengths. The delay involved in fighting at Sangshak completely wrecked the Japanese *31st Division*'s timetable for the march on Kohima, which allowed time for the 161st Indian Infantry Brigade to arrive from the Arakan. Intelligence about both the *15th* and *31st Divisions* gleaned by the 50th Parachute Brigade from the body of a Japanese captain provided the order of battle and intentions of the attack on Kohima and Imphal.

Meanwhile the situation at Kohima, which came within the bailiwick of Major General Ranking's 202 Lines of Communication Area, bordered on farce. Lieutenant Colonel Cree's 2nd West Yorkshires had been flown up from Arakan with the remainder of the 5th Indian Division, and formed part of the 9th Indian Infantry Brigade diverted to Dimapur, instead of being sent to Imphal. Cree arrived in Kohima, having motored

down from Dimapur. He had just finished putting the finishing touches
to a defence plan agreed with Colonel Richards, the garrison commander,
when Ranking came in and ordered the West Yorks back towards
Dimapur to hold the road in a series of company detachments. Cree:

> This was a most foolish thing to do. The road was jam-packed with
> vehicles trying to get out of Kohima and others trying to get in. If I
> had split the battalion into four detachments over 40 miles of road,
> I'd have had no control over them, couldn't have affected the battle
> at all, and would have been mopped up in detail. I disobeyed, and
> we went back to Milestone 10 and settled there for the night.
>
> Suddenly the general appeared. I thought, now I'm for it. How-
> ever he didn't mind at all. I explained what I felt, and he agreed, and
> said, 'tomorrow go back to Kohima and help defend it'. So back we
> went and took up positions around the place and prepared for a long
> siege.
>
> I occupied the matron's quarters in the former hospital. We
> found a harmonium there, which greatly pleased our padre, so we
> lifted it, and it accompanied us for the rest of the war. After a couple
> of days orders came that the West Yorks were to move to Imphal,
> and transport was being sent for us. Colonel Richards was rather
> dismayed, being left naked again without anybody to defend him,
> except the odds and sods of the convalescent depot. I couldn't have
> been more pleased.
>
> The vehicles arrived. We piled on to them, and went off down
> the road to Imphal like scalded cats. We were the last people to get
> through. We passed some military policemen on the way, and I asked
> them what they were doing. They replied 'directing traffic'. I fancy
> they must have been captured.

This order–counterorder *opéra bouffe* had not ended by the time the
next troops arrived in Kohima, consisting of Lieutenant Colonel Laverty's
4th Royal West Kents, part of the 161st Indian Infantry Brigade. The 4th
Royal West Kents were a very experienced battalion who had fought in
North Africa and in the Arakan, and were not in the least overawed by
the Japanese. The battalion and the rest of Brigadier Warren's 161st
Brigade, having arrived in Kohima on 29 March, was suddenly ordered
back on 1 April to Nichuguard south of Dimapur by Ranking, on whom
Slim had impressed that the defence of Dimapur was a top priority. The

immediate threat to Dimapur turned out to be a false alarm, although Slim did not know it at the time. Fortunately, as Slim wrote later, Sato turned out to be

> the most unenterprising of all the Japanese generals I encountered. He had been ordered to take Kohima and dig in. His bullet head was filled with one idea only – to take Kohima. It never struck him that he could inflict terrible damage to us without taking Kohima at all. Leaving a small force to contain it, and moving by tracks to the east of Warren's brigade at Nichuguard, he could, by 5th April, have struck the railway with the bulk of his division.[5]

Private Norman of 13 Platoon, C Company 4th Royal West Kents kept a diary recording events as seen from his level, including listing every meal he ate in loving detail (not every menu is repeated here!). On 4 April, at Nichuguard, he wrote:

> for breakfast we had B & B [bread and butter], tea, porridge, 2 fried eggs, bacon. For Tiffin (1230 hrs) we had B & B, tea and 2 fried eggs. For Dinner (1730 hrs) we had meat, 'Duff', potatoes, carrots and tea. Tonight I bought 1 pkt biscuits (14 annas [about 6 pence]) and 2 cups of tea (4 Annas [between 1 and 2 pence]) from the Padre. At 1830 hrs we were told that the 'flap' which was on when we were flown from the Arakan front was now 'off', and that we would stay here until something happened. At 2300 hrs we were told that we had to have our kit packed by 0630 hrs in the morning ready for moving forward. The 'griff' [rumour] was that one of the three Jap columns moving towards KOHIMA had occupied KOHIMA.

At dawn on 5 April the 4th Royal West Kents, the 20th Mountain Battery and a section of engineers moved to Kohima followed by the rest of 161st Brigade. As the West Kents and the mountain battery got into position during the afternoon, attacks started on Jail Hill, while the Deputy Commissioner's Bungalow was shelled and mortared, and the Japanese cut the road behind them; the garrison was isolated. Private Norman:

> We never had any tiffin, dinner or tea. There was plenty of firing all day and night, and at about 1730 hrs, the Assam Rifles hill was mortared, they started running away. Weather today, rainy, windy, very cold. Our valises and bed rolls were taken back on the trucks so

we hadn't anything to cover over us. Slept for only two and a half hours because of firing all night.

Warren decided that there was insufficient room on the Kohima ridge for a whole brigade, and instead of fighting his way into Kohima occupied a position near Jotsoma, about two and a half miles to the north-west, from where his artillery could support the garrison, and assist by counterattacks. His decision was critical to the defence of Kohima. By now the garrison, under the overall command of Colonel Richards, consisted of the 4th Royal West Kents, a battalion of Assam Rifles, two companies of the Burma Regiment, and about 1,500 non-combatants including sick, wounded, and convalescents. On the night of 6/7 April, Lieutenant Colonel Young RAMC, the CO of the 75th Field Ambulance, made his way into the perimeter, and took charge of all medical arrangements. On 7 April a company of the 5th/7th Rajputana Rifles from the 161st Brigade at Jotsoma got through, sending back out of the perimeter a platoon with 200 of the non-combatants. A patrol from the 161st Brigade, moving up the road towards Dimapur, reported that the Japanese had established a roadblock at Zubza, six miles north of Jotsoma: the whole brigade was cut off. The small garrison of Kohima was now to face the full fury of 12,500 Japanese soldiers. Major Winstanley commanding B Company 4th Royal West Kents recorded:

> The 4th Royal West Kents, the Assam Rifles and odds and sods defended Kohima against an entire Jap Division in a fourteen day siege. The perimeter shrank and shrank until it only included the Tennis Court and Garrison Hill where the final stand took place. At first B Company were only observers on Kuki Picket. After five days we were ordered to relieve A Company on the Tennis Court. My second-in-command, Tom Coath was taken to command C Company, whose commander had been wounded, so I had myself, two officer platoon commanders, Victor King and Tom Hogg, and Sergeant Williams commanding the other platoon.
>
> Garrison Hill was a pleasant pine-covered hill round which there was a 'ladies walk'. On a spur which ran towards the main road, cut into the side of the hill, was the DC's Bungalow, (the DC was an Indian Civil Servant). Behind the bungalow was a clay tennis court. On our side of the court was a small club house. Our position on Garrison Hill was on the fringe of the Tennis Court, and included a

mound above the Tennis Court occupied by my right-hand platoon, my middle platoon in the Club House, with my left hand platoon holding a bank that fell away from the Tennis Court. The Tennis Court was 'no man's land'. On the other side the ground fell away – that's where the Japs were. The Japs were only 50 yards away.

The battle took place on the Tennis Court – we shot them on the Tennis Court and grenaded them on the Tennis Court. We held the Tennis Court against desperate attacks for five days. We held because I had instant contact by radio with the guns, and the Japs never seemed to learn how to surprise us. They used to shout in English as they formed up, 'give up'. So we knew when an attack was coming in. One would judge just the right moment to call down gun and mortar fire to catch them as they were launching the attack, and by the time they were approaching us they were decimated. They were not acting intelligently and did the same old stupid thing again and again. We had experienced fighting the Japs in the Arakan, bayonetting the wounded and prisoners. So whereas we respected the Afrika Korps, not so the Japanese. They had renounced any right to be regarded as human, and we thought of them as vermin to be exterminated. That was important – we are pacific in our nature, but when we are aroused, we fight quite well. Also our backs were to the wall, and we were going to sell our lives as expensively as we could. Although we wondered how long we could hang on, we had no other option. We had no idea we were confronted by a whole Jap division and outnumbered some ten to one. We had no thought of surrender at any level; we were too seasoned soldiers for that. We couldn't taunt the Japanese back as we couldn't speak Japanese, but there were some JIFs on the other side, and we taunted them in English.

The other weapon that was so effective were grenades used by Victor King's platoon who showered them with grenades as they formed up. As Kohima was a depot, we didn't lack grenades, but we were very short of 3-inch mortar bombs. We were supplied from the air, and much of the loads went to the Japs. They had captured British 3-inch mortars, and most of the mortar bombs dropped for our use fell into enemy hands.

We had a steady toll of casualties mainly from snipers. Showing yourself in daylight resulted in being shot by a sniper. They also used their battalion guns in the direct fire role, in morning and evening 'hates'. This caused mayhem among the wounded lying in open slit trenches on Garrison Hill, so that many were killed or re-wounded. We heard that 2 Div were being flown in to relieve us, and we could hear the sound of firing to our north, as the division fought its way down to us. But it seemed to take ages.

After five days I was relieved on the Tennis Court by the Assam Regiment and moved to Hospital Spur [53 Indian General Hospital (IGH) Spur]. The Tennis Court position held, the Kuki Picket changed hands several times. We were in a filthy state.

The fighting at Kohima was often at close quarters, and far more personal than that experienced by most troops in other theatres of war, in Italy or North-West Europe for example. In one attack on Lieutenant Hogg's position at the Club House, the Japanese charged with fixed bayonets. Hogg, manning one of his Brens, aimed at the nearest one, and pulled the trigger, but the working parts slid forward too slowly to fire the weapon. The Japanese jabbed at him, luckily the thickness of his webbing belt stopped the point. Hogg hauled back on the cocking lever, and fired the whole of a twenty-five-round magazine into his attacker. The attack ground to a halt but not before it seemed that the Japanese would overrun the position.

Morale remained unshaken, despite unsettling and false rumours of imminent relief, and the added burden of realizing that even the most severely wounded could not be evacuated, but would share the horrors of the siege.

On DIS Hill, Private Norman noted:

Thursday 6th April, 1944
For breakfast we hard biscuits and 1 tin of blackcurrant jam which we scrounged from a basha. We were mortared all day today. We had no tiffin, only hard biscuits and jam for dinner. At 1800 hrs we were mortared again the Japs scoring two direct hits on Coy HQ injuring Major Shaw, and Privates Sharpe and Young. Major Shaw had a broken leg. At 2100 hrs the firing started and went on all night. At 2100 hrs we heard the clanging of picks and shovels and saw the Japs were digging in at the bottom of our feature. We opened fire on them, and Sgt Tacon ran down and grenaded them. 'Butch' [his great friend] told me afterwards that he counted 40 Japs with picks and shovels and 50 more behind them. When we fired on them they

scattered, and Cpl Webber's section shot ten of them, 'Butch' killing three; one had reached his pit and had his arm poised back ready to throw a grenade, when 'Butch' killed him. We heard a lot of firing in Coy HQ and 14 Platoon's area, and heard later the Japs had attacked 14 Platoon and Coy HQ occupying part of our feature, killing poor old 'Ginger' Judges, the cook, seriously injuring CQMS Jim Hayes and Sergeant Ward and two privates. Captain Watts was injured in the legs (stretcher case) and Cpl 'Jimmie' Beames had a bullet through the muscle of his shoulder, nothing serious, and these two stout fellows refused to be evacuated.

Friday 7th April 1944

Good Friday; the worst Good Friday I've ever spent. Stood to 0545–0615 hrs, to find that a coy of Japs (90 of them) had occupied the other half of our feature, so that C Coy was virtually surrounded in a space 200 yards by 100 yards. We started dealing with them at 1100 hrs. I was told to fire HE bombs [from the 2in mortar] on to the area occupied by the Japs. Sgt Tacon [platoon sergeant] and myself went out into the open, ten yards from our positions, without any cover from the few snipers on the feature in front of us, or the Japs on our feature. I fired 6 HE bombs on to the target and then Sgt Tacon left me to see if Capt Watts wanted any more bombs fired. He left me there for 15 minutes and I must say it wasn't pleasant. Shots were whizzing around everywhere, but I was lucky. For Tiffin we had hard biscuits and jam. At 1300 hrs we were told that two platoons of D Coy were working their way around the other side of the feature and were going to encircle the Japs. By 1500 hrs the game was on. There was plenty of firing and we set fire to the bashas the Japs and Jiffs were in, then the side-show started. They started running from the bashas and our lads fired everything at them. I saw Jap bodies falling everywhere. I was firing Ernie Thrussell's rifle and killed two Japs. This lasted for about two hours, and when the bashas had burned themselves out, we found approx 70 Jap bodies, and we searched the bodies for maps. We found there were quite a lot of milk tins open, and all the dead Japs had milk smeared on their mouths. We were mortared again tonight, and we fired at the Japs we could see in the moonlight. Capt Watts was wounded again (twice in the arm) and was evacuated to Battalion HQ much against his will.

Saturday 8th April 1944

At 1100 hrs a sniper hit Sgt Cathern right down in a forward trench, so I fired 6 smoke bombs to cover the stretcher bearers while they went forward to bring him in. They brought him in OK, but he was dead. I had no tiffin. At 1920 hrs 'Japie' started mortaring and attacked. There were about 200 Japs trying to capture our feature, but the four pits about 10 yards from the road stopped them, and after about three hours fighting in which they tried to put ladders on the side of our feature and climb them from the road (we were throwing grenades on to them) the Japs still hadn't captured any part of our feature and altogether they made three assaults. The bren barrels were getting red hot. We had to keep supplying the forward pits with ammunition. The Japs gave up at 2200 hrs, and when 'Taffy' Rees came up for more ammunition, he told me how Ted Wells, Skingsley and himself were enjoying themselves, knocking them down in 'batches'.

Sunday 9th April 1944

At 0030 hrs we heard digging, and at 0200 hrs a 3-inch mortar started firing at us, and a 75 mm gun shooting straight at our pits. He plastered us like hell. At 0245 hrs the barraged 'lifted' and the Japs started another attack. We started firing our 3.7 guns [mountain guns controlled by radio by a FOO with the company] but unfortunately one shell landed on Cpl Rees's pit killing poor old Ted Wells, and burying Rees and Skingsley. These two dug themselves out and came back to our pit.

Eventually by 0400 hours, the Japanese, having killed or wounded a number of C Company and overrun the forward weapon pits, gained a foothold at the bottom of the company's feature and dug in. By now the enemy also held a feature overlooking C Company, so in daylight it was extremely dangerous to stick one's head out of one's slit trench. Snipers were causing casualties when, according to Private Norman, they heard that:

Lance Corporal Harman, had volunteered to go on a one man bayonet attack past our pit to clear the Japs off our feature. He went down past our pit and killed some Japs. He was covered by Sgt Tacon who was in a pit well behind us and could move about. He killed a Jap who just going to throw a grenade at Harman. Harman killed the rest of the Japs, but instead of running back as we were shouting for him to do, he walked back calmly, and the inevitable happened. He was shot in the spine by a Jap machine gun and killed. [Harman was later awarded the VC posthumously.] Cpl Rees who was sitting next to me in the pit when Harman ran past, wouldn't stay in the pit, but stood on top of it. I tried to pull him back because the Jap had fixed lines on our pit, but he wouldn't let me, and while Harman was engaged in his action, 'Taffy' Rees was hit twice in the side. Sgt Tacon shouted 'hang on Taffy, I'm coming', but when he crawled towards 'Taffy' he was hit in the arm and leg (fracturing his leg) and just managed to roll out of the danger area. Although we couldn't help Taffy we did start talking to him because he was only about two yards from us down in a dip, but when he told us he was paralysed, we didn't think there was much hope. He was soon delirious, and for eight hours he was screaming and shouting calling for his Mum and Dad, and praying until he died. The company commander tried to get a smoke screen laid down so that Taffy could be evacuated by stretcher bearers.

An attempt to regain the lost positions failed, and the day ended with a cold and hungry C Company who had eaten nothing since breakfast the day before. The company was pulled off to FSD Hill on the morning of 10 April, where a head count on 11 April revealed that they were down to forty-six men in all, and were reorganized into two platoons.

By 11 April most of Major General J. M. L. Grover's 2nd British Infantry Division had arrived in Dimapur, a remarkable effort when one considers that when the Japanese were only 40 miles from Dimapur, the 2nd Division was 1,500 miles away by air, or over 2,000 by road and rail. On the same day, the Chindit 23rd Brigade was about to march forward to start attacking the Japanese line of communication to Kohima. This brigade had been held back by Slim from Wingate's second expedition. Lieutenant Highett, commanding the carrier platoon in the 2nd Dorsets in the 5th Infantry Brigade in the division, remembers his arrival at Dimapur:

The Japs were only 40 miles away. There were huge supplies of stores, which nobody seemed to be too bothered about. There are few things more unpleasant than a base in a flap. It was full of people who never expected to fight, and who couldn't wait to get out. 'Take what you like,' they said, 'just give us a signature if you've got the time'. We were pretty arrogant in 2 Div and were not impressed. I acquired two armoured cars, which proved very useful. We picked up masses of stores, ammo, food, drink etc. We could carry it in the carriers. The Dorsets and 2 Div weren't short of anything.

The 2nd British Infantry Division was indeed arrogant, consisting of battalions from some of the oldest and proudest regiments in the British army, many of them regular 1st or 2nd Battalions. The division detested the Indian Army, and was detested in its turn. Both had a great deal to learn about each other and the learning process was about to begin. In a series of actions the division started to fight its way along the road from Dimapur towards Kohima. In one of them, Major Allen's B Company of the 2nd Durham Light Infantry was sent to attack Terrace Hill, so called because it was terraced and planted with tea bushes. Company Sergeant Major McClane of C Company watched the attack, and listened to the reports on the radio. The stone-walled terraces presented the attacker with a seemingly endless succession of false crests. B Company infiltrated round the sides of the hill, covered by Brens, and, having cleared the hill, were reorganizing when Allen was killed by a Japanese who everybody thought was dead.

On another occasion, Sergeant Hazell of D Company 2nd Royal Norfolks was sent with his platoon to protect a tank laager at Zubza. He went to investigate a report from one of his corporals that 'Indian' troops were approaching, and nearly ran into Japanese: 'When I looked there was a bloody great Jap officer, big broad fellow and behind him I could see all these little hats bob-bobbing up and down'. He crept away, walking backwards, and went to warn the tank crews, who were so comfortable in their blankets under their tanks they were disinclined to pay much attention. Hazell:

I was thinking there were nine of them [the enemy] at that stage. I said, 'Nobody fire until I give the word'. I got my rifle and waited for the 'nine' to appear. It became nine, ten, eleven, twelve, thirteen,. . . . In the end we had 100 of them lined up. As the first one started to disappear from view into the woods again, I fired and everyone joined in with rifle and Brens.

Hazell's platoon accounted for at least thirty of the enemy.

In Kohima, as night followed day, the Royal West Kents, the Assam

Rifles and Rajputs fought off the Japanese attacks, and a steady stream of casualties thinned the number of men able to man slit trenches and fight back. One night Norman, on a water-collecting party, had to walk past the hospital.

> We kept falling over dead bodies which were black and decaying (there hadn't been time to bury them, and movement was limited in daylight. As we passed through the hospital the smell was overpowering. Col Young (the head MO) had designed a large pit covered by a tarpaulin which he used as an operating theatre, but hundreds of wounded were lying in open pits and this area was continually being mortared and shelled day and night, and the wounded were sometimes getting wounded a second and third time, and being killed.

> *Saturday 15th April 1944*
> We are no longer C Company, and have now been attached to A Coy. Yesterday and today, water and medical supplies were dropped by parachute, and these were accurate, and we lost only five out of 78 loads. 'Japie' didn't attack but he fired his automatics and discharger-cup grenades all night.

On 15 April an Assam Rifles and Assam Regiment composite company took over the DC's Bungalow position. Although Private Norman and others in the 4th Royal West Kents were dismissive of the Assamese troops, they were aggressive and innovative fighters who dominated the Japanese in their sector. It is possible that Norman mistook 'JIFs' for Assamese.

> *Sunday 16th April 1944*
> At 1045 we saw fifteen Indians climbing our feature, and they proved to be a patrol of Rajputs from Brigade sent by the Brigadier. They said our Brigade HQ had met the 5th Brigade from 2nd Division on the feature opposite us about two miles away. We knew then that relief wasn't very far away. For dinner (1800 hrs), we had a half tin of bully beef, hard biscuits, half a cup of cold tea. There was plenty of automatic fire and grenades exploding, but nothing else exciting. Pte Carlton was killed by a shell today.

> *Tuesday 18th April 1944*
> At 0300 hrs the 'odds and sods' behind D Coy and the Assam Rifles in front of D Coy ran back, so D Coy had to retire. CSM Haines was

killed and Capt Collett injured in the foot. As these lads retired, the
Rajputs who were holding C Coy cookhouse area also had to retire.
A Coy except our platoon went forward and took up positions on
the forward slope of Hospital Hill, facing C Coy Cookhouse area
now occupied by the Japs. At 0930 hrs Cpl Judge's section consisting
of Ptes Johnson, Thrussel and myself and Cpl Veal's section went on
to the road to help evacuate the wounded. It was my job to look at
the stretcher cases and if they were dead, I had to send the Indian
stretcher bearers round the back of the feature where they put the
bodies in a heap to be buried later. Among the walking wounded
were 'Butch', Hills, Gunter, CQMS Hales, Sgt Ward, Sgt Tacon, and
L/Cpl Liddell. At 1100 hrs the Japs started shelling us, killing Cpl
Judges and a large number of walking wounded, and seriously
injuring Capt Topham. As the shells exploded among us it was
terrible to hear the screams of the wounded (I saw trunks without
arms and legs, and bodies with heads blown off). I immediately ran
off the road up on to the feature, and the shells seemed to follow me.
It was some time before we ventured on to the road again and
continued the evacuation. Soon four tanks appeared on the road and
destroyed the Jap gun. At 1600 hrs we were shelled again, but this
time nobody was injured. We finished evacuating the wounded at
1800 hrs. We buried Cpl Judges and returned to our feature, passing
fifteen dead Japs at the bottom. We had no tiffin. For dinner (1800
hrs) we had half tin bully beef, potatoes, hard biscuits, tea. I've been
in the Army four years today.

The defenders of Kohima were now confined to Garrison Hill, and
expected a coordinated massed Japanese attack at any moment, which
even the most optimistic were doubtful of surviving. But, after a series
of piecemeal assaults had been hammered in their forming-up positions
and blasted off any ground they temporarily gained, Sato ordered his
men to desist and hold what ground they had gained, counterattacking
locally. Although the defenders did not realize, the 'high tide' of Sato's
offensive had been reached.

Wednesday 19th April 1944
Today Kohima was re-taken by our troops.

So recorded Private Norman, although it would be more accurate to
say that the siege had been broken; the 'retaking' of Kohima would take

a while longer. That morning the Japanese were 100 yards from the Dressing Station containing some 600 casualties, and the garrison was crammed into an area about 350 yards square, when up the road came eight Stuart tanks and a company of the 1st/1st Punjabis from the 161st Indian Infantry Brigade in Jotsoma. Norman continues:

> For Tiffin (1230 hrs) we had hard biscuits, baked beans, salmon, tea. For Dinner (1800 hrs) we bully-beef stew, tea, hard biscuits. At 0100 hrs [Thurs] 'Japie' put in three attacks on the DC Bungalow area, but they were all repulsed. There was plenty of automatic firing and grenades exploding, but our lads weren't attacked. Weather mild. Slept for 3 hrs.

> *Thursday 20th April 1944*
> For breakfast we had hard biscuits, baked beans, bacon, tea. At 0900 hrs we packed our kit and at 1200 hrs we were relieved by the Royal Berkshire Regiment. We were glad to get off the hill (Hospital Hill). 'Japie' mortared the road again but nobody was injured. We left the area in twos and threes. Some lads had to march four miles, but I was nearly last off the hill and luckily caught a truck.

After being trucked back to just south of Dimapur:

> We turned into our camp. The first thing we did was get a lovely cup of tea (hot), and then we had a lovely hot bath [in a 40 gallon oil drum slit in half] and shave. We felt much better after this. For dinner we had Bully Rissoles, Potatoes, Fried Tomatoes, Gravy, Meat, 'Duff', Treacle, Tea. I wasn't on guard tonight. Weather mild.

The garrison had suffered some 600 casualties, but Sato had taken far more, and he had failed to take Kohima. The 4th Royal West Kents had saved Kohima in a feat of arms seldom equalled and never surpassed. In saving Kohima, which should by all 'normal' military calculations have fallen on 6 or 7 April, the battalion had saved India from invasion.

The siege may have been lifted and the gallant defenders relieved, but the fighting for Kohima was far from over. Major Boshell commanded B Company 1st Royal Berkshires, in the 6th Infantry Brigade of the 2nd Division:

> My battalion was the first into Kohima, and my company was the leading company of the battalion. We took over from the 4th Royal

West Kent who had had a terrible time. To begin with I took over an area overlooking the Tennis Court, although only my left forward platoon could see the Court. The Dorsets were responsible for the position closest to the court itself. The lie of the land made it impossible to move by day because of Japanese snipers. We were in Kohima for three weeks. We were attacked every single night. On the worst night they started at 1900 hours and the last attack came in at 0400 hours the following morning. They came in waves, it was like a pigeon shoot. Most nights they overran part of the battalion position, so we had to mount counter-attacks. When part of my right hand forward platoon was overrun, we winkled them out with the bayonet. I lost two platoon commanders, but good sergeants took over, and did better. Water was short and restricted to about one pint per man per day. So we stopped shaving. Air supply was the key, but the steep terrain and narrow ridges meant that some of the drops went to the Japs. My company went into Kohima over 100 strong and came out at about 60.

Kohima had been relieved thanks to the efforts of the 2nd British Infantry Division, and the 161st Indian Infantry Brigade, but most of Kohima ridge remained in Japanese hands. They held a very strong position some 7,000 yards long based on a series of formidable features astride the road to Imphal. The flanks of the positions rested on high, forested ridges that guarded access to the features held by the Japanese. All positions were well prepared and concealed, and mutually support-ing. Among the tasks that lay ahead was to clear some elbow room, while holding on to what was already in British hands, while carrying out moves to defeat the Japanese 31st Division. By now the British were adept at doing to the Japanese what they had so successfully done to them earlier in the campaign in Burma: outflanking. While the 6th Infantry Brigade were fighting along the main axis in the centre, Grover ordered the 5th Infantry Brigade to approach the Naga Village and Kohima from the north via Merema.

Sato was also planning one more local attack, using his *138th Regiment* before it was detached to join the battle at Imphal. He decided to hit positions held by the Berkshires at the DC's Bungalow and the Durham Light Infantry on Garrison Hill. The Durhams were to have attacked the Kuki picket the next day, but the Japanese attack came from there first, consisting of a whole battalion of the *138th Regiment* screaming 'Banzai', wearing gas masks and throwing phosphorus grenades. C and D Companies of the Durhams were alongside each other expecting to attack at first light. CSM McClane of C Company 2nd Durham Light Infantry was woken by shouts from his company commander, Major Stock:

> green phosphorus was pouring into one end of the trench, I was covered in the stuff, which causes deep penetrating burns. I was rubbing the stuff off me with earth, then the Japs came in yelling and shouting. They were in among us and just ten yards away there was a fearsome looking man waving a sword.

Ammunition stored on Garrison Hill exploded, and parachutes from supply drops hanging in the trees caught fire. McClane: 'we stuck out like sore thumbs'. After fierce hand-to-hand fighting the position was cleared. McClane: 'My company commander, the runners, and the signallers were all dead. A shell had landed right into a shell hole where they were located'. Out of seven Japanese companies who took part in the attack, four were destroyed.

Wilson, who had been in charge of the 2nd Division's jungle battle school, was now the brigade major of the 6th Brigade.

> General Grover reckoned that the fighting on Garrison Hill was worse than the Somme, where he had fought in the First World War. 2 DLI had more casualties on Garrison Hill than anyone else. In A, C and D Companies there was a total of four officers left. Of the original 136 men in A Company, only 60 were left. The pioneer and carrier platoons also lost many killed and wounded. The fighting there was hand-to-hand. Men were kept going by training, regimental pride, and the will to survive. If you let those people in [the Japanese] you'd had it.
>
> At night the Japs sent fighting patrols in to beat up Brigade HQ, which were seen off by our defence platoon. The first morning we counted 20 dead Japs, including a young officer.

On the night 26/27 April, the 2nd Dorsets, temporarily under command of the 6th Brigade, were ordered to clear the northern side of the DC's Bungalow spur, thus opening the road to tanks to join the 5th Infantry Brigade. In order to understand this battle and the subsequent fighting for the DC's Bungalow, which lasted until mid-May, it will help to describe the ground as seen by Major, later Lieutenant Colonel, White of the 2nd Dorsets, who were to play the leading role in taking this position. The account illustrates in particular how difficult reconnaissance was in the whole Kohima battle, and how the infantry especially so often have to cope with the 'fog of war' as well as with the enemy:

On the top of the pass over the Kohima Ridge, where the Manipur Road swung right in a tight hairpin bend for Imphal, a side-road led left-handed up the side of Treasury Hill towards the Naga village. This road junction was dominated by a spur on which was situated the District Commissioner's [Deputy Commissioner's] bungalow. This spur rose roughly due west in four steeply terraced ridges to Garrison Hill, on the extreme top of which stood the Summerhouse which gave rise to the alternative name to this main feature.

The spur was divided into four main terraces, each separated by a steep bank varying in height from ten to forty feet. Starting from the top, there was the club square on which in happier days the members had played badminton. Ten feet below the club lay the tennis court. On the south side the tennis court was bounded by a large iron water tank and a long tin building which appeared to be servants' quarters. These were sunk so that only the roofs appeared level with the tennis court.

The next drop was a very steep and deep one of about thirty to forty feet to the terrace on which was situated the bungalow in its own compound.

Finally, below the bungalow, there was another drop which brought us to the lower garden, which overlooked the important road junction twenty feet below.

Viewed from the eastern side of Garrison Hill, the north, or to the Dorsets attacking, the face of the spur was extremely steep with a fall from the club square to the road of nearly a hundred feet in all.

On the south face of the spur lay various ornamental gardens, a drive in to the District Commissioner's [Deputy Commissioner's] bungalow, and the bungalow of the Commandant of the Assam Rifles.

. . . On the south side of the club (topmost) terrace rose a small 'pimple' about thirty yards long, fifteen broad and twenty wide.

An extraordinary feature of this whole spur was the impossibility of being able to see what was happening on the terrace next below.

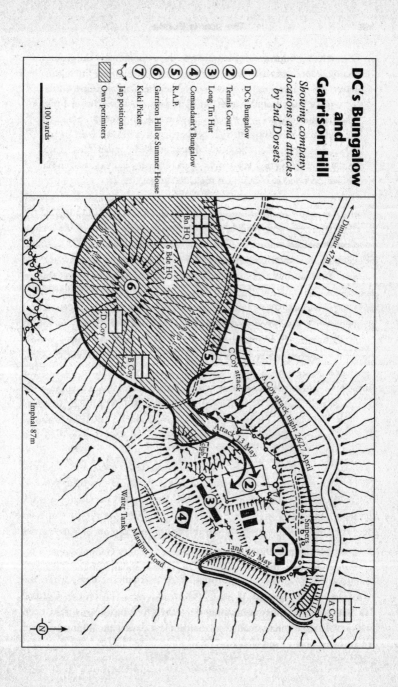

DC's Bungalow and Garrison Hill

Showing company locations and attacks by 2nd Dorsets

① DC's Bungalow
② Tennis Court
③ Long Tin Hut
④ Comandant's Bungalow
⑤ R.A.P.
⑥ Garrison Hill or Summer House
⑦ Kuki Picket

⤵ Jap positions
▨ Own perimeters

100 yards

Dimapur 47m
Imphal 87m

Bn HQ
6 Bde HQ
D Coy
B Coy
C Coy attack
A Coy attack nigh 26/27 April
Attack 13 May
Snipers
Tank 4/5 May
Water Tank
Manipur Road
A Coy

N

Owing to the thickness of the trees and the conformity of the ground, reconnaissance from a flank was practically impossible. Intelligence about this feature was almost nil. When the Commanding Officer arrived for his reconnaissance on 25th April even the Royal Berks, who had been fighting for some days on the club square, could tell him practically nothing of what lay beyond and below them. In fact, it was not until after the initial Battalion night attack that it was finally established that the tennis court was where it was, and not as we had been led to believe, on the club square.[6]

Only A and C Companies of 2nd Dorsets, and a company of the Royal Berkshires, were available for the attack, but in view of the lack of solid information about the terrain, they were amazingly successful. C Company lost their commander and all other officers, but under CSM Keegan, they and the company of the Royal Berkshires were able to consolidate around the club square and the 'Pimple'. The enemy were only fifteen yards away, and during the day of 27 April, the Royal Berkshires had seventeen casualties from grenades alone.

A Company had managed to fight its way past the Japanese positions between the road and the steep bank leading up to the tennis court and Bungalow, at one time establishing a toehold in part of the Bungalow. Although heavy fire forced them out of the Bungalow, the company held the tip of the spur overlooking the vital road junction, but only thirty yards from and below the Japanese on the terrace above. The tanks went through to the 5th Brigade, but the Dorsets had lost twenty-eight killed.

A Company held out against Japanese counterattacks on the night of 27/28 April, and the Dorsets never lost their hold on this tiny, exposed finger of vital ground. Over the next few days, a go at bulldozing a track up on to the position for a Lee-Grant tank failed, as did attempts to clear the whole DC's Bungalow complex with the support of Stuart tanks of the 7th Light Cavalry.

White, at that time the second-in-command of the Dorsets, was called forward to take over command for a couple of days, while the CO, Lieutenant Colonel 'Jock' McNaught, went to relieve Colonel Theobalds, the second-in-command of the 6th Brigade who had been responsible for the Kohima garrison, for a few days' rest. White recorded his first impression of Garrison Hill:

So close had been and still was the fighting, and so heavy the sniping, that it had been quite impossible to collect the dead even though, as in many cases, they lay just beyond a section post. Indeed in some places where the Jap had put in a 'Banzai' attack his dead lay piled deep where they had fallen in their assault on our positions. In a steep gully not forty yards from the club square, at the top of which lay one of our posts, were piled high the bodies of about a hundred and fifty of the enemy who had perished as they made one of their suicidal attacks against the Royal Berks.[7]

On arrival at Battalion HQ, White found

Jock McNaught trying to figure out whether to finish his half cup of weak compo tea or save the half-inch in the bottom to clean his teeth. We never did find a satisfactory answer to this problem, which was further aggravated a few days later when neither of us could stand being unshaven any longer and decided to improve our morale by occasional shaves. The only liquid available was the last of one's precious cup of 'char'.

On 3 May, A Company were relieved on their spur by B Company under the cover of a smoke screen. A Company, blackened and red-eyed, and reduced to 28 out of an original of 100, after five days' fighting had kept the road open.

Meanwhile Brigadier Goschen's 4th Brigade, consisting of the 1st Royal Scots and 2nd Royal Norfolks, had been ordered to carry out a daring flank march to the south of Kohima to cut the Imphal Road below the Aradura Spur. This was a distance of seven miles on the map, three or four times that on the ground, and it was estimated that it would take four days. The third battalion in the brigade, the 1/8th Lancashire Fusiliers, were on loan to the 5th Brigade, so the 4th Brigade had been reinforced by 143 Special Service (SS) Company, formed for amphibious operations in the Arakan, and stronger than a 'normal' company, as well as A Company of the 2nd Manchesters (the divisional machine-gun battalion). Captain Howard was the Intelligence Officer of the 4th Brigade:

Alastair McGeorge led with his [143 SS] Company that day [24 April] and 2 Norfolk with Bde HQ followed as it was growing dark. The country was difficult and for the final stage, we knew that there were no trails and that we should have to cut our own through the forest which covered the seven thousand foot ridge over which we should have to climb to reach the Aradura. Three hundred Naga porters carried the heavier loads of wireless sets and mortars and rations; when we arrived we were to be supplied by air.

Despite the porters, every soldier was heavily laden. Sergeant Hazell:

We were issued with 100 rounds of ammunition in addition to what we already had. This we carried in two bandoleers. Blankets were cut in half, and rolled up on top of our packs. Every third man was given a shovel, every third man a pick, and the other third two carriers of mortar bombs [a total of six bombs, each weighing 10lb].

Sergeant Fitt, a champion boxer and formidable fighter, commanded 9 Platoon in B Company, 2nd Royal Norfolks:

Around my web belt I had grenades all the way. I had five or six bandoleers. On top of that we had full ammunition pouches. We didn't expect the climb and the march to be quite as fierce as it was.

Lieutenant Horner, the signals officer of the 2nd Royal Norfolks:

The physical hammering one takes is difficult to understand. The heat, humidity, altitude and the slope of almost every foot of ground combine to knock hell out of the stoutest constitution. You gasp for air which doesn't seem to come, you drag your legs upwards till they seem reduced to the strength of matchsticks, you wipe the sweat out of your eyes. Then you feel your heart pounding so violently you think it must burst its cage; it sounds as loud as a drum, even above the swearing and cursing going on around you. So you stop, horrified to be prodded by the man behind you or cursed by an officer in front. Eventually long after everything tells you you should have died of heart failure, you reach what you imagine is the top of the hill; to find it is a false crest, and the path still lies upwards. And when you finally get to the top, there is a hellish climb down. You forget the Japs, you forget time, you forget hunger and thirst. All you can think of is the next halt.

Captain Howard:

On the third day [having covered four miles on the map] we stopped in a deep valley, west of the Pulebadze Ridge and close under the

9,000 [9,890] feet [Mount] Japvo. Here difficulties arose. The march was taking longer than had been anticipated, and rations had to be brought up via Khonoma by porter from the road. 'Death valley' as it was soon called, although no one died there, was a miserable place filled with huge trees covered in dripping moss. Sunlight rarely penetrated and rain was almost continuous. Here we lived on half light scale rations for three days. Light scale rations consisted of milk, tea, sugar, bully beef, and weavily biscuits. Here we received an order from Div HQ that instead of going behind the Japs on to the unoccupied Aradura Spur, we were to attack the flank of his known position on GPT Ridge, coming down on him from above. This entailed marching another two or three miles into country which he probably patrolled; it would be more difficult to achieve surprise in doing this than it would be to establish ourselves on Aradura and await his counter-attack which we knew we could defeat.

In Kohima the 1st Royal Welch Fusiliers had relieved the Durhams. Since the lifting of the siege, another eleven days of bombardment, hand-to-hand fighting, and bloodshed had passed. Water was rationed to one pint per man per day, and the monsoon was beginning, which would add to the misery faced by men in holes in Kohima or on jungle tracks high above the ridge.

In the thickly forested high ridges near Pulebadze, Goschen and his brigade were now faced with the problem of ensuring, as far as it was possible, that the attack did not run into unexpected opposition before reaching the objective, or even end up assaulting the wrong place. In the tangle of steeply forested spurs and valleys this was always a possibility, not least because it was difficult to establish exactly where they were. In this terrain, because of the thick foliage, standing on a piece of high ground does not necessarily guarantee a view over the surrounding countryside, and even if the final objective can be seen, what lies in between is probably obscured. A number of patrols were sent out, including one accompanied by Goschen himself, and including some Royal Norfolks. Captain Howard:

We could see absolutely bugger all. I suppose we were a couple of miles from the road and immediately below one was heavy jungle. I know it was clear [of trees] down by the road, but they were all reverse convex slopes and you couldn't see what was beyond the slope. It was too far away. I saw two chaps walking along the road, but even with binoculars you couldn't tell whether they were soldiers, Japs or Nagas – they might have been anybody.

Consequently the information on which the subsequent plan was based was flimsy in the extreme, and in some cases wrong. Because of this the leading battalion, the 2nd Royal Norfolks, was in effect committed to what in military parlance is called an advance to contact – you don't know what you are going to hit until you run up against it. When the battalion reached the edge of the jungle on GPT Ridge they were to inform Divisional Headquarters, who would order a comprehensive artillery programme on the objective before the final assault. The Royal Scots would provide protection to the rear, secure the forming-up position in the vicinity of a high knoll known as Oaks Hill, and also be available as brigade reserve, as well as exploiting forward to a small hillock, known as the 'Pimple', at the end of GPT Ridge.

Meanwhile, in the hours before battle, men had time to think. Private Fiddament, 2nd Royal Norfolks:

> Everybody's frightened. If he says he is not, then either he's a liar, or a bloody madman. Because nobody wants to die, but nobody. I certainly didn't. But you're pals together, there's a job to do and you get on with it the best way you can.

In those dark moments it is sometimes easier for commanders, at whatever level, busy making plans, or conscious of their responsibility for others. Sergeant Fitt:

> I was happy as a platoon commander. I wanted to go into battle with thirty men and come out with thirty men. About a couple of minutes before the attack, you'd get a sick feeling in the stomach, but immediately you moved, that sick feeling goes away altogether as far as I was concerned. Everybody, I don't care who he is, is nervous to a certain extent until the actual battle starts. But when it starts, then you've got one thing on your mind, it's the enemy that's going to get killed, not you or your men.

While the Royal Norfolks were marching to their forming-up position at Oaks Hill, two companies of the Royal Scots were in the process of occupying Pavilion Hill above it. Here they clashed with the Japanese who had almost forestalled them. For most of the night the Jocks of the

Royal Scots, the 1st of Foot, the senior infantry regiment in the British army, nicknamed 'Pontius Pilate's Bodyguard', fought the Banzai-yelling Japanese with grim ardour, using grenades, bayonets, rifle butts, and bare hands. In the morning there were dead Japanese all round them. Clearly the Japanese had reinforced this flank. But the Royal Norfolks' attack went well to begin with, and by 1230 hours, D Company had cleared up to the jungle edge. A and B Companies now waited on the start line for the artillery to fire on the far end of the ridge. The CO, Lieutenant Colonel Scott, decided that in order to maintain momentum, the advance would continue without artillery preparation. Overtaken with the itch to get forward to see what was happening and take a grip, which seizes many commanders in battle, he joined in the attack on a Japanese bunker. Sergeant Robinson:

> He lined us up with Bren guns. He was ill at the time with malaria, and all he had was his pistol and his cud stick.* His famous words were, 'Right-ho boys, let's go'. The instructions were to fire at everything, spraying up and down, some up and forward of course, because there was a bunker there. Up to that time I hadn't seen a Japanese at all. But hidden in this semi-clearing, low bushes, several got up and started running away. They didn't get far because the firepower was terrific, about 12 Bren guns. The bunker was taken.

Sergeant Fitt was leading the right-hand platoon of the attack.

> We went straight into the attack and took the position with the bayonet. I used this Bren gun [picked up from a casualty], for the remainder of the attack, running with it using it from the hip. The Japanese positions were facing outwards, so they had to come into the open if they wanted to fight us, and that suited us. We wanted them in the open so we could see what was going on. We tore down GPT Ridge as fast as we could. About half way down, I saw what looked to me like a flat piece of ground, and I thought it was a bunker facing the other way. I jumped on to this, and I was looking down the muzzle of a mountain field gun [a 70mm infantry gun]. I threw a grenade in. Three Japs got out, and my runner, a chap called Swinscoe, shot the first one that was running away from us.

---

* Khud means steep hillside, and a cud or khud stick is a stick with a metal point to assist one when ascending or descending the khud.

He twizzled him like a rabbit – a marvellous shot. We'd then got two prisoners.

I left them with one man, a soldier you could trust, and Col Scott came up. When I told him about the prisoners, he said, 'Where are they?' I told him they were being brought up by one of the chaps. 'Good', he said.

Well up came this fellow, no prisoners, so I asked him where they were.

'Back up the track'.

'What do you mean? They'll be gone'.

He replied, 'Never, they won't go anywhere. Remember my brother got bayonetted in hospital. When I searched them I took these badges off them. These are the Territorial badges what they had. [Badges worn by the TA battalions of the Royal Norfolks captured in Singapore.] Well I bayonetted both of them. I killed them'.

When I told the CO that we hadn't got the prisoners, he flew at me, and said, 'Bring the person who let them escape to me'.

I said, 'They didn't escape sir. He took these badges off them – they are officers badges of the 4th, 5th or 6th Battalions'.

'So what?'

I said, 'Well his brother was bayonetted in bed in hospital – he bayonetted them'

Colonel Scott said, 'That's saved me cutting their bloody throats'.

Captain Howard, Brigade Intelligence Officer, a fiercely loyal Royal Norfolk with many friends in the 2nd Battalion, but objective despite that, wrote later:

The Regiment's attack on GPT Ridge succeeded beyond our wildest hopes and the battalion reached the highest point below the trees at the point which became known as the 'Norfolk Bunker'.

The Norfolk Bunker was a complex of bunker positions starting about forty yards from where the battalion had finished its attack, and continuing right down the GPT Ridge towards the Imphal Road. Goschen did not commit his brigade reserve, the Royal Scots. Although some Royal Norfolks, and Captain Howard the Brigade Intelligence Officer, consider they might have taken the bunker while the enemy were still disorganized, the Royal Scots were already committed holding the high ground protecting the rear of the Norfolks, and with only two battalions, instead of the normal three, Goschen probably had no option but to go firm where he was. The fighting on GPT Ridge was to develop into a slogging match until the end of May, involving several attempts to clear the Norfolk Bunker, which blocked the direct route to Jotsoma. This meant that resupply of the 4th Brigade had to be by air drop or portered along the tortuous route along which they had marched. As badly wounded could not be taken along this route, they remained in the Regimental Aid Post.

On the ridge, reaction set in after the battle as the adrenalin drained away, and it was up to the leaders to maintain their men's spirits. Sergeant Fitt:

> We'd dug our foxholes and the next morning they were half full of water. It rained all night, and it was miserable. We'd had a hard day and a heck of a fight coming down here. All in all I think the spirits of the blokes were getting a bit down. But when they realised they had lost nearly all their senior officers and a lot of other people wounded, I think they all had the same feeling as I did. We'll annihilate them, come what may we're going to annihilate the Japanese.

The Royal Norfolks were blessed with a fine CO. Sergeant Fitt:

> He wasn't a man who just went and got in a dug-out and stayed there. Oh no, he went round his positions to make sure that everything was covered and he spoke to people as he went round. He was a great soldier, one of the finest soldiers you could ever meet. I always said that he should have had the VC.

Private Fiddament:

> Suddenly Robert Scott comes along. There we are crouched down in our holes. Scott says to us, 'Come on you chaps, there's no need to be afraid, you are better then those little yellow bastards.'

Scott was an Elizabethan character, who loved music and carried a pocket Shakespeare. Captain Howard:

> Robert Scott will always remain a legendary figure of Kohima. Two minutes with him and a man's fears were calmed, and mud and wet did not matter so much. His boots covered with mud, made his large

feet even huger. His trousers were covered with dried blood. Grenades, a pistol, and a dagger hung around his vast waist-line. His neck was muffled with a silk Japanese flag on which rested a stubby chin of greying black beard. His head was bandaged and his tin hat boasted a ragged bullet hole. He had lumbago and leaned on a long stick; he had a head ache and a vile temper. I doubt if he ever enjoyed himself more in his forty-eight years.

Most men change under danger: the man who appeared a fool develops a sound and bold judgment, or the man who was cool and level headed in peace may be changed by the imminent danger to life and limb and not have the power to impress his will on those around him. Robert's great power of leadership lay to a great extent in the fact that he hardly changed at all from peace to war. He shouted angrily and obscenely as before. He thought and moved slowly as usual: the usual entourage of batmen and gunmen continued to make tea. He lit his pipe with the same care as always. In the midst of chaos and mud, with friends being killed this one staple feature remained. His oddness and short-comings which had been abnormal before were still untouched by war, and became a familiar object on which frayed nerves could fix and adjust themselves. One thing however changed, his opinion of junior officers. He had thought them useless before, but none failed him in battle and many lost their lives most gallantly. He was still rude to those that survived, but there was a trust and affection in his voice which had not been there before.

He was, as we had expected, absurdly brave and inspired the same quixotic gallantry among many around him. His rumbling shout: 'Take cover you silly buggers, we're being shelled. Everybody down – except me – I've got lumbago, they can't get me.' had cheered many quaking hearts, and brought smiles to trembling lips.

His 'Oh dear', with a smile and a twinkle in his one good eye, 'We're all going to be killed', made the possibilities of death more remote.

Scott had been hit a glancing blow across the head. Sergeant Fitt:

When he got scalped, he shook his fist at the Japanese. He said, 'the biggest bloke on the damn position and you couldn't get him. If you were in my bloody battalion, I'd take away your proficiency pay'

Meanwhile the Norfolk Bunker remained untaken, and B Company of the Norfolks was ordered to have another attempt. Sergeant Fitt:

The plan was to attack the Norfolk Bunker from the front, it consisted of about seven or eight bunkers. My platoon was spearhead in [attacking] the centre, and 12 platoon on the right. Number 10 platoon was in reserve with a support platoon consisting of machine gunners and so forth from the Carrier Platoon commanded by Captain Dickie Davies. It was a frontal attack at dawn, and we had to climb a hill with very little cover through trees all shelled so the branches had been knocked off.

Lying on the start line just before dawn, Captain Randle, B Company commander,

came up and laid beside me. He said, 'I've seen all the horrible things that's happened to me in my past'. I said, 'So have I'. I think he had an idea that he wouldn't come out of that attack.

We moved and got about half way to the base of the hill. Captain Randle staggered twice before we ever got to the bottom, that told me he had been hit fairly heavily in the upper part of his body. I shouted to him to go down and leave it to me, you could see that he had already lost blood. He said, 'No you take the left hand bunker, I'm going to take this right hand one.' They were two light machine gun posts and they were carving up the company terrible.

I got mine by coming up underneath and before they could spin a gun on me I had a grenade in the bunker. After four seconds WHOOOF it went up. I knew that anyone in the bunker was either dead or knocked out. I immediately spun right because I thought I could have got to where Captain Randle was before anything happened.

I saw Captain Randle at the bunker entrance. He had a grenade he was going to throw into the bunker. I just stood there, I couldn't do a thing. If he had held on for about three minutes, I'd have got on top of the bunker, and knocked it out. But he had been hit again at point-blank range. As he was going down, he threw his grenade into the bunker and sealed the entrance with his own body. So that nobody could shoot from it. But he killed all the occupants. I thought, 'That's the end of Captain Randle'.

These two bunkers were only the outer edge of the whole complex, and Fitt charged to the next one, an open-topped slit, which he cleared with a grenade and used his last round of ammunition, from the Bren which he always carried. At the next bunker, a Japanese soldier rushed out.

He knew if he stayed there he was going to get a grenade in so he came out of the back door, which was behind me. I didn't see him when he fired. He got me through the side of my face, underneath my jaw, taking my top teeth out, fracturing my maxilla [upper jaw], the bullet burning alongside my nose. It felt like being hit by a clenched fist. It didn't hurt as much as a good punch in a fight in the past. I just spat out a handful of teeth, spun round, and he was a few paces away, facing me. He had a rifle and bayonet. I pressed the trigger, and I'd got no ammunition. As he came towards me, I felt it was either him or me. I was an instructor in unarmed combat. I let him come and threw the light machine gun in his face. Before he hit the ground I had my hand round his windpipe and I literally tried to tear it out. It wouldn't come – if I could have got his windpipe out, I would have twisted it round his neck. We were tossing over on the ground. I managed to get his bayonet off his rifle and finished him with that.

I stood up and had a call from 12 Platoon telling me they were pinned down from another bunker I couldn't see. I asked them where it was and when they told me, I threw a grenade. It went over the top, and a chap who could see, shouted a correction. I threw a second grenade, it hit the ground short, and bounced in, killing the occupants. There were still more bunkers. One of my corporals, Sculforte, spotted another bunker slightly over the crest. He started going for it. I yelled at him to stop, but he continued for four or five paces and was shot down.

Captain Davies, taking part in his first battle as a foot soldier, brought up his platoon, which had been providing supporting fire for the attack. He found Fitt, by now very shaken, but despite his wound still in control, and about sixteen others. Fitt shouted that Randle had been killed, and suggested that Davies take over, who replied, 'You know what's going on, I'll do anything you ask me to do.' Fitt, however, had to sit in the bunker and put on a field dressing, so Davies and his platoon set about trying to clear the remaining bunkers, which were facing away from them towards Jail Hill.

> You couldn't throw grenades at them, so you made a hole in the top with your bayonet, and dropped a grenade in. I picked up a Sten gun, thinking I'd carry that instead of a rifle. Four Japanese got out of one of the bunkers and ran down the hill, I pressed the trigger, and nothing happened. They always jammed, a useless weapon. I threw it at them.

Fitt was evacuated to the RAP, where Scott said to him:

> 'They got you then, Fitt? Let's have a look'
> The MO removed the field dressing. Colonel Scott stood in front of me and went, 'Ho, ho, ho! You never were any bloody oil painting'

Howard also saw Fitt:

> I saw Winkie Fitt, he was slightly [sic!] wounded and was being evacuated through brigade headquarters. I greeted him as he came up to the field ambulance. He said, 'I've had far worse bloody noses than this boxing, and they're trying to evacuate me'.
> I said 'Well Winkie, you'll have to go'. I myself think that if he'd been killed instead of Jack [Randle] the VC would have been the other way round.

Fitt was later awarded the DCM.

Davies with the remnants of B Company and his own platoon reorganized in the bunkers taken so far. Towards evening the mist came down. They were in captured slit trenches, in front of which the Japanese had placed tins with stones in as a form of early warning.

> We heard the tins rattling and the Japs shouting 'Are you there Tommy?' hoping we would shout back. It was horrible, I was very scared. We were soaking wet, we had no cover.
> The main bunker was full of Jap dead. They [the battalion] sent us some bully beef and my batman said, 'Let's have it'. He got his hankie out, it was filthy, and put it over the bare tummy of a dead Japanese. He pulled the warm bully beef out with his finger, put it on a biscuit, saying, 'Here you are Sir'. I couldn't eat it, I was sick.

Although not every part of the Norfolk Bunker position was yet in British hands, it no longer dominated all the ground around it. Contact had been established with the 4th/1st Gurkhas of 33rd Indian Brigade, so it was now possible to open up a track between GPT Ridge and Two Tree Hill leading to Jotsoma. Initial attempts by the 4th/1st Gurkhas to finally clear GPT ridge were unsuccessful, and among others cost the lives of Brigadier Goschen and Lieutenant Colonel Hedderwick of the Gurkhas. One of the problems encountered by troops attacking Japanese bunkers, here and elsewhere, was the fact that they were, to use a military term, sited in defilade, that is to fire to a flank, not to the front, and covered a neighbouring bunker or bunkers. A man attacking one bunker might have difficulty locating the firing slit, and while he was milling about, would be shot from another bunker.

By 7 May, after thirty-four days of some of the toughest fighting in the Second World War, the Japanese still held most of the key ground. The 6th Brigade had taken such heavy casualties in the fighting for the Kohima ridge that the Royal Berkshires and the 2nd Durham Light Infantry on Garrison Hill were formed into a composite battalion. The 5th Brigade on the left had reached the north end of the Naga Village. A column of the 23rd (LRP) Brigade had succeeded in cutting one of the Japanese *31st Division*'s supply routes on the Jessami track, but the whole brigade was not yet in action. Now followed a period of planning and readjustment at the highest level. Slim ordered Stopford to press forward to open the route to Imphal with two divisions (2nd British and 7th Indian), as soon as the 7th Division with its 114th Brigade had arrived from Arakan. It would take under command the 161st Brigade which had so gallantly stopped the Japanese in their tracks at Kohima. The 33rd Brigade, which had been detached to join the fighting in the Kohima battle, would also rejoin 7th Division.

In the meanwhile, the 33rd Brigade was involved in heavy fighting to capture Jail Hill, DIS Hill, and Treasury Hill, for the loss of over 400 casualties. After yet another attempt at clearing the Norfolk Bunker by the 2nd Norfolks, it was eventually taken by the 1st Royal Scots with tank support. On 13 May the 2nd Dorsets finally pushed the Japanese off the far end of the DC's Bungalow spur, at the second attempt, both with armoured support.

The first attempt on 11 May failed because the left hook of a pincer attack was delayed and surprise was lost. On the second occasion, on

13 May, the Dorsets had one troop of medium (Grant) tanks of 149th Regiment Royal Armoured Corps, one troop of light tanks of the 45th Cavalry, and an armoured engineer detachment. Lieutenant Highett took part in the attack riding in one of the Grant tanks, because he had a good idea of the layout of the land, having been using the armoured cars acquired at Dimapur to take ammunition up to the forward companies. Also, according to him, the Chief Royal Engineer and Commander Royal Armoured Corps had conducted personal reconnaissances in his vehicles.

> I was not the commander of the tank. One of the unsung heroes of Kohima was the driver [Sergeant Waterhouse]. He had to go down a vertical drop of six feet on to the Tennis Court. If the tank had been out of action on the Tennis Court it would have been a disaster. We were firing point-blank at the Jap positions from about 20 to 30 yards. I was firing one of the machine guns. The longest part of the operation for me personally, which took about two hours, was waiting on the edge of the drop down to the tennis court, while the driver made up his mind if he could do it. It was probably only a few seconds. But we were aware that there were anti-tank guns around, and we were stopped.
>
> Mopping up took time. D Company used pole charges. Richard Sharp of the BBC covered it live. Afterwards it was rather like a celebration, lots of people milling about, then the Jap artillery opened up, and the scrum of spectators dispersed rather quickly.

Sergeant Cook was platoon sergeant in 18 Platoon, D Company, 2nd Dorsets:

> My objective was a black water tank. I took one section with me, when I came under fire, I dropped off a Bren to cover the enemy, came under fire again, and dropped off another Bren. This left me with one Bren, another man and myself to take the black water tank. The tank [in support] had fired a few rounds into the black water tank, it was shot to pieces and there was no water in it. The Japs had dug trenches all round the tank, which was about 12 feet square, and underneath it. I had a pole charge, an eight foot length of bamboo with gun-cotton tied on the end with a fuse attached. When I jumped down into the enemy trench, and looked round the corner, there were three or four Japs There shouldn't have been

any left alive – the tank was supposed to have killed the lot. So I had no option but to put the pole charge in. We had been told that if you pushed the charge in before pulling the fuse, it would be pushed out by the Japs on to you, so I pulled the fuse, counted five, and put the charge in, and it must have blown the Japs to bits. Unfortunately I forgot to close my eyes, and I was temporarily blinded by debris being blown out from the fifteen inch gap between the bottom of the tank and the trench underneath. The explosion blew out a Japanese sword, and I could feel this thing, and said, 'there's something here'. A corporal said 'you've got a Japanese sword there'.

The other two sections had gone round the other way and did their work winkling out the Japs. I'd done my bit, but couldn't see so missed the mopping up. I was in the MO tent for four days, before they washed the dirt out, and I fully regained my sight after about a week.

People behave differently in action from their normal behaviour. One chap, Corporal Day, normally a mild-mannered man who wouldn't hurt a fly, had the Bren when we reached the black water tank. He stood on the top of a little trench shouting and cursing the Japanese, he was in another world.

Highett:

The Japanese were magnificent in defence. Every army in the world talks about holding positions to the last man. Virtually no other army, including the Germans ever did, but the Japs did. Their positions were well sited and they had a good eye for the ground. They relied on rushing and shouting in the attack. We thought they were formidable fighting insects and savages. We [the battalion] took few prisoners, about one or two in the whole war. We wanted prisoners [for information], but wounded men would have a primed grenade under them, so stretcher bearers were very careful.

The Japanese left about sixty dead, plus a large number of uncounted buried corpses. The final battle had cost the 2nd Dorsets only one dead and two wounded, but the whole eighteen-day slog for the feature cost the battalion seventy-five dead. As their war history says, 'If ever there was a feature that should be called "Dorset", it was that spur at Kohima, which was captured by Dorset grit and endurance'.[8]

During the fighting which led to the clearance of the Kohima ridge, Brigadier Theobalds, promoted from the 6th Brigade, and who had just taken over the 4th Brigade, was badly wounded and died later, and Brigadier Hawkins of 5th Brigade was severely wounded. Altogether the 2nd British Division lost four brigadiers in the Kohima battle, two killed and two wounded. Scott of the 2nd Royal Norfolks temporarily took over the 4th Brigade and to the intense frustration of the brigade staff insisted on commanding from his own battalion HQ.

Almost the last act in the Kohima battle was the battle for the Aradura Spur, which, it will be recalled, was the original objective for the flank march by the 4th Brigade a month earlier. The 1st Royal Scots and 2nd Royal Norfolks took part in a frontal attack on the north-east end of the spur, while the 6th Brigade were tasked with taking the south-western end, where their objectives were named 'Matthew', 'Mark', 'Luke', and 'John'. The 2nd Norfolks were now down to 14 officers and 366 Other Ranks, many very tired and suffering from dysentery. Lieutenant Horner, the signal officer of the 2nd Norfolks, was with all the other officers of the brigade when they were shown the ground from Treasury Hill. He thought:

> This is a straight forward nonsense from start to finish. There was a very steep hill, we knew the Japs were on top, we knew they'd be in a reverse slope position, and we were going to assault straight up the front – not a hope in hell.

Company Sergeant Major Gilding was with B Company, the leading company.

> The company were lined up on the base of the hill, it was all jungle covered, no tracks leading up to it and must have been about one in four. You couldn't walk up it, it had to be scramble up. The Royal Scots had a company on our left flank. Solid shot was to be fired from 25 pounders to break up the Japanese bunkers on the crest of the hill. The idea was to have two platoons forward, with one platoon back and company HQ including me and my party. With us was Colonel Scott. We were all within touching distance, there was no space to spread out. The artillery fired and this allowed us to start scrambling up the hill, bypassing a clump of bamboo, or round a tree, you couldn't go straight up. We could hear the thudding of the shot on the top of the hill. We got almost half-way up, when the

artillery stopped and then the fun began. Small arms fire, machine gun fire and grenades – we got the lot.

Second Lieutenant Franses, B Company, in his first battle:

then some Japanese grenades started coming down. So we threw our grenades up to the top. The ground was so steep, there was a great danger of our grenades rolling back on us. So I tried to land my grenades on the very top, or little further so they wouldn't roll back.

CSM Gilding:

The leading lads got within 20 feet of the crest. Robert Scott came up and he was with the leading troops throwing grenades, shouting, 'Get on, get on, get at 'em'. By this time I was about ten yards from him. I had a Sten gun and was firing, scrambling up grabbing hold of a tree, firing the Sten, going a little further, encouraging the lads. You couldn't see the bunkers or slits, they were so well camouflaged. I heard the stretcher bearers being called as people were getting hit.

Second Lieutenant Franses:

Robert Scott had always been a keen cricketer, and when he threw his grenades he reminded me of a medium bowler lobbing. He was being seen, it was a big help to us all, it certainly was a big help to me.

After a few minutes of this, a Japanese grenade came down towards Robert Scott and I think he decided to kick it away. He misjudged it slightly and it went off and brought him down.

CSM Gilding:

I saw him go down and the stretcher bearers come to try to pick him up. They cut his trousers open to put a field dressing on his wounds. This uncovered his bottom and through all the noise that was going on, Robert shouted out, 'COVER MY BLOODY ARSE UP'.

Private Cron, Carrier Platoon:

I had a go at the Japs with my Bren, kept their heads down while the stretcher bearers got him out. If somebody hadn't fired at the bunkers they'd have popped him and the stretcher bearers off. So I gave them two magazines of 30 rounds each. I got one through the arm – it didn't do much harm – it didn't stop me firing. By that time they'd got the old man on the stretcher and were getting him down to cover.

Although the battalion kept trying to reach the crest, the brigade commander, who was watching from Jail Hill, recognized that the situation was hopeless and called off the attack by radio. Major Murray-Brown, the senior surviving officer, brought the men down. The Norfolks could do no more for the present and they were sent back to Dimapur for a well-earned rest, although not for long.

The 6th Brigade attack was also unsuccessful. Wilson, the brigade major, had been sent up in a Royal Artillery Air Observation light aircraft to view the objective. He saw nothing because the Japanese positions were too well camouflaged.

The attack was on a one-man front in single file, with the Berkshires leading, followed by the Royal Welch Fusiliers. The Berkshires got up on to the objective before the Japs were aware of it, but the Royal Welch were ambushed. The Brigade HQ was at the tail end of the ambush. The Brigade Commander was wounded, and the engineer officer killed. The CO of the Royal Welch cracked up. I took over as Brigade Commander for 72 hours. Immediately I got through on the wireless to Div HQ, who told me to leave the Berkshires where they were, withdraw the Royal Welch Fusiliers, and form a defensive position with the Berkshires and DLI. Fortunately the Japs did not make any efforts to clear us off the ridge.

The end of May and the failure of the Aradura Spur operation marked another low point in the Kohima battle. The Japanese, by all normal standards, should have abandoned Kohima – they were sick, starving, and short of all supplies. If all the efforts expended so far had failed to prise them out of their last-ditch positions at Kohima, how on earth would they be turfed out of the many formidable positions they held all the way to Imphal? 33rd Corps would never reach the place at this rate. The battle that broke the 'log jam' was fought by the 4th/1st Gurkha Rifles under their twenty-seven-year-old CO, Lieutenant Colonel Horsford, capturing Gun Spur at the eastern end of the Naga Village. This cleared the way for further attacks by the 5th Brigade which prised open the enemy positions on Dyer Hill, Pimple (yet another), Big Tree Hill, and Garage Spur to the east of the Imphal Road.

On 4 June, now outflanked, the Japanese abandoned the Aradura

Ridge without a fight. The battle had lasted sixty-four days. The British had lost around 4,000 men, Sato over 7,000. The advance to Imphal was in full swing and it is now time to turn to events there, and for those, in the next chapter, we must backtrack.

6

The Japanese Main Assault: Imphal

Now is the time to capture Imphal. Our death-defying infantry group expects certain victory when it penetrates the main fortress of the enemy.

Lieutenant General Tanaka, *33rd Division*

Imphal, the capital of Manipur State, the most eastern province of India, consists of a small town and a group of villages on a plain about forty miles long and twenty wide, overlooked on all sides by high, jungle-clad hills, which afford an excellent view of the plain below. South of the town is the Logtak Lake, a shallow, marshy stretch of swamp and water roughly twenty miles long by twelve wide; its precise extent varied depending on the season, wet or dry. Here, as elsewhere in Assam, disease flourished, especially in the monsoon. Starting at the time of the retreat from Burma in 1942, Imphal had become a supply base for Lieutenant General Scoones's 4th Corps, and over the intervening two years the number of administrative units had multiplied to include hospitals, fuel and ammunition dumps, workshops, and airfields. Six routes converged on the Imphal Plain: from the north, at twelve o'clock, the Kohima Road; at one o'clock, the Iril Valley footpath; from two o'clock, the Ukhrul Road; from five o'clock the Tamu–Palel road; from seven o'clock the Tiddim Road; and from nine o'clock the Silchar–Bishenpur track.

When the Japanese offensive began, as many noncombatants as possible were evacuated from Imphal by road and air, including the inhabitants of the many villages. But the logistic support of the 4th Corps had to continue, whatever the Japanese were about, so many clerks, storemen, fitters, and other rear area 'wallahs', without whom any army grinds to a halt within days, had to prepare defensive positions and brace themselves for the fight.

The Japanese had been mounting probing attacks and reconnaissance in force, for weeks before their main force crossed the Chindwin in mid-March. On 29 January 1944 they attacked positions in the Chin Hills held by the 7th/10th Baluch, now one of the two reconnaissance battalions in Major General Cowan's 17th Light Division. John Randle, now a captain, was the adjutant:

Battalion HQ was at Saizang with a section of 25 pounders [two guns] under a British Sergeant, and the battalion mortars. We had A Company out near Vazang, and other detached positions. We had been shelled by Jap 155s from a long way off. At dawn, A Company was attacked and the company commander asked to speak on the wireless to the Adjutant. He was shouting 'London London London' the code for the 25 pounders to fire. So I shouted this to the Sergeant. The gun crews were all sitting around having a cup of tea. The sergeant leapt forward and pulled the firing lanyard and the guns opened up to support A Company firing the DF [Defensive Fire] SOS task on which guns laid all the time when not engaged on other tasks. It caught the Japs on the wire, and stopped them from overrunning the position. It was a brilliant bit of artillery support, it had an enormous morale effect on our soldiers. Some Japs did penetrate the wire and there was some hand-to-hand fighting. One sepoy got slashed right across the face by a Jap sword. He was patched up and came back to us.

When later we got orders to withdraw towards Imphal, we thought why should we, we've gone to all this trouble to build these good defensive positions? We pulled out of Saizang and harboured up in Tiddim. The Battalion was sent to Tonzang where the CO commanded an ad hoc force called Tonforce, [initially] consisting of our Battalion and a company of the 1st West Yorks. Our task was to provide a lay-back position through which the Division could retire. One of the positions we took over, called Richmond, had been prepared by the West Yorks.

The Japs attacked at dawn and overran one company, the company commander was wounded and we lost two good VCOs and a lot of soldiers. Another company was attacked in a half-hearted way by the INA. Our chaps jeered at them, 'we've come here to fight proper soldiers, not a lot of yellow deserters like you'.

Eventually the Japanese pressure on Tonzang, which covered the road from Tiddim to the important bridge over the Manipur River at Milestone 126, was such that Cowan ordered Brigadier Burton, commanding the 63rd Brigade, to reinforce Tonforce with the 1st/4th Gurkhas, and eventually take the force under his command. The 7th/10th Baluch took part in one more action on the Tiddim Road at the crossing of the Manipur River, and then force-marched to Imphal. But 17th Division had to fight more battles before it reached the Imphal Plain. One of these at Sakawng involved the 48th Indian Infantry Brigade, of which the 2nd/5th Royal Gurkhas were part. The 2nd/5th were commanded by Lieutenant Colonel Hedley, known as 'Deadly Hedley', a formidable personality, according to Lieutenant Martin:

> He smoked cigarettes in a long holder, and when in a 'mood', you always knew, he took the holder out of his mouth and very deliberately tore a strip off you. He kept the Battalion in fighting trim, insisting on the highest standards. No British officer could get away with being unshaven, and no Gurkha was allowed long hair, heads were shaved leaving just a top-knot. He was the finest type of commander in a crisis, later commanding 48 Brigade, and subsequently a division.

The Japanese had established a series of roadblocks covering some nine miles of the Tiddim Road, and captured stocks from a supply depot at Milestone 109. The 48th Brigade had to open the road and recapture the depot. Having taken part in a very successful brigade battle to clear the high ground overlooking the village of Sakawng, the 2nd/5th Royal Gurkhas were sent on an outflanking night march through the hills to clear two positions known as 'West Knoll' and 'South Ridge' astride the road at Milestone 105. C Company was to attack South Ridge, and Lieutenant Martin commanding D Company was ordered to secure West Knoll:

> I set off at 0230, ahead of me was the reconnaissance platoon commanded by Jemedar Netrabahadur Thapa, who subsequently was awarded a posthumous VC later in the Imphal Battle. C Company and Battalion HQ followed. The terrain was abominable. There was no track we heaved ourselves up the steep slopes tree by tree.
>
> Eventually we hit the unmetalled road to Imphal, on the other side was an earth cliff about 15 foot high, and above that the Japanese

position. We and the recce platoon dumped packs and shovels, and got ready to attack. The only way up this earth cliff was to make a ladder with bayonets and kukris. To our utmost astonishment we took the Japanese by surprise. Our attack 'roared' in and the Japanese fled leaving five dead and lots of equipment

The moment we started trying to exploit our success, we were subjected to sustained and accurate fire from medium and light machine guns, and by mortars. I told the men to dig in all round defence. We had left our picks and shovels with our packs and scratched and scraped with kukris and entrenching tools. Our casualties had been light to start, seven killed and wounded, but in a short space of time they had risen to thirty.

C Company passed through but their attacks failed on each occasion. The company commander and two VCOs were killed, and all the havildars wounded. The Adjutant sent up to take command was badly wounded. Ammunition was getting low, and an attempt during the day by the QM to send ammo and food up on mules failed. We had no food until a patrol found a lorry on the road containing tins of pilchard in tomato sauce – not my favourite food.

The wounded suffered greatly, we had to keep them overnight in a collecting post. If hit in the stomach, their chances of surviving were nil.

Between 2nd/5th Royal Gurkhas and the main body of their brigade and the 17th Division was a strong intermediate block nicknamed 'Bunker Hill'. The deadlock was broken by a force consisting of the commando platoons from all the battalions in the brigade under Major Parry, seizing Bunker Hill, which caused the Japanese to withdraw from the whole block position, opening the way for 17th Division.

The 2nd/5th Royal Gurkhas played an important part in the final brigade attack to breakthrough to Imphal, encountering a block held by the best part of a battalion which had had a week to prepare the position. Martin:

A Company ran into trouble, but eventually succeeded by excellent infiltration. B Company gave a magnificent example of tenacity in their attack. In the first of the major road block battles, the Battalion lost 37 killed and 67 wounded, and in the second, 13 killed, 46 wounded and two missing. In the four months starting with the withdrawal in March 1944, to the end of the Imphal battle, we had

800 casualties, including about 180 killed, the highest in the whole of 17th Division.

The division had conducted a brilliant fighting withdrawal, confounding the enemy, who, based on past performance, confidently expected a smashing victory. The Japanese had deluded themselves to the extent that their radio reported that the 17th Division had been annihilated no less than three times, describing in vivid and moving terms its panic-stricken last moments. The aggressive handling of the Japanese by the 17th Division is epitomized by the exploit of Jemedar Kishenbahadur Gurung at Sakawng. During a grenade-throwing battle, a Japanese officer jumped from his trench, ran forward, and killed a Gurkha in the forward platoon with his sword. The jemedar, from a reserve platoon close behind, leaped forward, wrenched the sword from the Japanese, and killed him with it.

Although this account has dwelt on the exploits of the 17th Light Division, the withdrawal of other formations on the various Japanese invasion routes was equally aggressive and well handled. These efforts and feats such as the Sangshak battle by the 50th Indian Parachute Brigade, covered in the previous chapter, all contributed to delaying the Japanese offensive and making them pay dearly for ground gained.

By 4 April 1944, the withdrawal of the 4th Corps to the Imphal Plain was complete, with Scoones's troops dug in on all the main tracks and roads on a ninety-mile arc from Kanglatongbi about ten miles north of Imphal town, through the 5,833 foot high double peaks of Nungshigum, to Yainganpokpi on the Ukhrul Road, Wangjing and Tengnoupal on the Tamu–Palel road, Shuganu south of Logtak Lake, and Torbung on the Tiddim Road. Major General Cowan's 17th Light Division (the 'Black Cats', from their formation sign) were in corps reserve situated just north of Imphal town, with their 63rd Brigade at Kanglatongbi. Major General Briggs's 5th Indian Division (the 'Ball of Fire', or 'Flaming Arsehole') was responsible for Yainganpokpi and Nungshigum, while Major General D. D. Gracey's 20th Indian Division (whose sign was an upthrust curved dagger) guarded the Shenam Saddle on the Tamu–Palel road. Major General O. L. Roberts's 23rd Indian Division (the 'Fighting Cocks') held the Tiddim Road. Scoones had no intention of sitting waiting for the Japanese, and regrouped ready to take the offensive. In essence this involved ordering the 17th Light Division to take over responsibility for the Tiddim Road, thus releasing the 23rd Division for operations to clear the area south of Ukhrul. Meanwhile the 5th Division was to strike north and seize the high ground at Kangpokpi on the Kohima–Imphal road. The 20th Division was to remain where it was. Regrouping sounds so easy playing war games at staff colleges far from the attentions of the enemy, but the Japanese were not sitting waiting to be attacked, and as the moves by the 4th Corps were in train, two regiments of the Japanese *15th Division* attacked Imphal from the north, while the *33rd Division* mounted an offensive from the south.

The fighting that ensued was to last for over three months, and, it cannot be said too often, was confused, bitter, and mainly an infantry-man's war. Although the battles tended to be along, and for control of, the six main routes, moves were made all over the 'clock face', as units outflanked each other, and were outflanked in their turn. Often the Japanese, driven off the roads and tracks, took to the hills, where they were followed and destroyed. Space does not allow us to follow the fighting in detail. For simplicity, the story will follow events as they occurred route by route, although in reality it did not happen neatly like that, but in several directions at once.

On 6 April the Japanese pressure in the north became so intense that Scoones withdrew the advance stores base at Kanglatongbi. The next day a company of the 3rd/9th Jats was driven off Nungshigum Hill, but a counterattack by the rest of the battalion regained it. However, the view from the top of the hill over Imphal airfield and town was so command-ing that the Japanese mounted a successful effort to seize it again on 11 April. It was the nearest the enemy were ever to get to Imphal, other than patrols, but close enough and the most dangerous; within four miles of corps headquarters. During the fighting for Nungshigum Hill, Jemedar Abdul Hafiz of the 3rd/9th Jats was awarded a posthumous VC.

On 13 April the hill was hit by air strikes from Vengeance dive-bombers, Hurricane fighter-bombers (Hurribombers), and artillery. An attack by 1st/17th Dogras supported by Lee-Grant tanks of B Squadron the 3rd Carabiniers (Prince of Wales's Dragoon Guards) followed. Corporal Arthur Freer was the radio (wireless) operator in B Squadron Leader's tank:

> Nungshigum consisted of two false peaks and one main peak. The
> feature was about 1000 feet above the plain. The whole of B Squadron

was involved. Two troops were to mount the ridge climbing from two different places [up two spurs]. Half of B Squadron HQ and the Squadron Leader, and the Squadron Sergeant Major [SSM] would go up as well. The Squadron Leader, Major Sanford, was 27 years old, the gunner was 'Sherley' Holmes [abbreviation of 'Sherlock'], the loader Joe Nussey, I was the driver/operator, the driver Paddy Ryan a London bus driver, the 75 mm gunner Ginger Whitely. I can't remember the loader's name. [The remaining two troops stayed on the plain.]

We got to the foot of the hill very soon, driving across the paddy fields with infantry walking on either side, consisting of two companies of the 1st Dogras: A Company up the left hand spur and B Company up the right hand spur each with a troop of tanks. The Squadron Leader's tank and the SSM's tank went up the left hand spur. A sapper officer Lieutenant Ryder?????, from Edinburgh guided the tanks to where the slope suddenly became very steep. He walked ahead of the tanks giving signals to the drivers who couldn't see very much. He walked backwards looking over his shoulder guiding the tanks till the Japs saw him and started firing. This told us where they were. We fired a few rounds and we thought they had run away.

As we got closer some of them ran out of the bunkers, and ran up to the sides of the tanks carrying sticky bombs attached to a bamboo rod, they stuck the bomb on the side of the tank and as they ran off they pulled the pin and the theory was it would blow the tank to pieces. We managed to deter them from sticking them on by firing machine guns along the side of the tank [one tank covering each other]. I fired the front Browning which could not traverse but only elevate or depress. If I could have traversed it I could have killed a lot more Japanese. We started hearing [over the squadron radio net] of people being killed, usually 'number 9 [OC] hit in head'. These were the tank commanders with their heads out of the turret looking for the way forward. As they instructed the drivers [over the intercom], they were firing their pistols and throwing grenades at the Japanese. They were exposed to rifle fire and were shot in the head. I heard a thump at the side of me, called up to 'Sherley' Holmes, 'what's happened'. He said, 'Dizzy's been hit in the head'. That was the nickname for our Squadron Leader, and I looked into the turret, because my head was on the level of the feet of anyone standing in the turret, and I could see the Squadron Leader lying on the floor.

I asked 'how badly is he hurt?' 'Sherley' Holmes said 'its gone into his head, and he won't survive'. I passed two morphine tubes back and 'Sherley' injected him with both in case he was in pain.

Paddy Ryan the driver was still driving forward and by now we were in the lead. We had left one bunker, still occupied by Japs. Paddy was asking the gunner on his right [the sponson gunner] 'can you see the bunker in front have a go at it?' We had no tank commander now. I told 'Sherley' Holmes to close the lid, we didn't want any grenades in the tank. The gunner fired a few rounds at the bunker, and I fired my machine gun at them. We went right over the top of the bunker. I told them to stop we must report what was happening, I reported to the CO on the radio that number 9 was hit. He said, 'what do you mean by number 9'. I said, 'our number 9, Dizzy'. He asked if he was alive. I told him he'd still got a pulse, but was not in pain. The CO said try to get down.

We could still hear reports over the wireless of the others being killed. Paddy Ryan went over the peak, and down to the far tip, and it was a sheer drop. So I ordered him to reverse, and told 'Sherley' to turn the turret round and guide him back. 'Sherley' had forgotten the tank was going backwards and was saying 'left a bit left a bit', when he meant right a bit. The tank ended up on the ridge rocking on its tracks with a sheer drop in front and behind. Paddy Ryan, a brilliant driver, put enough power on each track to get back on the ridge, and we moved back past the other tanks. We got away and got down. By that time all the officers were killed, and four men who had replaced the tank commanders. The Sergeant Major was left in charge.

In the Dogras the Subedar Major was in command; all their officers were casualties as well. So SSM Craddock was left with the job of finishing the battle, which he did very efficiently. The tanks fired into the bunker slits, and we learned afterwards that there were 250 Japanese bodies found later that afternoon when the position was taken.

The Squadron Leader was hit by a bullet under the chin and it came out of the top of his steel helmet. Under his body we found a grenade, which he had been about to throw, without a handle [i.e. about to explode within four seconds], and we had had it in the tank with us amongst all that ammo 120 rounds HE, and couldn't understand why it hadn't exploded. Paddy Ryan started to unscrew the baseplate to look inside. I told him to get outside the tank while he did it. So he walked off into the paddy, took the base plate off, the cap had been struck, and the fuse burnt all the way round to the detonator and burnt out. Fortunately for us it was a dud fuse.

We left two tanks up on the mountain, one had slipped down a ridge, and another one – both recovered. The only casualties were to tank commanders or men who took over. One tank lost three men. At the time I thought why did they stick their heads out. The reason was because the drivers couldn't see where they were going, the slope was so steep that the tank was up at an angle.

From my position in the tank I could look through a port hole on the left hand side about three by four inches by raising the plate, which I didn't do often. I also had a periscope to aim the Browning. The Japanese on Nungshigum were not little chaps, as we had been led to expect, they were strapping big six footers, formidable foes.

My first reaction on coming down was relief, instead of the rattling of rounds hitting the armour on the side of the tank, and noise of the guns going off, it was quiet.

The Lee-Grant was a superb tank in these conditions, with tremendous fire power. The only weakness was that being a riveted tank, if a shell blew off the head of the rivet, the rivet could fly off inside the tank and kill or wound the crew. I had friends killed in this way. We were using the tanks as mobile artillery pieces [assault guns].

That night Colonel Younger [the CO] came round to our tank, bubbling with the success. Although he had lost some of his bright young men, he looked upon this as one of the risks of war. I was new to it. He had fought with the 7th Hussars in North Africa and in Burma in the retreat. Here each squadron of the Carabiniers, fought individually. The CO didn't have a great deal to do. I wrote in my diary 'I have had my first taste of action and I don't like it'. The others felt the same. But from then on everything was better.

The next day we had a lot of work cleaning up the tanks and oiling guns, replenishment of ammo etc. The tracks were clogged with bits of Japanese uniforms, bones and bits of meat.

The 5th Division, having secured Nungshigum, handed over responsibility for the area, including the Ukhrul Road, to the 23rd Division, and concentrated on clearing the Iril Valley as a prelude to its operations on the Kohima Road. This involved pushing the enemy off the Mapao Spur between the Iril Valley and the Imphal–Kohima Road. The operation was only partially successful, as to begin with the Japanese clung to the northern part of the spur, but the threat to Imphal was greatly reduced. It marked the turning point in the northern part of the Imphal sector, for the Japanese stopped trying to break through at Sengmai on the Imphal–Kohima road, ordering their forces to switch to the defensive. Scoones now realized that he had gained the initiative on his northern sector. By mid-May, Briggs's 5th Division had pushed north up the Kohima Road by holding the Mapao Spur with one brigade, and using another brigade to attack in a series of short hooks from the Iril Valley, while punching directly up the road with his third brigade. On 21 May, having entered Kanglatongbi to find most of the stocks in the depot intact, his division continued its offensive to the north.

The 23rd Division, after flushing the headquarters of *15th Division* out of the hills south of the Ukhrul Road, cleared the road to within fifteen miles of Ukhrul. The *15th Division Headquarters* escaped, but, discomfited by relentless harrying, it was not well placed to coordinate operations; the British were now paying the Japanese back in their own coin. During the first half of May, the 23rd Division dominated the enemy over the whole of the Ukhrul Road sector.

Although by mid-April the Japanese had gone over to the defensive in the north and north-east of Imphal, in the south they were still attacking, as they had been from the outset of the battle. On the Tamu–Palel road, the 20th Division was one brigade light, with its 32nd Brigade in corps reserve. The division was responsible for twenty-five miles of front from Tengnoupal through Shenam to Shuganu. Gracey did not attempt to hold every yard of ground, but instead concentrated on holding key features and passes, including those traversed by tracks and paths, dominating the intervening ground by aggressive patrolling. Here they faced Major General Yamamoto's column, equivalent to a brigade group supported by artillery and tanks. He was tasked with opening up the main road to Imphal, after first destroying the 20th Division. Yamamoto was under pressure from Mutaguchi to complete his task, and switch his artillery and armour to take part in operations elsewhere on the Imphal front. He accordingly battered the defences covering the Tamu–Palel road.

The 1st Battalion The Devonshire Regiment (the Bloody 11th) were to play a leading part in the fighting around the Shenam Saddle on the Tamu Road, and their Regimental history describes the scene of their actions:

The Shenam Saddle, 45 miles from Imphal and 30 from Tamu, rises to between 4,000 and 5,000 feet above sea level: cool and lovely in the hot season a blessed relief from the suffocating heat of the plain, its character changes in the Monsoon when it is cloaked in mist and often achingly cold.

The area around Shenam was essential to the defence of the Imphal stronghold. From the saddle the road carved out of the jungle runs for a time almost due east through a number of steep hills covered in vegetation with sharp and, viewed from any distance, knife-edged summits. Although unnamed except perhaps in local folklore, they are marked on 14th Army maps, Brigade Hill, Recce, Gibraltar, Malta, Scraggy, Lynch, Crete East, Crete West, Cyprus and Nippon. The crest of Nippon Hill lies on the 5,000 contour line.

... If the Shenam Ridge fell into enemy hands he could have Palel, its excellent airstrip and dumps, an open door for an assault on the Imphal Plain and, thanks to the monumental works of the road-builders, the means by which he could bring up his reinforcements. Every inch of these hills was important, with Nippon[,] garrisoned by a detached company of the 2nd Borders, dominating – a fact grasped by the Japanese who, after a stiff battle on 1st April, took it in force.

... For the next seven days the Japanese strengthened their grip on Nippon: frenzied, unceasing digging had turned the crest, the upper forward and reverse slopes into a human warren.[1]

Six attempts were made to retake Nippon Hill. The seventh was allocated to the 1st Devons. Accounts by three private soldiers and an NCO in the 1st Devons in the 80th Indian Infantry Brigade give some idea of the fighting at the Shenam Saddle. The two other battalions in the Brigade were 9th/12th Frontier Force Regiment, and 3rd/1st Gurkha Rifles. The 1st Devons, a good battalion, understood very well the value of ensuring that reinforcements were properly looked after. Private Palmer joined the battalion before the withdrawal. Here he met the CO, Lieutenant Colonel Harvest:

He had a bush hat and carried a rifle and to begin with you wouldn't have known he was an officer. He said, 'Tomorrow we shall be withdrawing over the hills. I don't want to separate you from friends, so when I ask for so many people for a certain company, stay together in your groups'. He called out A Company, and then B Company, which I joined. He wanted 12 people for B Company, and there were three of us friends, who'd been in England together [in 9th Devons], and travelled out together, Bill Clements and Sid Holder. At B Company we met the company commander. He said 'stay together with friends you know. I want three to go to 21 platoon'. So the three of us were in the same section, with Corporal Devonshire, and private Noble we were a five-man section.

For the attack on 11 April, Harvest planned to use three companies: A and D Companies with the guerrilla platoon to assault from the north, while C Company made a frontal attack from the east. After capturing the hill, it would be handed over to A Company. At 1000 hours a Hurribomber strike would go in, followed at 1010 hours by artillery and mortar concentrations. The rocky soil of Nippon Hill had been so fought over and subjected to so much artillery and mortar fire that it was unusually bare. Corporal May was a medical orderly in the 1st Devons:

The night before [the attack] the lads were playing monopoly, I was putting up battle boxes, ammunition boxes with dressings and other medical kit in each to prepare for dealing with casualties. Our MO was a dour Scotsman, Captain McNicholl, but very nice when you got to know him. He had trained us that the first chap to get to a wounded man saved his life. He used to say 'the finest surgeon in the world can do nothing with a corpse'. The stretcher bearer or medic is the most important live-saving chap. We had 24 stretcher bearers, all well trained in first aid. We worked in groups of four.

That morning we established the RAP in Dead Mule Gulch. Our mortars put a couple of smoke rounds very accurately right on top of the hill, then three Hurribombers came in and dropped 250 lb bombs and raked the hill with cannon fire. While they were attacking, the companies were advancing up the slopes. When the Hurris left, the artillery opened up.

The Hurribomber attack was devastating and 'the whole bloody top of the hill was blown away'.[2] A direct hit on one bunker removed the roof and blew the Japanese into the air. So devastating was the fire support that D Company reached the top without a shot being fired. However, once over the crest, hand-to-hand fighting began when Japanese not eliminated by bombing and shells fought back from deep warrens and gullies. While A and C Companies worked forward around the flank to clear the enemy reverse slope positions, the guerrilla platoon was called in to deal with bunker positions. Private Savage:

We left our positions at about 0300 hours for the march to Nippon Hill. The Hill was in stark contrast to everything else around. It was brown and stripped of vegetation. The attack due to start at 0900 hours [sic].* We felt apprehensive, it was pretty certain someone was going to get hurt. The attack started with three Hurricanes coming over to drop two bombs each on the hill, followed by strafing. This was the signal for us to be on our way. We were making quite good progress. Mortar bombs were dropping round us. There was a huge bang, and I was disorientated, I was hit by shrapnel on my left leg, breaking it. Our orders were that no one was to stop to assist the wounded. Lieutenant Atkinson my Platoon Commander, just stopped and asked if I was all right. I said 'yes'. He pushed on.

My next thought was to get back on the track where I might get some help. I had to push myself down a gully and on to the track. I was worried that our own troops following up behind us would shoot me by mistake when I put my head above the ridge. It turned out all right. I made my way down the track using my rifle as a crutch, and got patched up [at the RAP?]. From here I was evacuated to the CCS, and eventually to Calcutta.

The Regimental history describes the bloody and confused fighting on Nippon Hill as a 'rat hunt'. A soldier would pick his target before dashing forward to stick his bayonet down a foxhole. An officer was seen sitting on the ridge, putting grenades into the holes like marbles – some of the Japanese galleries ran for twenty feet beneath the surface. By 1400 hours the position was in the Devons' hands. The Japanese lost sixty-eight dead, from the count of bodies that could be found. The Japanese company holding Nippon Hill was annihilated, but at a price. All three Devon company commanders were wounded, two other officers were

* This may have been the time his platoon left the assembly area for the forming-up position, or his memory may have been at fault.

killed; the battalion suffered a total of eighty-seven casualties. Corporal May:

> I remember Sergeant Major Jimmy Garvey of D Coy. They brought him into us dying, he charged leading the men with the bayonet. He said 'don't waste time on me'. Couple of our chaps got DCMs. No other awards were given.

The hill was now a mass of churned-up earth. A Company remained while the remainder of the battalion withdrew to its original position on Patiala Ridge. That night A Company beat off three Japanese counter-attacks, being relieved the next morning by the 9th/12th Frontier Force Regiment (FFR).

No sooner had A Company of the 1st Devons withdrawn down the hill, than a furious attack was put in by the Japanese on the 9th/12th FFR, not only from outside the perimeter, but amazingly from inside as well. 'The crest was, by then a stinking homogeneous pile of soil and human remains under which lurked still living Japanese, surviving for days without food and water, who were able to cause casualties by suddenly emerging to throw a grenade before they were gunned down.'[3] After several days of fighting, including tank attacks, the 9th/12th FFR were driven from the crest. General Gracey decided to let Nippon Hill go, rather than spend more lives on it.

B Company 1st Devons was moved up to 'Crete' where it was heavily attacked, beating off two assaults in bouts of hand-to-hand fighting. Between the attacks the Japanese tried to persuade the company to surrender, by promising fair treatment. It is possible that these blandish-ments were the work of a Japanese officer found hanging on the wire by Sergeant Leech and Corporal Venner, who were out looking for a live prisoner. When Leech tried to pick him up, he buried his teeth in Leech's hand. When Venner bashed him with his steel helmet, he still clung on, until Venner drew the officer's sword and killed him.

Just before this the 1st Devons had taken over all the 9th/12th FFR positions and now occupied Cyprus and Scraggy, as well as Crete. The Japanese had turned their attention to Crete East. During the fighting for Crete East Palmer picked up a Japanese flag:

> The Japs attacked in daytime. I could see the Jap carrying this flag attached to his rifle and bayonet. Three or four of us shot at him.

Everyone of us claimed him. We decided that the one that got to him first would claim the flag. When the fighting died down a bit, I went over the top and collected the flag off the Jap. I got roasted by my platoon commander for going. I had to go about 20 yards. There was blood on flag.

The flag is now in the Imperial War Museum. Another 1st Devon reinforcement, Private 'Ray' Dunn, was on

Crete East when Japs put in a night attack. On the features we fought on we did not have wire or mines. The majority of Jap attacks were night attacks. The Japs had soft shoes, and the first thing you were aware of was when the Japs were almost on us, well within grenade-throwing distance. It was so surprising that they were on you so suddenly. We had shortcomings, we had nothing in front to give us warning. Sometimes we had trip grenades fixed up: a grenade in a tin with pin out and connected to a trip-wire.

On one night Japs got to within ten yards of our bunker. I woke up to shouts and firing, from the other man in our bunker. This was followed by the Brens and Tommy Guns firing, and our 3 inch mortars. I was the 'bomber', with a grenade-projector on my rifle. The others got out their grenades. We also used phosphorous grenades. The bunker I was in exploded. They were roofed over with timber and earth. The other two men were very badly wounded. Our rifles were on the floor under the earth. The firing stopped and I didn't know if the Japs had taken the position. It was a long night. I wasn't sure whether to stay there and be bayonetted to death, or be off. I knew the Japs bayonetted the wounded, and I didn't want to leave the wounded men in my bunker. My best friends were in the other bunker, and one was killed, the other so severely wounded he was invalided out of the Army. I was ill prepared for the ferocity of the Jap attacks. We had been told to fight to the last man and last round. The Company Commander eventually gave the order to what was left of us to evacuate the position, contrary to what we had been told. The CO was not best pleased. But if this order had not been given, I would not be here today.

Dunn was wounded later in the battle and flown out from Imphal by Dakota:

In bed next to me in hospital was Harry Taylor, the sole survivor of a Jap attack on Lynch's Pimple, overrun by the Japs, who bayonetted the wounded. He had feigned death, and had a watch taken off him without him moving. They threw him with the others over the side of a hill, where he was found by a Gurkha patrol.

The 1st Devons were pulled out of the Crete positions on 25 April, but remained in the Shenam Saddle area. The loss of Crete East isolated Cyprus, which Gracey ordered abandoned. The forward defences now became Crete West and Scraggy, which were to be the scene of bitter fighting for the next three months. Crete West was subjected on 7 May to no less than eight Japanese assaults, during the course of which a platoon position on Lynch's Pimple, named after a platoon commander in 1st Devons, was overrun, and Crete West threatened. A counterattack on Lynch's Pimple failed and only six wounded men could be rescued from the overrun platoon. On that one day the battalion lost one officer and twenty-two men killed, and two officers and forty-eight wounded. D Company still clung to Crete West, but only just, in the face of wave after wave of attacks. On 10 May, the 3rd/1st Gurkhas attacked Lynch Pimple with two companies, aiming at breaking the Japanese threat to Crete West. 'The sustained fire of well dug-in Japanese machine guns was too much even for the Gurkhas and the attack failed', recorded the Devons' Regimental history.[4] There was one bonus, the enemy's attention was so concentrated on the Gurkha attack that D Company managed to withdraw to Scraggy with all their walking wounded and carrying nine stretchers. Crete West was now gone, and Scraggy became the forward position which the Gurkhas fought grimly to hold until relieved by the 2nd Borders. Between 1 and 10 May, the 1st Devons alone had lost 200 men, killed, wounded, and missing. The Japanese had lost about 1,000 men. Both sides were exhausted and Scoones took advantage of the ensuing lull to replace the 20th Division, which had been under great pressure for over two months, by the 23rd Division, which was at full strength with three brigades.

The 'Jiffs' of the *Gandhi Brigade* of the INA had also featured in the early phases of the fighting in this area. One can only comment that to name a fighting formation after a man who preached nonviolence seems somewhat bizarre, and their performance in battle was no less so. When a large party of 'Jiffs' from this outfit were ambushed, they fled into the surrounding countryside and wandered about disconsolately, attempting to surrender.

In battle quick thinking, boldness, and initiative often pay off, and perhaps there is no better example than that displayed by Major Dinesh Misra, an Indian King's Commissioned Officer. It is worth interrupting the narrative to give a little of this remarkable officer's background. Commissioned into the Indian Army before the Second World War, he was captured in Hong Kong in 1941 with the 5th/7th Rajputs, and despite being subjected to considerable pressure, refused to join the INA. He eventually escaped from Hong Kong and after many adventures in China ended up back in India, where he joined the 5th/6th Rajputana Rifles as second-in-command.

A Japanese force infiltrated well behind 23rd Indian Division's defended localities, and seized a hill, which Misra calls 'Lone Tree Hill'. Nothing stood between Lone Tree Hill and Divisional HQ. The 5th/6th Rajputana Rifles were ordered to clear them off. Misra:

> The CO sent for me and said I will take two companies and you stay in rear. I begged him to let me take the two companies. He let me take them. I mounted a frontal attack, because I thought speed was of the utmost importance, as the Japanese were in the middle of preparing positions. We got to within 30 yards of the objective and were grenaded back. We withdrew and took up a defensive position, spending all night there.
>
> Next morning, the RAF Liaison Officer [with a radio to talk to strike aircraft] arrived and asked what he could do to help. We were so close to target that any shorts from artillery would risk dropping on us. During shelling the Japanese would withdraw down the reverse slope, and come back when artillery stopped. I said to RAF Liaison Officer, 'you bring in air strikes in a north–south direction. When your aircraft have dropped their bombs, don't let them go away. Get them to turn round and attack in dummy runs while we advance'. The aircraft did this, and during the dummy runs we got on to the top of the hill without any firing. I told the Company Commanders 'get your LMGs out in front facing the direction which enemy would come from'. After about ten minutes, the Japanese appeared chatting away. We let them come within 30 yards and opened up with everything. They dropped like flies. The survivors withdrew.
>
> By then it was getting dark. I told the Company Commanders to

expect a counter-attack about two hours after dark. Sure enough it
came at that time. Everything opened up. We beat it off, we had
taken a few casualties. I knew that in the early morning there would
be a final counter-attack. It came and in the hand-to-hand fighting
we had more casualties. I felt detached, but hatred for the Japanese,
and determined to kill them. We were shouting our battle cries, and
the Japs shouting '*Banzai*', the officers had swords. The Japanese
withdrew and I knew we had won. There was a tremendous feeling
of joy and relief. We counted about 150 Jap dead. The Hill became
known as Rajputana Hill.

Misra was awarded the MC, and later attended the British Army Staff
College at Camberley.

*

The defence on the Tiddim Road–Silchar track routes was centred round
Bishenpur, held by the 32nd Indian Infantry Brigade, transferred from
the 20th Division to Cowan's 17th Light Division. The Silchar track in
Japanese hands would have been a direct threat to Bengal and India.
Even holding the eastern end of the track allowed the enemy access to
the hills overlooking Imphal, and an axis of attack on to the plain. The
hinge was Bishenpur, protected by the marshes of the Logtak Lake.
The brigade's right flank rested on Point 5846 on the Silchar track, and
its left was guarded by the marshes. Cowan, with Scoones's permission,
had acceded to the request that the 32nd Brigade should hold there and
not at Moirang, some eight miles further south. But there were disadvan-
tages. The Japanese would be allowed to advance within eighteen miles
of Imphal, and more important would gain access to a number of rice-
growing villages. Anticipating this, the sappers attached to the 32nd
Brigade destroyed some 90 per cent of the rice stored in the villages
before withdrawing north; one method was to mix the rice with cement.
It will be remembered that Mutaguchi had based his logistic plans on
capturing rice, so denying the village stocks to his men was a key factor
in his defeat. By mid-April the Japanese rice ration, their staple food,
was reduced by a third, and by the end of May by another third.
Although the force attacking Imphal did receive some supplies, unlike
the troops investing Kohima, the long drive from Kalewa on the
Chindwin, the shortage of transport, the appalling road, and the mon-

soon all combined to drastically reduce the supply tonnages reaching the Japanese, and most of it consisted of ammunition.

The Japanese attacked the Bishenpur position in their by now familiar three-pronged formation. One column demolished a suspension bridge on the Silchar track. Although this was not back in service until mid-June, its destruction made little impact on the British. One column seized 'Wireless Hill' on the right flank of 32nd Brigade, and had to be driven off. Two days later the Japanese were back on Wireless Hill again, and this time tanks of the 3rd Carabiniers supported the 3rd/8th Gurkhas attacking the hill for a second time. The slope was so steep that one tank overturned and rolled all the way to the bottom, killing the troop commander, but luckily not the rest of the crew. The attack was called off. More serious however was the realization that a Japanese regiment was about to attack Point 5846 and 'Wooded Hill' adjacent to Wireless Hill, with another regiment threatening to advance to the Tiddim Road north of Bishenpur.

Cowan decided to reinforce the 32nd Brigade with the 1st/4th Gurkhas and the 4th/12th Frontier Force Regiment, just in time for the Japanese occupied the villages of Potsangbam ('Pots-and-Pans' to the British soldiers) and Ningthoukhong, between the Tiddim Road and Logtak Lake, threatening the 32nd Brigade's left flank. Two attacks supported by tanks failed to turn the Japanese out. The fighting was bitter, and the British lost seven tanks, irreplaceable until the road from Kohima was open.

The 1st/4th Gurkhas, normally part of the 63rd Indian Infantry Brigade of 17th Division, had been loaned to the 32nd Brigade, consisting of 1st Northamptonshire Regiment, 9th/14th Punjab Regiment, and 3rd/8th Gurkhas. On 27 April, the 1st/4th Gurkhas were sent to relieve the 3rd/8th, who had been under constant attack on Wireless Hill, part of a long ridge over 5,000 feet high astride the Silchar track, where the Japanese *215th Regiment* was attempting to advance east along the track to Bishenpur. For the first mile and a half from Bishenpur the track passed through open paddy fields, before climbing along the spurs of the main hill features reaching down to the Imphal Plain. The spurs and hilltops were open and grassy, but the lower slopes were wooded, sometimes with almost impenetrable bamboo clumps, and the valleys between the spurs were dark with tangled wood and undergrowth.

The 1st/4th Gurkhas found that reaching Wireless Hill would not be plain sailing as the Japanese had already established blocking positions along the track between Bishenpur and the hill, starting with one near the village of Toulang. An attack by B and C Companies of 1st/4th Gurkhas failed with the loss of two dead and twenty-seven wounded. The CO, Lieutenant Colonel Oldham, withdrew B Company with a view to putting in another attack the following day. C Company beat off three Japanese attacks during the night. Lieutenant Evans was with C Company:

> Early in the evening on return from a patrol, when fired at by one of our sentries I had called out 'It's Evans Sahib'. The Japs must have heard, because after the first Jap attack, our LMGs opened up on a Jap patrol, at which one of them called out 'Evans Sahib'. The Gurkhas were not taken in and continued firing.

The next day Oldham appeared with two companies and a troop of Lee-Grant tanks from the 3rd Carabiniers. After a hard fight, lasting two days, the force managed to outflank the Japanese, who withdrew, at a cost to the 1st/4th Gurkhas of ten dead and forty-six wounded, including two company commanders. The battalion dug in for the night, and set off the next morning for Wireless Hill, establishing piquets (which were subsequently given appropriate names) on the prominent features en route. Meanwhile a company of the Northamptons from Point 5846, at the other end of the Wireless Hill feature, battled towards the advancing 1st/4th who were having to fight a series of actions to clear Japanese off blocking positions on the track. Lieutenant Evans:

> I was sent with a platoon of C Company (equivalent to two sections in strength) to attack a knoll where the Japanese were sited in reverse slope positions. I did not like this at all, you had to get over the crest before you could attack the position. I decided to outflank the enemy with one party, while distracting them with another.
>
> I could see the outflanking party move round, so we crawled forward, gradually until we could see the enemy trenches. I could see my Jemadar popping up, aiming his rifle, firing, ducking down. I got out a grenade and raised my self on my elbow, he came up on aim, I threw the grenade, and at that moment I was hit.
>
> A Gurkha piper came up and put a first field dressing on me, saying 'it's a small hole Sahib. You'll be all right'.

He turned me and his face fell. He must have seen the exit wound. He gave me morphia. I felt light headed as I walked back to the ambulance.

Evans is being modest. He had already tried once to take the position, and been driven back by a shower of grenades. Undeterred he tried again, with support from tanks and by sending one section round to a flank, as he describes above. With only seven men, he attacked the position. 'It was', said Major Simpson of the 1st/4th Gurkhas, 'the finest thing I had ever seen'.[5] It was left to Naik Pritam Sing Rana to finish the job. Shouting at the top of his voice, he hurled grenades into bunkers still occupied by Japanese, and at the backs of retreating enemy. Twenty-eight Japanese dead were found. The feature became 'Evans's Knob', and was occupied by A Company for the night.

The Japanese, never ones to give up, harassed A Company all night from a nearby position. In an attack to remove this irritation, A Company's commander and two Gurkha soldiers were killed, and nineteen wounded. By now the order to relieve the 3rd/8th Gurkhas had been cancelled, it being apparent that keeping the Silchar track open would occupy the whole attention of the 1st/4th Gurkhas. The Japanese attacked the piquets night after night. Usually they failed, and the citation written for Jemedar Gajbir Pun, by Oldham, a few days before he himself was killed, gives some idea of the savagery of the fighting:

On 8th May 1944, Jemedar Gajbir took over command of the platoon piquet 200 yards north of the water point at MS 21.6 on the Silchar Track. That night the Japs made a heavy and sustained infantry attack on the piquet preceded by a twenty minute bombardment from two 75-mm guns. Although the barbed wire round his perimeter was shattered by the weight of shells which fell in the area and several of his bunkers received hits which restricted their fields of fire, Jemedar Gajbir successfully repulsed a very heavy attack made by about 200 Jap infantry on his isolated platoon. The enemy assault began shortly after dusk and continued till 0300 hours and was directly supported by MMGs as well as by a high-velocity gun firing at less than one hundred yards range from the jungle edge. When dawn broke, no less than twenty-five enemy dead as well as a considerable quantity of arms and equipment were found outside the piquet's perimeter.

But one feature, called 'Scrub Ridge', fell after the jemedar in command had been badly wounded. Oldham decided to retake it at once. At 0430 hours, Major Hammond attacked with A Company, but he and three Gurkha officers were wounded immediately, and the attack stalled. Lieutenant MacLeod, who had just joined the battalion, at once volunteered to go forward and take over the company, but was killed as he rallied the men who were pinned down close to the enemy position. Captain Frankenburg, a day short of twenty-one years old, seeing what was happening from an adjoining piquet, went off to lead the company in one more effort, but was killed as they advanced. Major Brodrick-Pittard was called upon to try again, and he led a charge which reached the enemy wire, where the attack lost momentum, and he was killed. Losses for this attack, in addition to the three British officers dead and one wounded, were two Gurkha officers wounded, six riflemen killed, and thirty-six wounded. The Japanese held Scrub Ridge for a few days, and then slipped away to take part in operations that will be described shortly. The 1st/4th Gurkhas had successfully frustrated the *215th Regiment* in its mission, thus restoring the situation on the Silchar track. The *2/215th Battalion* had been destroyed, and the *215th Regiment* from a starting strength of around 4,000 was down to about 900. But the 1st/4th Gurkhas had suffered heavily, with a total of four British officers and 46 Gurkhas dead, and seven British and nine Gurkha officers, and 146 Gurkhas wounded. The only British officers left in the battalion were the CO and three others.

At this stage both Mutaguchi and Scoones resolved that a decisive blow must be struck to break the deadlock before the monsoon descended. Mutaguchi chose a major effort by the *33rd Division* to break through at Bishenpur, and on to Imphal, using all his artillery, tanks, and four reinforcing battalions. Scoones opted for an attempt to destroy the *33rd Division*, and reinforced Cowan to do so, stripping his corps reserve with the exception of two battalions. Cowan's plan was to move the 48th Brigade east and south of Logtak Lake and establish a block on the Tiddim Road around Torbung, south of the *33rd Division*. This would be the anvil. The hammer would be his 63rd Indian Infantry Brigade assaulting Potsangbam and Ningthoukhong and driving the *33rd Division* against the anvil at Torbung.

The move of the highly trained and well-led 48th Brigade (2nd/5th Royal Gurkhas and 1st/7th Gurkhas, 21st Indian Mountain Regiment (artillery), two mule companies, and medical and stretcher bearer detachments) went well thanks to excellent planning by its commander, Brigadier Cameron. Soon after first light on 17 May, the leading battalion, 1st/7th Gurkhas, had just established a roadblock about a mile south of Torbung, when they saw four enemy light tanks approaching. At this stage the Japanese had not used tanks on the Tiddim Road since losing five in one fell swoop at the Battle of Tonzang, so the 48th Brigade had not brought any anti-tank guns with them. They did however have a few PIATs (Projector Infantry Anti-Tank), a shoulder-fired weapon which projected an armour-piercing bomb, effective at close range. PIATs had recently been issued to infantry battalions in the Fourteenth Army, and had been received by the 1st/7th Gurkhas only a month before. B Company of the 1st/7th Gurkhas opened fire with small arms, but the tanks came on, and it seemed that nothing would stop them, when Rifleman Ganju Lama moved close enough to knock out the two leading tanks with a PIAT. This turned the scales, and the two undamaged tanks retreated. During the day the sappers laid anti-tank mines on the road, and the Gurkhas improved the block. At about midnight four more tanks appeared, again from the north, and were driven off by PIAT bombs, damaging three. This was followed by a convoy of eight trucks from the south, loaded with rice and fifty-two men. The lorries were destroyed, the rice taken for consumption by the Gurkhas, and the men all killed. Patrols were sent out by the 2nd/5th Royal Gurkhas to try to find the Japanese gun positions, but were unsuccessful. Attacks were mounted on other Japanese locations in the vicinity, but again without much success, mainly because the light shells from the mountain guns supporting the attack caused little or no damage to the strong enemy bunkers. A cannon-firing Hurricane did however attack one of the Japanese tank harbours, and no more tanks appeared from the north of the block.

The brigade was supplied by air-drop adjacent to where brigade headquarters (the gunners, sappers, and infantrymen not on the roadblock or patrol) were located. Later generations would call this a Fire Base. Light aircraft were also flown in to a strip constructed by the sappers, allowing seriously wounded men to be flown directly to Imphal. Casualties were dealt with in the advanced dressing station, which had moved forward with the 48th Brigade, and until the airstrip was built, were then evacuated by mule and stretcher bearer five miles across country to Kumbi, from where they were floated in country boats some ten miles down river to Shuganu, and thence by ambulance to Imphal. All but the most seriously wounded continued to be taken out this way while the block was in position.

On the nights of 19/20 and 20/21 May two successive attacks by an enemy battalion on the 48th Brigade block were driven off with heavy losses. The Japanese lost around 200 killed, including leaving 116 bodies round the wire. On the following two nights the Japanese attacked, but were beaten off each time. Six days had passed, but there was no sign of the drive from the north by the rest of the 17th Division. The Japanese had inconveniently chosen this moment to attack as well, thus disrupting Cowan's plans, and Brigadier Cameron learned by signal that attacks on the two brigades at Bishenpur were so serious that there was no question of any offensive by the division for the present. Cameron was ordered to be prepared to move back to join the remainder of the division at Bishenpur. He decided to return by fighting his way up the Tiddim Road to Bishenpur rather than by the route round Logtak Lake, because in this way he could take the Japanese attacking the rest of the division in the rear, and perhaps overrun the enemy artillery in the process.

The move north went well initially, Japanese positions encountered were successfully dealt with at considerable loss to the enemy, and the 48th Brigade established another roadblock at Moirang, some eight miles north of the original one. Meanwhile the Japanese attacked the abandoned block, where a number of them were killed and wounded by booby traps left by the sappers of the Indian Engineers. The night of 25/26 May saw the start of the monsoon, and the slit trenches at the Moirang block soon topped up with water. Cameron was now ordered to move north to Ningthoukhong, but decided to hold the Moirang block for one more night.

On the evening of 26 May, 2nd/5th Royal Gurkhas were attacked by four tanks preceded by artillery fire. One was blown up on a minefield laid by the battalion, one ran into the position, while the other two sat on a bund and fired down into the position. The battalion took about fifty casualties before the two tanks on the bund were destroyed. The wounded were lying in waterlogged trenches, while Captain Sanyal, the MO, did his best for them, in the dark, being unable to show any light. The wounded were evacuated back along the route round Logtak Lake, but from then on, casualties would have to be carried with the brigade main body on mules or stretchers.

On 27 May, the 1st/7th Gurkhas secured Siphai, two miles to the north, and the brigade column closed on this area for the night. The 2nd/5th Gurkhas extracted themselves from Moirang after heavy fighting. And so the move continued; while one battalion cleared an area to the north, the other remained in position covering the guns and the wounded, who were all carried with the column, and fighting off the Japanese from the south as well. There was no rest for anyone, day or night.

From then on the fighting encountered as the 48th Brigade battled its way north became more intense, and, held up by Japanese bunkers in Ningthoukhong, Cameron ordered an outflanking march by his brigade. Reconnaissance had found a track through the edge of Logtak Lake, only about three feet deep in water and fairly well screened by rushes and reeds. Arriving at Potsangbam, ambulances were waiting to evacuate the wounded. On 30 May, while the 1st/7th Gurkhas held off the enemy, assisted by air attacks, the remainder of the brigade column made its way through the lake, to rejoin the road south of Potsangbam, where ambulances were waiting for the 150 or so wounded. As they were loading they were subjected to heavy shelling from Japanese artillery which caused several casualties. Among the killed were two ambulance-loads of wounded including Lieutenant Colonel Outram, who had taken over from Hedley as CO of the 2nd/5th Royal Gurkhas when the latter was promoted to deputy commander of the 48th Brigade.

The battle of the Torbung blocks has been covered in some detail as a demonstration of the impressive progress in battle skills made by the British and Indian armies since the dark days of the 1942 retreat and abortive First Arakan campaign of 1943. Air superiority made the kind of bold tactics used by Cameron possible. But more than anything the key to success was an attitude of mind that refused to accept that the Japanese were invincible. Man for man, the Indian, Gurkha, and British soldiers at Imphal, as at Kohima, more often than not beat the best the Japanese could throw at them. It was not easy; fighting the Japanese never was. In the Torbung battle, the 48th Brigade lost 120 killed and 301 wounded. The 2nd/5th Royal Gurkhas alone lost two British officers, and seven Gurkha other ranks killed, and four British officers, one Gurkha officer, and 109 Gurkha other ranks wounded, and seven missing. Japanese casualties, confirmed by post-war reports, were around 450 dead and 700 wounded, plus six tanks destroyed.

The Japanese offensive at Bishenpur, which had frustrated Cowan's plan to destroy the *33rd Division*, resulted in fighting which lasted until the end of June. The phase of the battle that ended on 27 May saw the destruction of two Japanese regiments, and the British positions untaken. There had been some close calls when Japanese outflanking moves had cut in behind the Bishenpur position, overrun the 32nd Brigade's administrative area, attacked 17th Division's headquarters, and established roadblocks between there and Bishenpur. The fighting had again been savage and at close quarters.

The nature of the fighting and life for the soldiers engaged in the battles up and down the Tiddim Road is clear from accounts by participants. At one stage, the best part of a Japanese battalion seized most of a feature known as Red Hill just south of 17th Division's HQ. The highest part of the hill, Point 2926, was held by a platoon of 7th/10th Baluch under Subedar Ghulam Yasin. Randle:

> We spent quite a few days getting rid of the Japs. The monsoon had started by then. The objective was north of the artillery positions which were quite a long way south, so we had problems with fire support. The 7th/10th Baluch put in a counter attack with two companies, which succeeded in capturing most of the central part of the hill. But we had a lot of casualties, including officers. The Japs put up a fine show. Their commander deserved a DSO. They were very skilled in camouflaging positions.

Eventually the position was cleared by the 3rd/1st Gurkhas. The operations to clear Red Hill had involved forming an ad hoc force under Brigadier Woods, the commander of the remnants of 50th Parachute Brigade; his nickname in the Indian Army was 'Lukri' (wood), so the force was known as Lukriforce.

Arthur Freer also spent some time at Bishenpur:

> A Squadron in Bishenpur and Potsangbam had had a rough time, so B Squadron was sent down to help. We were in action almost every day. It was paddy on both sides of the road, on one side was the Logtak Lake. Troops would go out and conduct shoots on Jap positions indicated for them by the infantry. Squadron HQ usually went each time too, so we had a lot of trips out. We had a new Squadron Leader from A Squadron, quite a character Huntley-Wright, everybody called him Huntley. We loved him, he was a

wonderful leader. He made the mistake of getting out of the tank at the wrong time – much later.

The Japs would fortify the villages with bunkers and use the bunds as defensive positions. At night having half cleared a village, we would remain guarded by a platoon of the Bombay Grenadiers [3rd/4th Bombay Grenadiers allocated to tank protection].

At this time we all got the 'runs'. There was a latrine [in the squadron laager] at Bishenpur, a four seater, always occupied, so you would have to go elsewhere. It was a communal meeting place, and you would chat and have a cigarette. It stank. The MO ordered that it was to be covered with oil daily to seal it off. This was OK until we were short of oil, but we had plenty of high octane petrol, because the tanks had aero engines, and someone put that down. Someone lit a cigarette, dropped the match, and up went the petrol burning the backsides of the four men sitting there. With the rains of the monsoon the dusty tracks would become ankle deep in mud in an hour. Prickly heat drove you mad. The best way to relieve it was to stand out in the rain.

The thing I remember most is being stuck in the tank day and night when I had the 'runs'. There were three of us with the runs at the time and I was the worst. To sleep in the tank you sit in your seat. To crap you got the 75 mm gunner, who was standing on the escape hatch [in the floor of the tank] on the other side of the tank, to move to your seat, and you lifted the hatch and crapped on the ground a few feet below. You then got the driver to move the tank a bit away from the stench. Put the lid back again. Nobody slept. We all stank to high heaven, we were all unwashed. There was always a revolting stench in the tank. At dawn you stood to, the tank guard would move away, and we would go into action again. It could go on for three days and nights at at a time.

The Japanese were very skilled at the rapid preparation of a defensive area. One night they penetrated the mule lines and killed the drivers and mules. We had been standing to since 4 o'clock in the morning, and we were faced by a strong force of Japanese (300 to 400) with bunkers all round them about 40 to 50 yards from where the tanks were. One half of the Squadron under the 2ic (Captain Murphy known to us all as 'Spud' Murphy) was ordered to clear the mule lines.

There was no breakfast for anyone because, the major said he was going to take Numbers 4 and 5 Troops with half of Squadron HQ north to Buri Bazaar where the road to Imphal had been cut by the Japanese. This was a trap for the Carabiniers we learned later. We were a menace to their success. They cut the road knowing that the Carabiniers would be sent to clear it. But they had also hidden three medium guns near Buri Bazaar. They could knock out a tank with these. It was a week before the squadron was together again.

We found a troop of 7th Indian Cavalry in Stuarts in the paddy fields, in a little triangle with a cooker going brewing water to make a cup of tea. They waved to us to join them, we ignored them, because as we drove across, three Jap pieces of artillery opened fire and knocked out the tanks of the leading troop. We had one troop left who opened fire on the gun flashes, and the first round from this troop hit the stock of ammo for all three guns, wiped out the three guns and their crews. The Japs had ignored the light tanks they wanted the Carabiniers. It took us a couple of days to get two of our tanks with tracks blown off repaired and replace the knocked out tank.

From here we were ordered to another battle where an Indian infantry battalion was pinned down. We set out without a cup of tea, nothing to eat since the night before. We called for a water wagon from Imphal but it never arrived. We were fighting for a week like that. Some eventually came up, but we neither washed nor shaved for a week. We had one Chagul [water bottle] of water each per day. We killed a lot of Japanese. We got back in the early morning a week later to our original positions, parked the tanks, and I took a water bucket and was going round looking for some clean water to wash in. We were all in rags, we stank. I crossed the road saw a stagnant pond with thick green water, and I was just scraping this away, to try to get some clean water. A jeep pulled up and the CO got out. He had come from Imphal, having driven through a Japanese roadblock. His uniform was immaculate, brasses shining and I stood in front of him like a scarecrow. He asked me what I was doing, so I told him. He asked me where the Major was, I said, 'He's in the next pond looking for water'.

The CO came back and inspected us two hours later. We had changed into our spare jungle greens.

The other half of the squadron had been taken to the south side of the mule lines and plastered all these Jap bunkers. The infantry were told to attack from the north side. So our overs hit them. The

Squadron 2ic took the two troops round to a flank, but had two tanks knocked out losing tracks. After three days, some of the Japs moved into the gunners box, capturing some 25 pounders before the gunners killed them. It took about five days fighting to clear all the Japs. The bodies stank so high, the tank crews tied handkerchiefs over their mouths. The bodies were buried in pits dug by bulldozers.

Although by now it was apparent to Mutaguchi that hopes of taking Imphal were a delusion, he tried again, thus playing into Slim's hands.

It was at this stage that Lieutenant General Tanaka, who had taken over command of the *33rd Division* in the middle of the second phase of the battle for Bishenpur, confided to his diary that his division was about to be wiped out. Nevertheless he issued an order of the day, part of which is quoted at the start of this chapter, and which continued:

The coming battle is the turning point. It will denote the success or failure of the Greater East Asia War. You men have got to be fully in the picture as to what the present position is; regarding death as something lighter than a feather, you must tackle the task of capturing Imphal.

For that reason it must be expected that the division will be almost annihilated. I have confidence in your firm courage and devotion and believe you will do your duty, but should any delinquencies occur you have got to understand that I shall take the necessary action.

In the front line rewards and punishments must be given on the spot without delay. A man who does well should have his name sent in at once. On the other hand, a man guilty of any misconduct should be punished at once in accordance with the military code.

Further, in order to keep the honour of his unit bright, a commander may have to use his sword as a weapon of punishment, exceedingly shameful though it is to have to shed the blood of one's own soldiers on the battlefield.

Fresh troops with unused rifles have now arrived and the time is at hand – the arrow is about to leave the bow.

The infantry group is in high spirits: afire with valour and dominated by one thought and one thought only – the duty laid upon them to annihilate the enemy.

On this battle rests the fate of the Empire.

All officers and men fight courageously!

One officer who fought the Japanese in Burma was of the opinion that an order, couched in such uncompromising terms, would hardly have appealed to any Western army. But then, as Slim remarked, 'there can be no question of the supreme courage and hardihood of the Japanese soldiers who made the attempts [to capture Imphal]. I know of no army that could have equalled them.'[6]

The Japanese attacks, mostly for control of the Silchar track, ended in utter failure, but not without savage fighting for features such as 'Mortar Bluff', 'Dog', and 'Water Piquet'. Martin of the 2nd/5th Royal Gurkhas:

> Mortar Bluff was held by a platoon reinforced to a strength of 41 men under Subedar Netrabahadur Thapa. At about 8 pm in pitch dark and torrential rain, the Japanese attacked. There were good communications to Battalion HQ, and the attack was broken up by supporting fire. In the early hours of the morning another attack came in and succeeded in penetrating the position. Savage and confused fighting followed, and the Subedar called for defensive fire from guns and mortars, but the position was almost overrun. Arrangements were made to send up reinforcements with extra ammunition, but they were wounded carrying it up, although some ammunition was retrieved. The Subedar had been killed by a grenade leading a counter-attack. Only six unwounded men remained on Mortar Bluff. These collecting as many wounded as possible, withdrew to BP Piquet. When the Subedar's body was recovered his kukri was found embedded in a Japanese.
>
> The next morning most of the Battalion moved off at first light to re-establish the piquet, and had a hell of a battle. A major who had rejoined the battalion the previous day, three havildars, and others were wounded. During this attack, Naik Agansing Rai stormed through the wire with his section, knocked out the crew of a medium machine gun, which had been causing many casualties, and led his section against a 37 mm battalion gun, capturing it. The enemy shattered by the artillery barrage and the very aggressive attack pulled out. Naik Agansing Rai was awarded the VC.

The 7th/10th Baluch also fought on the Silchar track, where the hardest fighting in this phase of the Imphal Battle took place. Randle:

16. Ground crew arming a Hurribomber on a forward airstrip

17. Two bombs fall away from a Hurribomber attacking a bridge on the Tiddim Road.

18. The pre-eminent Chindit Brigade commander, Brigadier Mike Calvert (centre), with two Chindits.

19. Soldiers of the 11th East African Division enter Kalewa on the River Chindwin, in December 1944. The division pushed on to Shwegyin, from which the British had withdrawn back into India in May 1942.

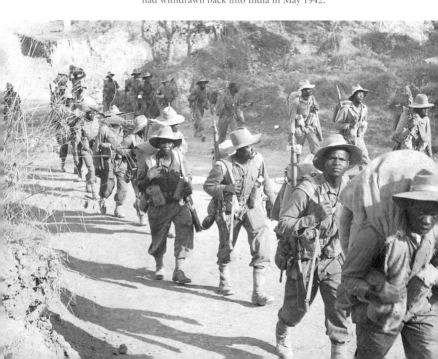

20. Christmas dinner by air drop from a Dakota.

21. Men of the 81st West African Division crossing the Matamuhari River at Alikadam in the Arakan, at the start of their return for the 1945 offensive in the Kaladan.

22. Stuart light tanks of the 7th Light Cavalry cross the Irrawaddy.

23. A Lee-Grant of 3rd Carabiniers crossing the Irrawaddy at Myinze.

24. A rifleman of the 4th/6th Gurkha Rifles wading from his craft after crossing the Irrawaddy. He is carrying his load in the Nepalese manner on a head strap. He is a 2in mortarman. The mortar is folded on top of his pack, and in his pouches are the bombs. A Vickers machine-gunner is just visible to his left.

25. Swimming mules across the Irrawaddy.

26. The 1st/6th Gurkha Rifles in action at Singu with Lee-Grant tanks in support.

27. Major Scott of the 8th/12th Frontier Force Regiment during the advance on Mandalay.

28. Machine-gunners moving up for the battle on Pear Hill.

29. A 5.5in gun firing point-blank at Fort Dufferin in Mandalay.

30. The moat round
Fort Dufferin.

31. Sepoy Hali Ram of the
19th Indian Division drinks
from his chagul outside
Mandalay.

It was rather like the Western Front, dug in wired positions, with the Japs only about 50–60 yards away. Everyone was mixed up. For about three weeks there was very intensive fighting. The scrub was thicker than in Chin Hills, and very wet. It was a very hard infantry slog. The Japs attacked then we counter-attacked. Positions changed hands several times. I was the controller of the fire support, guns, mortars, 25 pounders, and 5.5 inch mediums, also some AA guns in the direct fire role. We shared a Command Post with 5th Gurkhas.

Water Piquet, Mortar Bluff, etc. were pimples or hills occupied by companies or even platoons, and mutually supporting. Subedar Netrabahadur Thapa on Water Piquet called for fire through me. Spoke in Gurkali, but switched to Urdu when realised he was not talking to Gurkha officer. He was overrun – got a VC.

Next day 2/5 RGR got another VC, Agansing Rai, only time I've seen Gurkhas go in with the kukri. An awe-inspiring sight. They were counter-attacking the position and took it back. It was the most close fighting I ever saw in Burma.

Japanese attacks tended to come up and close the last few yards with bayonets. In a counter-attack we gave enemy positions a really good pasting, then fought our way in, clearing enemy positions with grenades, Tommy Guns, Gurkhas with kukris, and our chaps used a bayonet.

Casualties were high in this period. The 1st/4th Gurkhas had 300% officer casualties. There were 12 officers in a battalion, so they had 36 officer casualties.

We had no morale problems. We had good officers, and were experienced. We thought we were winning. We had far more artillery than the Japs, and the RAF were in evidence all the time. Rations came up. The wounded were taken out by the American Field Service. There were none of the uncertainties of the retreat.

In addition to the two VCs just mentioned, two more were awarded for the fighting round Bishenpur: one posthumously to Sergeant Hanson Turner of the 1st Battalion West Yorkshires. The other was awarded to Rifleman Ganju Lama who had already won the MM for knocking out two tanks with his PIAT at the Torbung roadblock. During the fighting in Ningthoukhong, two bogged but serviceable Japanese tanks held up the advance of two companies of the 1st/7th Gurkhas sent to assist the 2nd/5th Royal Gurkhas. Ganju Lama crept forward and knocked out both with his PIAT. By now badly wounded in the legs, he despatched the tank crews with grenades as they tried to escape.

While Tanaka had been furiously attacking in the Bishenpur sector, Yamamoto on the Tamu–Palel road continued to hammer away, so it was fortunate that the stronger 23rd Division was now holding that part of the front. On 9 June, after what was reckoned to be the most intensive bombardment put down by the Japanese in the entire Burma campaign, they overran Scraggy, held by a detachment of the 3rd/3rd Gurkha Rifles, who were almost annihilated. Counterattacks failed to throw the Japanese off. But this was as far as Yamamato was to go.

Meanwhile the 33rd Corps, consisting of the 2nd British and 7th Indian Divisions, had been fighting their way towards Imphal from Kohima, as the 5th Division pushed north to meet them. The Japanese were relying on a very strong position at Mao Sonsang with a covering position at Viswema to prevent the 33rd Corps from reaching Imphal.

Captain Howard, the Intelligence Officer of the 4th British Infantry Brigade in 2nd Division advancing down the main road from Kohima, remembered this as a trying time, as the brigade had just lost its second commander in the Kohima battle:

> The next few weeks were chaotic. Colonel xxxxxx was appointed Brigade second in command and took over. He had been a most successful CO of a battalion, but was strange as a Brigade Commander. I think he was likely to crack up or die winning a VC; the former being most likely. After a fortnight living with this man night as well as day, a man who never stopped talking and woke every time a shot was fired within a mile, which was frequently, I was beginning to go mad myself from the time of the break-out from Aradura to the end of the battle of Viswema. I do not think I was much use to anyone. Fortunately Jock McNaught [ex-CO of the 2nd Dorsets] took over in the middle of the Viswema battle although too late to save the mess in which the Brigade had become involved.

Howard then turns to his own battalion, 2nd Norfolks, in the same brigade:

> Robert Scott [see previous chapter] was in hospital at Dimapur. The Regt had lost all its original company commanders and had been taken over by Jock Carroll who had emerged for the purpose from HQ Fourteenth Army. The next few months of the battalion's history

were unhappy. At Viswema they were badly committed by the 'Bograt' [the temporary Brigade Commander before McNaught took over], too late in the day and on insufficient information. No patrolling had been done. Jock Carrol's actions did not retrieve the 'Bograt's' original mistakes and the Regt got stuck in close contact with the enemy on top of a thickly forested spur and remained in an absurd box for about a week. Cherub Swainson, Jerry Myler, Dickie Davies and a newly joined officer were hit. Cherub died a week or two later.

After Viswema we did not play a large part in the battle of the Imphal Road, although we got a good haul of documents when we captured all the kit of HQ 31 Divisional Infantry Group at 87 Milestone. I stayed up half the night sorting them out. We were in an extraordinary position, Brigade HQ, three battalions, and about five batteries of guns in an area a half mile square. The guns fired over our heads all night and kept blowing out the hurricane lamps.

Wilson, the brigade major of the 6th Brigade, working for a first-class brigade commander, is more cheerful:

We took Mao Sonsang 5 Brigade did a brilliant operation at next delaying position. We went through and met the Imphal garrison coming north.

We were clearing road blocks quicker than Japs thought we could. The Japs would blow the little culvert between two ridges, and sit on other side; they could be anything up to battalion strength. There were no bunkers, but foxholes and they fought hard. The technique was to fix them in the front and climb above them, and outflank them. It could take a day to three days to clear. Marram was the major battle in breakthrough. The Japs were getting short of men. Artillery support was very important. Sometimes the guns fired direct over open sights. The Jap artillery was very sparse. They were an army in disarray, but it didn't mean they didn't fight.

On 18 June Slim visited and I had an argument with him. He and Bill Smith, my new Brigade Commander, a highly professional Australian soldier were great chums. Slim said to me 'this is different to what happened to you in Malaya'.

I said 'Because in 1941/42, we had no air supply, no wireless, and had to hold the road to be supplied'.

Slim said 'we don't bother about the road now'.

I replied 'why are we in such a rush to open the road?'

He laughed and said 'you shouldn't argue with Army Commanders.'

He was in great humour, and knew perfectly well how important the road was. The point was that in Malaya once you'd lost the road you'd had it, whereas in Burma you could exist for quite a long time without it – although not indefinitely. Of course Slim realised this.

By 18 June the leading troops of 33rd Corps and 4th Corps were forty miles apart, with 2nd Division near Maram, and 5th Division approaching Kangpokpi. On 22 June the tanks of the 2nd Division met infantry of the 5th Division at Milestone 109. The way to Imphal was open, and a convoy of trucks waiting for this moment, surged down the road, the first supplies to reach Imphal by road since the end of March.

Slim had no intention of allowing his army to rest on its laurels after what he described as the first decisive victory of the Burma campaign. It was clear to both him and the Army Group Commander, Giffard, that the reconquest of Burma would have to be mounted from Assam. The landing craft and shipping for an amphibious assault on Rangoon, or anywhere else in the theatre, were not available, being entirely employed in the great landings in Normandy followed by those in the south of France. Slim's first priority was to finish the destruction of the Japanese army in Assam. By 7 July, General Kawabe ordered Mutaguchi to withdraw from the Imphal front. On the same day, Slim, having moved his tactical headquarters to Imphal, ordered 33rd Corps to take responsibility for operations down the Tamu Road, while 4th Corps advanced down the Tiddim Road.

Yamamoto's force was in a desperate state. His men were reduced to half a pint of gruel a day, mixed with grass and bean paste. He decided on a last attempt to infiltrate forces through to Palel, and attack the dumps and important fighter strip. Most groups were unsuccessful, but one attacked the fighter strip on the night of 3/4 July, destroying thirteen aircraft and numerous stocks. Slim commented, 'a very fine effort'.[7] On 13 July, Yamamoto was ordered to withdraw to the Kabaw Valley.

By 8 July, Ukhrul was captured, but it took until 14 July for a large force of Japanese holding out in a perimeter on the Ukhrul–Imphal road to be eliminated. The remnants of the *15th* and *31st Divisions* were now in headlong retreat towards the Chindwin, although rearguards still fought on.

On both the Tamu and Tiddim Roads, the *33rd Division* (the White Tigers, from their divisional sign), fought hard, nowhere more so than on the Tiddim Road: although they had been short of food, they were in nothing like the condition of the other two Japanese divisions who had taken part in the Kohima and Imphal battles. To begin with the advance led by the 17th Light Division had to clear a succession of Japanese strongpoints south of Bishenpur. The Japanese were dangerous even in defeat. For example, a company of 1st West Yorks was cut off in the village of Ningthoukhong Kha Khunou, and attacked by Japanese supported by two medium tanks. When the wounded company commander eventually broke out with twenty-six men, half of whom were wounded, he left behind two officers and twenty-three men dead. The village was eventually taken after one of the biggest artillery preparations in the whole campaign. Sixty-two dead Japanese were found in the ruins of the village. One dazed survivor lurched off ahead of the assaulting troops and was shot. The final battle of Imphal was the taking of Thinunggei, the last objective for the 17th Light Division. Following this they were withdrawn to India to refit and retrain, no longer as a light division, but as a mechanized formation ready for the recapture of Burma. The *33rd Division*, now soundly beaten by their old adversaries, was unquestionably in full retreat. The 5th Indian Division took over the follow-up.

The Japanese blew all bridges, and held up the advancing 5th Division at every possible place. Sometimes they would delay for twenty-four hours before pulling out, sometimes for longer. They never abandoned a position until it was outflanked. Although malaria was kept in check with mepacrine, over 500 men caught scrub typhus, for which there was no prophylactic. It took a month to clear the fifteen or so miles of road from the high ground at the end of the Tiddim spur to 'Vital Corner'. The road climbed the Tiddim spur up 'the Chocolate Staircase', thirty-seven hairpin bends cut in the dark earth, which the monsoon rain turned to the consistency of melted chocolate fudge. In the bitter fighting for this part of the road, Subedar Ram Sarup Singh of the 2nd/1st Punjab Regiment won a posthumous VC, the sixth to be awarded for the fighting on and around the Tiddim Road in the Imphal battle. On 12 November the 5th Indian Division marched into Kalemyo, having descended some 7,000 feet into the foothills guarding the Burmese plain.

Here they met the 11th East African Division (the Rhino Division, from their formation sign), at the end of their long trek down the Kabaw Valley from Tamu. Ahead lay the Chindwin and Central Burma. The Tiddim Road was now abandoned and allowed to revert to jungle, while the engineers built a road down the Kabaw Valley which had fewer curves and steep gradients.

The 11th East African Division had taken over from the 23rd Indian Division at Tamu, and carried out a two-pronged advance to Sittaung on the Chindwin (36 miles) and to Kalemyo via the Kabaw Valley (100 miles). The division consisted of three East African brigades of King's African Rifle (KAR) battalions from five British East African colonies, Uganda, Kenya, Northern Rhodesia (now Zambia), Nyasaland (now Malawi), and Tanganyika (now Tanzania). Many of the officers and soldiers were battle-hardened having fought in Abyssinia. The main thrust was down the Kabaw Valley, which had been the original and only 'main' route between Burma and India. Lieutenant Colonel Collen, the CO of 22nd KAR, recorded:

> The advance started at the very height of the monsoon. The tarmac road Palel–Tamu was almost completed but beyond Tamu there was no road in any direction – simply unbridged cart tracks. Rainfall was frequently five inches in a day.
>
> On 7 August I went forward with the GSO 1 [the general staff officer of the division] to watch the Argylls and Sikhs [sic] of 23 (Ind) Div, mopping up Tamu village. Tamu was one of the most dreadful sights I had ever seen, dead and dying Japs several deep in each house. These were the remnants of Yamamoto Force and the 15 and 31 Divisions, dying in thousands from beri-beri, dysentery, malaria and starvation after retreating from Kohima and Imphal. Finally it became essential to burn the whole village with flame-throwers.
>
> On 9 August, 26 EA Brigade started the main thrust from Tamu down the Kabaw [valley], encouragingly referred to by 23 (Ind) Div, who had been holding it for 14 months, as 'Death Valley' or the 'Green Hell of Asia'. The advance was initially led by a composite force called 'Petforce' under Major P G Molloy MC, until they reached Yedoc, 20 miles down the valley.
>
> The track was such that a jeep with a chain on each wheel, often took 12 hours to do 5 or 6 miles. The road was built every step of the way, by the infantry themselves, on the 'corduroy' system: placing

logs side by side, pegged with long stakes. Without the skill of the Askari [East African soldiers] with their pangas, it would have proved impossible. Every few yards we came upon either a skeleton or a hut with a dead body in it. Jap troops who could go no further, built a small hut of branches, and in it lay down to die.

Meanwhile the 25th East African Brigade followed up the retreating Japanese on the Sittaung track. The first real organized resistance was by a Japanese company on a small hill, later called Jambo Hill. On 18 August, 11th KAR attacked this position and overwhelmed the opposition. This early success was good for morale.

The first serious opposition on the Kalemyo Road in the Kabaw Valley was at Yazagyo, part of the Japanese defensive line after the 1942 British retreat. Collen's battalion carried out the attack:

> On 24 September, the battalion moved up with no transport as the road was impassable, carrying three day's rations, to a point one mile short of Yazagyo. The next day was spent in recce, and the attack launched on 26 September. It was a complete success as absolute surprise had been obtained. In this action the battalion had no support weapons bigger than our own 2-inch mortars, as the 3-inch mortar platoon had been formed by Brigade HQ into a mortar company, and was then twenty miles away on the wrong side of a flooded chaung. 22 KAR was fifteen miles ahead of the next battalion.

Just after this battle a war correspondent with the East Africans, encouraged by the battalion commanders with the division, wrote an article pointing out how badly off the African troops were for cigarettes, and other welfare items. Collen:

> Nothing was provided for the Askari, not the fault of East Africa, but because of faulty arrangements in back areas [in India]. 14th Army were notoriously bad in their efforts to do anything for African troops, who did not have the local support of Indian Divisions, or the vociferous clamour of British Divisions. After this there was a considerable improvement.

Operations by the 21st East African Brigade between the Kabaw Valley and the Chindwin resulted in some of the hardest fighting by troops of the Rhino Division. At Leik the 4th KAR lost nineteen dead and 102 wounded. This was followed by 2nd KAR attacking a feature known as Longstop Hill, during the course of which the battalion lost seven askari killed, and three Europeans and thirty-three askari wounded. Here Platoon Sergeant Major Silika Walani from Nyasaland was awarded the DCM. His citation reads:

PSM Silika engaged a dug-in Japanese light-machine gun at ten yards range with a Bren gun while his platoon attempted an outflanking movement, until his ammunition ran out and he withdrew. From a fresh approach he renewed the assault and silenced the light machine-gun with hand grenades. Heavy and concentrated fire came from several directions and PSM Silika decided more grenades were needed to resume the fight. With fresh supplies of grenades, he rallied his platoon, and showing the utmost determination and outstanding leadership, went forward with grenade and bayonet. At this stage showers of grenades and heavy enemy fire blasted several of the men off their feet, and wounded PSM Silika. Having collected his wounded and as time was getting late he was ordered to withdraw.

The toughest battle in the Kabaw Valley involved an attack by the 26th East African Brigade following an abortive operation by the 36th KAR at Kantha. The key part in the attack was played by 22nd KAR, as Collen later wrote to his wife:

The 26th and 27th October will live in my memory. For two whole days my dear battalion hammered at a Jap position of very great strength. By incredible guts and determination, first D Company on the 26th, then A Company on the morning of the 27th, and finally C Company about 1700 hours on the 27th fought their way to the top, only to be blasted off by MMGs, LMGs and grenades. I was so terribly proud of them, but it was just too agonising. I was only about 300 yards behind in my tactical HQ. I couldn't see them, it was so fearfully thick, smoke and dust from the shells. But I could hear them whooping and yelling 'Sokalai, sokolai, Yao – oo – oo', the Nyasa war cry. When we made the final count this morning, though pretty sickening, it wasn't as bad as I thought.

You will, I know be awfully sorry to hear that Hugh Mills was killed – most gallantly at the head of his platoon. And so much for my dear, brave, faithful askari who paid the supreme sacrifice – who I knew and loved so well.

22nd KAR lost one officer, one CSM, and eleven askari killed, and two officers and fifty-three askari wounded. Corporal Wisiki Bauleni was awarded the DCM. In spite of being wounded 100 yards after crossing the start line, he continued to lead his section. He was wounded twice more before reaching the objective. Despite weakness and loss of blood from three wounds, he refused evacuation and continued to direct the fire of his section on the Japanese counterattack. After this was beaten off, during the course of which Corporal Wisiki was wounded for a fourth time, he was finally evacuated unconscious. Collen, to his wife:

Hugh was buried between two of his men, Lance Corporal Jeffery and Private Ulanda. I have found out now what happened. Hugh was killed almost the moment they crossed the start line by a grenade fired by four Japs from a bunker. To avenge him, four of his men led by Ulana and Jeffrey crawled up to the bunker to throw their grenades through the aperture. Ulanda and Jeffrey were killed before they could get there, but Petro and William Chimowa got there safely, threw their grenades and killed all four Japs.

The 21st Brigade reached the Chindwin at Mawku on 1 November, and by 11 November had advanced to Mawlaik. On the way, the 5th KAR had carried out a spirited attack without any artillery support, and with Tommy gun, grenade, and panga cleared a series of enemy bunkers at Letzagan. From here the brigade advanced on both banks of the Chindwin.

The advance by the 26th Brigade down the Kabaw Valley encountered a succession of stubbornly defended positions, and months of toil on the road, followed by a month of intensive fighting in the enervating climate, sapped the energies of the soldiers. By this time the effect of the operations of the 5th Indian Division on the Tiddim Road began to react in favour of the Rhino Division. Japanese flushed out by the 5th Division began to bump the right flank of the East Africans. The 25th Brigade were brought up to capture Kalemyo and effect a junction with the 5th Division. Both the 25th and 26th Brigades were now supported by the divisional artillery.

22nd KAR had some hard fighting round Indaingyi, before the Rhino Division faced the last leg of the advance to Kalewa on the Chindwin. The road ran along the bottom of the Myttha Gorge, with steep cliffs on each side, where deep clefts offered many excellent defensive positions,

which the enemy used to advantage. After more hard fighting, 13th KAR
entered Kalewa at the head of the division on 2 December 1944. There
now remained the task of bridging the Chindwin. Collen's account:

> 34th KAR [of 25th Brigade] crossed on the night 3/4 December and
> on the 4th established a precarious bridgehead. The Japs had not
> disputed the crossing, but were holding three enormous features
> known as 'Tom', 'Dick' and 'Harry', which completely dominated
> the whole bridgehead. On 5 December, 22nd KAR reinforced 34th
> KAR. In spite of broad daylight and intermittent shell fire, we had
> no casualties and by that night had taken over and consolidated the
> whole of the right sector, astride the road. For two exciting days we
> were out of touch with Brigade or Division on the other bank. Owing
> to the unpleasantness of the crossing, visitors were nil, and Lt Col
> Trimmer of 34 KAR and I ran the war as we thought fit, disregarding
> occasional ridiculous orders from Div who had entirely lost their grip
> of the situation. On 9 December our patrols had established contact
> with patrols of 4 KAR, the leading battalion of 21 Brigade which had
> been steadily working down the east bank of the Chindwin for over
> a month. 11 Div's task of forming a bridgehead for 2nd British
> Division to pass through Ye-U and Mandalay was nearly done.

On 8 January 1945, the 11th East African Division was withdrawn to
Imphal after a splendid job done. Lieutenant Colonel Birkbeck, the CO
of 11th KAR, wrote:

> In spite of the terrific physical bashing we all had, morale was
> terrifically high, and we were all very pleased with ourselves. We had
> carried out a fighting advance all through the torrential rain of the
> monsoon and over almost impossible country. Everything we wore
> or ate had come down to us from the air, and we only had with us
> what we could carry on our backs and what would go into 12 jeeps
> and trailers which were our only transport. I dropped from my
> normal 15 stone to 10 and a half, but had never been fitter.

The Japanese soldiers paid for Mutaguchi's logistic gamble. Of some
85,000 who marched on Assam, half died in battle, and a further 20,000
of malaria, dysentery, and starvation on the retreat to the Chindwin.
Only around 100 prisoners were taken; the senior officer captured alive
was a captain. Few survivors would be fit to fight again. They suffered

far more than the British had in 1942. The tone in Japanese diaries reveals their stoicism and their suffering. A report on Japanese morale in the 17th Division narrative of operations comments on intelligence assessments mid-April/May 1944 as follows:

It would be false optimism to imagine that Japanese morale was appreciably lowered by their early reverses in this campaign [Imphal]. Some thought the presence of 16 PW significant after all the months that the Div had spent trying to capture a single Jap. It was not particularly significant because:

(a) 90% of these taken were wounded when captured

(b) 4100 were killed before 16 PW were taken.

The diary of a Jap NCO captured at NUNGSHIGUM was interesting for its insight into the hard conditions under which the invaders were living. It was comforting to know that even the Japs did not like being bombed, and had doubts as to whether the war would ever end. But the fact that these grumbles were committed to paper does not necessarily show a loss of morale. The British soldier loves to grumble, the difference being that he does not often write it down, because there is no restriction on him talking about it if he wants to and it relieves his feelings adequately.

Apr 1/2. Am always being scolded by the CO. He seems to think I'm dumb. He is quite unreasonable at times, also I think the men are getting browned off. If this keeps up the operations are bound to be a failure.

Apr 7. The enemy are bombing us *again*, what the hell are our planes doing?

Apr 9/10. The attack on the airfield by 10 Coy has been stopped and they have come back ... I wonder how important this present operation is, I can not readily understand how pressed we are. I wonder when the independence of India will come into effect. I cannot see how it can be done. At this rate the war will go on for ever. In the end the only results are loss of men by each side and there is no end to this bloody affair.

A diary was taken from a corpse on the Tamu Road; the dead man was the MO of *1/60 Regiment*.

3 Apr 44. We have crossed the Arakan and set foot on the soil of India. Already Lieut Goto, and 9 others have been killed. I am

sure they will become the guardian deities of our country. We out in the front line are too busy to pay our respects to the spirits of the departed, for we too, owe everything to the Emperor to carry out our duties to the utmost.

19 Apr 44. From the chilling of the stomach and the cold nights in camp arise many cases of diarrhoea and dysentery, and there are many cases of beri-beri. Still the willpower of the Japanese soldier is high, and he can withstand this with ease.

25 Apr. 5,000 feet up in the mountains there is no water. We cannot fight without water. Days pass when you only get rice and salt to eat. Sweat soaks through your underwear, and the stench of your body is appalling.

6 May. Bombing by a large enemy formation is mortifying.

18 May. Am I the only MO left? More than ever then I must try to do my utmost.

23 May. God I hope it doesn't rain tonight. I'll never forget this life of slopping around in the slime of filthy streams and drinking foul waters. Well I've got amoebic dysentery now. My wound is discharging pus, but if I weaken and fail what is going to happen? Am I not the only MO left now? Come on now, I must put all my efforts into it.

As the Japanese waited to cross the Chindwin the RAF machine-gunned and bombed them. No sooner had the aircraft pulled away than the vultures piled in to feast on the heaps of corpses. Utterly crushed, and reduced to a rabble, it was the greatest disaster the Japanese army had ever experienced. On 8 December 1941 Winston Churchill had recorded his feelings on learning that America was now an ally following the Japanese bombing of Pearl Harbor: 'As for the Japanese, they would be ground to powder'.[8] He was now being proved right.

7

The Second Chindit Expedition

> Our task is fulfilled. We have inflicted a complete surprise upon
> the enemy. All our Columns are inside the enemy's guts... Let
> us thank God for the great success.
>
> Major General Orde Wingate

Wingate sent this signal to his men while one of his brigades was
marching in to Burma, and at the culmination of the fly-in of around
9,000 men, 1,350 mules, 250 tons of stores, a light anti-aircraft battery,
and a 25pdr battery into the heart of Japanese-held north Burma. It had
taken seven nights and 650 transport aircraft and glider sorties. Wingate
had reason to be proud of his achievement. There were moments in the
preceding months when it seemed that his dream of long-range penetration on a hitherto unprecedented scale would never see the light of day.
Not everyone was fired up. The war diary of the 2nd Battalion The Royal
Leicestershire Regiment, part of Wingate's Special Force, whose CO had
not fallen under Wingate's spell, recorded: 'Long message from Force,
impossible to decipher, but something in it about guts and God'.

While the fighting in the Arakan and Assam was at its height, the
largest behind the lines operation the British mounted in the Second
World War was in progress. The operation, codename THURSDAY, was
born as a result of the conference in Quebec in August 1943, attended
by President Roosevelt, Winston Churchill, and the Anglo-American
Combined Chiefs of Staff. Wingate had been summoned home personally by Churchill, and taken across the Atlantic to attend. The Prime
Minister had been persuaded by Wingate's report on his first expedition
that he was the man to transform the gloomy situation in Burma, where,
in mid-1943, nothing seemed to be going right.

Wingate's eloquence at the Quebec conference convinced the Combined Chiefs of Staff that a large long-range penetration operation could

play a crucial part in the war in Burma. Although, as discussed in Chapter 3, the Americans had not the slightest interest in the reconquest of Burma in order to restore it to British rule, it will be remembered that they were convinced that if they supplied and supported the Chinese Nationalist leader Chiang Kai-shek, he would play a major part in the defeat of the Japanese. Their hopes were never fulfilled, but in mid-1943, Chiang Kai-shek's real aim – defeating the Chinese Communists once the Japanese had lost the war – had yet to be revealed. Eventually, after many changes of plan, Wingate's role was refined to assisting the American Lieutenant General Stilwell in his mission of advancing south from Ledo, to take Myitkyina, and connecting Ledo with the old Burma Road into China. Wingate's LRP force was tasked with cutting the line of communication of the Japanese opposing Stilwell. He was given two other subsidiary assignments: creating a favourable situation for the Chinese army in Yunnan (not under Stilwell) to advance across the Salween, and inflicting maximum damage on the Japanese in north Burma. Privately, Wingate nurtured a scheme to reconquer Burma south to a line roughly corresponding with the 24th parallel of latitude, including Indaw.

For his Force, Wingate was given his old 77th Indian Infantry Brigade, and the 111th Indian Infantry Brigade, which had been training for the LRP role under Brigadier W. D. A. 'Joe' Lentaigne, who was not a Wingate fan. Most controversially, he was also given the very experienced 70th British Division, which was broken up to form columns and LRP brigades. Finally he was allocated the 3rd Brigade of the 81st West African Division. As a deception his Special Force was named the 3rd Indian Infantry Division. In effect Special Force was a small corps of two understrength infantry divisions, commanded by a man who had never commanded a battalion in battle, let alone a brigade. Special Force looked like this:

3rd West African Brigade
(Brigadier A. H. Gillmore, succeeded by *Brigadier*
'*Abdy*' *Ricketts)*   (Column 10)
6th Battalion Nigeria Regiment   (Columns 39 & 66)
7th Battalion Nigeria Regiment   (Columns 29 & 35)
12th Battalion Nigeria Regiment   (Columns 12 & 43)

14th British Infantry Brigade (ex 70th Division)
(Brigadier Thomas Brodie)   (Column 59)

54th Field Company Royal Engineers	(Support)
1st Battalion The Bedfordshire & Hertfordshire Regiment	(Columns 16 & 61)
7th Battalion The Royal Leicestershire Regiment	(Columns 47 & 74)
2nd Battalion The Black Watch	(Columns 42 & 73)
2nd Battalion The York and Lancaster Regiment	(Columns 65 & 84)

16th British Infantry Brigade (ex 70th Division)

(*Brigadier Bernard Fergusson*)	(Column 99)
51/69 Field Regiments Royal Artillery (as infantry)	(Columns 51 & 69)
2nd Field Company Royal Engineers	(Support)
2nd Battalion The Queen's Royal Regiment	(Columns 21 & 22)
2nd Battalion The Royal Leicestershire Regiment	(Columns 17 & 71)
45th Reconnaissance Regiment (as infantry)	(Columns 45 & 54)

23rd British Infantry Brigade (ex 70th Division)

(*Brigadier Lance Perowne*)	(Column 32)
60th Field Regiment Royal Artillery (as infantry)	(Columns 60 & 68)
12th Field Company Royal Engineers	(Support)
2nd Battalion The Duke of Wellington's Regiment	(Columns 33 & 76)
4th Battalion The Border Regiment	(Columns 34 & 55)
1st Battalion The Essex Regiment	(Columns 44 & 56)

77th Indian Infantry Brigade

(*Brigadier Michael Calvert*)	(Column 25)
Mixed Field Company Royal Engineers/Royal Indian Engineers	
1st Battalion The King's Regiment (Liverpool)	(Columns 81 & 82)
1st Battalion Lancashire Fusiliers	(Columns 20 & 50)
1st Battalion The South Staffordshire Regiment	(Columns 38 & 80)
3rd Battalion 6th Gurkha Rifles	(Columns 36 & 63)
3rd Battalion 9th Gurkha Rifles	(Columns 57 & 93)
	(to 111 Bde later)
142 Company Hong Kong Volunteers	(Support)

111th Indian Infantry Brigade

(*Brigadier 'Joe' Lentaigne* succeeded by *Major 'Jack' Masters* and *Brigadier 'Jumbo' Morris*)	(Column 48)
Mixed Field Company Royal Engineers/Royal Indian Engineers	
2nd Battalion The King's Own Royal Regiment	(Columns 41 & 46)
1st Battalion The Cameronians	(Columns 26 & 90)
3rd Battalion 4th Gurkha Rifles	(Columns 30 & 40)
4th Battalion 9th Gurkha Rifles (MORRISFORCE)	(Columns 49 & 94)

Other units included:

BLADET (Commando Engineers) (*Major Blain*)

DAHFORCE (Kachin Levies) (*Lieutenant Colonel Herring*)

2nd Battalion Burma Rifles

Four troops 160th Field Regiment Royal Artillery (in gunner role)

Four troops 69th Light Anti-Aircraft Regiment Royal Artillery
    (in gunner role)

Logistic Units

Despite the lessons of the first expedition, the unwieldy column organization was retained for the second, although some battalion commanders made their own changes to it, as best they could. Columns were formed by splitting battalions in half. The CO commanded one column and a senior major the other. A typical column organization is shown in Appendix B. The numbering of some columns followed the old battalion numbering system (for example the Black Watch was formed in 1881 from the 42nd and 73rd of Foot), others were combinations or permutations of regimental numbers (the Bedfordshires were the old 16th Foot, the King's Liverpool the 8th), or from the number in the Army List of the original column commander's regiment (columns did not change number when other officers took over when the original commander was killed, wounded, or went sick). Each brigade headquarters made up one column.

Although Special Force consisted of Gurkhas, West Africans, and Burma Rifles, it was predominantly a British formation, and exceptional for the Burma campaign both in that respect and, remarkably, in not including any Indian units. This was a reflection of one of many Wingate misconceptions, in this case that Indian troops were second-rate, which was rooted in his irrational dislike for Indian Army officers, both British and Indian. His prejudice did not extend to Gurkhas, partly because they had no caste requirements where food was concerned. Despite this, for the 3rd/2nd Goorkhas, his first expedition had not been a happy experience, largely because his 'Old Testament' leadership style did not work with them, as any British officer of Gurkhas could have told him had he bothered to ask.[1] Most British officers of Gurkhas loathed Wingate, not least for their perception that he considered everybody under his command was his to dispose of as he wished, and was expendable into the bargain. The chapter in the regimental history of the

2nd Goorkha Rifles relating to the experiences of the 3rd Battalion in Wingate's first expedition is larded with phrases such as:

> [Wingate] declared that unless trained in this fashion his force would not be able to fight in this fashion. The onus for proper preparation therefore rested squarely on the Chindit commander's shoulders . . .[2]

and later in the same regimental history:

> From the standpoint of the Gurkha Brigade the training was faulty. Here the onus must be borne by the Chindit commander. He was well aware that his forces would be subjected to particularly hazardous employment in which the psychological factor might dictate success or failure. The Gurkhas should have been taught not only what they had to do, but why they were doing it . . . The failure to appreciate general principles [on Wingate's part] was accompanied by a similar failure to instil the fundamentals of jungle warfare . . . It was beyond the province of British officers of the Third Battalion to re-adjust training policy.[3]

Despite this failure by Wingate to play to the Gurkhas' strengths, Calvert was to write later, referring to the 3rd/2nd Goorkhas: 'they outfought and outmarched troops who were first class and tenacious enemies'. Opinions of Wingate before his second expedition, as on his first, varied. Major Carfrae of the 7th Nigeria Regiment in the 3rd West African Brigade remembered the disappointment engendered by a shambolic figure arriving to inspect the battalion, eyes cast down, and mumbling:

> Then alert at last and looking straight into our faces, Wingate began to talk. He talked quickly and passionately, words tumbling from his mouth in short staccato phrases, his mind so teeming with ideas and images that his thoughts seemed almost visibly to leap ahead of his speech. The fixed determination, the power of personality that radiated from, and transformed this wolfish and unmilitary-looking man are impossible to describe. I can only say that when he stopped speaking there was not one among us who had any doubts as to what was expected of him, not one who had a question to ask, not one but would follow wherever Wingate might lead. We never saw him again.

The majority of Chindits would agree with this assessment, but a minority would adhere to the contrary view, such as that expressed by Lieutenant Colonel Rose of the Black Watch, and commander of Number 42 Column, when he described Wingate's qualities as 'lack of common humanity, ruthlessness, and a determination to have his own way at any cost'. The last two are the prerequisite for any successful commander: it is the first that many believe made Wingate such an unattractive person; that, and his tactical and strategic myopia, failed to impress some intelligent, open-minded, thinking soldiers, such as Major 'Jack' Masters, who later commanded 111th Brigade.

For a while Wingate also had command of a 3,000 strong American infantry regiment (about a brigade in size). Officially designated the 5307th Provisional Unit, it was more romantically known as 'Merrill's Marauders', after its commander Brigadier General Frank D. Merrill, a Stilwell disciple. Merrill's men were clawed back by Stilwell well before Wingate's Force moved into battle, and Wingate raged at the American officer bearing the order, 'You can tell General Stilwell he can stick his Americans up his arse'.

Wingate came back from Quebec with a priceless asset. The Chief of Staff of the US Army Air Forces (USAAF), General Arnold, had been so horrified by Wingate's accounts of leaving wounded and sick behind during his first expedition that he immediately agreed to provide light aircraft for casualty evacuation. He went further, exceeding Wingate's wildest dreams by sending Colonel Cochran's Number 1 Air Commando to India tasked with supporting Special Force for ninety days. For major troop lifts, resupply tasks, and close air support, the RAF and USAAF Troop Carrier Command would be needed too, but Chindit morale soared when they heard that Wingate had secured a private air force. Best of all was the realization that wounded and sick would no longer be left to the mercy of the Burmese villagers and the Japanese. Number 1 Air Commando consisted of thirteen C-47 Dakotas, twelve C-46 Commando transports, twelve B-25 Mitchell medium bombers, thirty P-51 Mustang fighter-bombers, 225 WACO gliders, 100 L-1 and L-5 light aircraft, and six helicopters.[4]

Originally Wingate intended that his columns would march in to Burma as they had on his first expedition. Once inserted, each brigade was to choose a stronghold as a base of operations that would be inaccessible to wheeled vehicles, but including, or at least dominating, an airstrip and a dropping zone (DZ) for supply by parachute. The enemy was to be induced to attack the stronghold, and while doing so, would be attacked in his turn by 'floater columns' operating outside. Wingate wrote in a Training Memorandum dated 20 February 1944, 'The stronghold is a machan overlooking a kid tied up to entice the Japanese tiger.' This was not a particularly good metaphor. The aim of luring a tiger by live bait to the area of a machan (a hide in a tree) is to enable *the hunter sitting in the machan* to shoot the beast; not for it to be engaged by a band of roving riflemen on the ground. Floater columns were not a Wingate creation, but had been devised by Scoones commanding 4th Corps; when Wingate first raised the stronghold concept with Slim, he sent him to talk to Scoones.

On the whole the training before the second expedition was an improvement on the first, as was the quality of the soldiers, many of them battle-experienced. Columns were still dependent on mules to carry the heavy loads: no less than ten mules in each column were fully committed to carrying the heavy valve wirelesses then in service. Readers accustomed to palm-size mobile telephones and military radios not much larger should bear in mind that each number 22 wireless for communication within the column, and, most important, with its own reconnaissance platoon, required three mules to carry the set, the batteries, and charging motor. The radios were vital for requesting air drops and for communicating with brigade HQ, other columns, and within columns. Transmissions over longer distances were by Morse key, laborious and time-consuming. Most messages had to be enciphered. The West African brigade had one advantage which speeded up transmissions: the ability to pass messages in Hausa, the lingua franca of West Africa in those days, which the Japanese were unable to comprehend.

Learning from his first expedition, Wingate also insisted on comprehensive river-crossing training. Lieutenant Dell, then a platoon commander in 21 Column, remembers: 'We did our watermanship training on a large lake. Two thirds of our other ranks could not swim – we taught them all'. Lieutenant Colonel Peter Vaughan, who commanded the 7th Nigerian Battalion and Number 35 Column, wrote:

> For crossing minor rivers the drill was that all troops who could swim did so. Their rifles and packs were made up into section rafts from the mens' groundsheets stretched and tied with jungle twine

round a simple bamboo framework. These were pushed ahead of strong swimmers, while the weak and non-swimmers held on and were thus ferried across.

Getting the mules across was much more of a problem. Every mule *can* swim, and swim strongly. But the difficulty is to induce the reluctant mule not only to enter the water, but, once in, to swim to the opposite bank, and not, as the obstinate ones always tried to do in a circle back to the near bank. We soon discovered which were the reliable mules, and these were always shoved into the river first, usually crossing without trouble, their muleteers hanging on to the headrope and letting their charge drag them across.

Having seen their mates cross safely, most of the remaining mules, after a little physical persuasion to actually get them in the water, would follow suit. The really obstinate ones – and my God they could be obstinate – were coerced into crossing by such tricks as allowing them to watch their pals enjoying a good feed on the far bank, or by thrashing them with bamboo rods, which were always conveniently handy, until they got the idea.

For crossing a really broad river, such as the Irrawaddy, special river crossing equipment could be dropped to columns on demand. This consisted of inflatable rubber dinghies driven by outboard motors, and additional rafts to be towed behind. Mules were attached to the dinghies by nooses round their necks, allowing the mules to swim, but being towed in the right direction.

There was still room for improvement in the training, largely because Wingate had no experience of infantry fighting. Lieutenant Taylor, a platoon commander in the 45th Reconnaissance Regiment in the 16th Brigade, was of the opinion that 'we did too much marching during training and were already tired before we even started the operation. We did not concentrate on preparing for action and our operational role'. In the case of the 45th Reconnaissance Regiment this deficiency was especially acute because before it joined the Chindits it had been a mechanized unit equipped with tracked vehicles and trained in reconnaissance duties for an armoured formation. Now it was required to operate on foot, and radically alter its tactics and outlook on soldiering accordingly.

The Force was issued with the American K Ration, and many accounts echo Vaughan's description, 'The nauseating monotony of our daily food is the most unpleasant memory which I retain of the entire campaign'. It lacked sufficient calories, and was no more nutritious than the ration issued on the first expedition, so sickness caused by under-nourishment and the near starvation of heavily laden men, required to march long distances for months, was commonplace in the second.

Chindit soldiers of all ranks carried heavy loads. In addition to normal battle order, grenades, ammunition, weapon, and water bottle, each man carried a large pack weighing about 40lb. These were standard issue 1937-pattern web equipment packs modified by having two extra pockets sewn on each side. They lacked all the features that present-day soldiers, or hikers, regard as normal: padded straps, waist-belt, internal frame, quick-release buckles, compression straps, chest straps, adjust-ment and bungee straps, waterproof lining, and draw-string closure. At Appendix C is a typical Chindit load.

In mid-January, Brigadier Lentaigne reported to Wingate that the Japanese had closed up to the Chindwin in strength, and were keeping close watch on all crossing places south of Homalin. Although neither Lentaigne nor Wingate knew it, this was in preparation for Mutaguchi's offensive into Assam, and nothing to do with the Japanese suspecting a repeat performance by Wingate. However, this caused Wingate to fly in his Force, except for Fergusson's 16th Brigade, which would be trucked to the roadhead on the Ledo Road at Tagap Ga, and march to cross the Chindwin just up-river from Singaling Hkamti, well over a hundred miles north of Homalin.

Wingate chose three main objectives: Indaw (in some accounts given as 'Rail' Indaw to distinguish it from 'Oil' Indaw just east of the Chindwin), the railway from Mandalay to Myitkyina, and the road from Bhamo to Myitkyina. The fly-in brigades would be taken by glider and Dakota into four landing zones (LZs) named Piccadilly, Chow-ringhee, and Broadway (after three famous streets in London, Calcutta, and New York), and Templecombe, a Somerset village. Early glider loads would carry light bulldozers and sappers to construct airstrips for the Dakotas. The LZs were some distance from brigade objectives, and Wingate was thus disobeying the cardinal rule of airborne operations: land right on or close by your objective to make the most of surprise and shock. Instead, he relied on brigades approaching their objectives under the cover of the thickly wooded and rough terrain. His plan was as follows:

Fergusson's 16th Brigade, march from the Ledo road, starting in February, and secure the two airfields at Indaw. On the way he was to destroy the Japanese garrison at Lonkin, on the right flank of Stilwell's route south.

Calvert's 77th Brigade, land by glider and Dakota at Broadway and Piccadilly, and having marched to the railway, set up a block.

Lentaigne's 111th Brigade, land by glider and Dakota at Piccadilly, and head for the area south of Indaw, and by road blocks and demolitions, to protect the southern approaches of 16th Brigade's operations there. Bladet was to operate in the same area and demolish certain railway bridges.

Morris's 4/9th Gurkha Rifles (Morrisforce), land by glider at Chowringhee, march to the mountains east of the Bhamo–Myitkyina Road and carry out raids on the road.

Herring's Dahforce, land by glider at Templecombe, raise guerrilla bands from the Kachins, and support Morrisforce.[5]

The remaining three brigades, 14th, 23rd, and 3rd West African, were kept for a second wave, which at the time was planned as a relief for the first wave above, in about two or three months; the rationale being that ninety days was the maximum that Chindits could spend behind the lines without relief. Some soldiers were promised that they would be flown out after ninety days, which was unfortunate, because in many cases they were in for much longer. In the event, the back-up brigades were flown in much earlier than planned.

*

On 8 February 1944, the 16th Brigade set off from Tagap Ga to march to the Chindwin across some of the roughest terrain in the world. After an alarming journey in American trucks with Chinese drivers, each column spent the night in the forest. Captain Dell was now administrative officer of 21 Column, who led the brigade:

Next day in pouring rain the march started. It took us a whole day to get the column up the first mountainside, it was as steep as the roof of a house. The sappers had cut steps in zig-zags, but they crumbled before half the column had passed. In places the slope was so steep that the mules had to be unloaded and their loads passed up hand-to-hand. It rained all the time. At least we in the leading column got to the top by nightfall. We bedded down on the saturated ground. It was very cold, and we slept in pairs to try to keep warm.

We had been issued with super light-weight blankets, which became so saturated, the next morning they were all abandoned because they were so heavy.*

Despite the rain, and saturated ground, we were short of water. We could hear the streams thousands of feet below. I had to indent for an air drop of water in order to have enough for the mules.

It took nine days to cover the first thirty-five miles over hills sheeted with mud, humid by day, and bitter cold at night. Captain White was the second-in-command of Number 54 Column, part of the Reconnaissance Regiment:

A typical day consisted of getting up in the dark at 0530, saddling the mules, and moving off just before first light. After thirty minutes we halted to tighten the girths. Mules did not like tight loads and blew themselves out, passing wind for the first part of the march – I can still smell it.

At this halt we had breakfast, before walking for four hours. At midday we stopped for lunch, and sent radio messages, because this was the best time for wireless conditions, which were always bad to impossible after dark. After lunch we marched until it was dark. So a day consisted of ten hours marching.

Every fifth day we stopped for a supply drop, and the parachutes often got caught in the trees. I had been a Physical Training Instructor pre-war, and once when one of the parachutes got hooked up in an especially tall tree, I thought I knew best and swarmed up, to cut the rope to the load. It fell on me, smashing me to the ground. I broke my left arm. A couple of days later a light aircraft was called in to evacuate a casualty and my CO told me I was to go. I refused. My arm was in plaster. I couldn't have faced my comrades had I gone.

By 5 March Fergusson's already weary men reached and crossed the Chindwin. They still had a very long way to go to reach their objective; 150 miles as the crow flies, but actually double that toiling up and down the steep mountains, and along winding ridges.

---

* Yet another example of poor discipline, and inadequate training and preparation for the conditions that would actually be encountered.

That same day, the move of the fly-in brigades was begun in an atmosphere of high drama, largely because of three decisions by Wingate that actually increased the risks faced by his men. First, he would not use parachute troops to seize, secure, and mark the LZs before the arrival of the gliders. In a typically sweeping statement, based on no experience whatever of airborne operations, he declared that parachute troops were outmoded – this was in early 1944, before the three greatest airborne operations in history (Normandy, Arnhem, and the Rhine Crossing).

Second, he banned all air reconnaissance after 12 February, despite the ability of the RAF to fly high-level air-photographic missions which would not betray to the enemy which areas were of interest. He was therefore inviting Cochran's leading glider pilots to fly at night into unmarked, insecure LZs.

Fortunately Cochran courageously chose to ignore the edict banning reconnaissance, and without telling Wingate, despatched an aircraft to take photographs of Piccadilly and Broadway. When photographs of Piccadilly revealing the area blocked with logs was shown to Wingate at Hailakandi airfield, where Calvert and his men were waiting to emplane, he lost his head, panicked, and refused to go ahead. Eventually, Slim, who was also present, calmed him down, and, having first ascertained that Calvert was willing to fly his complete brigade into Broadway, ordered him to proceed. Wingate turned to Slim and said, 'The responsibility is yours'.[6] Scott had evacuated sick and wounded from Piccadilly during the first Wingate expedition, so it was not unreasonable to assume that the Japanese had blocked the LZ. In fact the logs had been laid out to dry by foresters, although Wingate was not to know that at the time. To this day, Wingate supporters claim that it was he who persuaded Slim to allow him to go ahead, not the other way round. Those who knew both men believe Slim's account. Wingate wrote a report two weeks after this incident, in which he claims credit for the decision and also, by inference, for the last-minute air reconnaissance mission. In a letter to Mountbatten he makes the same claims, although by then it was known that the Japanese were not responsible for blocking Piccadilly.

Wingate's third decision was to allow each Dakota to tow two gliders. This was the subject of heated discussion up to the very time of take-off: involving Cochran, who supported the idea, Brigadier General Old, the commander of Troop Carrier Command USAAF, who did not, and a number of other airmen, both RAF and USAAF, who favoured one side or the other. The ultimate responsibility for sanctioning the scheme was Wingate's as the commander of the troops being transported into battle.

The leading four Dakotas, each towing two gliders, took off at 6.12 p.m., followed fifteen minutes later by more Dakotas towing gliders with Calvert's advance HQ of the 77th Brigade. Although there had been trials of one tug aircraft towing two gliders, there had not been sufficient time to rehearse all Dakota pilots. Many had never tried in daylight, let alone at night. Many gliders were overloaded, as troops took equipment not listed on the manifest. To clear the high ground astride the Chindwin on the route from the two departure airfields of Hailakandi and Lalaghat, the aircraft had to climb to 10,000 feet, straining and overheating engines, and developing faults, so that some pilots realizing, they would never make it, cast off their tows. In the nick of time, lights were laid out just before the arrival of the main body of the brigade. Deep ruts in the long grass caused many crashes, and the mayhem was increased by gliders running into the ensuing wreckage after landing. Of the first wave of fifty-two gliders, thirty-four landed at Broadway, killing two men and wounding thirty-four. Of the remainder, four broke loose soon after take-off, and four were returned to base. Eight gliders landed in enemy territory; from these some men marched in to Broadway, some back over the Chindwin, and some were taken prisoner; the loads in two were never traced. Two gliders were prematurely released near Broadway, crashing half a mile from the LZ and killing all but two of the troops. Of the second wave of nine gliders, eight were recalled, and one containing a bulldozer landed across the LZ, but the two crew got out unhurt.

At dawn on 6 March, some 400 troops were at Broadway. But Calvert sent a signal delaying the fly-in of the rest of his brigade until the strip could be improved. By last light, the strip was ready to receive Dakotas, and at 8 p.m. the leading aircraft, piloted by Brigadier General Old, touched down on Broadway.

That night the fly-in of the 111th Brigade began. This brigade was destined for Piccadilly, but rather than switch the whole formation to Broadway, which was becoming congested, Wingate ordered them to go to Chowringhee. Unfortunately this LZ was on the other side of the Irrawaddy from the brigade's objective. By first light on 8 March, 111th Brigade HQ, the 4th/9th Gurkhas (Morrisforce), and the 3rd/4th

Gurkhas had arrived at Chowringhee. Wingate, visiting on 9 March, changed the plan, and ordered the rest of the 111th Brigade (1st Cameronians and 2nd King's Own) to fly into Broadway. Wingate's decision was probably correct because the Japanese had overflown Chowringhee, and they had an airfield only fifteen miles away. Dahforce was also ordered to Broadway, because conditions at Templecombe were too uncertain. The outcome of this order–counterorder was that Dahforce, Brigade HQ of 111th Brigade, and the 3rd/4th Gurkhas had to cross the Irrawaddy before reaching their operational areas. The additional distance that the Cameronians and the King's Own now had to cover, thanks to the change of plan, meant that they were too late to attack Japanese marching north to attack Fergusson moving on Indaw. 111th Brigade's crossing of the Irrawaddy was so badly held up by the reluctance of the mules to swim the mile-wide river that after two days, with reports of Japanese approaching in strength, Lentaigne stopped it. Number 40 Column with most of the mules and support weapons, still on the far bank, were told to march east to join Morris, while Number 30 Column and Brigade HQ set off westwards to join the Cameronians and King's Own.

Meanwhile Calvert was marching to set up his block near Mawlu in the railway valley, along which were transported the supplies to the Japanese division facing Stilwell. It is important to understand that Calvert was about to establish a block not a stronghold, because by Wingate's definition the latter should be sited in a place where access by the enemy in road or rail transport was difficult, preferably impossible. Nowhere in the railway valley fulfilled that requirement.

With Calvert were the 1st South Staffs and the 3rd/6th Gurkhas. The two columns of the 1st Lancashire Fusiliers had independent tasks to be carried out en route, on completion of which they would become the 'floaters' for the Mawlu block. He left the 3rd/9th Gurkhas to garrison Broadway, with the 1st King's (Liverpool) as 'floaters'. From the Special Force Battery, a composite sub-unit of field and anti-aircraft gunners, a troop of four field guns, 25pdrs, and a troop of six 40mm Bofors anti-aircraft guns were flown in. The Japanese air force attacked Broadway on no less than six occasions, with mixed-sized raids of up to forty-nine aircraft each. The Bofors did good work, destroying several. As well as ground attacks, the enemy also tried infiltrating, and, recorded the battery captain of the Special Force Battery, on one occasion posing as Gurkhas marched in good order inside the perimeter. The ruse was successful only for a moment. A short, fierce struggle took place and the invaders were all killed. In the battle which preceded and followed this incident, all gunners, both field and anti-aircraft, used their small arms with good effect. One related afterwards how he had carried out a friendly conversation with a 'Gurkha' who stood on his gun-pit wall. The deception was discovered by a true Gurkha who shot the impostor dead, but the incident left the gunner a little surprised at the rapidity with which the 'Johnny' had disappeared.*

Calvert was unquestionably the finest of Wingate's brigadiers. Despite his pugilistic appearance (he was an Olympic-class swimmer and University and army boxing champion), he had a first-class brain, and in modern parlance was a 'lateral thinker'. Major Carfrae describes him:

When he made mistakes he never tried to excuse them; when he was successful – and he was nearly always successful – he never strove to take the credit for himself. His personality was dominant and colourful; above all else he was enriched by a gift for leadership. Calvert was also a dreamer, his manner could be rambling and vague. In the middle of giving operational orders to his column commanders, he would sometimes begin to talk about birds, or life at Cambridge, or some other irrelevant topic; and this could be quite disconcerting. Like all of us he had his idiosyncrasies and would become moody, irritable and garrulous by turns; but in the darkest hour his courage never dwindled and proud men followed him without a word. I have met no soldier more admired by those he led, nor under whose banner I would rather serve; and although war's atmosphere is emotional, breeding unreasoning loves and hates, I do not think Calvert's qualities were over-estimated. To us he was a hero without peer, and praise from him was music.

Calvert was not afraid to challenge Wingate's concepts, and in his turn was one of the handful of people to whom Wingate would give a moment's attention. Already Calvert was becoming convinced that the column organization was unsuitable for the tasks being demanded of

---

* 'Johnny' Gurkha was the British troops' affectionate nickname for Gurkhas.

the Chindits, and was soon to change it. On arriving at the village of Henu, just north of Mawlu, he had a stiff battle to turn out the Japanese, during the course of which he personally led charges with rifle and bayonet and a satchel full of grenades. After fierce hand-to-hand fighting, and Japanese counterattacks which alone cost the South Staffords fifty-nine casualties, Lieutenant George Cairns of the South Staffs was subsequently awarded a posthumous Victoria Cross.

Here the block was established, soon to be nicknamed 'the White City' because of the festoons of parachutes from supply drops. The soldiers roofed their dugouts with sleepers torn from the railway line. A strip was constructed, sandbags and barbed wire were dropped, engineer plant flown in, and a formidable block was soon constructed, complete with four 25pdr guns, six light anti-aircraft guns, and four anti-tank guns. Again the gunners played a key part in the defence of the block. The first morning after their arrival the guns were in action. The following morning

the field guns fired smoke at the enemy guns to indicate them to the planes which gave direct air support. As the planes flew over the target, half a dozen enemy anti-aircraft guns opened up. During the day, the ground attack developed steadily and both field and anti-aircraft gunners had their hands full. The latter, until they had completed defensive positions within their gun pits, deployed each night to infantry positions and fought as infantry. They acquitted themselves well in this role; and one of them performed an act of outstanding devotion by standing on a grenade which had rolled back into the weapon pit whence it had been thrown, until it exploded. Fortunately, he escaped with nothing more than a numbed leg.

Besides assisting with beating off enemy attacks, the field guns fired in support of operations outside the White City, whenever targets were within range. On seven days, Japanese air raids took place. Captain Brown: 'A total of 1073 Bofors rounds were fired with five enemy aircraft destroyed, and eight damaged.'

By now Fergusson's 16th Brigade had completed its slog south. At one stage Wingate ordered Fergusson to make for Henu to assist Calvert, but changed his mind when it became clear that no help was required in that direction. Wingate's obsession at this juncture was seizing Indaw and its two airfields, Indaw West and Indaw East. He hoped by taking these to force Mountbatten, and through him Slim, to fly a whole division into Indaw. He told Fergusson that he was to establish a block at Aberdeen some fifteen miles north-west of Indaw, into which he would fly the 14th Brigade, and from where the attack on Indaw was to be mounted. At that stage the 14th Brigade was not at Wingate's disposal; he had asked for it to be released to him, but Slim had refused. Wingate had lied to Fergusson, not for the first time. When Slim did allow the 14th Brigade to fly into Burma, Wingate sent it to Alezu, fifty miles south of Indaw, but without telling Fergusson, who had set off for Indaw under the firm impression that the 14th Brigade was available to support him.

Wingate's command and control of a formation battle, the first and only of his career, was not a success. Fergusson's brigade was exhausted by its long march, and ten days behind schedule. The 111th Brigade was badly delayed by its last-minute change of LZ, and was not in a position to attack the Japanese to the south of Indaw in time to assist the 16th Brigade. To press on with the plan under these circumstances was foolhardy. Giving the task of capturing what he clearly regarded as his operational ace card to a brigade that had to march 400 miles to get there also calls into question his tactical acumen. Indeed one might ask why he marched in one of his brigades at all, when by using gliders and Dakotas he had the means to land close by and seize Indaw by coup de main. But his obsession with guerrilla warfare, and conviction that this was the way to defeat the Japanese, clouded his judgement, a point to which we will return.

At Indaw, Fergusson was also commanding his first and only brigade battle. Through no fault of his, the attack was too late; by then the Japanese had a strong brigade there. His most serious error was failing to carry out any reconnaissance. He had the whole of the 45th Reconnaissance Regiment in his brigade, but did not use it properly. For example, during the approach, the reconnaissance troop of one of Number 45 Column (one of the Reconnaissance Regiment columns) was detailed off to guard the mule harbour at the rear. The result of this oversight was that not only was he unable to fix the enemy positions properly, but he was unaware that there was a complete lack of water on the route to Indaw from the north. His force needed some 3,000 gallons a day for men and mules. Dell of Number 21 Column:

On our approach march we finished up on a ridge, where there was no water to be found. We scratched around in a dry stream bed, and I got about half a cup full. There was none for the mules.

Fergusson approached on four axes: nothing wrong with that, but he did not attack concentrated. The attack failed, although the 2nd Royal Leicesters, a superb regular battalion, nearly took Indaw East. Their CO, despite being wounded, refused to be evacuated, and fought a model battle. He had modified the column organization, and fought as a battalion. For two days his soldiers, veterans of North Africa, and with the support of Cochran's P-51s, cut down a succession of '*Banzai*' charges by massed Japanese. Had Fergusson coordinated the efforts of the rest of his brigade to come to the Leicesters' assistance, they might have captured the airfield. But Aberdeen was reported, wrongly, to be under attack from 1,000 Japanese, so the 16th Brigade was pulled back to the stronghold. The long travail of their march had been for nothing.

Aberdeen probably received as much attention from the Japanese air force as any other block or stronghold. There was no field artillery flown in, but a mixture of Bofors and .50in heavy machine-guns supplied the anti-aircraft defence. The detachment commander was Captain Moody:

My entry into Aberdeen on 23rd March with thirty men and ten .50 calibre guns on the direct orders of Duxbury [Commander Royal Artillery Special Force (CRA)], notwithstanding, made me wonder what I had done wrong. I was detached from the bulk of my troop, all my Troop HQ staff and remaining officers, when I had already prepared all Bofors and men for the fly-in to White City. I would have been quite happy to send Braid or Poppell with the .50 calibres to Aberdeen and remained with the balance of my Troop [bound] for the White City.

After landing at Aberdeen the pilot said he hated the strip which was too short and lethal to any plane where the wheels touched down more than fifty yards before the start of the strip. Hastily we unloaded and I started to site the guns.

Fergusson told Moody that for the next thirty hours he was virtually the only defender of Aberdeen as his column was resting in a safe harbour to the north.

Meanwhile planes were coming in all night with troops and stores. Next day more of Fergusson's brigade came through and many light planes with wounded and sick for evacuation. Aberdeen was now busier than any other strip in the Chindit area, according to the RAF pilots I spoke to and I witnessed the tragedy of the plane crash killing West African and British other ranks. The plane first circled the strip, then came in with its own landing lights on, but was too high near the touchdown so boosted its engines and tried to climb, succeeding in clearing the first row of trees near the dispersal area but its wheels caught the taller trees behind, crashing almost immediately and bursting into flames and exploding.

During this period we had constant Jap air attacks each day, but no sign whatever of Jap ground attacks.

Moody was mentioned in despatches for his good work at Aberdeen, and sent to join the light anti-aircraft troop at the White City after his stint at Aberdeen. The fly-in of the 14th Brigade to Aberdeen, at short notice, was chaotic. Lieutenant Colonel Wilford, CO of the 7th Battalion the Royal Leicesters (47 and 74 Columns), and commander of 47 Column wrote in the Column diary:

27 March
Column arrived Lalaghat, ostensibly to carry out 6 weeks training, glider other airborne instruction. On arrival informed that the Black Watch who had preceded us, were being flown in next day, followed by the battalion. Chaos. All Column baggage lost by Indian railways, no transport, no information. New weapons issued prior to entrainment still to be fired [and zeroed, training carried out etc.].

Before emplaning for Aberdeen, Wilford was briefed on a brigade plan, which was swiftly overtaken by a second plan. By 31 March the concentration of 47 Column was complete at Aberdeen, which was defended by the West African Brigade and the anti-aircraft gunners. Here Wilford received the third version of the plan, which was to relieve the pressure on Calvert by disrupting the Japanese line of communications to the south. Fergusson's brigade was re-forming at this time at Aberdeen after the unsuccessful attack on Indaw.

On the railway, Calvert had increased his elbow room, while the 14th Brigade and 3rd West African Brigade were starting to fly into Aberdeen. The sixth Chindit Brigade, the 23rd, was switched to operate against the line of communication of the Japanese attacking Imphal, as we saw in Chapter 6. At this point, Wingate was killed in an air crash.

He had visited Broadway on 24 March and had called in at Imphal on his way to Lalaghat. The B-25 in which he was flying never arrived. A search party sent out to investigate reports of a crashed aircraft found wreckage and Wingate's Wolseley pattern solar helmet. There were no survivors. To this day the cause of the crash has never been established beyond doubt, although bad weather may have been to blame. For most Chindits Wingate's death came as a great shock, not least to his Chief of Staff and great friend, Brigadier Tulloch, who wrote in his diary, 'God what enemies we have & now we shall have to fight them alone'. He was referring to 'enemies' of Wingate's own making within the army.

Slim appointed Lentaigne as his successor, regarding him as the most experienced and balanced of his brigade commanders. Lentaigne was a regular Indian Army officer, an Irishman with a very short fuse, who had commanded the 1st/4th Gurkhas with distinction during the retreat in 1942. He had been appointed to command the 111th Brigade well before the huge expansion of Special Force on Wingate's return from Quebec. He was not a Wingate admirer, and disagreed with many of his views on tactics.

The command of the 111th Brigade, in the Chindit role, was given to Major Masters, Lentaigne's brigade major. Three different officers each informed Slim that Wingate had told him he was to be his successor should one be required. Slim wrote, 'I have no doubt at all that they were speaking the truth.'[7] As events turned out, it might have been better if he had selected Calvert.

The battle round the White City continued unabated. Part of the 3rd West African and 16th Brigades were flown there to allow Calvert to operate in a mobile role outside the block. 'Far from besieging, the encircling Japanese were in frequent uproar, when perambulating Chindits pounced from nowhere, took a smack, and withdrew at speed', wrote Sergeant Shaw, the British machine-gun platoon sergeant of Number 12 Column of the 3rd West African Brigade.

On 5 April, the advance party of the 7th Nigeria Regiment was flown into the White City, while the main body landed at Aberdeen, and made for the White City on foot. Lieutenant Colonel Peter Vaughan went with the advance party to see them into their positions outside the block.

From here they would eventually enter the White City, and report to Calvert for orders. Vaughan recorded in his diary:

> [I] returned to Lalaghat in an American piloted Dakota with my sole companion in the huge machine a dog – the pilot's mascot.

6th April
A day of immense flap to begin with, as there were no less than five changes of detailed plan before we are finally allotted 30 planes for flying in the battalion tonight [to Aberdeen]. A mild attack of fever – quickly overcome by doses of quinine did not help matters for me personally. (in West Africa we always referred to Malaria as 'just fever').

An amazing spectacle of confident security miles behind the enemy's frontiers [sic] greeted us on arrival [at Aberdeen]. Planes, lights, men and stores were everywhere to be seen. Further planes kept pouring in all night, and I stayed up showing our troops into their positions until by 3.0 am most of the battalion was in. I got an hour's sleep near the strip just before 4.0 am.

7th April
My first day proper in Jap-occupied territory – Good Friday.

Vaughan now received orders to march from Aberdeen to a position outside the White City. Although he does not make it clear in his diary, his battalion was not flown into the White City, because it was destined to operate outside the perimeter as a 'floater'. On 8 April, he set out from Aberdeen with part of the 12th Nigeria as well as those of his own battalion who had arrived for the brigade RV. By 10 April he had arrived at the RV, but was unable to make contact with the White City. He had sent out a patrol to attempt to contact Calvert, whose commander reported back that they had got close enough to hear orders being given in English, but because of the battle raging all round could not get in. Vaughan sent him back, telling him not to return until he had got through. A second patrol was sent in later with the same instructions. Meanwhile as Vaughan recorded in his diary he was in the following, not altogether happy, position:

> (1). Being out in the Burma jungle completely without orders for three days – i.e. since my original orders from Brig Argy (Brigadier Gillmore);

(2). Unable to get wireless communication with either our own or any other HQ;

(3). Without information of the result of the battle we heard raging at the nearby stronghold [White City]

(4). Only one day's ration per man left;

(5). Our water point possibly compromised.

Vaughan was about to go to sleep, when to his delight, he heard a challenge. It was the patrols, and his advance party which he had taken into the White City four nights previously, including Major Carfrae, now in command of 29 Column. They also brought orders with them.

So we celebrated the occasion with some of the unofficial contents of 'Office Box' – a small quantity of rum had been included in it – and I went to sleep feeling very satisfied with the events of the day however belated their appearance.

Having moved to his RV as ordered, Vaughan's men took a supply drop, and constructed a light aircraft strip, into which Calvert flew to give orders. Vaughan's two columns, temporarily under Calvert's command, were to take part in an attack on the Japanese to the south of the White City; with the 3rd/6th Gurkhas and the 1st Lancashire Fusiliers, from the White City garrison, and the 45th Reconnaissance Regiment switched from the 16th Brigade at Aberdeen. Gillmore was now in command inside the White City. Vaughan's part in the attack was to take and hold part of Mawlu. Unfortunately Calvert, unusually for him, had not carried out a proper reconnaissance, and the Japanese locations were not where he expected them to be. A fierce battle ensued, which ended in Calvert ordering the withdrawal of the attacking force back to the harbour at Thayaung, held by one of Vaughan's companies. However, considerable casualties were inflicted on the Japanese, mainly by rockets and bombs from Cochran's Mustangs. Vaughan expressed satisfaction at how well his Africans had done in their first battle at the cost of one officer and one African killed, and thirty-two Africans wounded, ten badly. Four days later, still under Calvert's command outside the White City, Vaughan's battalion laid an ambush on the road supplying the Japanese. He was

Strolling along to see Charles Carfrae and his Column just before evening stand-to, I had no sooner arrived than we all heard the sound of an approaching car engine. The next ten minutes were the tensest in my life. A quick warning and in a flash sixteen Europeans and 200 Africans got into our holes in the ground and remained absolutely motionless. We heard the leading lorry come up to the ford across the river where it stopped with its engine running. A Japanese officer got out, walked forward along the road right under our noses, prodded at the road with a stick (testing it for mines), and was apparently satisfied. He took a very cursory glance at the hill on which we were crouching, shouted an order or two, and strolled back to his lorry.

Still not a man of ours moved, though Denis Arnold [platoon commander in Carfrae's column], who had the Verey pistol with which to give the order to fire was quivering with excitement. We heard the leading lorry engage bottom gear, saw it crawl slowly forward out of the ford and up the slope towards us. Just at the correct moment when it had come forward about another thirty yards, Dennis fired the Verey pistol. The result was staggering.

Two PIAT bombs hit the leading lorry and it burst into flames, while everything else we had – machine-guns, Bren guns, grenades and rifle grenades went smack into the Japanese troops, whom we could see standing in the back of the lorry.

The scene was now of the burning lorry – we could discern two others behind it in the failing light – burning fiercely and lighting the sky for miles, but not a sight or sound from the Japs who had been in the convoy – if indeed any out of this inferno still remained alive. But as it was now dark, it would have been madness to go and investigate, so this must wait until the morning.

18 April

Dawn revealed we had bagged not three but five lorries. Soon after dawn the Japs survivors started sniping at our position on the hill. So ordered Charles to send out a platoon to mop them up.

The count of the result of last night's affair:

    1 Japanese officer killed
    38 Japanese soldiers killed (including ten killed in this morning's mopping up operation)
    5 wounded and taken prisoner.
    Total 44 – and 5 heavy lorries bagged.

It was a most satisfactory outcome to the night's work, and good for morale; there is nothing like a successful battle early in a campaign to get soldiers' tails up. The other brigades and columns had also been busy. Morrisforce had demolished the bridge over the Taiping River, and damaged the Bhamo–Myitkyina road, while Dahforce ambushed enemy columns. The 14th Brigade destroyed the rail bridge at Bongyaung (Bonchaung), cut the railway in sixteen other places, and destroyed fuel and ammunition dumps. The two 7th Royal Leicester columns were ordered to protect the flank of the 2nd York and Lancasters, who had been ordered to blow the bridge over the Bonchaung gorge. The attack was postponed, so Wilford, the CO, decided to blow another part of the line where a new bridge had been built to replace one destroyed earlier by the RAF. The block set up to carry out this operation had to be restricted to two platoons because of lack of water in the area. The narrative in Number 47 Column's diary shows that the Japanese were rarely supine, and if stirred up reacted speedily and violently, but also that the Chindits, as with the rest of the Fourteenth Army, were a match for them:

16 April
(1) Block shot up armoured trolley on railway and Jap infantry patrol.
(2) In the evening Captain Newbould despatched to the block with orders for the commander Major Booth [infantry company commander in 47 Column] for the intended attack. While at the block it was attacked at dusk by a Jap company.
(3) After inflicting some 50 casualties, block was ordered to disperse to the near RV where the balance of the column had since moved. Captain Newbould led back one party to the RV, and then choosing eight men, returned to facilitate the withdrawal of the remainder of the garrison should the necessity arise. He encountered a Jap platoon moving east with the obvious intention of cutting off the withdrawal. This he attacked, and a running fight ensued throughout the night. Enemy casualties approx 28 for the cost of two dead.
(3) Meanwhile Major Booth commenced withdrawal of remainder of block, but was delayed by fact that during the night 16/17 April, four Jap columns each approx 400 strong, passed along the road moving east.

Booth and his men did not manage to rejoin the column until the afternoon of 18 April after a most difficult cross-country march with no water. After a number of plan changes, the 7th Royal Leicesters were ordered into the White City where they remained from 29 April to 10 May.

The little party called Bladet had also had some adventures, as related by Lieutenant Binnie:

Bladet was Blain detachment. It consisted of 6 Junior Officers and 60 men who had volunteered from Recce Patrols of individual Columns of Special Force. The Unit was trained as a sort of personal arm of Wingate's to be used for duties such as sabotage, reconnaissance, diversion etc, wherever desirable during the main operation. Engineers trained in the use of explosives were attached, a couple of Signallers and 3 mules to carry wireless and charging machine [sic] were also on strength, as was a Burmese interpreter. The Unit was commanded and trained by Major Blain who had been a Sergeant-Major in the first Wingate expedition, who had been highly thought of and was, I believe, promoted in the field to Officer rank and awarded the DCM.

The Unit's first and only action [involvement in the campaign] was in March/April of 1944 when it was landed west of the Irrawaddy in 5 gliders, by night, on rather an indifferent paddy field landing strip, prepared by some of Brigadier Lentaigne's Gurkhas. [At Aikma between the Irrawaddy and the railway line on the night of 19/20 March 1944.] The landing was a successful shambles. The gliders were piloted by Americans of Cochran's Commandos. The first glider with Blain and myself in it overshot the strip and tore into the jungle shedding its wings and splitting open throughout the length of the fuselage. The troops within were able to step out of the wreckage, alarmed but relatively unharmed. The remaining gliders performed with equal acrobatic flair and the one carrying the mules actually looped the loop very near the ground, pancake-landed and the mules walked daintily out over the wreckage and calmly started to graze. The Unit bivouacked for the night in nearby jungle, the bivouac including the American pilots who were to be flown out by Light plane at first light. They were very unused to jungle and I don't think they slept much, seeing 'lions, tigers and Japs' everywhere. During the night Blain realised that he had been injured in the glider crash and was incapable of undertaking a long march in enemy territory. He was therefore to go back with the US pilots and I, by chance, the senior lieutenant, took over command. This was, initially, quite a shock, as apart from CSM [Company Sergeant Major] Chivers and a couple of engineers, the remainder of the detachment were new to action and it had been anticipated that Blain's experience would be essential to the success of the operation. I was fortunate in having CSM Chivers to lean on throughout the patrol as he had been with Blain in the first expedition and was an excellent Wingate-type soldier.

Anyway the troops were of good quality and my fellow officers were keen and enthusiastic. We set about our objective to reach a bridge over the railway near Kawlin [sic] on the Mandalay–Myitkyina railway line, blow it up, and throughout the patrol give the impression to native Burmese – knowing that the information would be passed to the Japs – that there was a biggish Chindit Force this far south.

The operation which took about 6 weeks was a success and we blew the bridge [six miles north of Kyaikthin] and a nearby pumping station, and cut the railway line in several places [and carried out demolitions on the Wuntho–Tawmo road]. During the patrol the mule carrying the wireless set went over a cliff, falling about 200 feet and we were incommunicado for most of the patrol. Eventually it [the wireless] was resuscitated enough to permit contact with India and we arranged one supply drop without which we would probably have perished. We were congratulated by Wingate just before his untimely death and told to move on to Aberdeen.

This was quite a hike and we became very exhausted and hungry. A period of marching through dry belt very nearly caused madness due to thirst and one got to the stage of planning the murder of one's best friend for the sake of the small residue he might have in his water-bottle. At one stage we got very lost and hunger and thirst were so affecting us that it was proposed by CSM Chivers that we should take a free vote as to whether we should go on looking for Aberdeen or allow small groups to go it alone and head back over the Chindwin to India. I think that Chivers felt that having done it himself before, that he could do it again.

Fortunately, the problem was solved by the sudden appearance of two Gurkha soldiers at the fringe of the jungle. Our saviours were in bivouac about quarter of a mile away – Tim Brennan's Cameronians, The King's Own and a couple of Columns of Gurkhas [part of the

111th Brigade by now commanded by Masters]. We were made very welcome, fed with bully beef and peaches and cream [condensed milk?] until we were sick and allowed to sleep the sleep of the just.

Tim Brennan got a message that we were to move on, when ready, to Aberdeen and be flown out as we were too exhausted to participate in any further action. A day's rest and we were on our way. We were ambushed by some excitable Japs a short distance away from the bivouac, but they were as anxious as we were and we escaped with one Engineer shot through the knee-cap, John Urquhart, my second-in-command, with a bullet burn right across his left breast – lucky fellow – and otherwise shaken but intact. Two days of tough marching saw us in Aberdeen, happy, but very very exhausted.

We eventually arrived in Shillong in Assam, where we were to recuperate. Within 24 hours every single member of the Unit was in Hospital – after an enormous celebratory binge – suffering from malaria or dysentery. I was unconscious for 3 days with malignant tertiary malaria. I thought the initial symptoms were merely those of a gigantic hang-over. This extraordinary medical situation was of great interest to me after the war when I trained to become a General Practitioner and wasn't understood until one heard of Cortisone and how, in desperate states, our Adrenal glands produce masses of Cortisone in an endeavour to keep infection at bay and maintain necessary bodily function in the effort to survive under extraordinary circumstances.

Bladet was disbanded at this stage and individuals returned to their parent Units when their health was restored. I then had the dubious pleasure of being trained to command a small detachment of 12 man-pack flame-throwers and soon took them into Mogaung to be used by Brigadier Calvert. We were used, I believe, rather unskilfully in a night attack on a village near Mogaung. However, although the tactics were discredited, their use was such a shock to the Japs that the village fell into Calvert's hands with minimal casualties to our attacking force. In this action I lost the sight of my right eye from a Jap grenade, one soldier was killed and the remaining ten soldiers were all wounded to some degree.

By relating the final chapter of the Bladet story, we have got ahead of the narrative. Indaw West was finally taken, but it was neither drained nor surfaced, so was useless. Fergusson was ordered to abandon it.

Meanwhile on 9 April, Slim, after a visit to Stilwell, had told Lentaigne that all Chindit brigades, less 23rd Brigade still being held under Fourteenth Army command for operations in the Imphal area, were to assist Stilwell directly in his battle for Mogaung and Myitkyina. Lentaigne decided that to fulfil this task, all brigades should move north. The 16th Brigade, which was burnt out, and had achieved very little, was to be flown out India, after which Broadway, Aberdeen and the White City would be abandoned. He also decided that a block would be established near the railway near Hopin, to be nicknamed 'Blackpool'.

On 17 April, the Japanese made their last attack on the White City. Major General Yoshihide Hayashi, the commander of the *24th Mixed Brigade*, was killed leading the attack on a white horse. The Japanese penetrated the defences but were killed by machine-gun fire and in hand-to-hand fighting with the South Staffs and West Africans. In the fighting around and in the White City, a Japanese force of near divisional strength had been defeated by seven battalions: four British, two West African, and one Gurkha.

The evacuation of the White City was carried out successfully. Lieutenant Colonel Wilford of the 7th Leicesters, who as part of the 14th Brigade had been ordered to act as 'floaters' for the block at Blackpool, recounts:

10 May
White City evacuated during the night of 9/10 May without interference in spite of fact that Japs had ranged landing strip during previous afternoon. Dakotas flew in at dusk with limited reinforcements and took out fortress stores and guns, and sick and wounded. 49 sorties flown.

Battalion moved out at 0300 hours leaving Commando platoons to booby-trap and destroy non-essential stores. Subsequently and on return to Column, Commandos reported Jap reinforcements with tanks were moving up from the south.

Note. Just prior to leaving, plan changed and Battalion ordered to move with all speed to [RV] with intention of securing and holding it until arrival of remainder of brigade.

Captain Moody, the senior gunner at the White City, wrote later:

I was the last person to leave the White City: the fortress was empty and I had already evacuated five guns. The Japs were within small-arms range of the end of the strip and the pilot would not allow me to pick up the final box of ammunition. I booby-trapped it with a grenade and we took off. Just airborne we had small-arms fire and the fuselage was holed in several places. The plane was however still airworthy and no one on board suffered any injury.

Seventeen hours later this troop was in the air again, on the way to Myitkyina. As so often happened the Japanese were following up aggressively, and on the night of 12/13 May hit 47 Column. Wilford:

13 May
at 0420 hours Column attacked in bivouac by Jap patrol with ponies estimated 30 strong. Original intention to stay until first light, and then clean up [and take supply drop]. Japs however made excellent use of cover, and as they were inflicting casualties on men and mules, and it was not known whether they were an advance party of a bigger force moving up behind, it was decided to pull out.

Main portion of Column moved down boulder-strewn chaung with precipitous sides. It eventually became necessary to leave the chaung. This necessitated off-loading the mules, and man-hauling the loads up the side for some 200 feet. Japs failed to follow-up, probably due to their officer being killed. Arrived bivouac. Own casualties:

> *Killed*: Officers – two
>   WOs – one
> *Missing*: Rank & file – five
> *Wounded*: Rank & file – thirteen
> *Animals killed*: one pony; two bullocks; thirteen mules.

This brisk night-time skirmish cost the column twenty-one casualties, a large slice of their animal transport, and the RAF radio set for requesting supply drops. As a result the column was without rations for four days.

*

On the night of 16/17 May, Stilwell assumed command of the Chindits, and told Lentaigne that he was to operate to the south of Mogaung, while keeping a base at the Blackpool block. In the opinion of Lieutenant Richard Rhodes-James, the cipher officer of the 111th Brigade,

The choice of location was disastrous. 'Jack' Masters chose it, it was the best of a bad bargain. It was too far from the railway, and too close to the enemy front line. It was surrounded by terrain easily occupied by the enemy which dominated our position.

The Blackpool block (again not a stronghold, for the same reasons as the White City), was established by the 111th Brigade on 7 May, and the first Japanese attacks started that night. Although beaten off, the preparation of the defences was carried out under sporadic small-arms and artillery fire. As the days passed the attacks became more determined, following the arrival of the fresh Japanese *53rd Division* (Lieutenant General Takeda). With the abandonment of the White City, this division was able to move north without hindrance to attack Blackpool, before it could be supported and reinforced. Although an airstrip was built, a combination of heavy rain and low cloud severely hindered air strikes and supply sorties, consequently the Japanese were able to establish artillery and especially anti-aircraft guns in a position to dominate the strip and its air approaches, so that supply missions had to be stopped. However, a troop of anti-aircraft and a troop of field guns (initially only three guns) were flown in to Blackpool before the strip could no longer be used. They were soon being engaged by Japanese artillery, as extracts from a narrative by Captain Brown relate:

Soon after nine o'clock, the gun position was shelled for fifty-three minutes; three gunners were hit, one of whom subsequently died of wounds and a lance bombardier and a fourth gunner were badly shocked.

The enemy now settled down in earnest to shell the area of the Stronghold. His fire was backed by bombardment from the air, all three guns suffered slight damage, but nevertheless, at twenty to twelve, they fired a total of sixty rounds of HE on the Troop fire plan.

On 19 May [the fourth gun had now arrived] the tempo of the battle was quickening and rose to a crescendo over the next four days. Neither high explosive nor direct air support could stop the momentum of the Japanese assault. On the 24th after a desperately busy morning, the Troop Commander, Captain Young was killed in his OP, and a subaltern wounded. The latter took over command of the Troop and at half past seven on the morning of 25 May, ordered a temporary evacuation of the gun position – the firing mechanism and sights being first removed. But five minutes later the enemy burst over the ridge behind which the guns had been sited, and engaged the Troop with mortar bombs and grenades from discharger cups. There were a number of casualties which were so serious that they had to be abandoned in the face of overwhelming enemy pressure, in the direction of Brigade Headquarters.

The anti-aircraft troop had similar experiences:

During enemy shelling on 14 May [the day after arrival], the CRA Major Duxbury had been killed, and the Troop Commander wounded. Several of the gunners had been hit; one killed outright, another so badly wounded that he died. The Troop Commander was evacuated (he was replaced almost immediately by another officer). It was an ominous enough beginning.

When the final breakthrough came, the guns on the strip were overrun before they could be destroyed, but essential parts were removed by the detachments before they withdrew. These men fought bravely and well as they fell slowly back, and one of their number was subsequently awarded the Military Medal. The remaining anti-aircraft guns were, with the possible exception of the two Hispanos, disabled and all the gunners lined the main ridge with the infantry. It was here that heavy casualties occurred. The enemy brought down high explosive on the ridge, which tore the defenders limb from limb, and then mercifully turned his machine-guns on the dying. During this slaughter Captain Braid [replacement Troop Commander] was hit many times. His batman and another gunner carried his unconscious body back with them in the withdrawal that followed this disaster, until they were ordered to abandon him by a Medical Officer.

Eventually, almost out of ammunition and supplies, Masters had to abandon the block on 25 May. The fighting was at close quarters, as the Japanese came racing in for the kill. Scott, now a lieutenant colonel commanding the 1st King's Liverpool, was in the block at the end, and covered the withdrawal:

I was under a tree, which although it had lost its top branches to artillery and mortar fire, still had a substantial trunk. Two lieutenant colonels, I and Thompson commanding the 2nd King's Own, with a few men were by the tree. I was firing round the right hand side of the tree, and Thompson the left. I threw grenades up hill at the advancing Japs, which kept rolling back and missing the enemy. Suddenly there was a gasp of expelled air, and Thompson went down with a wound in his left shoulder. I bent to pick him up, was hit, and felt warm liquid gushing down my leg. I looked, it was water, my water bottle had been hit as my bottom stuck out round the tree when I bent down. When we pulled out, the Japs only followed us for about 300 to 400 yards. I don't know why. I think they were exhausted too, and were glad to let us go.

Masters gave orders that wounded so badly injured that they would be unlikely to survive were to be shot to avoid them falling into the hands of the Japanese who would have tortured them before bayoneting them to death.

Stilwell was livid and accused the Chindits of cowardice. According to Rhodes-James, he is alleged to have said, referring to the Chindits, 'You are yellow. You are not tired. I am going to run you into the ground'. Now began the unhappiest period in the Chindit story. The root of the problem was Stilwell and his sycophantic staff, and – it has to be said – Lentaigne's failure to stand up to him. To some of his soldiers Lentaigne was known in rhyming slang as 'Calamity Jane', which is probably unfair. However he visited his Force in the field only once, and was not well placed to argue their case against Stilwell's constant jibes at their expense. Rhodes-James, who had been Lentaigne's cipher officer, said, 'Lentaigne was a charming man, who had made a very good reputation as the CO of the 4th Gurkhas in the retreat in 1942. But he was totally unsuited to command an LRP brigade, and even less so to command the Chindits, especially as he did not agree with Wingate's views'.

Stilwell was equally harsh with Merrill's Marauders, and under his direction they ceased to exist as a fighting force. If anything the Americans hated him more than the British did, and at least one officer in the Marauders expressed the hope that an opportunity would arise which would enable him to shoot Stilwell during a visit forward.[8] Slim got on well with him, and said that he liked him.[9] He was one of the few British soldiers who did. The British Chief of the Imperial General Staff, Field Marshal Sir Alan Brooke, had no time for him at all, and considered that he had little military knowledge and no strategic ability of any kind.[10] One Chindit, Major Ramsay of the 7th Nigeria Regiment, an acerbic officer whose diary entries we shall encounter later, wrote a song which gives the Chindit view of Stilwell, sung to the hymn tune 'The Church's One Foundation':

> We are Joe Stilwell's army, no bloody use are we,
> For our Commander's barmy, as barmy as can be:
> And whether we attack boys, or whether we defend,
> It's 'Better we go back' boys and stop this lease and lend.
>
> Old Sahmaw's chaung is deep boys, and Sabaw's Bum is high,
> We starve and never sleep boys, our clothes are never dry,
> But Chindits they can take it – so says 'Lantana Joe' –
> But whether we can make it, we don't profess to know.
>
> And now we're on our chinstraps, our eyes towards Myitkyina
> Our nerves are wearing thin boys, you know what whizzbangs are,
> We start at every shot boys and leap at every shell,
> And Ricketts he can rot boys, and Stilwell go to hell.

Ricketts was the new commander of the 3rd West African Brigade, and by all accounts he was not popular. The Marauders seized Myitkyina South Airfield, but the Japanese held the town in strength. Stilwell refused the British offer to fly in the fresh 36th Indian Infantry Division; he did not want to share the honour of taking the place with the hated 'limeys'. Meanwhile the Chindits, weakened by long marches, malaria, and malnutrition, desperately battled on to take objectives selected off the map by Stilwell's staff. Columns were down to less than 100 men in some cases, and companies were smaller than platoons. Lieutenant Colonel Scott, who had been a column commander on the first Chindit expedition, considered that his men were in worse condition than on that occasion. Space does not allow us to follow the story of more than a month of marches and small engagements which drained away the strength of the Chindits, mainly through sickness. Had it not been possible to evacuate the large numbers of sick and wounded from Indawgyi lake by Sunderland flying boats, hundreds more would have died.

Vaughan, CO of the 7th Nigeria, tells the story of one of these engagements in his diary, having set out with a patrol to conduct a reconnaissance:

June 17th

Just as we started we heard shooting from the direction of the lantana patch. On reaching it, I found Charles Cowie and his Burma Riflemen had fired at two Japs who had appeared on the edge of the patch. I called up two more sections to act as escort to the recce patrol which consisted of Mike Llewellyn-Davis, Charles Cowie, Bungy King and myself. We had gone about four hundred yards along the track when suddenly hell broke loose. During the few minutes taken to get up the additional sections, the little devils of Japs had obviously quickly improvised an ambush on the track.

In the first burst of automatic fire, I got one bullet straight through my right upper arm and was knocked clean off the track by the force of the impact down a slope into cover bordering the path, which almost certainly saved my life. My arm felt numb, I was bleeding badly, and I had dropped my carbine from my numbed right hand. My feelings were of bewildered fury at being so stupidly caught out. One of the nearby Africans shouted *Babbun Baturi sun buga shi* (The Big Shot, they've got him). I shouted to Sergeant Alhasan Giri who was crouching near me, 'Right flanking and drive the bastards out of it quick'. Which he did admirably without further loss to us. He was subsequently awarded the DCM for his determination and aggressive spirit in this and other actions.

I was half led and half carried until I found I was not too badly damaged to walk along a piece of dead ground with bullets still whistling over our heads to a track to the rear. Here my shirt was cut away and a field dressing applied to my wound, before walking to column HQ where Bob Murray the MO cleaned and re-dressed my wound under a shot of morphia.

Here I heard the tragic news that Mike Llewellyn-Davis had also been hit in the opening burst of fire and killed outright. After the heroic struggle which he had put up against dysentery and malaria for many weeks, during which he had refused to miss a single day's duty with his company, this is a tragedy, and we all felt shocked and depressed. He was one of the best officers in the battalion, and loved and respected by his brother officers and the Africans alike.

A fresh platoon was sent out and the Japs tried no probing

attacks, although we expected it, during the rest of the day. An examination of my arm which was hurting me a good deal, revealed that although the bullet had gone clean through, and had actually grazed the bone, there was no serious fracture. (in fact the bone had been fractured though I did not know this until it was X-rayed in hospital in India weeks later). The main damage was a nasty jagged hole with a few torn muscles on the side where the bullet emerged.

After three more days of beating off Japanese probing attacks and moving to take a supply drop, which failed to materialize but necessitated a halt, Vaughan recorded:

June 20th
Jan Szysych (Polish Brigade HQ Doctor) took advantage of this halt to do a clever operation in the field on my arm. It was already starting to heal cleanly, but some of the muscles had been sawn in half by the emerging bullet, and Jan's operation was to catch the ends and sew them together. He had no anaesthetic with him and the four stitches he put in were extremely painful, though when he had finished he seemed very pleased with the result, and the general condition of the wound.

In early July, the scourge of typhus was added to the other problems being borne by the Chindits in the 3rd West African and 14th Brigades.

Perhaps one of the Chindits' greatest feat of arms was the capture of Mogaung by Calvert's 77th Brigade. But it was at a price: at the end only 300 of his men were fit to fight. Between 17 May and 26 June alone, while operating in support of Stilwell, the brigade had 950 battle casualties and 150 men evacuated sick (the 77th Brigade suffered 1,811 battle casualties in the second expedition; almost equal to the other four brigades in total). After the battle for Mogaung two Victoria Crosses were awarded: one posthumously to Captain Allmand, Indian Armoured Corps, attached to the 6th Gurkha Rifles, and the other to Rifleman Tulbahadur Pun 3rd/6th Gurkhas.

Calvert heard on the BBC that the Americans and Chinese had captured Mogaung. He sent a message to Force HQ, copied to Stilwell, saying the 'Americans have captured Mogaung, 77th Brigade is proceeding to take Umbrage.' Stilwell's son, who was his Intelligence Officer, said, 'They've taken a village called Um-bra-gay which we can't find on the map.'

On 13 July, by which time Mogaung had fallen to Calvert's 77th Brigade, Carfrae's Number 29 Column was ordered to take part in a brigade attack near the road east of Mogaung, in which Vaughan's column did not participate, but about which he comments having monitored progress on the brigade wireless net:

> The unjustifiably (I think) over-confident and obstinate Brigadier Ricketts appears to have rushed into the attack against an enemy position not properly reconnoitred, and relying on the most inadequate supporting fire. The attack was a complete failure, the Brigade suffered many casualties, and every fresh message we heard confirmed the degree of failure of this assault, which early opinion on Brigadier Ricketts's part had summed up as 'just brushing them aside', but which soon became known as 'Ricketts's Folly'.

Major Ramsay, Carfrae's column second-in-command and rifle company commander, recorded in his diary:

> *Wednesday 12th [July].*
> Dickie [2ic] reports he contacted the 12th Nigeria on main road. They have bumped a strongish dug-in position by the main road on a small hill. Tomorrow Ricketts is going to attack it. We are to go and cut the road behind it and ambush them as they run away. Dickie says the Chinese are there with artillery, a light plane OP, and ambulances. Also rice and spuds etc. What a relief to have an L of C again [i.e. the prospect of no longer having to rely on air supply].

Carfrae's column moved into position, although not without taking casualties. Ramsay:

> The attack went in with, to our great surprise, not a round from the Chinese guns, and no direct air support, although planes were hovering and asking if they were wanted. Ricketts said 'no'. He also refused the artillery support offered by Colonel Dupuy (US Army [under Stilwell]). We kept on calling brigade, but Tony Crown at the other end said he had no news. For about six hours there was no news or control whatsoever. If he [Ricketts] had bothered to find out where we were we might have linked up with 12 Nigeria and taken the hill. They did get on the ridge near it, but were driven back again. The whole show was unco-ordinated.

The hill that the 3rd West African Brigade had just failed to take became known as Hill 60, and they had been told that it would be the brigade's final battle. A further attack was also unsuccessful. Ramsay's diary entry for 15 July:

Charles [Carfrae] got on the blower and for the fourth time explained where we were, as he was sure brigade had not taken any interest. True enough, XXXXX [illegible] said did not know where we were and spoke as if we had never told him. He said Bde HQ were due east of Hill 60. We said, 'Nonsense, we are'. XXXXX went to prove us wrong and returned and admitted they were not due east of it. Actually they were much nearer north.

The attack was a failure again.

Peter [Vaughan] came out to see the battlefield. His arm is getting bad.

Carfrae recorded:

In the morning we were paid a surprise visit by Peter Vaughan. He was near to fainting with exhaustion. His wound which refused to heal was giving him much pain; the long walk in the sun had tried him hardly and for several minutes he was unable to speak. Yet he had left his own column to see for himself whether he could help us, and without a word from me had brought food and extra ammunition. I remembered, to my shame, that when I had disagreed with some of his decisions, I had not failed to say so, sometimes illnaturedly, and asked myself if I would have done as much for him as he had done for me.

Ramsay recorded on 16 July, 'Peter is being evacuated at last.' The last act in the Chindit story was the taking of Hill 60 by the 12th Nigeria of the 3rd West African Division, and the 9th Royal Sussex and 6th South Wales Borderers of the 72nd Indian Infantry Brigade Group, 36th Indian Division. Carfrae's column was in a supporting role. Ramsay:

About 0300 hours firing started. Quite a lot of it. I learnt afterwards that Ricketts tried to spoil the plan by suggesting that one of our companies and the R Sussex companies occupy the ridge after the direct air support – to save artillery barrage. The CO of the Sussex said no, he thought it was a poor idea, but Aslett [Commander 72nd Brigade] (a tough looking little man, but maybe not over-clever and inclined I should think to be easily influenced) ordered him to do so. They got on OK, and moved along the ridge to the west. Early this morning they were counter-attacked and driven off with about 20 casualties. Their CO and R Sussex officers were very angry about this.

We moved off at about 0700. The barrage late in starting, this is disturbing after wireless silence as it looks as if a change of plan has taken place. However half way there the barrage started – a oh boy what a barrage. The 105s and 155s pounding away (six of each)* and probably the 4.2-inch mortars the Chinese have now got. Salvos bursting in very rapid succession, fountains of earth and dust, and a terrific smell of cordite. The rapidity and number of shells is astonishing and slightly horrifying. We got to the cross track RV and put out protection. At zero hour the barrage stopped, then nothing heard for a bit, then one or two bursts which took us a few minutes to realise were Tommy gun.

We moved to the road and took up a temporary position astride it. Then Charles, Coggy, Dickie and I went up on to Hill 60. A most amazing sight. How anyone lived there I do not know. Many died there. The hill was completely bare of cover and pitted with bomb and shell craters, with about 20 Jap bodies lying about. One Jap officer with a Jap bayonet still through his eye, and another with a bayonet wound through the centre of his forehead. Charles pulls them about and searches them – which I can't.

From the hill we watched the South Wales Borderers battle about 800 yards away. Their mortars putting down a lot of smoke. On their night advance they blundered into some Japs – the advance guard halted, and the rest of the battalion closed up on them – all in the open in short grass. The Japs opened up with light machine-guns and a lot of medium machine-guns and the South Wales Borderers were literally pinned – the slightest movement brought a hail of bullets and no cover for them. They were too close for artillery support, so they put down 2-inch mortar smoke and withdrew under cover of that. They then put 3-inch mortar smoke on the enemy which served as an indication to the gunners who got on to it.

12 Nigeria already digging in on the hill. We are to go from the Sahmaw Road to a tree about 400 yards off, however Ricketts wants to push us forward. For once he has got local protection – a platoon

* Not actually very many in the circumstances.

in front, they were told to open up and advance on either side of road. Troops a bit dumb, as they have forgotten about open warfare. Jap bivvies all the way and tons of equipment.

The 3rd West African Division spent the next three days in the Hill 60 area, and a further week in helping build an airstrip, before marching to Mogaung to entrain for Myitkyina and there emplaning for India. Ramsay:

Wednesday 16th [August]
Mogaung at 0530. Coggie found two very nice steel-shafted golf clubs in a Jap bunker. Lot of shooting – it's the Yanks keeping Chinese off the supply drop area. Crossed the railway bridge and waited for our Jeep train, shared with 36 Div casualties – mostly first go malaria – they would not like Long Range Penetration. Guarded the train with one platoon with fixed bayonets – the Chinese have made trouble and drawn guns and grenades on the 6th Nigeria when turned off [the train]. Had to turn off three Chinese. No trouble. Filed on the six trucks (270 of us), and off we went. The train after us shot a couple of Japs on the journey. Arrived Myitkyina. Bare and blasted, full of Jap positions. Stink of Jap dead. Marched to transit camp. The next train after us encountered four Japs, they shot two.

Thursday 17th
Emplaned at Myitkyina airfield. Coggie carrying his two golf clubs – much to the surprise of the Yanks.

The 14th Brigade who also left Burma by the same route noticed the same problems. Wilford:

Much trouble caused on Mogaung–Myitkyina Railway by complete lack of any form of discipline displayed by our Chinese allies. They succeeded in derailing at least three trains by placing rocks on the permanent way, and changing points etc.

So ended the second LRP expedition, very differently from the original Wingate concept. But it was almost inevitable that Special Force should be used in the fashion it was, not least because Wingate was constantly trying to drive Allied operations in north Burma down paths which were outside his training and experience. Wingate had no idea of just how tough the Japanese army was in a conventional battle, because he had never fought, much less commanded so much as a platoon, in such a battle. But he persisted in dreaming up schemes that would result in his Special Force being pinned down in what one author called 'death-grapples with the Japanese', a role for which they were not equipped.[11] When the Chindits were pulled north to support Stilwell, which was inevitable, bearing in mind that support for him was their agreed task, and was precisely why the Americans had sent Cochran's Commandos to Burma, their misemployment in a conventional infantry role became even more frequent.

The Chindits achieved much on a personal level in courage, endurance, and sacrifice, and for that we should salute them. Less clear is what they achieved in the overall operational-level picture in Burma. In Slim's opinion the effects of Wingate's Special Force 'compared with those of a normal corps . . . were painfully slight'.[12]

The Chindits required an enormous air effort to keep them in action. There is no doubt that they assisted Stilwell in his advance to Myitkyina, and especially because of the capture of Mogaung by Calvert. But a more economic use of the same size force might have been achieved by employing a standard division, say 70th British or 36th Indian, on the main axis, and on road supply. The effect of the Chindits on the Imphal front was negligible. Here, the twenty Chindit battalions occupied the attentions of around eleven Japanese battalions, only one of which was withdrawn from Mutaguchi's *15th Army*, and returned to that formation at the end of March. The damage done to Mutaguchi's supply dumps was insignificant. Fergusson directed the RAF on to one near Indaw, and the 111th Brigade over a period of two weeks destroyed 'nearly 200 tons of stores and 20 vehicles, and inflicted 430 casualties'.[13] The last figure is problematic and, being a round number, highly suspect. Most post-battle reports exaggerate enemy casualties, and often the true figure is not known for years afterwards, if ever. The only infallible 'score' is one arrived at by physically counting the 'bag' at leisure: captured equipment and prisoners. Body counts of dead, often completed in haste, and under fire, are usually wrong, and guesstimates based on the weight of fire to which the enemy has been subjected are specious, as the Americans were to discover twenty years later in Vietnam.

As we have seen in the previous chapters, the Japanese ran short of supplies, but the main cause of this was self-inflicted by Mutaguchi in sending his divisions into battle over some of the most challenging terrain imaginable with a mere twenty days' supplies, gambling that the bulging depots at Imphal would be his for the taking. The Japanese scuppered their own logistics, not the Chindits.

Slim, despite his judgement quoted above, saluted the Chindits' courage, and their magnificent achievements, especially at the White City and Mogaung. But that does not alter the fact that the Special Force was a costly, and on the whole non-productive, experiment. This does not in any way detract from the bravery and endurance of the thousands of Chindit soldiers, or diminish their personal achievement. But that should not be allowed to cloud the issue. Rhodes-James's view is that:

> Although we [the Chindits] did have an effect [on the campaign], it was not cost-effective to achieve this with six brigades. The 77th Brigade achieved great things, the other brigades did not. Two or three brigades would have been enough to commit to the LRP task, Slim could have used the other three more brigades to much better effect in the main battle.
>
> When people find out I was in Burma, they often ask if I was a Chindit. The romantic stories of the Chindits are often the only thing people remember about the Burma campaign. At times you see and hear in the media that 'Wingate turned the tide in Burma'. He did not turn the tide, it was turned at Imphal and Kohima by the Fourteenth Army.

One of the Force's major drawbacks was its lack of mobility once troops had deplaned from Dakota or glider. As has been stated elsewhere, once on the ground, the Chindits had the mobility of the boot. The Wingate contention that columns had inherently greater mobility than the Japanese was utter nonsense, as Lentaigne wrote afterwards:

> A column has NOT got superior mobility to the enemy in the jungle. The rations and supplies carried by the man are heavier than that carried by the enemy, while the heavier weapons and W/T [radios] which make the column self-supporting entail a mule train, which inevitably slows it down and also renders it very vulnerable when attacked on the march.[14]

The casualty rate in Special Force was out of all proportion to its achievements and by far the greatest number of casualties were caused by sickness. It can be argued that the high numbers of sick were caused by poor training and lack of discipline.[15] The highest ratio of sick to battle casualties was in the 14th Brigade, with over seven men evacuated sick for every man killed or wounded. For example Wilford reports that the two columns of the 7th Royal Leicesters, 47 and 74, had a total of 15 officers and 328 other ranks *evacuated* sick out of a strength of 38 officers and 796 other ranks. The battalion suffered 69 battle casualties (killed, wounded, and missing), and 50 who died either of wounds or sickness, Wilford does not say which, but probably mostly the latter.

The lowest ratio of sick to battle casualties was in 77th Brigade, who had by far the highest number of battle casualties in Special Force, and just over one man sick for every battle casualty, an indication of the standard of leadership and morale in Calvert's brigade; and moreover his brigade did more fighting than the other four put together. The second lowest sick to battle casualty ratio was in the 3rd West African Brigade at just over two men sick for each battle casualty.[16] These figures are a tribute to the West Africans and their officers. In this context it is perhaps fitting to end this chapter by quoting from a captured Japanese document:

> The enemy soldiers are not from Britain, but from Africa. Because of their beliefs they are not afraid to die, so even if their comrades have fallen they keep on advancing as if nothing had happened. They have an excellent physique and are very brave, so fighting against these soldiers is very troublesome.

8

The Battle of the Irrawaddy Shore: Mandalay and Meiktila

It is possible that the Allied Chiefs of Staff did not appreciate the scale of the Japanese defeat in Assam, for in its aftermath the mission given to the Fourteenth Army was, in Slim's view, too modest. In essence he was told to mount an offensive to join up with the Chinese (Northern Combat Area Command – NCAC), in the vicinity of Maymyo, level with Mandalay – Operation CAPITAL. Rangoon was to be captured by an amphibious and airborne force, not under Slim's command – Operation DRACULA. Slim, believing that the fruits of his great victory should not be so lightly discarded, told his staff to prepare plans for his Fourteenth Army to capture Rangoon overland, known to his staff as Operation Sob – 'Sea or Bust'.[1]

Slim sought to bring the Japanese army to battle as early as possible, in a place of his own choosing, where his superiority in armour and air power could be used to best advantage. He judged that the Japanese would fight hard to stop him reaching the Irrawaddy, and this would give him the opportunity to destroy them on the Shwebo plain, north of Mandalay, between the Irrawaddy and the Chindwin. Operations by the 15th Corps in the Arakan, to which we will return, were to be shaped to help the Fourteenth Army after it had taken Mandalay, by capturing air bases at Akyab, Cheduba, and Ramree, while holding down the maximum number of Japanese in the Arakan.

By now there had been some key command changes. In mid-October 1944, Stilwell was relieved. Slim was sorry to see him go, but his views were not shared by anyone who had been unfortunate enough to serve under him. The American 14th Air Force openly celebrated his removal.[2] Of far more concern to Slim was Giffard's replacement as 11th Army Group Commander by Lieutenant General Sir Oliver Leese, fresh from commanding the Eighth Army in Italy, where he was not popular – for, according to the CIGS, Field Marshal Sir Alan Brooke, his departure was 'greeted with considerable joy'.[3] He came at Mountbatten's request, in the newly created post of Commander-in-Chief Allied Land Forces South East Asia (CINCALFSEA). Leese was an able soldier, but his relationship with Slim was cool. Leese did not help by bringing a flock of Eighth Army staff with him, who did not bother to conceal their patronizing air towards Fourteenth Army. They, in their turn, resented being told what to do by a bunch of people whose experience of fighting in Burma, and especially the Japanese, was nil. Slim's operations were conducted with scant regard for Leese and his staff at ALFSEA.

*

The command change that was to have the profoundest effect on Slim, or rather his plans, was the replacement of Lieutenant General Kawabe by Lieutenant General Hyotaro Kimura as commander *Burma Area Army*. Kimura was highly intelligent and subtle, unlike his predecessor. Kimura aimed to treat Slim as he had played Kawabe and Mutaguchi at Imphal: lure him on to ground of his choosing and smash him. To this end he resolved not to hold the Chindwin in strength, but pull back behind the Irrawaddy. Here, when Fourteenth Army was committed to crossing this vast river, he would fight what he called 'The Battle of the Irrawaddy Shore'. Kimura aimed to isolate part of Slim's army on his side of the river and destroy it. His plan was strongly influenced by the directive from Field Marshal Count Terauchi, C-in-C *Southern Command*, that the security of southern Burma was the first priority, if need be at the expense of the rest.

Slim launched Major General T. W. Rees's 19th Indian Division (Dagger Division), under command of 4th Corps, across the Chindwin to take Pinlebu, exploit towards Wuntho, and link up with NCAC in the railway valley north of Mandalay. Here Rees would make contact with the 36th British Division, who had been operating under NCAC, and together make for Shwebo. Thus 4th Corps would be the anvil to the hammer provided by 33rd Corps, strong in armour, advancing east across the Shwebo plain from Kalewa. By mid-December the 19th Division had taken Pinlebu, and 2nd British Division had relieved the 11th East African Division on the east bank of the Chindwin. All was now set for the battle of the Shwebo Plain.

Captain Howard, Brigade Intelligence Officer of the 4th Infantry Brigade, 2nd British Division, wrote:

The 6th Brigade [one of the other brigades in the division], broke out of the Africans' bridgehead at Christmas and advanced along the Kalewa–Ye-U road very fast, without meeting any opposition for about forty miles, until they hit a Jap position in the Wainggyo Gorge which held them up for about two days. After this they went fast again, smashing more Jap resistance, burst out into the Ye-U plain and went hell for leather for the Kabo Weir which controlled the irrigation system of the whole Shwebo plain.

The first week of the new year we spent in catching up with the battle. The infantry marched mainly by night when it was cool, and the seventy miles was done in a week. Not spectacular marching, but good steady progress which toughened the men without tiring them unduly.

We made contact at Payan half way between the Mayu River and Shwebo, where the Royal Scots captured the village just as it was getting dark. I went up with the old man [brigade commander Brigadier R. S. McNaught] to see the CO [Royal Scots] at his Tac HQ during the attack. He was dug in on the embankment of a bridge on the road, the one place high enough above the flat country for it to be possible to see anything. Needless to say it was equally obvious to the Japs that this was the only viewpoint, and the arrival of our jeep soon drew some shelling. Fortunately they all landed in the river and mud two or three hundred yards to the south. A false alarm of 'down' from Dick Crockatt [Intelligence Officer 1st Royal Scots] sent me under the bridge where I stumbled into the one patch of water deep enough to get a ducking. I hadn't heard the shell myself and was livid when I found it had landed far away. Since that ignominious soaking, I have usually trusted my own ears rather than other peoples', in the matter of judging where things are coming.

One of the unpleasant features of visiting units is that they know the habits of the enemy gunners and have the 'length of the ball', and know when to duck; also they have holes and the visitor hasn't. Jock McNaught appeared to attract shells, for nearly everywhere we went there was always a 'plonk – swish – bang'. When I went out with him, I used to take it for granted that we would be shelled and was quite pleased and surprised when we were not.

Although the Japanese were retreating, it was not a time to drop one's guard. Arthur Freer, the radio operator in the Squadron Leader's tank, B Squadron 3rd Carabiniers:

The advance to Shwebo was through teak forest and jungle. Nothing happened until we started to get into thicker jungle. There were signs that we were catching up on the Japs, food left behind and so forth. I asked the Squadron Leader 'shouldn't we net in on the sets to talk to the infantry'? He didn't do anything about it. On 23 December 1944, we came upon a Jap roadblock, and came under small arms fire. He couldn't speak to the infantry CO on the wireless, and got out of the tank to do so. That was the last we heard of him. A troop leader, Capt Swann, called us eventually, telling us that the Squadron Leader was badly wounded [he eventually died]. I took off my headset, I was sat next to the driver, and climbed into the turret to take command of the tank. I put my head out, and I felt a heavy bang on my head, and woke up on the floor of the turret. My head was hurting, there was no blood, but a lump the size of the egg. The sniper's bullet had hit the turret outside chipping off something which hit me, but I got away with it.

I ordered the turret gunner to spray the trees above us and around. Capt Swann came on the air and said he was taking command of the squadron, and why was I firing. I told him I was trying to spray the sniper. He told me to leave him alone the infantry would sort him. We were told to by-pass the Japs and press on.

The next day we burst through a Jap cookhouse smashing a huge pot of boiling rice which burst all over the tank. We were hungry and the rice smelt delicious, but we couldn't stop. By now we were out of the jungle and smashed through the Jap roadblocks. Each day another battalion, from 2 Div, took over the lead.

As in other formations, the battalions of the 19th Division engaged in a series of encounter battles as they advanced. The 2nd Royal Berkshires, a pre-war regular battalion, had been in India since before the outbreak of war in 1939; the advance to Shwebo was their first experience of battle and despite years of training there was a great deal to learn. Major Hill, a twenty-six-year-old regular, commanded B Company. After the company's first little encounter, which concluded successfully for the loss of one sergeant, the company continued the advance. Almost immediately the leading platoon made contact with the enemy; the leading soldier was fired on across a small clearing, but was untouched. B Company's well-practised battle drill swung into action: supported by 3in mortars, the leading sections probed to right and left of the enemy. At that moment, the 4th/4th Gurkhas, advancing down a railway line to the right of, and slightly ahead of, the 2nd Berkshires, reported they were under mortar fire. The railway line converged to meet the track down which they were advancing, so to avoid what is now called a 'blue-on-blue', it became, in Hill's words,

vital to make quite certain that the troops to our front were Japs not Gurkhas. The Commanding Officer came up and said, 'STOP'. Within minutes the Brigadier crawled up alongside us and said, 'STOP'. As we peered through our binoculars at the far side of the clearing, up walked General Rees, wearing, as always, his bright red scarf in our Division colours and a Gurkha hat, he had fought in the desert with the 4th Indian Division and yet, here he was hardly properly attired for the jungle war within yards of the enemy. There was a breathtaking pause while the General joined us, and said, 'You'd better make sure'.

The men who had been leading the advance were called in to a short conference about fifty yards from the edge of the clearing. Meanwhile no firing came from the enemy across the clearing, and apart from the leading sections crawling forward, round the edge of the clearing nothing else was happening.

The following conversation took place:

Private Mason; 'I goes quiet like thro' the bushes by the clearing and I 'ears a sound just beyond. I comes out of the bush and there staring at me standing up was a Jap'.

General: 'How do you know it was a Jap?'

Private Mason; 'he was wearing a Jap steel helmet, he had long puttees, he talked Japanese at me, he was a Jap, and he looked like a Jap, sort of yellow'.

Me; 'What happened?'

Private Mason; 'He hops into his trench and fires, only nothing happens, his rifle isn't loaded'.

General; 'What did you do?'

Private Mason; 'I fires at him, and hops into cover quick'.

General; 'Did you hit him?'

Private Mason; 'No Sir, I missed'. (Rather crestfallen and a big anticlimax).

A second man was questioned. He had also seen a Japanese, who had fired at him, and he had returned the fire. Hill was certain his men had seen Japanese, while the General was doubtful, and believed the Berkshires had been firing at Gurkhas. The General, Brigadier, CO, and Hill crawled forward and started shouting in Urdu, Gurkali, and English for about ten minutes with no response. The General waved his hat. Eventually Hill gave the order:

'The advance must continue – they are Gurkhas'.

One section moved fast over the clearing, and halted – no sign of Japs, only one empty trench. By now the General was getting impatient, and with his escort of one Sikh and his Adc, he dashed ahead of the section. While I was telling the Platoon Commander what to do, the General nipped into the jungle on the far side of the clearing and shouted that he had found a trip-wire and a booby trap, and another unoccupied trench, and to come on. Running back across the track, he had just got into some bushes, where my leading man had originally seen the Jap, when a light machine-gun at about twenty yards fired straight down the track, killing instantly the leading platoon commander 'Jock' Ridley, who was about to continue the advance and wounding one of our men and the General's escort.

The gathered 'company' went to ground, and it is of interest to record who this lot were. Apart from myself and the leading platoon, within fifty yards of the Japanese were:

The Divisional Commander with his bright red scarf and bush hat with red general's band round it.

His Adc

The Brigadier

His Intelligence Officer

The Commanding Officer

The Commander Royal Artillery (CRA)

The Regimental Commander Royal Artillery [the CO of the field or mountain artillery regiment supporting the brigade]

A divisional liaison officer

The Battalion O Group, including, as it does, all the commanders [company commanders, mortar platoon commander etc.] in the

battalion with their escorts and runners, various other officers, either
infantry, gunners or sappers.

The first five above mentioned were the nearest to the Japs with
the exception of one dead officer, one seriously wounded private and
one man of my company. What a party. Suffice it so say that all
crawled back to safety. We could now get on with the job. The
tension created by Pete Rees' presence was over. He had come up
because he undoubtedly wanted us to move faster. I think he knew
that he had not helped us and we really did know what we were
about. My feelings at losing quite uselessly one of our subalterns,
were of anger rather than sadness. The incident was known thereafter
as 'Pete's folly'. Pete was our nickname for our much admired and
respected General, who inspired us all, whatever our colour or branch
of the service to great heights of achievement, and who gained for
the 19th Indian Division an enviable reputation for getting the better
of the Jap.

The incident served to remind us that advanced guard and patrol
actions against the Japs were not the easy 'bumming' along the road
or track until held up by umpire-induced 'fire' which was the usual
routine on training.

From now on we fought our normal battle. Mortars ranged, and
the Gurkhas discovered that it was the Japs who were mortaring
them not us.

At this stage in the advance towards the Shwebo plain ominous
signs appeared that the Japanese were not about to dance to Slim's tune.
The enemy had not always been up to their normal aggressive form,
and although Kimura had left covering forces west of the Irrawaddy, the
advance of the 19th Division, for example, despite some brisk engagements, had been unexpectedly easy. Slim realized that if he was to
destroy the Japanese he must do so east not west of the Irrawaddy, by
getting across their line of communication south of Mandalay. Over a
period of forty-eight hours, without asking Leese, merely informing
him, Slim changed the plan. Stopford's 33rd Corps was to take 2nd,
19th, and 20th Division under command, and concentrate in the Shwebo
area with 254th Tank Brigade (Lee-Grant and Stuart tanks) and the
268th Independent Infantry Brigade, while the 4th Corps (now commanded by Lieutenant General Messervy) was to move secretly down
the Gangaw (or Myittha) valley and cross the Irrawaddy at Pakokku,

over ninety miles as the crow flies south-west of Mandalay. The Corps was to consist of the 7th and 17th Indian Divisions, the 255th Tank Brigade (Shermans), the Lushai Brigade, and the 28th East African Brigade. In the second phase of what was now called EXTENDED CAPITAL, 33rd Corps was to seize bridgeheads across the Irrawaddy on each side of Mandalay, while 4th Corps burst out of its bridgehead at Pakokku and dashed the fifty miles for Meiktila, an important road and rail centre, with numerous depots, hospitals, and supply dumps.

To deceive Kimura into believing that Fourth Corps was still moving into the Shwebo Plain, a dummy HQ was established at Tamu from where radio transmissions were made, and all signals from 33rd Corps to the 19th Division, originally in 4th Corps, were relayed via the dummy HQ. The actual 4th Corps was to maintain radio silence while it moved, and until command and control necessitated the passing of messages. Even then it was to simulate the HQ of the 11th East African Division (which had actually been withdrawn) mounting a deception flanking move. This part of the hoax was assisted by the inclusion of the 28th East African Brigade in 4th Corps, and Messervy's plan that it should lead the trek down the Gangaw Valley, so the Japanese would report contacts with African troops. The deception was so dazzling that Field Marshal Terauchi, believing the east side of the Irrawaddy immune from attack, made the grievous error of transferring the Japanese *2nd Division* from Meiktila to Indo-China.

Slim's stratagem involved one of the boldest and most quickly planned manoeuvres in the history of warfare – the move of 4th Corps alone along 328 miles of tracks was daunting enough in itself. The concept was brilliant. The late-twentieth-century military vogue phrase 'manoeuvre warfare' was not invented, but Slim was to prove himself a master of the art years before the term acquired the cult status it now enjoys at staff colleges and with military-minded academics. Lieutenant Marshall, 4th/5th Royal Gurkhas:

After Christmas we got the word that the advance into Burma was to take place. We went from Tamu to Kalewa, down Kabaw valley, and news came we were to march down Gangaw Valley at night as the whole movement of the division [7th Indian Infantry] was to be kept secret. The Gangaw Valley we found was one of the most unhealthy places in Burma, fortunately it was not during the monsoon. It was very hot even at night, dry and dusty. We marched 300 to 400 miles, and took the whole of January 1945. Marches generally started at 2200 hours and lasted for 11 to 12 hours. It was tiring for the British officers because Gurkha have short legs and march at between 2 and 3 mph. Whereas the British Army marches at between 3 and 4 mph. So it takes longer. By the time we had finished this marching we could say that everybody was fit.

None of this would have been possible without air power. The whole enterprise nearly came to a grinding halt at the outset, well before Slim changed CAPITAL to EXTENDED CAPITAL, when, in mid-December 1944, some seventy-five American Dakotas allotted to Fourteenth Army were suddenly ordered to China. The Fourteenth Army needed some 7,000 air lift supply sorties a day, and the loss of these aircraft would have been a disaster. Fortunately Mountbatten persuaded the Americans to release just enough Dakotas to keep the Fourteenth Army supplied. To ease the load on the air forces, Slim and his logisticians decided to make maximum use of the Chindwin and the Irrawaddy for supply. Starting at Kalewa on the Chindwin, his engineers constructed craft from the abundant stands of teak near the river. Forestry units and Colonel William's Elephant Company were put to work supplying the necessary timber, and by the end of the campaign some 541 craft were manufactured. Prefabricated shallow-draft tugs and lighters had also been sent by rail to Dimapur from India, and trucked from there to Sittaung, being used for the first time by the 19th Division to cross the Chindwin.

Stopford advanced south with 20th Division on the right, 2nd Division in the centre, and the 19th on the left. Each small battle produced a trickle of casualties. Hill was with the 2nd Royal Berkshires after a contact at Kin-U about twelve miles north of Shwebo which cost his company

Company Sergeant Major Staples, Privates Horton, Jones, Armsby and Hall killed, Lance Corporal Heath died of wounds, sad losses to us all. The Japs lost a warrant officer and seventeen other ranks killed (including two sergeants) in Kin-U village and two other ranks killed outside by the patrol of the night before. It was evident from bloodstained packs that there had been three more wounded who had got away. No prisoners were taken.

The position had been held by about one and a half companies, and captured diaries and maps indicated another 300 men with mountain guns and medium machine-guns in the general area. The attack had been entirely successful, being mounted from an unexpected direction. The days of frontal attacks, except when unavoidable, had long gone, but the inexorable seeping away of experienced men would make innovative tactics more difficult to accomplish. Hill:

> Kin-U was a good example of infantry tactical technique and owed its success to training and the ability of all ranks. From now on we began to find how much more difficult it was to operate with depleted numbers, as casualties mounted and trained NCOs and men disappeared. Semi-trained reinforcements with little or no battle experience could never satisfactorily replace the existing wealth of skill and knowledge.

By mid-January, Monywa had been overrun by Gracey's 20th Division after a sharp three-day battle, and Shwebo finally taken by Nicholson's 2nd Division. Lieutenant Noakes was in the 1st Northamptons (in the 32nd Brigade of the 20th Division):

> I now commanded number 4 Company as a Lieutenant. We had marched about 250 miles. We had to put in an attack in the afternoon, and to cross a railway line in full view of the enemy, it was the first time we had seen a railway for long time. The idea was to rush the Jap positions and seize the road running from Monywa to Shwebo. I was right flank company, and never got there. We were met by heavy machine-gun and rifle fire and we dug in that night. We didn't have much to eat or drink. The left flank company commanded by Peter Cherrington managed to get the Japs out of Budalin, where there was a railway station. Peter Cherrington was awarded the DSO. He was killed later. He was a lovely chap, who played cricket for Leicestershire.
>
> When we came to Monywa I still commanded number 4 Company, until the company was taken over by Donald Eales White, a major, and I became second-in-command – again. We attacked through a mango plantation. The Japs were in trees and foxholes. Donald got wounded, I took over again; for the third time. Monywa was taken and the Japs retired post-haste to defend the passages over the Irrawaddy.

Freer, with 2nd Division:

We entered Shwebo from the north. We took a war correspondent in our tank. He had been the last British person to leave Shwebo [in the retreat in 1942]. We came to a gateway where there was a dry moat crossed by bridge. There was no sign of life, but there were Jap bunkers on the other side of the moat. The leading tank crossed and others behind him noticed wires leading from the bridge over the moat to the bunkers. Everybody was told to halt, and our sapper officer went forward and found some 500 Kg bombs fixed for setting off by men in the bunkers, but they had been abandoned because we had sprayed the bunkers first. We went into the town, which was dead, with a few chickens running around, but no Burmese or Japs.

The war correspondent produced a report which he showed me, and the only thing I could recognise was the names and addresses of the tank crew. The rest of the report was his imagination.*

Rees seized the opportunity to swing left and push part of his 19th Division over the Irrawaddy at Thabeikkyin and Kyaukmyaung. At Kyaukmyaung Captain Rowley of the 5th/10th Baluch Regiment found that

Crossing the Irrawaddy was the longest swim I ever had. I was charged by my divisional commander to take my rifle company (A Company, Punjabi Mussalmans) across the Irrawaddy, four miles higher than where the main crossing was to be, and we had to swim it. I had some Indian Sappers who helped us build bamboo rafts to carry our weapons and kit. We also took our 18 mules. When we came to look at the Irrawaddy at close quarters it was quite a fast-flowing river, and we had to work out how far we had to start upstream to hit the bank on the other side where we wanted to be. I took one platoon to start with, and I got across reasonably all right. I was able to signal the rest of the company to come plus the mules. Mules are very good swimmers, we crossed dressed except for our boots. All the mules got across. I was very relieved, a mule swept away down the Irrawaddy would have given away the fact that we were there to the Japs, who were unaware of our presence. In fact they did not know we were there for several hours. I moved

---

* Nothing ever changes.

downstream to where the main crossing was to be. We joined the main bridgehead.

The original slender foothold at Kyaukmyaung, about a quarter of a mile in length along the eastern bank, was being slowly and painfully enlarged. Two vital tactical features had to be secured. One of these, 'Pear Hill', was a barren peak rising sharply about 800 yards from the river bank and parallel to it. It was about 2½ miles from the main bridgehead, and dominated it. Both these features were key OPs for Japanese artillery. Captain Rowley:

I was having a few hours rest, having rejoined the battalion, when I was summoned to Divisional HQ, to our magnificent commander Pete Rees, who said to me, 'I want you to get Pear Hill, and hold it'. When you are told by your General that's what you've got to do, you say, 'OK Sir, I'll do it'.

I went back and sorted out my company. We left the bridgehead, which was quite risky because the Japs had surrounded us and were potting at us and I didn't want to get too close to where they were. I got out with my company in single file along the river bank. Several hundreds yards along, we got to the bottom of Pear Hill. I left my company at the bottom, and climbed with my Subedar Major, my orderly and my signaller. I wanted to recce and see what was up there. It was very rugged, and I was trying to keep as quiet as possible. It was quite lightly wooded. I got on top, and there was no sign of the enemy. I turned to my Subedar Major and told him to bring the rest of the Company up. Like an idiot I had taken my equipment off with my revolver, to my horror I found myself looking straight at a Jap OP position close by. I shouted to my men. The Subedar shouted 'Sahib'. There was a Japanese officer rushing towards me with sword raised to knock my head off. He got to within three yards of me, fortunately my Subedar Major shot him. He was a magnificent chap, but was killed later. We killed the OP party all of them. We could hear the gun position calling up the OP on the telephone. We didn't know what they were saying, but we could hear them calling up. I told the Subedar Major to get the company up as fast as possible, and I laid them out ready for an onslaught which we knew would come without question.

I sat on a rock and had the most appalling anguish and was not happy where I was. I was not religious at that time. But I sat saying,

'Lord Jesus what is wrong'? And I listened, the most important thing when you pray is to listen, and this is what staggered me. I got a message, not a voice, but a message, and it said, 'You're not on the top of the hill'. I thought oh my God. I walked forward. We were short of the top by about 80 yards. And there it was the Jap emplacements totally empty. I shouted to my chaps, get up, advance at once. We secured that place. And in due course the Japs belted us. But it would have been a massacre if we had been in the original place. We held the hill. Another company joined us the following day. The Japs did us a lot of damage. But we did more. I was up there for four nights. The rest of the battalion for more. The Japs threw more artillery at Pear Hill than anywhere else in Burma. In the OP there were maps of the Jap positions. I said 'send a gunner up'. The following morning, along with Paddy and his Dogra company, a captain and subedar of Indian gunners came up. As I was explaining the situation to this captain, he was hit by a huge piece of shrapnel.

The aggressive moves by the 33rd Corps, particularly Rees's enterprising crossing of the Irrawaddy, persuaded Lieutenant General Masaki Honda, commanding *Thirty-Third Army*, that this was the main thrust, and he launched a series of fierce but unsuccessful attacks on the 19th Division bridgeheads. The fighting here was some of the bitterest in the whole Burma campaign. An especial threat was the Japanese lodgement on the west bank of the Irrawaddy at Kabwet between Rees's bridgeheads at Thabeikkyin and Kyaukmyaung. Rees sent the divisional machine-gun battalion of the 11th Sikhs (not to be confused with 1st/11th Sikhs) and his reconnaissance regiment to contain the *51st Regiment* of the *15th Division* until arrangements for its elimination could be made. It was as well he did, because the Japanese were planning to use their toehold at Kabwet as a springboard for a counterattack on the Shwebo plain. The Sikhs now found themselves cut off in their turn at Kabwet. They had fought off the Japanese using the considerable firepower of their Vickers guns but were in a tight spot, so the 2nd Royal Berkshires were sent to reinforce them. Hill, whose company was leading, was clear:

There was little time to lose. At about 3 p.m., we found one company of the 8th/12th Frontier Force Regiment which had been placed under our CO's command already in contact with the Japs on the main track which entered the Sikh perimeter.

The now familiar crack and thump of rifle and machine gun fire rose and fell spasmodically ahead of us as we moved forward on our feet. Getting closer, the long staccato bursts of the uniquely recognisable Vickers machine guns engaging the encircling Japs sent sprays of bullets away into the distance.

We deployed to carry out a right flanking move to enter Kabwet from the West whilst the 8th/12th Frontier Force company attempted to make contact on the main track from the North.

In all our advance to contact operations, we carried 60lb packs on our backs with some 100 rounds of .303 ammunition in belts (or equivalent for sten gunners) round our waists. We were wearing steel helmets with our bush hats strapped to our packs. In addition were the Bren guns, their loaded magazines, and our reserve ammunition. All had to be carried, adding to the weight [on the men] when the mules hadn't caught up – as now. To be ready for battle, the first few men left their large packs on my Jeep and Trailer already loaded with impedimenta, later to be brought up as required. The Jeep and trailer was an invaluable maid of all work for carrying extra ammunition and a vital supply of water in chagals strung round it.

It was already late (nearly 5 p.m. before my company began the move). Hopefully we could cover the one and a half miles to the Sikh perimeter before dark. If the Japs were dug in, it would be lethal to try to push ahead and make contact after dark. We would have to see how the situation developed. As usual tracks were non existent through the open scrub and trees. Compass bearings, pacing and the sound of bullets were our guide with the Irrawaddy River bank becoming visible ahead of us.

Having experienced 14 days of continuous close contact with the enemy up to now, I wondered how and when the next test of our battle worthiness would come and how our weakened numbers would affect our skills. In these close quarter skirmishes and actions it was our junior leaders who were taking the brunt. Finding, engaging and killing the enemy, especially when dug in and with little fire support, was made more difficult by the need to maintain pressure on the enemy and press on as quickly as sensibly possible.

By 1800 hours with dusk already blurring the light, we made out the edge of huts and a banana plantation some 150 yards ahead. The leading men moved forward steadily. Frogs croaking, the chirping of cicadas and the rustling noises which are common features of dusk in the East provided a subdued orchestral background to our silent progression through the bamboo thickets and low thorny shrubs.

The Company were by now almost head to tail behind the leading men and me; the noise of firing had temporarily ceased when all three men ahead of me quietly dropped to the ground. Behind me the column halted, closed up as I crawled forward in the gloaming. 'An empty bunker, Sir – and the Japs' smell' whispered the Lance Corporal of the leading section. Looking and bending down we could see another foxhole nearby astride the track. No-one made a sound. Suddenly from about twelve paces distant a man's hissing urgent voice said something like 'Whurre, whurre, wer?' It was certainly neither English nor Urdu. No-one moved; the voice repeated its challenge. Should we answer back? Should we rush in? I already had the pin of my grenade in my hand. Should I throw it? I confess my heart pounded with anxiety.

These are not the kind of happy questions that in these circumstances had a set piece answer. Almost anything we did would probably be wrong! And my three armed men were also twitching alongside me, directly in front of a probably dug in, enemy position.

Behind me some 80 men were now crouching alongside the ill-defined track in the dark wondering what was happening. A cough, a jingle of equipment almost any noise could bring catastrophe on us, whether the man or men in front of us were Japs or our own Sikh machine gunners. It was no good shouting the password if – as seemed probable – the voice we had heard was the enemy's.

Ending the suspense for us four in front, I left a bren gunner to cover us and motioned the others to crawl to the rear. On reaching the rest of the company, I had already decided to set an ambush on the track. It was a racing certainty that we were on the administrative supply path used by the Japs – why hadn't they fired? We could, with luck, catch them using the track during the night if this was their supply route.

Those who have military experience will know that to turn 80 men round, silently, by night, give orders and lay an ambush within close proximity of the enemy is an ambitious move requiring high technical skill and training from all ranks. B Company lived up to all I expected of them.

By 8 p.m. we had established the ambush and now I could send a three man patrol to try to contact the Sikhs along the river bank fifty yards to the South. Within half an hour they returned having been shot at, to report Jap positions on the bank and almost simultaneously once again the sharp staccato sounds of the Vickers machine gun bullets tore through the air close above us. It now became clear that we had run into the Jap positions encircling the Sikhs in Western Kabwet. Reporting over a telephone line which we had reeled out behind us, the C.O. decided that casualties were not justified by a unreconnoitred night attack or by rushing unseen into the Jap posts. We now settled down in the ambush. Desultory firing and occasional shouts from the Japs brought intense long burst of fire from the machine gunners crackling over our heads.

At about midnight, from the edge of our ambush area there was loud shout, a shot and two grenades burst with bright flashes in the centre of the ambush. Within feet of all of us two figures were seen to fall. Then silence. I crawled over to Sergeant Barratt of 5 platoon just as one of the figures moaning and shouting leapt to his feet and to the accompaniment of burst of LMG fire stumbled off into the night. Sergeant Barratt showed me a Jap corpse almost alongside him. 6 platoon under Sergeant Godley had let the two Japs come right into our ambush hoping others would follow but they were unable to wait longer before dealing with these two. Several Japs were heard running away helped by fire from Sergeant Godley and 6 platoon. Sergeant Barratt had thrown the grenades which killed a Jap Sergeant Major, as we discovered in the morning – still carrying his sword, the symbol of his rank and no doubt to be used for summary executions not only on captured prisoners, but also probably on any recalcitrant soldier in his own army.

Although the moon had now begun to appear, it was not practical to move about except in a very limited way. Crawling between various posts only when vital to communicate was about as much as was possible. We could not adjust our ambush area by night without causing uncertainty and confusion, so when I heard sounds of talking and of boats oars on the river we had to wait for events to develop. Meanwhile a few shots of rifle fire and the burst of grenades from the perimeter of the Sikh defences, interspersed with the rattattatting of the Vickers Machine Guns, continued through the night. Bullets swishing through the air less than 6 ft. above us.

At about 4 a.m., at first light, behind us on the river bank at about 100 yards distance we heard the noise of men chopping wood, and talking and laughing – suddenly a fire flared up not more than seventy five yards away right on the edge of the river. I sent an N.C.O. – Sergeant Davies and two men to investigate – they reported the most astounding thing – thirty to forty Japs brewing tea, lying about on the ground and cooking rice. While he was there about fifteen of them moved off to the north. This was too good to be true – we would never catch them if we waited any longer, so I detailed Sergeant Davies with 6 Platoon to go for them and beat them up. To the accompaniment of groans, screams and the noise of boats – he accomplished his task and returned, leaving, most unfortunately, one badly wounded man who made a lot of noise. A party went out and fetched him in but he had already died. When we were able later to search the area, we found upturned mess tins, rifles, steel helmets and a lot of blood on the ground and three Jap bodies. As this target was 'sitting' [sic – static?] the Japs must have been able to withdraw their wounded.

Almost immediately after this episode, the dawn began to break and the plan which I had hatched during the night was carried out. We were in a very exposed position for day, within sight probably of a strong Jap position and in full view from the east bank, in addition, the noise we had made by night would undoubtedly have attracted attention to us. We moved about 400 yards north-west into some cover and started to dig ourselves in. At about 8 a.m. a sentry reported 'Jap approaching' – everyone got into cover and a Jap was seen about 100 yards off, running in with one arm clutching his shoulder. We motioned for him to put his hands up. We stood up and shouted to him to put his hands up. No-one could see what he was clutching in his hand and we all thought it was a grenade. The Jap grenade rather smaller than our no. 36 mills grenade, was activated by striking a protruding cap against any hard object. After a short pause, the grenade would be detonated. This man showed no sign of a wish to surrender despite signals from us to raise his hands. He came running in, his arm against his shoulder, his hand clenched. We had visions of a hara-kiri death not only for him but for some of us. The command fire was given when he was thirty yards away and he fell. On being brought in he had no grenade but was only covering a bullet wound in his shoulder. Now he was nearly dead and died about half an hour later. He had wanted to give in – he was in a poor physical state and had nothing in his satchel except bandages.

He was probably one of the party of the night before. Everyone of us was encouraged to know that at least the Jap was prepared to surrender in isolated cases. No-one felt sorry that he had been killed.

At about 9 a.m. just as we were probing forward again to contact, the C.O. phoned to say that A Company had gained contact with the 11th Sikhs on the main axis into Kabwet and that the Japs had withdrawn many of their encircling posts.

We were withdrawn to the Battalion area where we remained in reserve for the 17th being able to eat and rest. On the 18th we moved into Kabwet to relieve the Sikh Battalion who had had a very harassing time – the Japs had completely cleared off from Kabwet village itself and were nowhere to the east. The Battalion moved three miles west to Yonbin to make sure the Japs had gone and not just moved west a few miles. Although recently occupied we found empty Bunkers but no Japs were seen.

There were however strong Japanese positions on Hill 152 across a chaung east of Kabwet, consisting of two battalion HQs, five companies, and guns, with more bunkers and guns west of the chaung. The Royal Berkshires spent some twelve days in contact, patrolling and making local attacks to gain information. Hill's company was now down to 80 all ranks (from a starting strength of 120), despite having been reinforced with men from C Company, which had been disbanded to provide men for the other three companies in the battalion. Only one platoon in B Company was commanded by an officer. Hill was wounded in the foot during this period, but 'strapped up by the stretcher bearers with a sulphonamide dressing I was soon back in my OP'.

A Company, carrying out a local attack, resulted in the loss of the company commander and five men missing. Two officer-led patrols trying to find the missing men ended with both officers dead, and several soldiers killed or wounded. Hill:

> When the area was finally overrun, the bodies of a number of officers and men were found stripped of their boots, tied upside down to trees with electric light wire, assaulted and beaten. This was the first occasion we had experience of brutality which only served to harden our hearts still further against the Japs.

On 28 January the first phase of the final attack to eliminate the Japanese at Kabwet succeeded in clearing ten bunker positions, but some still remained. It cost the lives of the Royal Berkshires' most experienced company commander and several soldiers. Now Hill 152 must be taken. Hill:

The 29th dawned and the plan for what was hoped would finish Japanese resistance was based on an H-Hour of 12 noon. The fire plan included four squadrons of B-25 bombers dropping 1,000 and 500lb bombs from H minus 25 minutes to H minus 10 minutes; one squadron of Hurribombers from H minus 10 to H-Hour and completing their bombing runs by strafing the enemy positions.

It occurred to me that this huge weight of firepower on enemy in open country even if dug in MUST kill them and so demoralise them that we would have a simple task. It had not occurred to me that there would be much of a firefight. I was even looking forward to taking prisoners. How I was mistaken!

Our friends from 115 Field Regiment, the Sikh machine gunners and our own 3-inch Mortar and small arms were to give covering fire over our heads from H minus 10 to H hour.

During this time the Battalion was to move to a Start Line about 50 to 100 yards short of the enemy held hill. Very close up, B Company on the right, D Company on the left. The Hurribombers would make dummy runs on the enemy position after H hour to keep the Japs heads down and the Artillery and Mortars would lift their fire, being controlled by wireless, 100 yards at a time. H hour would be signalled by firing Red Verey Lights.

Huge columns of smoke and dust signalled the results of the bombing from the B25's which arrived on time as we moved forward from our Assembly area to the Start Line, everyone with their bayonets fixed.

All went according to plan and we found ourselves fifty yards from the enemy position, all had been briefed thoroughly and in front of us lay a bare brown hill with enormous craters 20 feet across a few tangled bushes and trees. We were lying down waiting for the Red signal with the noise of aircraft and the continued rattatting of the Vickers guns overhead. The time was about 1152 and I looked for a few seconds at the aircraft as they swept in spitting viciously at and beyond the hill. As I looked at one just overhead, to my horror a bomb suddenly detached itself and came straight on us. I shouted 'down' – we were already quite flat! The next minute it hit the ground with a dull thud and nothing happened! I breathed again. The bomb was obviously not fused. The fortunes of war were with us.

The red lights were up and we were up and suddenly the noise of the Vickers swung to our left flank, no more sharp flat cracks immediately overhead. We rushed madly up the hill gaining courage with every yard, on the right someone firing. The right platoon going slowly, the left platoon going well and now half way up the hill, the right platoon going again, more firing, a man hit – there are Japs. Damn, thought I, having hoped they would all be killed or give in. Another hit to my right the right platoon held up, a Jap Light Machine Gun and grenades The Little B—someone firing back, the Platoon sergeant, Davies, of 6 Platoon with blood on his shoulder holding it. Suddenly finding myself looking at a Jap just about to fire at me, ten yards off! Instinct – fire back, one dead Jap. Still on again, another Jap, a grenade out and into his hole, explosion and groans, on again, bayonet – and now the platoons are moving again. In with the bayonet shouting, and sticking a third Jap in the chest – more shooting and no more Japs to be seen, good work that was almost fun!

Those chaps in 6 Platoon were very 'sticky' and ought to have done better. On my left 4 Platoon on the position two dead Japs – no casualties. On my right 6 Platoon on the position about eight dead Japs and three casualties.

We were there! So were D Company to our left and just in front at about 200 yards range were about twenty Japs running away. A crescendo of firing – more Japs running. By now we had started reorganising on the objective; tools [picks and shovels], ammunition, collection of wounded, patrols forward, a good deal of return fire on anyone exposing himself forward and two of our men hit whilst running about on top of the hill.

We were right to take this hill. We now dominated the whole Jap position down to the river but visibility was still constrained by trees and scrub. The whole area was bomb cratered with trees, shrubs and debris everywhere. Quickly coordinating new platoon defences on and beyond the ridge one of our men said with a twinkle in his eye 'none of them surrendered then Sir?' they all knew we wanted some prisoners but had ambivalent views about taking them. Carl Reynold my 2 i/c was searching for identities having dragged out one dead

Jap from a foxhole, he suddenly saw movement in another a few yards off and as he came up – a Jap put his face up and bared his teeth and snarled at him making an almost inhuman sound in his throat. Disposing of him with his sten gun he then discovered that the Jap had been hit by a grenade and had both arms broken, apart from numerous injuries to his body. Yet this Jap had been capable of snarling a last defiance before passing on to join his ancestors! All those Japs who fired at us after the most terrific hammering by all the implements of modern war, were fanatically brave and we always had the utmost admiration for them in defence, where in all cases each individual fought till he was killed.

We expected the counter attack but it never came and by dusk we were well established in their positions.

After this battle we were hopeful next day of taking the remainder of the Hill feature to the east where there were two Pongyi Kyaungs [monasteries] untouched by the bombing, and so on 30th we withdrew again while an air strafe with bombing took place.

Very unfortunately the air attack missed its appointed target and we and D company found ourselves committed with virtually no support. Needless to say the attack failed, but in failing we had a very serious list of casualties. Sergeant Barratt, Corporal Bailey, and Private Lea killed. The Sergeant was a magnificent leader, an old regular who knew his job and was brave and very cool headed. Corporal Bailey – a young and promising N.C.O. and Lea who had done good work with his light machine gun throughout. Sergeants Edwards and White wounded. Private Birch wounded and died of his wounds later. Edwards was very keen and a good N.C.O. having trained for the Chindit operations and falling sick just before they went into action he had had extremely good training experience and Sergeant White had been with us in all our Jungle Training. I could ill afford to lose four first rate N.C.O.'s in one battle, at this stage in the campaign and in this Theatre.

Dodd was again 'cited' for distinguished and brave conduct in bringing in wounded under fire and reorganising the platoon when all the N.C.O.'s on the spot had been killed or wounded. He later was mentioned in dispatches for his work here.

The lessons of this attack became obvious. If fire support fails to neutralize the target, with our present depleted numbers the attack should have been called off before it began. I think at Battalion HQ there was a feeling that all was over bar the shouting and that two companies would be adequate; also that we should press home our successes of the day before and clear the Japs up quickly and finally. I think Harold Finch [the CO] learnt that there were limits to what we could achieve with our numbers and fire support in what amounted to a set piece attack against entrenched opposition. I think Brigade HQ wanted to get Kabwet out of the way as quickly as possible. We had been there a long time.

In the attack, I needed to remind our sergeant platoon commanders and our NCOs that if a man was hit, whoever he was, he could not be rescued or looked after until the attack was over. There had been a natural tendency to want to help a comrade immediately he was hit. This I explained was what our excellent stretcher bearers were for. It was paramount with our weakened numbers to maintain the momentum of forward movement at all costs, if we were to kill the enemy and seize their ground. The stretcher bearers understood and carried out their task in quickly reaching wounded men which did much for morale.

On the night of 30th – 31st January a motor boat was heard on the river and the noise of explosions and people talking and shouting on the east bank. We harassed them with gun fire which silenced the noise and caused the boat to chug off down the river.

On the 31st January a dummy air strike was laid on. We smoked the area but did not withdraw, the plan being to catch the Japs out of their positions as it was suspected that they had evacuated their position before the air strike on the previous day. At the same time as the aircraft arrived on the previous day, we moved in and now to our amazement found the whole Jap position empty. They had had enough at last. Among others we had again seen off the Japanese 58th [51st] Regiment perhaps for good.

After sixteen days of continuous fighting and contact the objective had been attained, costing the 2nd Royal Berkshires nine officers and ninety other ranks killed or wounded in this action alone. It was now just over a month since the battalion's first battle and Hill's company was down to fifty all ranks, despite having absorbed reinforcements from C Company. No one should be in any doubt that losses in the fighting in Burma could equal those on the Western Front in the First World War.

Others had also been fighting on the Shwebo plain before crossing the Irrawaddy, and there were as always moments of farce, dangerous nevertheless. Freer:

After Shwebo, we had a few more actions in villages in the area between the Irrawaddy and Chindwin. The tanks were wearing out, and we had tracks dropped to us by air which we fitted within hours. Food was also dropped by air. It was announced on Squadron orders in mid January, that Christmas Day 1944, will be on 15 January 1945. The cooks produced some chickens and we had Christmas Pudding.

After that it was sorting out road blocks again. On one occasion we were clearing a village with a company of Royal Scots. The tanks were in the lead. I saw two Japs jump into a slit trench just ahead. The Squadron Leader told me to guide the driver to it. I opened my little port, just as a grenade landed beside the trench, about five feet away from my port. It was the Squadron Leader who had thrown the grenade. It killed the Japanese, but a splinter from the grenade had cut the wire that ran under the tank wing to the wireless aerial. The set wouldn't work. So the Squadron Leader ordered me out to repair it. I asked him to turn the tank sideways to give me cover. I climbed out and with a pair of pliers, and jackknife. I looked under, found the two wires, repaired them, but not before I got a tremendous [electric] shock, because the Squadron Leader was transmitting, using me as an aerial. The fighting continued and we had tiffin on the move, eating cold baked beans out of the tin.

We then went back to the slit we had attacked earlier. We lifted up the Jap bodies and took the papers out of their pockets. Just then machine guns opened up and rounds cut up the ground around us. I recognised the sound of a tank Browning. We all threw ourselves to the ground. I said, 'It's one of our tanks Sir.'

He said, 'Well go and stop it'.

That's when the 100 yard record was broken for the first time. I jumped into our tank, and picked up my headset to hear a troop leader, say, 'I still think there's some movement there, give them another burst or two'.

I said over the radio, 'Able 5, were you were firing your Maggie?' [machine-gun]

He said, 'yes, I'm engaging some Japanese, over.'

I said, 'Cease firing.'

'Why, over?'.

'You are firing on number 9 and his crew, over'.

There was a horrible hush, then 'Wilco out'.

The CO had been listening and chipped in, 'I want a report on the situation within minutes. Out'.

I looked out of the tank, and the other six members of the crew were walking back.

Next day following the same routine one of our troop leaders wirelessed back to the Squadron Leader 'there are some boats crossing the Irrawaddy' He replied 'sink them then'. They were laden with troops, and were sunk.

That was the end of that phase. We relaxed, swam, and fished with grenades to improve our diet. Then we were told we were going to cross the Irrawaddy, and go to Mandalay.

Slim kept a tight hand on the timings of the operation, not allowing 20th Division to cross the Irrawaddy west of Mandalay until the 4th Corps was ready to cross far away to the south. On the night of 12 February, the 20th Division crossed and seized a bridgehead at Myinmu, followed by breaking out and cutting the Japanese communications at Kyaukse south of Mandalay. Noakes was with the 20th Division:

My company was the reserve company for crossing the Irrawaddy. The attack, at night, was by numbers 1 and 3 Coys. When no 3 got into their boats to go, the boats sank. The company commander ordered his men out and on shore. The CO was fed up, and ordered me up and to get my boys into boats that were made available. And we set forth like a crocodile of rubber dinghies with an outboard motor on the front one, which kept on conking out. We were met by machine-gun and mortar fire which was not very effective. A couple of nights before we crossed, a young officer was sent out to the far bank with two or three signallers in a rubber boat with an Aldis lamp as a guide to us. He was told to put a red filter in the lamp. The Irrawaddy current is quite fast, so navigation across at night is difficult. The red lamp was a brilliant idea. The RAF were asked to send their noisiest plane to patrol up and down the river to cover the sound of the crossing. This seemed to work.

We landed on the far bank after a while. When we got out we found ourselves in four feet of water. We waded ashore, and dug in on the beachhead. Two days later the whole battalion was across, the

Japs reacted by shelling. We came up against the infantry guns, we called them 'whizz-bangs'. The guns were manhandled up to the front line and skilfully handled by the Japs. The gun had a very flat trajectory which did not give any warning of the approach of the shell.

After a few days, it was decided to extend the bridgehead, and my company was sent to a chaung, a tributary of the Irrawaddy, which was used as an OP by Jap artillery. So we turfed them out, dug in, and we were shelled every day. The area was all elephant grass. It crackles as you walk through it. The Japs attacked one night, didn't come through the elephant grass, but up the chaung. Fortunately we heard them. They are great chatterers. I put up parachute flares from 2 inch mortars, and we beat off the attack. There were plenty of trees round our perimeter so we had a two strand barbed wire fence round our position which was a godsend. We also had a section of Medium Machine Guns from the 9th Jats. We had a very big attack two or three nights later. The Japs employed smoke to cover their attack against the light of the parachute flares. They brought up smoke canisters. At first we thought it was gas, and we had left our respirators in India. We had 4.2 heavy mortars in support. These fired through the smoke, also the Medium Machine Guns were very busy. The Japs brought up Bangalore Torpedoes made of bamboo, with which they attempted to crawl up to the wire. But we never allowed them to get close enough to do that. We found a lot of Jap dead near the wire. I found one dead Jap officer, called Lieutenant Yamamoto, beautifully dressed with a sword, which I still have.

I never saw Mandalay until later, from about 5 miles away. We advanced across open country, and saw no Japs until we got behind Mandalay. The Japs were evacuating the city, and we ambushed a party of them. It was a Jap warrant officer who was Head Clerk of Army HQ in Mandalay, carrying a case of documents, which we passed back. We shot him, and he crawled away. We heard him moaning, I told one of my platoon commanders, 'put him out of his misery'. As he approached, this warrant officer shot himself.

Rees passed the rest of his division across the Irrawaddy and pushed south. Captain William Rhodes-James (brother of the Chindit) commanded B Company 1st/16th Gurkhas in the 64th Indian Brigade in a succession of advance to contact battles. On one occasion

We had Grants in support. We formed up on the Start Line and were shelled by the Japs which was disconcerting. I rode on the tank until the bullets started to bounce off the armour. We found the Japs dug in, the tanks seemed to hypnotise and cow them. My men sorted them out, while the tanks stopped to let us clear them out. My left platoon found two battalion guns dug in ahead. My right hand platoon commander rushed forward and captured both.

As we advanced south, following up the Japs as they withdrew, I was wounded. There were a lot of Jap bullets flying about, and a Jap grenade landed in the road, the shrapnel hit my forehead, and filled my eyes with blood. It was not serious, in the same battle Mike Cowan, General Cowan's son, was badly wounded.

In the meantime the 2nd Division crossed at Ngazun, between 20th Division and Mandalay. Captain Howard did not look forward to it:

Having very little to do the day before crossing, I found my imagination was roaming around too much. With no facts for an appreciation of the situation, the imagination was making one without the facts, and remembering the hammering 19 Div had taken in their bridgehead, the imagined situation was unpleasant. Not even the thought that nothing could be worse than Kohima, which I survived unscathed, was reassuring.

In the morning, I don't know whether Jock [his brigade commander] did justice to his breakfast, but I made little headway with mine.

From the moment of landing [on the far bank], my spirits rose rapidly and my appetite returned. For the next few days I felt at the top of my form. Before crossing, I had been scared stiff, but now I was over, I felt as happy as a sand-boy – well almost.

The 33rd Corps were now marching on Mandalay from three directions, and Kimura was convinced this was the main British thrust.

Meanwhile the 4th Corps had been marching south on the Gangaw track, their armour on transporters, and with road gangs improving the going behind the leading formation. Messervy ordered the Lushai Brigade, a lightly armed formation which had been operating in a LRP role in the Lushai Hills for over a year, to take Gangaw; he chose it because he did not want to rouse Japanese suspicions by too great a show of force. The first attempts were unsuccessful, but a massive air strike dropping several tons of bombs for every Japanese defender did the trick. The 28th East African Brigade took over the advance and screened the remainder of the corps as it slogged down the Gangaw Valley. All the while, Slim hoped that the Japanese eyes were fixed on Mandalay, while the 4th Corps approached the Irrawaddy. He steeled himself to avoid taking counsel from the fears which assail most commanders in the lull before the next enterprise:

> Success depended on what? Luck? A Japanese pilot streaking across the tree tops in his Oscar, an enemy agent with a wireless set crouched above the track counting tanks, or a prisoner tortured until he talked – and Kimura's divisions would move, the muzzles of his guns swing towards our crossing places. Imagination is a necessity for a general, but it must be a *controlled* imagination. At times I regained control of mine only by an effort of will, of concentration on the immediate job in hand, whatever it was. And then I walked once more among my soldiers, and I, who should have inspired them, not for the first or last time, drew courage from them.[4]

The Irrawaddy in the latter half of the dry season has receded from its full monsoon flood, but is still a mighty river, and where the Fourteenth Army was about to cross was an average of 2,000 yards wide, and well over 4,000 at the junction with the Chindwin. As the river shrinks after the monsoon, it exposes broad stretches of soft sand on each bank which are difficult to traverse in wheeled vehicles. Dotted about throughout its course are islands and sandbanks, whose position changes with every flood. This meant that the best route across was not necessarily the shortest, and craft had to pick their way through the channels between sandbanks, sometimes doubling the distance from bank to bank. The equipment available to Slim to move his army across was rudimentary, and in a poor state of repair after years of use and long journeys in trucks over appalling roads. There was a shortage of outboard motors. The local boats could carry a good load, but were very difficult to handle by anyone other than the Burmese boatmen, many of whom declined to participate. Slim had nothing like the resources available to the armies in Europe, who were readying themselves to cross the Rhine at about the same time.

Messervy planned one main crossing place at Nyaungu, with deceptions at Chauk (by the 28th East African Brigade), a large one at

Pakokku, and another at Pagan. Lieutenant Farrow, the Intelligence Officer of 1st/11th Sikhs, noted in his journal:

> The far bank of the river, except at Nyaungu town itself consisted of cliffs intersected by the mouths of dry chaungs every few hundred yards, and appeared to afford complete observation over the low-lying cultivated near bank.

As the 114th Brigade approached Pakokku, Lieutenant Marshall, the commander of the 4th/5th Royal Gurkhas' mortar platoon, recalled, 'Our patrols found a heavily defended position at Kanhla', eight miles west of the town. A quick attack by the 4th/5th Royal Gurkhas made some headway but a second 'bite' was necessary.

> The Japs were well dug in in prepared positions. It took all day, but eventually we overran the position at about 1600 and many Japs were finished off in their holes, as they refused to surrender. During the battle, our new CO, Lieutenant Colonel John Turner was giving orders, and was hit by a sniper in the stomach. I was taking orders about three feet away from him.

The CO of the 4th/5th Royal Gurkhas died the next day. The 114th Brigade were ordered to clear the west bank of the river, and mask Pakokku, which was strongly held, to prevent the garrison interfering with the crossings. The 89th Brigade reached the west bank opposite Pagan, and Farrow of the 1st/11th Sikhs

> established an OP on the east side of island facing Pagan where we could observe activity on opposite bank. This island was separated from the west bank by about three hundred yards of water.

> *10th February 1945*
> I go to B Company with air photograph which will assist Jim Merrick's [the company commander's] planned recce into Pagan.

> *11th February*
> B Company had managed to get a small reconnaissance patrol across the river in the southern end of Pagan. It was well concealed and reported by wireless at odd times on enemy activity.

> *Monday 12th February*
> Locals report large enemy forces actually in Pagan. 300 JIFs with 20

to 30 Japs and field gun, MMG in Bupanga Pagoda. Our recce patrol over there confirms this information, which is something of a surprise as the place had earlier been reported empty. During the night the entire battalion with a battery of mountain artillery concentrated on the island.

Tuesday 13th February

Tonight's the night we are to go across the river. The plan is for A & B Companies to go across in the first wave. We have 17 country boats ranging from 2 to 10 tons and these were placed under my control. Due to many of the boats springing leaks on loading we were only able to get B Company away. The boats were obviously not accustomed to carrying too much weight during their normal duties on the Irrawaddy river.

B Company go off into the night, rather like a cluster of leaves falling into a fast moving stream. We could see them turning first one way then the other as they disappeared into the darkness. Suddenly all hell is let loose as three MG's, rifles, and grenade dischargers open up from the opposite bank. We attempt to neutralise using MMG's and mortars but firing still goes on. B Company must be having a terrible time and we hear on the radio from midstream that as soon as the firing started the Burmese boatmen refused to proceed further. Despite threats, beatings and near miss revolver shots the boatmen brought their craft back to the island. After all that exchange of fire we discover that we only suffered three wounded, however we are all seething with rage at our failure to get across in strength.

Wednesday 14th February

As dawn broke the battery of mountain artillery (3.7 guns) who were with us managed to get off some good shots in the area of the Red Pagoda. We could see numbers of Japs and JIFs on the other bank quite plainly.

Meanwhile preparations for the main crossing at Nyaungu were in train. It was to be the longest opposed river crossing attempted in any theatre in the Second World War. Soundings and reconnaissance by the Special Boat Section (SBS) charted the channels. As they were making the final reconnaissance of the far bank, the SBS encountered two Japanese swimming, who were shot to stop them escaping, and it is

likely that this alerted the enemy. Despite this, one company of the 2nd
South Lancashires managed to cross without any opposition on the night
of 13/14 February and dig in on the cliff top. The daylight assault by the
remainder of the battalion was, however, driven back by enemy machine-
gun fire from positions in the cliffs. Farrow was opposite Pagan:

Wednesday 14th February [continued]
On several occasions during the morning we were greatly saddened
to see a number of assault boats drifting past our position, some
empty but many contained dead officers and men of The South
Lancashire Regiment and Royal Engineers. These were some of the
heavy casualties sustained at the main crossing at Nyaungu, six miles
north of our position. Main problem was engine malfunction with
the result that number of boats just drifted out of control downstream and past Japanese entrenched positions on far bank. We were
able to collect several of these badly shot up boats and the bodies
were moved back to Myitche.

Our abortive attempt to cross the previous night must have
drawn enemy attention away from the main crossing further north.
I return to Bn H.Q. at Taunghansu. Air strike goes into Pagan using
VCP (Visual Control Post) complete with RAF officer and wireless
operator in their own jeep. We are sending fighting patrol over to
Pagan to-night. Message from Brigadier Crowther that we will get
across somehow and supported by General Messervy with 'Throw
your heart over and your body will surely follow.'

Thursday 15th February
Early in the morning we were surprised to see two men on the
opposite bank carrying a white flag. They were of the Indian National
Army, and they crossed to our position by country boat. They
reported that the Japanese who had been with them on the far bank
had moved north, leaving a company of INA to hold Pagan. It was
obvious that our fighting patrol which had gone across to Pagan the
night before had been most successful as the INA company wanted
to surrender!

Jim Merrick immediately volunteered to take B Company across
the river. Only three country boats were available and the local
boatmen nowhere to be found. Jim took over one of his platoons in
the first wave and the INA filled up the boats and brought them back
to us. Their weapons were laid down in dumps on the far bank as

Jim and his platoon took up defensive positions. We gradually got his other two platoons over, but found that we officers had to do much of the rowing as our men had no experience and very little idea. Not much rowing done in the Punjab. By evening both A and B Companies plus Battalion HQ were established in Pagan and dug in for any counter attack. The remainder of the Battalion, less C Company, were to join us the next morning plus the mountain battery.

The 92 INA men are now on the other side of the Irrawaddy and the captured equipment included two Vickers MMG's which will be very useful for us in holding the bridgehead. The equipment is obviously that taken by the Japs in Singapore. I learnt from the INA company commander that they had all been captured in Singapore and by joining the INA had considered it the best means of getting back to our forces. The Japs had executed several who were reluctant to join in public parades after the Singapore surrender.

We found several INA (JIF) bodies in Pagan which were no doubt the result of our fighting patrol the previous night.

Friday 16th February
Battalion less C Company now complete with mountain battery and consolidating in Pagan.

Saturday 17th February
Twenty-six INA surrender to us with more old Singapore captured arms. Early in the day we had contacted troops from the main crossing at Nyaungu and the battalion had been assigned the job of protecting the right flank of the bridgehead. Later we moved two miles south to Myinkapa, and dug defensive positions covering the main road to Chauk. Patrolling commenced and we were soon getting reports of contact with large groups of Japanese moving north to oppose the bridgehead.

As Slim comments, the surrender of the JIFs at Pagan 'was, I think, the chief contribution the Indian National Army made to either side in the Burma War'.[5]

Meanwhile, the 33rd Indian Brigade, led by the 4th/15th Punjabis, had started to cross at Nyaungu under massive supporting fire from artillery and aircraft. By nightfall on 15 February the whole brigade was dug in on the east bank, and had sent a patrol to link up with 1st/11th

Sikhs at Pagan. Although as Farrow records the Japanese moved up from the south to attack the lodgement, they did not give it their full attention. Their eyes were fixed on the 33rd Corps's crossings around Mandalay. The following day the crossing at Nyaungu was in full swing, and guns, tanks, mules, and men poured across while attacks towards Chauk and at Pakokku drew away the Japanese reserves in the locality of the crossings. Farrow:

Sunday 18th February
B Company started moving south down the main Chauk road, but were soon halted when one of their patrols encountered a Japanese company in the vicinity of a ruined pagoda. Two men of our patrol were wounded but B Company pushed on and the enemy withdrew to a large red pagoda about half a mile further south. Due to the very open ground, fairly flat but dotted with many small ruined pagodas Jim Merrick considered he was unable to move further forward without additional support. Captain Pritam Singh with a section of his mortars moved up in support and a request was made to Brigade for tanks to assist the advance. The latter was a difficult request to negotiate as there were not too many tanks in the bridgehead on this side of the Irrawaddy. One troop of 116 RAC. (Gordons) (Sherman Tanks) was obtained with the remark that if they were not extensively used we were in serious trouble. B Company started moving again as soon as the tanks arrived around 1100 hours and cleared down to a village called Monatkon. In the meantime the CO and the mortar section had moved down to a Red Pagoda. It was unfortunate that B Company in their sweep forward had concentrated their attention towards the east side of the Chauk road. At Twinywa, a village on the west side of the road, some hundred or so Japanese were hiding and attacked the Red Pagoda after the tanks and B Company had passed by.

The ground in this area is very broken with many small dry nullahs and the fighting became very close and confused. Japanese were popping up and running all over the place as Battalion HQ was suddenly under direct attack. Captain Pritam Singh (Mortar Officer) was badly wounded in the first few minutes and although Dick Webster and Harold Proudlock made every effort to carry him away, he had to be left behind in a very exposed position. Nevertheless he had a very lucky escape by playing dead when approached by a

Japanese officer brandishing a sword. After a close study the officer moved on.

Bn HQ were able to use the 15 cwt truck belonging to the Mortar Section, to reach B Company and the CO then ordered them to turn around and attack the Red Pagoda. B Company and tanks engaged the enemy in and around the pagoda and inflicted extremely heavy casualties in fierce fighting. The 75 mm guns of the Sherman tanks were too hot to touch after all the firing. Their machine guns also took heavy toll when they caught many Japanese in the open.

After the engagement over 30 bodies were counted with our casualties being three killed and 14 wounded. Late in the action Jim Merrick was hit in the stomach while using the 'house' telephone on one of the tanks and directing tank fire. Throughout the entire action Pritam Singh continued to lie in the same original very exposed position and all attempts to rescue him had failed. Finally he was spotted by a tank and recovered. Sepoy Pertap Singh (15 cwt truck driver) throughout the engagement drove around the battlefield behind the tanks, often under fire, picking up our dead and wounded. One Jap was seen banging his fists against the side of a Sherman tank in his rage and frustration at not being able to do anything. Needless to say he was quickly shot down. Instances were reported of Sten guns jamming but as one VCO said they 'make satisfactory clubs'.

Monday 19th February

Terrific Japanese night attack on our positions which lasted for two and a half hours. They followed up with subsequent attacks to recover their dead and wounded. With the exception of one body they recovered all their dead outside seven to ten yards of our forward trenches. We captured three wounded Japanese all belonging to *5 Company 2 Battalion 153 Regiment of 49 Division*. They were quickly passed back to Brigade headquarters for treatment and interrogation. D Company (Major Tom Dykes) who were located at the village of Thutekan claimed 20 plus Japanese killed with eight bodies actually recovered. We lost communication with them for a time during the night.

Tuesday 20th February

Visited Field Hospital at Myitche but was greatly saddened to find that Jim Merrick had died of his wounds and had been buried on a small knoll a couple of hundred yards from the tented hospital.

Meanwhile Messervy had pushed two brigades of the 17th Division (48th and 63rd) and the 255th Tank Brigade through the Nyaungu bridgehead, in readiness to advance on Meiktila. In the north further crossings by the 33rd Corps kept Kimura's eyes firmly fixed in that direction, and he ordered the maximum concentration of force against the 33rd Corps in the vicinity of Mandalay. He stripped troops from other fronts to concentrate some eight Japanese and one and a half INA divisions against what he perceived as the Fourteenth Army's main thrust. But the Japanese did not let up in the vicinity of the crossings by 4th Corps. Farrow:

Friday 23rd/ Saturday 24th February
Expected very determined Japanese attack came in our main positions during the night and lasted for four hours. They brought up 70 mm gun to 500 yards from our positions and their 250-man attacks were also supported by mortars and MMGs.

On 21 February Cowan's 17th Division and 255th Tank Brigade (in total two regiments of tanks, about 100 all together, and a regiment of armoured cars, a self-propelled battery, and two lorried infantry battalions) advanced on Meiktila on two routes. By 26 February, Thabutkon airstrip, twelve miles north-west of Meiktila, was in 17th Division's hands, and the fly-in of their 99th Brigade (Brigadier G. L. Tarver) began. Strong Japanese opposition on the route to Meiktila was overcome by a tank attack on a wide front. This was the first time the Japanese in Burma, and probably anywhere, had ever encountered armour used in such quantities, exploiting its speed, shock, and firepower in open country. They had no idea how to cope and were routed, hunted down, and killed in droves. Lieutenant Colonel Pettigrew, the GSO 1 (de facto chief of staff) to Major General 'Punch' Cowan, remembered that on one occasion

Punch Cowan had a real rush of blood to the head, because he cut straight across country with the whole of Div HQ. It was highly exhilarating, the whole lot in jeeps, signals trucks etc. driving over fields, and leaping over bunds. We reached a road just as it was getting dark, cut back along it to regain the main road to Meiktila. Punch Cowan told me to get on and find areas for the brigades. So with liaison officers from the brigades, I set off realising I was leading the whole division. I told the liaison officers where to put their brigades, and everybody occupied their positions in the pitch dark. I'm sure there were Japs about. I said to 'Punch' Cowan, 'you remember we had a good saying on the Frontier, "you must make camp two hours before dark", and I reckon this applies here'. He was a very wily old chap, and I had some disagreements with him.

In fact, as the 17th Division account relates, the area was

infested with snipers, so the layout for the harbour area for the whole force was delayed, and dispositions in the case of some units were not occupied till after dark. But the JAP [sic] had taken a terrific knock and well over a 100 had been killed by one bn [battalion] alone, and a peaceful night ensued.

Cowan had advanced eighty miles and now had to take Meiktila. This had to be done with the utmost speed before Kimura could react. Major General Kasuya commanding the administrative area of Meiktila had about 13,500 men at his disposal to defend the locality. Some were 'cooks and bottle washers' in base units and dumps, but they were ordered willy-nilly into the firing line, including sick and wounded, even men with one leg. The town itself was held by 3,200 men, well dug in with artillery and anti-aircraft guns in the ground role. Wide lakes and canals provided obstacles for armour in the south and west of the town, so Cowan decided to block the main approaches to Meiktila, to hold off any reinforcements, while the Tank Brigade with two infantry battalions hooked round to the north and came in from the north and east. On 5 March, after four days of bitter fighting, Meiktila fell to Cowan's men. The Japanese resistance was fierce. In one position the fifty or so surviving Japanese jumped into a lake to drown or be killed. In another locality, about 200 by 100 yards, 876 Japanese bodies were collected. According to the 17th Division report:

1 March saw the bitterest fighting of all. Progress was slow but one by one bunkers and positions in houses were overcome and all the Japs in them killed. The enemy casualties were very great, but so many were buried in bunkers by air, artillery and tank attack, that only a part could be found and counted.

During operations by the 63rd Brigade, as it was clearing the western section of Meiktila, Major Randle commanding the Pathan Company of the 7th/10th Baluch Regiment found a Japanese hospital on fire. Tanks had been bunker-busting in the hospital compound, which was heavily defended, and an air strike had started the fire:

> It was like a scene from hell with flames and screams. It was a base hospital full of wounded and sick, in a filthy state smelling ghastly.
>
> We were pushed on at dawn the next morning, given an FOO and a tank in support. My leading platoon commander was killed, the FOO was killed. I couldn't get on, so another company [A Company] was put in with a whole squadron of tanks, and succeeded. Naik Fazal Din was awarded the VC for this action.

Two VCs were awarded for the battle for Meiktila, one to Lieutenant Weston of the Green Howards, attached to 1st West Yorkshires, the other to Naik Fazal Din, part of whose citation reads:

Naik Fazal Din was commanding a section on 2 March 1945 during A Company's attack on the Japanese bunkered position ... During this attack, the section found itself in an area flanked by three bunkers on one side and a house and a bunker on the other. This was the core of the enemy position and had held a company attack made earlier in the morning. Naik Fazal Din's section was accompanied by a tank but, at the time of entering the area, it had gone on ahead. On reaching the area, the section was held up by Light Machine Gun fire and grenades from the bunkers. Unhesitatingly Naik Fazal Din personally attacked the nearest bunker with grenades and silenced it. He then led his section in a blitz against the other bunkers. Suddenly six Japanese, led by two officers wielding swords, rushed at the section from the house. The Bren gunner shot one officer and a Japanese Other Rank, but by then had expended the magazine on the gun. He was almost simultaneously attacked by the second Japanese officer who slashed with his sword and killed him. Naik Fazal Din went to the Bren gunner's assistance immediately but in doing so was run through the chest by the Japanese officer, the sword point appearing through his back. On the Japanese officer withdrawing the sword, Fazal Din despite his ghastly wound, tore the sword from the officer and slew him with it. He then attacked a Japanese Other Rank and also killed him. He then went to the assistance of a sepoy of his section who was struggling with another Japanese and killed the latter with his sword. Then waving the sword, he continued to encourage his men, thereafter staggering to Platoon

Headquarters about 25 yards away to make a report. Here he collapsed and was evacuated to the Regimental Aid Post. He died here soon after reaching it.

Naik Fazal Din's VC was the sixth won by the 17th Indian Division in the Burma campaign.

The Pathans of Major Randle's company had a grim sense of humour:

We were under strict orders not to hurt the Burmese. One of my patrols came across some Japs having it off with some Burmese girls. The girls ran in one direction, the Japs in another. The men were shot. There were more Japs in a bunker with some Burmese girls. We managed to get the Burmese girls out, before my chaps threw in some phosphorous grenades and burned the Japs to death.

The attack on Mandalay began on 8 March. Rees's 19th Division assaulted the city, while 2nd Division took Ava and Tade-u, and 20th Division advanced on the road running south through Kyaukse to Meiktila. The core of the defence of Mandalay was Fort Dufferin. This was a huge construction, two miles square, with brick walls twenty-three feet high, banked with earth ramps and surrounded by a forty-foot moat. Air and artillery attack seemed unable to do anything other than scratch the huge embanked walls, and no breaches were made. A silent attack by the 64th Brigade in rubber-soled shoes and with flamethrowers was mounted in rubber boats across the moat. A toehold was achieved, but at daybreak Rees reluctantly ordered a withdrawal. So far no Japanese had attempted to leave the fort, and not so much as a British patrol had entered it. At this point Rees received information from a prisoner which indicated that the Fort Dufferin garrison was small and had been ordered to hold out to the last man as relief was impossible. He therefore sealed off the exits, and concentrated on taking the remainder of the city, while subjecting the Fort to almost nonstop artillery and air bombardment. Major Hill, B Company, 2nd Royal Berkshires:

My company's order was to clear the west of Mandalay City. A Company was on our left. The enemy had organised a house-to-house rearguard operation. We were now in a standard street fighting operation with a minimum of fire support from artillery and mortars. Snipers were everywhere. Bullets whined and ricocheted among us as we returned fire and inched forward by short bounds.

Harold Finch [the CO] visiting the forward companies to urge us on, cut across from A Company through the remains of bombed-out houses. Taking a short cut he ran through an area being sniped at by the Japanese. Arriving during a lull in the firing, he stood looking down at one of my men under cover and asked what he was doing. When told, 'pinned down by fire', he said, 'press on'. Before anyone could reply, three shots in quick succession hit the ground right by him, and he took cover rapidly. Confirming my orders, he began to understand we were not just sitting around.

I was usually about ten yards behind the leading men, and my batman and runner sometimes found ourselves having to sort out Japs who had been overrun. On one occasion we came upon a Jap in a clump of grass who leapt up almost under our feet having fired a shot at us. He had a stubbly beard and filthy long hair, shouting something like 'Banzai' he tried to run into a house beside me, but my single rifle shot caught him and we finished him off with a grenade thrown over a low wall behind which he had toppled.

During the advance by B Company, Sergeant Heywood commanding 6 Platoon captured an ammunition dump by the railway line. Hill:

The Jap guards, wearing white gloves were unaware of his approach and were despatched speedily before they could occupy their positions. One blew himself up with a grenade. Perhaps they had never had their orders countermanded and continued with their ceremonial guard mounting as if nothing had changed from their peace-time role.

As a result of this day's fighting L/Cpl Brown, Private Jenns and Private Dodd MM were killed, Private Cullen died of wounds, and there were 11 wounded including two platoon commanders. Private Dodd was killed trying to bring in a wounded man – he had been magnificent throughout the campaign – never more than a private soldier, he was quiet and unassuming, yet bullets and action and danger seemed to stir him into life and make him a superman among his platoon – he had no outward fear and was the inspiration of his platoon if not the company. His death was a heavy blow to us all. This day's fighting only accounted for eighteen dead Japs, a bitter day.

On 12 March, Mandalay Hill to the north of the city was finally taken. Meanwhile, on 14 March, Hill's B Company was still involved with the force clearing Mandalay City. With his company was a troop of tanks of the 7th Cavalry. The tanks had far more casualties during the Mandalay fighting than at any other stage of the campaign so far. Hill:

The Japs contrived to retain a gun and a little ammunition round every corner and with Shermans as our strongest tank it did not need anything bigger than a 75 mm at point-blank range to put them out of action. During the fighting in Mandalay we invariably captured a field gun whenever we overran a Jap position.

On 14th March the Company was ordered to capture a road junction level with the east wall of the Fort. After capturing a 75 mm. gun manned by Japs who ran east we were fired on from some ruined houses about 150 yards short of the objective. The tanks were signalled up and ranging by artillery of 115 Field Regiment and mortars from 33rd Anti Tank Regiment commenced, together with a recce of the area to be attacked.

While we were doing this one of the tanks was hit by a direct hit at about 100 yards range from a 75 mm. and set on fire. At the same time Japs had crept round to our south and were lodged in houses sniping at us in the Assembly Area causing casualties and preventing free movement. The attack had to be called off while these snipers were cleared. Meanwhile the tank was burning fiercely and ammunition was exploding everywhere from it.

The crew of the tank were in the most shocking state. Right under our noses they baled out one by one through the burning turret, each one more badly burnt than the next, and for some reason there were seven of them which is more than the normal crew. I shall never forget watching them helplessly as we all were, the first man had no hair and his clothes were half burnt. It needs no language to describe the last man. They all died later in hospital – those who got as far. Tanks in built up areas are very vulnerable to anti tank and field guns fired at close range.

The snipers to the south were proving very troublesome. In the upper stories of a group of houses, they could see any movement in the area and yet they were some 600 yards distant well outside our objectives. I sent Sergeant Heywood with his platoon to deal with them. In his usual efficient way, he withdrew his men quickly and within minutes was on his way round to the south. Just before he left the area he was hit in the thigh by a piece of shrapnel from a Field gun firing at the burnt Tank. It took about 20 minutes to get him under cover. He died of his wounds about five hours later, we were told, having been evacuated to the advanced dressing station north of Mandalay. The platoon under a Corporal with smoke and mortar covering fire continued without Sergeant Heywood and to a timed programme rushed the group of houses and killing one Jap saw the other three running towards the Fort. They returned without loss and the CO decided that the enemy in front of us were more than one company could take on. We withdrew some 100 yards into some rough ground while C and D companies planned an attack for dawn next day. During the night the Jap abandoned the cross roads and C and D Companies successfully attacked the area around the houses by the cross roads.

Sergeant Heywood's wound and subsequent death affected everyone. He had so clearly been outstanding in all he did. Even those men whom he had cause to discipline from time to time realised we had lost not only a true professional but also a cheerful and intelligent companion. He had already been given the DCM as an immediate award for all his work up to now. An award he never lived to receive. We also lost Sergeant Cox commanding 4 Platoon wounded by rifle fire during the assault on the cross roads. So our platoons were commanded now by one Sergeant – Godley – and two Corporals. NEVER TAKE COUNSEL OF YOUR FEARS – The enemy were undoubtedly in much worse shape than we were and I felt despite our losses we were tactically superior and certainly fitter, better equipped and fed.

And to cap this day we lost our Company 2 i/c [wounded for the second time in the campaign]. Times were indeed getting harder.

On 20 March, six Burmese with a white flag left the east gate of the Fort and reported that there were no more Japanese left in the fort; remarkably the enemy survivors had slipped away. Among the first troops to enter the Fort were Rowley's A Company of the 5th/10th Baluchs:

We went in all ready because we didn't trust the Japs. We crossed the moat, and climbed over the rubble [caused by artillery and bombing attempting to breach the walls] into what had been a prison courtyard. We knew there was a prison where we entered, but not that it was empty and the doors locked from outside, so we could not get out [of the courtyard]. I had to use a machine-gun to blow the lock away. We were going along gingerly, when we heard and saw a figure about fifty yards away. As it got closer, it didn't look like a Japanese. I shouted a challenge, and he turned out to be an American from Shwebo [airstrip] who had just driven in in his jeep to look for souvenirs. He said, 'The gates were open. I'm on holiday, on leave'.

Meanwhile Kimura, reacting with unusual flexibility, unlike most Japanese generals, ordered a swift regrouping to recapture Meiktila. This involved moving troops from a number of dispersed points, and Fourteenth Army's response was aggressive action to destroy the enemy as they concentrated. Farrow's account of operations with 1st/11th Sikhs operating in the vicinity of the Singu–Kyaukpadaung road gives a flavour of the fighting at company level at this time, mostly unreported in official histories:

Two D Company patrols returning in the early morning to their main position stumbled on to a small party of Japs. Thinking it was just an ambush group, the fifteen Sikhs fixed bayonets and charged. Unbeknown to them the Japs were about 150 strong, but the fierce Sikh charge took them right through the Japanese position and out the other side. They killed 14 [sic*] en route, but regrettably only seven Sikhs got through, and they were all wounded. Really magnificent performance, but absolutely typical of these tremendous warriors and it is a great honour to serve with such men.

And five days later:

Extremely heavy night attack on A Company positions in Tetma village area. Japanese Captain led the assault waving his sword. He was shot and caught in the wire, where he stayed shouting and crying for most of the night. When he was approached at dawn, he committed hara-kiri with a grenade.

During these Japanese assaults it took several hits to stop these fanatical infantrymen. Sometimes it was almost as if they were

---

* I doubt that the surviving seven Sikhs who had just charged through about 150 Japanese stopped to count the bodies on the way.

wearing protective clothing, and even the odd head wound, showing brain, still found them very much alive and dangerous.

Slim's excellent radio-intercept service and air reconnaissance pinpointed the enemy as they marched to Meiktila, and they were harried and struck from the air and ground. The Japanese had been helped by Chiang Kai-shek suddenly and arbitrarily withdrawing his Chinese divisions from NCAC. This left the 36th British Division as the sole Allied contestant on the Northern Front. It had captured Mongmit after a hard battle two days after the fall of Meiktila, but Chiang Kai-shek's obtuseness allowed Kimura to move the bulk of Honda's *33rd Army* south in the effort to destroy the British at Meiktila. The Japanese meanwhile cut the road between 17th Division and the Irrawaddy. But, Cowan, now on air supply, never lost the initiative for a moment. He mounted a series of attacks on the Japanese communications and bases, buying time for the remainder of the 4th Corps to break through to him. The 9th Indian Infantry Brigade, in the 5th Division, was flown into Meiktila airfield to reinforce Cowan. Part of the brigade landed while the airfield was under Japanese attack. At one stage the Japanese held the edge of the airfield, and supplies, particularly ammunition and fuel, were low; reinforcements could not be brought in, nor casualties evacuated. Corporal Wilks of B Company 2nd West Yorks:

> As we were landing the Japs were shelling the airstrip. The American crew said, 'We're not stopping, we'll land and taxi along, and as we taxi, you lot jump out. As soon as you're out, we'll take off again'. It was a bit of a shambles, with men and packs all over the airstrip.
>
> After landing we went into a defensive box, which was about the first time in the whole campaign I'd seen barbed wire. The Japs shelled us. Our job was to get out and clear the airstrip before the next lot of planes could land. The Japs were in trees each side of the strip, sniping at us. We couldn't see all of them, so we let go with bursts of fire into the trees. When we shot a Jap we had to search them for diaries, letters and the like. We kept watches if we could find them. I still have a Jap silk flag. We only took one prisoner, wandering along in a coma. If it had been one of us [taken by them], we'd have been used for bayonet practice.

Cowan, not for the first time since taking command of 17th Division three years before, found himself fighting a savage battle, cut off from

32. After an air drop. Mandalay hill in the background.

33. Dry season in central Burma: Lee-Grant tanks in the dried-up bed of a chaung.

34. A human mine: a Japanese soldier shot while sitting in a hole with an aircraft bomb awaiting a tank.

35. The 255th Tank Brigade at Meiktila.

36. The 6th/7th Rajputs at Meiktila with a Sherman tank.

37. A Lee-Grant with infantry south of Mandalay.

38. Major General 'Punch' Cowan GOC 17th Indian Division, with cigar, and Brigadier 'Deadly' Hedley Commander 48th Indian Brigade, with cigarette holder, confer outside Meiktila.

39. A Sherman of the 19th Lancers with infantry of the 25th Indian Division pushing up the road from Ruywa to Tamandu in the Arakan.

40. Gurkhas attacking in a burning village after crossing the Irrawaddy.

41. Three commanding officers of the 5th Infantry Brigade, British 2nd Division. The brigade led the division's crossing of the Irrawaddy at Ngazun west of Mandalay. Left to right: Lieutenant Colonel Mcalester 1st Queen's Own Cameron Highlanders, Lieutenant Colonel O. G. W. White 2nd Dorsetshire Regiment, and Lieutenant Colonel T. A. Irvine 7th Worcestershire Regiment. By this stage in the war, unfit and incompetent COs had been weeded out.

42. This picture shows about two sections of 1st Sikh Light Infantry charging with the bayonet during the battle for Pyawbwe. Possibly a posed picture, or taken of one of the rear companies, as the photographer is unlikely to have preceded the advancing troops, unless he had suicidal tendencies.

43. The 4th/10th Gurkha Rifles enter Prome, the third largest city in Burma. A Chinthe stands on each side of the temple steps.

44. Captured 'Jiffs'.

45. A rare sight before the end of the fighting in Burma – a Japanese surrendering to soldiers of the 5th/10th Baluch Regiment.

46. Preparing for the drop on Rangoon: rigging up Gurkhas of the composite parachute battalion formed from 50th Indian Parachute Brigade (last in action at Sangshak near Kohima). The drop went well, but Liberators attacking Elephant Point, one of the objectives, bombed short inflicting thirty-two casualties on the Gurkhas, who went on to take the objective. Of the thirty-seven Japanese holding the position, only one was taken alive. The Gurkhas suffered a further forty-one casualties, bringing their total losses to twenty-one killed and fifty-seven wounded.

47. After the fall of Rangoon: (left to right) Lieutenant General Sir William Slim GOC-in Chief Fourteenth Army, Air Vice-Marshal S. F. Vincent commanding 221 Group RAF, and Major General H. M. Chambers GOC 26th Indian Division which carried out the seaborne landing at Rangoon.

the main force. At its climax, he learned that his son Mike, a company commander in the 1st/6th Gurkhas, had died of his wounds. Clearing the Japanese away from the airfield took several days of fighting by tanks and infantry. Randle, with 7th/10th Baluch:

> I was sent out on an independent operation with armour, my first with a squadron. We rode on the tanks, I was on the Squadron leader's tank. He drove over a mine attached to an aircraft bomb, wrecked the tank and blew me off the tank. The driver had his legs broken and the tank was smashed. I took ages to clear the thick stuff with my company. The squadron stayed outside. The squadron leader didn't appreciate how long it would take, and got impatient and pushed off. We didn't get the degree of smooth integration that they had in Normandy or the Desert. Tank's attitude was we are the chaps who clear everything, and you're just the poor bloody infantry. This might have been OK in NW Europe, but not in thick country. Tanks couldn't understand why we took so long to clear thick stuff. We were taking casualties. They had a 'hack on' attitude. It was lack of their experience. Somebody should have worked out how to communicate with them. We never really cracked it.

The telephone on the back of the tank was one way of communicating, but risky when the tank was under fire. Getting through by radio could not always be relied on in heavily wooded country.

When the Japanese ran out of anti-tank mines, they replaced them by human mines, consisting of a soldier crouching in a hole with a 100kg aircraft bomb between his knees, holding a large stone poised over the fuse. When a tank came over, he would hit the fuse with the stone, to blow up himself and, he hoped, the tank. When infantry found these human anti-tank mines first, sometimes they made no effort to defend themselves, '.... or strike the bomb, when our men looked down on them. They only peered up, seemed to say to themselves, "A man! I'm waiting for a tank," and again bow their heads, in which position they were shot'.[6] Sergeant Wood, a platoon commander in the 2nd Durham Light Infantry, was moving on foot up a dried-out water course with his platoon, supported by tanks, when

> In the middle of the river bed we saw a pile of fresh straw. I contacted the tank commander through the tank telephone, and suggested he gave the heap a burst with his machine gun. This was lucky, because

no sooner had he blasted at the straw, than a Japanese jumped out of the hole. When we got there, he was sitting, dead, cross-legged in the hole, with a huge shell between his legs. He had a stone with which to hit the detonator when the tank went over the top.

At Meiktila it took until 29 March to clear the Japanese right away from their artillery positions dominating the airfield, and on 1 April the airfield was open for use without interruption. By now the 20th Division had passed through Wundwin on the road south from Mandalay, and on 30 March made contact with the 17th Division.

Meanwhile the rest of the 4th Corps had been fighting hard to open the road to Meiktila and capture Myingyan. With the latter in Slim's hands, supplies could be brought down the Irrawaddy from Kalewa on the Chindwin. Fierce fighting was required to achieve both these objectives, but no sooner was the road open, than Honda attacked from the south from Kyaukpadaung, towards the bridgehead at Nyaungu. His troops included INA, who fled when they encountered a brigade of the 7th Division coming south to meet them, but the Japanese units put up a stiff resistance, as they also did north of Chauk on the west bank of the Irrawaddy. Earlier the 4th/14th Punjabis had been detached to assist the East African Brigade, who were in trouble in the area of Letse on the west bank of the river. Here Major Gadsdon of 4th/14th Punjabis recalls an attack by the *153rd Regiment*:

The shelling was just the preliminary to the anticipated attack, which came in on the rear perimeter of the Letse Box on the night 19/20 March. I listened from my slit trench forward of the defended area with mounting apprehension. The amount of shelling combined with the noise of an infantry attack was enough to make any reserve Company commander feel that he would soon be called upon. The area attacked by the Japanese housed our Battalion mules the reserve ammunition and all the Battalion stores. This equipment had a small party of fighting men to look after it, together with the cooks, tailors, sweepers and other followers of the Battalion who were not recruited from Indian fighting classes. Some enemy got inside the barbed wire and occupied the pits in which the ammunition was stored. From there they were evicted at first light by mopping up parties in which our followers took an active part. The overall situation was, however, desperate. The enemy had taken a number of points on the high ground overlooking our Box and were sniping at anything that moved. The African troops were becoming increasingly demoralised under the shelling.

At dawn my call came. 'Take all available troops and report to the Brigadier.' So off we set to try to restore the situation. As we got near the Box it was apparent that there was still quite a battle going on, but it was mostly our troops firing on the far side of the perimeter. So I crossed my fingers and made for the barbed wire gate sealing the track, when a large African askari stepped out and saluted smartly. The result was that I was caught by a sniper who got off two rounds before I found cover in the ditch, swearing vehemently. It was good shooting at fairly long range.

The Brigadier's instructions were explicit, 'Clear the northern perimeter, remove all enemy from Songon village and patrol as far north as Wayonbin.' As on a previous occasion, I thought the orders a bit ambitious as the Japanese 153 Regiment, or what was left of it was somewhere out there. At full strength they numbered about three thousand men and I was taking out two platoons, about seventy strong. Off we went across the Letse Box to our starting point, where the attack had come in during the night. Our mule lines were on the way. Here the shelling had caused havoc, leaving only seventeen animals standing out of our full complement. Beyond the mules the reserve ammunition lay in pits. This was as far as the attack had penetrated. The odd enemy soldier had been eliminated there at dawn, in a spirited attack by our non-combatant cooks and camp followers who were looking after the dump. Enraged by the continuous shelling of the last twenty-four hours, they were only too willing to have a go when called on to eliminate the enemy inside our wire. We found the gate in our wire, and here a macabre sight met our eyes. The perimeter wire was three coils of Dannert [spiral barbed wire] laid two on the ground and one on top. This is a formidable obstacle to penetrate without wire cutters, or a 'Bangalore Torpedo' to blow it up. On the wire were draped the bodies of forty-nine Japanese unable to go forward because of the wire and unable to go back because machine guns were enfilading the wire a few feet outside our defences, and firing on fixed lines at night. Thus the enemy were trapped, and a number of them took their chosen way out, with a hand grenade down the shirt front. Since all Japanese prisoners were considered dead by their families, this form of 'hari kiri' was a quick way out and a passport to Heaven. It was not a pretty sight, nor one calculated to improve the morale of a small mopping up force, as we spread into open formation with a rather hollow feeling in our stomachs.

We were now clear of our defences, looking across four hundred yards of flat open plain to a small tree-covered hill on which stood the village of Songon. I checked that the safety catch on my Orderly's Thompson sub-machine gun was 'off' [sic], as he was a bit trigger happy, and fixed a bayonet to the rifle that I always carried. I much preferred that weapon to the alternative of a .38 Smith & Wesson revolver, having done the Sniper's Course, and it was also a simple matter of self-preservation. We moved forward in bounds, with one Platoon covering the other, with no artillery barrage or supporting fire, and without knowing whether somebody was watching us over the sights of a medium machine gun which the Japanese carried well forward. In fact there was one in Songon village, but it was beyond the crest of the hill in front, so my luck held once more. I do not recommend that walk to anyone with a lively imagination.

As we went we passed the casualties of the night's action, but none of them stirred. Suddenly I saw movement under a bush ahead. Throwing up my rifle I took a snap shot and charged in, accompanied by Waris Khan, whose Tommy gun had acquired a life of its own, spraying bullets in all directions. We had captured a Japanese officer, too badly wounded to escape with his retreating comrades. He was sent back for interrogation, after I had relieved him of his Samurai sword. At the time prisoners were so rare that a reward of Rs.100 and a fortnight's leave was offered to anybody who took a prisoner. I never got either, maybe because my prisoner only survived long enough to say that this was D-day and that he was from 153 Regiment. In any case, nobody was going to get leave in our situation.

We had now reached cover at the foot of the hill and paused to reform. Not a shot had been fired by the enemy. We worked our way up the ridge through the village, killing some ten Japanese stragglers who stayed to fight it out. They would not be taken prisoner, preferring to die fighting. One wounded Japanese lay just beyond the crest of the ridge where my orderly and I came on him in the act of throwing a hand grenade. As I shouted he stopped, and I thought that we had another prisoner, but each time that we approached he made to throw the grenade and eventually blew himself up. I could see my right-hand platoon closing up to the ridge when, suddenly, firing broke out on my left. I hurried along the dead ground below the summit of the hill and found my men engaging an estimated ten Japanese, with one of our men wounded and lying in the open. I could clearly see two Japanese getting a machine gun into action about 100 yards in front of us across a dip in the ground. The situation called for the usual tactic of holding the enemy in front and working round to attack in the flank or the rear. I gathered up the right-hand platoon and set off to carry out the manoeuvre. Some time later, guided by the sound of firing, I got into position, gave final orders, and put in a charge. To my amazement I quickly found that we were attacking about a hundred of the enemy who were attempting to dig a defensive position. As we ran forward a machine gun opened up, down went two of my men, and I was on my face in the sand, with a long crawl out to cover, assisted by the machine gun crackling overhead.

Once I was clear, in the dead ground, I wirelessed back for help from the artillery whilst we stayed in position to stop the enemy from getting away. I was also given a platoon of Africans who were to be used for a further flanking move. When they appeared they made it quite plain that they were not going any farther, so I put them into my platoon's position on the crest, and, once more, gathered up my men for another attempt to dislodge the enemy. By now it was nearing mid-day and arrangements for covering fire from the guns took some time, so the attack would be in the heat of the afternoon.

We set off again, somewhat more warily, to try to outflank the position. Coming over some rising ground I spotted their defence line some seventy-five yards away, with one Japanese standing in his slit trench, looking to his right, the shape of his helmet being clearly outlined against the sand behind his trench. It was, for all the world, like one of the snap shooting targets that suddenly appeared as you advanced up the Stickleback range at Bisley on the Sniper's Course. Instinctively I threw up my rifle and fired as I steadied the sights. That will square the account for my friend Chris Edelsten, who they killed in the Arakan, I thought. A spurt of sand shot up behind the trench, the helmet turned slowly and disappeared into the bottom of the trench. One more enemy would take no further part in the day's engagement. Realising that the artillery had their range, and that they were about to be attacked again, the Japanese left their trenches and charged us. The platoon on the left received the main attack and killed sixteen Japanese without a single casualty on our side. At that, the enemy decided to quit, and about forty got up and ran wildly for the cover of the trees behind their trenches. They ran across the front of a section placed to stop them and ten more were eliminated.

The firing then died down and I was able to deal with our wounded and recover the body of the one Sepoy who had been killed. It had been a long hot day, but I reported to the Brigadier that Songon village was clear of the enemy and that we had killed some fifty Japanese. The total count of enemy dead in the area turned out to be 235. I noticed that the Brigadier seemed more than relieved that the immediate threat to his base at Letse had been removed. At the time I was not aware that the shelling inside the perimeter had shaken the Africans to the extent that they were close to running away, and any further attack could have been the last straw. At any rate he was grateful, and showed it three weeks later when I received the immediate award of the Military Cross. The Naik, who recovered the body of the dead Dogra under a smoke screen, and another NCO were both given the Military Medal.

My small skirmish did not decide the outcome of the battle. The Japanese had taken Point 534, overlooking part of our defences, and were using the position to shoot at anything that moved inside our perimeter. It is true that victory and defeat are often finely balanced in war, and this occasion was no exception. The Brigadier sent for his unit commanders the following day and told them that he could no longer rely on the Africans to stand and fight. In the circumstances he must issue preparatory orders to bury our ammunition, be prepared to break up into small parties, and find our own way back to the main force miles in the rear. These orders would be activated if necessary. Back with the Battalion a white-faced Colonel repeated the preliminary orders. We listened aghast. I could still hear the screams of the Somerset Light Infantrymen, a year before in the Arakan, when the Japanese butchered their wounded. I went back to my trench, pulled a blanket over my head in the dark, and chain smoked furiously while saying a sincere prayer not to let it happen. We had held our positions around Letse for a month. We had to fight it out; to do anything else would be suicide.

By morning the situation in the African lines had sorted itself out, but one platoon each from A and D Companies was sent back to Letse to strengthen up the defences. This left me somewhat short of manpower on my exposed hill at Ywathit. Rations were also short and we were forced to open some of the sealed tins in which emergency rations were stored. These consisted of hard biscuit, processed cheese and a pack of dried fruit. Unfortunately, the latter had some livestock [weevils?] in them which, at first sight, made them unacceptable. However, hunger soon taught us to remove anything that stirred by day and then eat the fruit at night. We suffered no ill effects.

Point 534 plainly had to be retaken and C Company was given the job. It was the usual advance down a ridge and John Davis, the Company Commander, was killed almost at the outset. Our Battalion Second in Command, Neville Williams, then went forward and took over. He was a tall Regular Officer who had won the Military Cross on the North West Frontier, where fighting the British Raj was a way of life with the Pathans. In order to find out what was going on he went right forward to do a reconnaissance and was killed by a machine gun. The loss of two British officers in one engagement was a severe blow to the morale of the Battalion, and we began to wonder just who was winning our part of the war. However, the 2nd South Lancashire Regiment was sent down to reinforce our garrison and arrived on the same day as we had our officer casualties. Point 534 was not recaptured by us, but the enemy knew that we had their location and their situation was not tenable unless they captured the Letse Box. Two days later one of our patrols found that the position had been abandoned.

On 1 April, the Japanese conceded defeat in the battle of Meiktila and Mandalay, and rearguards were ordered to cover the retreat of the remnants of *Fifteenth* and *Thirty-third Armies*. The casualties suffered by the *Fifteenth Army* are not recorded, but were probably similar to those in *Thirty-third Army*. The *18th Division* lost about a third of its strength and twenty-two out of forty-five guns. The *49th Division* took 6,500 casualties out of 10,000 with which it had started the battle, and lost forty-five of its forty-eight guns. In the words of the British official historian, '*Burma Area Army* had virtually ceased to exist as a fighting force'.[7]

Unsurprisingly, fighting the formidable Japanese, Slim's stunning victory had not been won without loss to Fourteenth Army. Let us look at B Company 2nd Royal Berkshires, who have figured prominently in this chapter, and were by no means atypical, as Hill relates:

> Of the original B and C Companies amalgamated after Kin-U, who started from Imphal in November [1944], i.e. from a total of 196 all ranks there were only 26 left in the Company. I was the only officer.
>
> In the first phase of our battles from 25 December [1944] to 25 March [1945] we had 16 days of close contact on the approach march. At Kabwet another 21 days of actual combat, and now a further 30 days of direct close involvement with the enemy.
>
> We were ready for a breather before chasing the enemy further south in the next stage of the campaign. In another theatre, we would probably have been taken out of battle altogether and even possibly disbanded to reinforce other units. With the long lines of communication with every aircraft, boat and lorry loaded with supplies for subsistence this was not an option in Burma in the Spring of 1945.
>
> Mend and make do and soldier on. Nothing had changed.

While the 4th Corps concentrated at Meiktila, the 17th Division made preparations to assault Pyawbwe, where the enemy were preparing strong blocking positions on the road and railway to Rangoon. The enemy would fight hard to hold these, to stop the Fourteenth Army from bursting through to Rangoon before the monsoon closed most airfields and made movement by armour and wheeled vehicles impossible except on hard-top roads. From Slim downwards, the Fourteenth Army was determined to reach Rangoon before the rains came. Before relating the story of the advance down the Rangoon Road, we must fast rewind to events in the Arakan.

9

The Arakan: A Watery Maze

The perversities of weather and terrain imposed even greater strains than the malice of the enemy. Life during the monsoon necessitated the transformation of each soldier from mammal to near-amphibian ... The oozy troughs of the chaungs, the matted thickets of the hillsides, the sodden glades and naked peaks alike inflicted a stark and sub-human routine on all ranks. Days and nights coalesced in an undemarcated nightmare of sleeplessness, fouled food, soggy clothing, rusting accoutrements, mouldy blankets and unending tension ... To wait, to march, to fight, to hunger and to thirst, to bear burdens, to wait, to march and to fight again – such was the interminable ambit of the days.[1]

Although Slim had ordered Christison's 15th Corps to pull back from Buthidaung into more easily defended localities with the onset of the monsoon of 1944, this did not preclude aggressive patrolling by his battalions. Lieutenant Neill, the Intelligence Officer of the 3rd/2nd Goorkhas, took out many patrols; one of them was tasked to seize a Japanese prisoner from behind their lines. The Brigade Intelligence Officer, Captain Val Meadows, was to accompany the patrol, whose soldiers came from 5 platoon B Company, with their platoon commander, Subedar Manbahadur. Neill was summoned to Brigade HQ for briefing, where he found a V Force officer called Maurice Budd. Neill:

The plan was to board a small coastal steamer at Maungdaw, steam down the Naf River by night, towing three large country boats to a point about five miles south of the river entrance, where we were to get into the country boats, and row ashore. Having left a section to hold the beach, with the heavy radio to Brigade HQ, we were to advance about 1,000 yards to the village of Ponra, to set up an advance patrol base with the co-operation of Maurice Budd's V Force villagers.

We boarded the steamer at 2200 hours wearing cap-comforters instead of bush hats, and hockey boots to aid us in silent movement. We took rations for fourteen days, but relied on the V Force villagers to supply us with rice on repayment. The main load was ammunition and grenades, which we grossly underestimated. We had all experienced deep penetration operations under Wingate in 1943, and this was very much in our thoughts, because it had been a bad year for the Battalion, and an alarming baptism of fire for many of us. At an early age we had been introduced to bad superior commanders, conducting an ill-conceived plan, and we had not enjoyed the treatment.

At about midnight, in an ominous swell, we climbed, heavily laden, into the country boats, which were about the size of a fairly large rowing boat. The mens' faces in the moonlight were studies – if I was afraid how much more must the men been in the fear of their lives as not a single one could swim. After a nightmare 500 yard journey in the boats, we all landed safely and spent the rest of the night on the beach.

The following morning Maurice Budd left to join the V Force patrols. When we arrived at Ponra, we found a message from him saying he would make contact later. The villagers were all Muslim, pro-British, fiercely anti-Japanese, and loyal friends throughout.

Our first contact with the enemy came on 1 July [having set up a patrol base forward of Ponra]. We were patrolling the village of Lambaguna, which was in two parts. As we were moving through the northern part, the villagers said the Japs were occupying the southern part, but did not know their strength. We were taking up a position overlooking a strip of paddy between the two halves of the village, when three Japs stood up from behind a small mound about three-quarters of the way between us and the far side of the paddy. After a few minutes, perhaps they were suspicious, because they took up fire positions behind the mound, but still clearly in sight, as they were out to our flank. We watched fascinated for another minute, as they lay exposed about 75 yards away.

We had never had the chance in 1943 to study Japs at leisure, at short range. We made the most of this opportunity and then killed them. I fired first with my Thompson SMG, and my Bren gunner shot the other two. There was no reaction from the enemy in the southern sector. But we should have been given bad marks for moving out into the open to search the Jap bodies, furthermore we were few in number and a long way from home.

Learning that the Japanese were still in the vicinity, and guessing that they would follow up, Neill decided to ambush the track. After spending a night without sound or sight of the enemy, he pulled back to his patrol base. The following day he learned from villagers that a Japanese patrol was approaching the base.

Silently we ran to our stand-to positions, but in our haste, I had forgotten to give out specific orders about opening fire. The enemy were about 400 yards away, and it was too late to put this right. There were nine of them, bunched up in single file, with rifles with fixed bayonets slung on their shoulders. They were moving idly and talking among themselves. I was surprised at such laxity, which was unusual. We watched like cats watching mice, but these mice were dangerous. I grinned at the soldier alongside me and he grinned back. When the Japs were about 75 yards away, and I was saying to myself that they were not quite close enough, a long burst of Bren fire shattered the silence. Excitement had obviously got the better of the left hand section's gunner.

The Japs took cover behind the bund like lightning, and I doubt that any were hit. Everybody fired without any control orders from me, with all the horrors of the Wingate campaign of 1943 bubbling up in our minds, the sight of our enemy pinned down in front of us drove us berserk, and we fired and fired until the barrels of our weapons became red hot raking the bund. Occasionally a Jap shoulder or rump would appear momentarily above the bullet-torn paddy, and we would fire wildly at such an attractive target. I had fired nearly three out of my five magazines, and not hit anything, before changing to single shots. A Jap tried to crawl away, I fired quickly two or three times, seeing hits on the wet shirt on his back. A wet rump poked up for a moment, and I fired three quick shots, one hit and flung the Jap back into the flooded paddy. As I hit him with another shot, I remembered that our mission was to take a prisoner, and if I didn't act soon, all candidates for the POW cage would be dead. I screamed above the din to the left-hand section to give me covering fire, ordered the section with me to cease fire, fix swords [bayonets in rifle regiments are called swords], draw kukris and charge.

Over the bund we leapt, and plunged into the knee-deep water of the rice field, yelling blue murder. I could see the strike of the shots from the supporting section hitting the field ahead. Suddenly two enemy broke cover and tried to make a dash for it. I fired at one – too short – magazine empty, how many more mistakes, how many more lessons to learn? I knelt and guiltily changed magazines, switched to automatic, determined to kill the Jap. The other fleeing enemy stopped and flung up his hands in surrender I was not gaining on the other man, my chest was heaving, my Tommy gun muzzle was going up and down, my eyes full of sweat. I fired three bursts and could see the rounds hitting the man's back, flicking away pieces of shirt and flesh. I had not realised the hitting power of a .45-inch bullet before. The Jap shot forward like a rag doll hit with a sledge hammer. I went over to him and took his rifle.

I told my men to check the remaining seven bodies for signs of life, and that I wanted to search each one for documents. The Japs were great ones for keeping diaries, which disclosed useful information. I started on the body of the man I had been chasing. His documents told me that he was a first class private of the 143rd Regiment, as were all the others. He was young, about my age; we had come a long way from our respective homes to meet under such violent circumstances in a flooded field on the remote coast of Arakan. In his wallet there was photo of a young girl and two tiny children – his wife and babies. In the years since I have often thought of the young woman I made a widow and the children I made fatherless. Then I think what he would have done to me had our positions been reversed.

I walked back to where the prisoner was standing among the dead and the reddening rice water. We had shot them to ribbons. We were exposed and asking for trouble to remain long.

We had not been back in Ponra long, before the Japs attacked us. The first thing we heard was the slow tock-tock-tock of Jap MMG fire, covering enemy infantry coming at us. We stood to, but there was not sign of the enemy. Shots struck the leaves of the Peepul tree over my head. I told the Subedar to give me an ammunition state, knowing full well that our previous wild and uncontrolled firing would have left us in a precarious state. I nearly had a fit when he told me that all Brens and Tommy Guns were down to one or two magazines, and riflemen about 20 rounds each.

At that moment I saw the Jap infantry doubling over the paddy some 800 yards away. The full enormity of my failure to control fire earlier struck me. Had we had ammunition we could have stayed to fight and give the Japs a bloody nose. As it was we might have to fight to hold the beach while waiting for the steamer. In the meantime we had no alternative but to get out of Ponra as soon as possible.

On our way to the beach, we missed our route, finding ourselves in deep tidal mangrove swamps, followed by having to cross a 25-yard wide chaung. I had to swim each man across, which was time-consuming and exhausting. Altogether we had to cross four more such chaungs in this fashion before arriving at the beach, where we found the reserve section waiting anxiously, having heard the firing.

I sent a brief message to Brigade HQ telling them what had happened and asking for the divisional artillery to fire on likely Jap approaches between Ponra and Lambaguna. As the artillery opened up, the Subedar told me that Rifleman Bharsad was missing. In the heat of the moment, his section commander had failed to check him in at the RV. Clearly Bharsad was still in Ponra, dead or a prisoner. I sent a section to check if the enemy were still in occupation of the village, and lady luck smiled, because they came back with the 'lost sheep'. His story made us laugh with pride. He had never got the order to withdraw, and when he realised he was on his own, and had not specifically been told to withdraw, he assumed I had wanted him to stay. So he remained fighting his private battle with the Japs. After a while the Japs marked his position, so that he was finding it difficult to aim and fire his rifle, so he made a hole in the bund with his bayonet to fire through. Fortunately the artillery fire came down in the nick of time, driving the enemy back from the paddy before they could reach his position.

We remained that night at the beach, but did not sleep easily. The following day the steamer arrived with the rest of B Company. Before returning in the steamer, I took the company commander to Ponra, which was empty of Japs, and showed him the details of the action. A few days later we learned that our prisoner was a JIF, which was disappointing, but later V Force patrols reported that the Japs had buried a total of 34 dead as a result of our two contacts and the artillery fire.

Lieutenant General Christison, commanding 15th Corps in the Arakan, wrote:

By November [1944] the monsoon was over and the country gradually drying up, and I keenly awaited orders from XIV Army. But on 15th November I got a new directive, not from Slim, but from Oliver Leese, C-in-C ALFSEA. My Corps was to leave XIV Army and become an independent Corps under ALFSEA.

My Corps was given a defensive role to hold Maungdaw on the coast and keep the Naf River open to navigation, while protecting the airfields at Cox's Bazaar and Chittagong etc from Jap raids. I was terribly disappointed and urged Leese to alter my role. He pointed out that I could not be supported logistically in an offensive role, but when I unfolded my plan to use sampans to carry troops and supplies, guns, ammo etc., down the Kalapanzin, he saw Mountbatten and they agreed to let me mount what offensive I could with what I had. Meantime we secured Hill 1433 which overlooked Maungdaw and the Naf River, after heavy fighting and defeating determined counter-attacks, and the West Africans drove the Japs off the Indian frontier to deny raiding bases from which to raid our airfields.

The 3rd/2nd Goorkhas took part in the fighting for Hill 1433,

a peak on the main spine of the Mayus three miles to the south of the Maungdaw road. Here the Japanese were ensconced on a narrow saddleback with precipitous slopes falling away for 1,200 feet on either side. The enemy's dispositions consisted of a main force established on Point 1433 together with a substantial covering group at Tiger, a feature 500 yards farther north.[2]

The CO of the 3rd/2nd Goorkhas, Lieutenant Colonel Reggie Hutton, had specially asked to revert from brigadier to take command of the battalion after its disastrous experiences on the first Wingate expedition. He tasked Neill, still Intelligence Officer,

To accompany all reconnaissance patrols on the objectives. The purpose was to find suitable routes for the assault companies, and an area for a firm base east of the Mayu Range for the reserve company. It took me about fourteen days to get the required information. I went out every day, although I had fresh troops each time. But it was very tiring in thick jungle and the steep terrain. Once near the Japs, I could hear them talking among themselves, and the adrenalin flowed in streams. Luckily the second-in-command noticed my condition and told the CO a new patrol commander was required. The

CO said, 'Not a bit of it, I will take the last patrol myself'. He took a strong platoon of picked riflemen, and came back with all the information. I thought him so ancient and liable to drop dead – he was probably in his mid thirties. He did the right thing.

He then told me to take an ambush to a north–south track between Tiger and Point 1433, and to get a prisoner. 'Knock him out and bring him back. Take an entrenching tool helve [handle] and stun a Jap'. This is not a suitable implement to deal with a ferocious enemy. I could not hit on a suitable way to get a prisoner undiscovered. Fortunately the CO changed his mind, and said, 'We'll do without a prisoner'.

For the assault on Tiger and Point 1433, Neill and the CO were in adjoining slit trenches in Battalion HQ about 200 yards from Tiger:

A Company under Dicky Clarke assaulted 1433 from the south, and C Company under Steve Stephenson probed the same feature from the north. At the same time, Adrian Hayter's B Company was to hit Tiger from the east. Adrian was a New Zealander, a pre-war regular. D Company was in reserve in a firm base.

I heard the battle begin. After the guns opened fire, then the mens' awe-inspiring roar of 'Ayo Gurkali'. This was the first time I had heard a whole company of Gurkhas give tongue in battle. Within moments the mens' brave cries were silenced by Jap LMGs, rifle and grenade fire from their log-covered bunker on Tiger. I was astonished at the intensity of the Jap fire.

The fire-fight between B Company and the Japs went on for an hour or so. We had reasonable radio contact with A and C Companies on 1433, and learned they had encountered impenetrable bunker positions. Then we lost contact with A and C Companies, but still had line contact with B.

Next I remember a patrol from B Company bringing in a blood-covered Adrian Hayter. He had been hit by countless rifle grenade fragments and the blood was flowing freely from his many wounds. He told the CO that the attack had come to a halt from LMG cross-fire from flanking bunker positions and a never-ending shower of grenades rolled down from hill-top bunkers.

I took him aside to try to dress his wounds. Suddenly our tough 'Kiwi' Adrian flung his arms round me and wept like a child. He was a fine brave man, tested to the limit weeping on a friend's shoulder for his men who had died or been wounded in bitter battle. Six months later on Snowdon East, it became my turn to weep on Adrian's shoulder.

A few minutes later, the C Company Jemedar came up to say that his Company second-in-command was badly wounded, one platoon commander was dead, and Steve Stephenson had taken a patrol to link up with B Company on Tiger, to see if he could assist as his own operation had not been successful. Steve had been killed attacking a bunker on Tiger. Having given his report, the Jemedar returned to take command of C Company. Poor Reggie was greatly affected by Steve's death and the fact that his carefully planned attack had failed. He loved his men dearly, and it was tragic to see the look in his eyes as he reported the situation to the Brigade Commander on the radio.

As a result of the CO's report, the GOC of 25th Division ordered that a siege was to be laid to 1433 and Tiger, followed later by another assault. For this purpose a company of the 4th/10th Baluch was to come under command to bolster A Company on 1433, and another company from the 17th/5th Mahrattas would assist our D Company to strengthen the firm base east of Tiger.

Two days later, on 10 September, I was told to take a platoon from B Company, now partly withdrawn from Tiger, and carry out mock attacks on Tiger as soon as possible after first light on 12 September. Reggie was meticulous in his orders, even checking out my Nepali vocabulary in order to ensure that I could give out his orders to the men without fault.

On 11 September I went forward to B Company to give out orders for the mock attack, where I found that 6 Platoon under Havildar Thapa had been nominated as my mock attack force. We would advance, but before reaching the first line of bunkers, we would halt and take up fire positions, and open rapid automatic fire on the bunker slits to draw Jap fire and ascertain where his MMGs were located. If no enemy fire was returned, we would advance cautiously to check physically for signs of enemy occupation.

At first light we set off, and started to ascend the steep slope. There was an eerie silence, no sounds of Jap chatter from the invisible bunkers. Then we caught the stink of the bodies of our own dead. The light was improving, and we could see the bodies of Steve's party. I had seen many dead bodies before, but the sight of his corpse on Tiger took me aback.

At that moment I saw what could be a bunker roof 20 to 30 yards ahead of us. I gave the order to fire. All of us were yelling obscenities at the Japs to try to get them to disclose their positions. After five minutes, and with no indication of enemy occupation, I ordered cease fire and we advanced in open order to the summit of Tiger. We passed more of our comrades dead bodies, finally reaching the bunker consisting of strong points with overhead log covering. We searched but there were no Japs anywhere. Their smell was everywhere. All positions were strongly built and I estimated that Tiger would have held an infantry company or more.

I searched our dead for identification. All their bodies were a shiny, translucent black, and bloated like a Michelin man. I came across a corpse only two yards from the bunker entrance. I saw a yellow lead pencil sticking out of his pocket, this was Steve's hallmark, he always carried them so. I gingerly turned him over. He had been hit by an LMG burst as his entrails were hanging out. He was still wearing his signet ring, and I thought I would take it from him so Reggie could hand it to his widow. With great care I started the awful task of taking the ring off Steve's decomposing finger. I got it partly off, when skin and ring fell into his exposed entrails. I was nearly sick on the spot. With the ring out of sight within Steve's poor body, I had neither the heart nor the courage to delve inside to find and recover the ring. I decided it would remain with Steve.

As we withdrew from Tiger, we came across a badly wounded rifleman from B Company who had hidden from the Japs, and carried him down.

On hearing that Tiger was clear of Japs, Reggie told Dicky Clarke to check if 1433 had been similarly evacuated, it had. Much to our joy, we knew that Reggie had won at last his carefully planned battle. He was given an immediate DSO.

Stephenson died two arms-lengths from the Jap bunker, no one except his small party saw exactly what he did. They all died too. For my money I would say that Steve's actions were the stuff of what VCs are made. Why did he do it? Why did he attack that bunker single-handed? Pride in his Regiment? Unless and until a man has fought in bloody, terrifying battle in total war against a highly trained, experienced enemy, he will never truly know the meaning of pride in his regiment.

Neill does not mention that he was awarded an MC for his work both before and during the battle. Hutton was promoted shortly afterwards to command the 51st Indian Brigade in the division.

Meanwhile Christison's earlier disappointment at the prospect of lack of employment for his corps was overtaken by his new directive.

It had become clear that Slim's 14th Army could not be supplied in its long advance except from airfields in Akyab and Ramree, the only possible sites in Arakan. Mountbatten therefore formed an HQ consisting of Naval Force W (Rear Admiral Bernard Martin), 15 Corps (myself), and 224 Group RAF (Air Vice Marshal the Earl of Bandon ('Paddy')), and a specially equipped HQ ship, HMS *Phoebe*, a cruiser was put at our disposal. The staff of all three services shared messes, and lived in the jungle, except when combined operations from the sea were taking place.

Our task: to drive the Japanese out of the whole of Arakan, and secure airfields for 14th Army at Akyab and on the large island of Ramree. We were to destroy as many of the enemy as we could and prevent them escaping in any strength to reinforce central Burma. This entailed landings from the sea to get behind the enemy, but in 100 miles of coastline, the only beach was Akyab. To defeat the Japanese 28th Army which opposed me in Arakan and which would contest every step was a formidable task.

Following the successful conclusion of this offensive, Operation ROMULUS, Christison's corps, consisting of 25th Division, 26th Indian Division, 81st and 82nd West African Divisions, the 3rd Commando Brigade, and the 50th Indian Tank Brigade, would be released for other operations, notably DRACULA (the amphibious assault on Rangoon). In fact, Operation ROMULUS was based on a false assumption, that the Japanese would fight to the death to hold every inch of ground in the Arakan. Actually Lieutenant General Sakurai commanding *Twenty-eighth Army* was ordered merely to delay the British advance to allow the Japanese main body to withdraw to the Irrawaddy Delta, to meet the principal threat: Slim's Fourteenth Army.

The offensive on the Mayu Front began on 12 December, and the 82nd West African Division took Buthidaung before opening the route to the Kalapanzin River. Hundreds of small craft were taken by road over the Mayu Range to the Kalapanzin and were to prove invaluable in the supply of the West African advance south. Christison had earlier sent for his chief engineer,

> and told him that we needed about 800 sampans, with oars for the small ones, perhaps 150, and outboard motors for the bulk, say 650. No sampan must be bigger than can be carried on a 3-tonner [truck], and must be able to be transported through the Tunnels, but one or two could be larger and we could use tank transporters. I want these arriving at Maungdaw by 15 November.
>
> 'But we have no sampans', he said. 'The Japs either sank them or took them down river for their own use.'
>
> 'Well you must get them from the country between Chittagong and Calcutta', I replied.
>
> The sampans, dug-outs and outboards were procured in time, and then came the Herculean task of ferrying them the 14 miles over the jungle-clad mountain pass, through the tunnels, and down to the secret assembly areas as close to Buthidaung as possible.

Meanwhile the 25th Division advanced to Foul Point. Neill, now a captain and commanding B Company of the 3rd/2nd Goorkhas, recorded:

> Reached Donbaik Christmas Day 1944 – dug in on the sea shore.
> Boxing Day – advance south continued, arriving 1 January 1945 at Foul Point.

Thus were the objectives for the first Arakan offensive, two years earlier, for which so many men had died in vain, finally taken, with little effort. Christison visited Donbaik, 'and saw the three Valentine tanks lost in the 1943 attack still lying in the anti-tank ditch. The Japs had not even bothered to remove the bodies of the crews. One tank was sitting on top of another'.

Christison was keen to press on to Akyab, when he had a signal from Mountbatten stating that

> landing conditions would be impossible, in view of cyclone warning involving bad flying conditions and waves 10 to 15 ft breaking over shoals, consider Operation Lightning [Akyab landing] should be postponed, but having turned over responsibility for this operation to Force Commanders leave the final decision to them. Admiral Martin and I were sitting on high ground near Foul Point, when we

saw the transports and supporting warships turning about. I said that Mountbatten in Ceylon could not possibly know our local conditions. The sea was dead calm and no sign of a break [in the weather]. We must go on as we would lose any chance of cutting off the Japs later. Admiral Martin saw the point, and at that moment signals could be seen coming [by light?] from the HQ ship, HMS *Phoebe*, where the Admiral's Chief of Staff, Eric Bush was on board. 'What's he saying, "Flags" [his flag lieutenant]', said Martin.

'Sir, he says he has orders from Supremo to return to Indian waters as Operation Lightning is being postponed'.

'Tell him I can't read his bloody signal, and he's to turn back again on course'.

Having signalled Leese in Calcutta that he proposed to ignore the signal and press on, Christison heard that

a young Royal Artillery pilot [spotting for naval guns and artillery] had just come back from a flight over Akyab and reported no signs of Japs. [Air Vice Marshal] Paddy Bandon and I flew in ourselves in two light planes, piloted by Dennis David and an American, and landed in a paddy field. Some locals came over and told us that the last Japs were just pulling out at the east end of the island. They took us down to the beach and showed us which parts were mined, and which clear. We returned with this information and the troops landed the next day with everything ready to fire. I again flew over early and guided the Royal Marine assault parties [from the 3rd Commando Brigade] on to the un-mined beaches. Their surprise at being welcomed by the Force Commander only equalled their relief at landing unopposed. Throughout the next three days steady landings of men, ammo, and stores went on, while the RAF got local labour to repair the airfield. But not all the Japs had left. A number remained in the north-east corner of the island waiting for craft to take them over to the mainland. 53 Brigade came up against them, and the York and Lancaster Regiment [9th York and Lancasters, in 25th Division] was containing them and cutting off their escape. I told General Wood to hold them, while he sent troops from 74 Brigade to round them up. At 2200 hours on 9th January, I heard heavy firing from the north-east. The Japs were surely not going to attempt to re-capture Akyab. I thought it highly unlikely in the circumstances, though it would have been in accordance with their tactics.

We now knew that part of his IIIth Regiment and some AA detachments were those trapped. During the night four Japanese armoured landing craft each carrying 50 men with heavy and light machine-gun support landed troops which at once tried to drive off the York and Lancasters so they might rescue their stranded comrades. This strong party of Japs was led by an officer who came forward shouting in English, and when challenged by sentries replied in Urdu. Thinking this was Japanese the sentry shot him, and then all hell broke loose. For an hour there was close-quarter fighting in the dark which ended when the Japs ran for their boats. But the Japs were most persistent. Two nights later, some of the York and Lancasters were sleeping in their boats and sampans, when about 40 Japs rushed them, throwing grenades. Our men formed a strong point among the boats and beat them off. But this was only a feint. About 100 yards away a covering party came ashore from landing craft while another party landed on Akyab Island and started to rescue their comrades. Suddenly a large 70 foot armoured motor launch appeared and was thought to be ours. But it put on a searchlight and opened fire on our men with 2-pounder guns and medium machine-guns. With it there were three landing craft. This was a brilliant effort by the Japs, a copy-book little operation, but it cost him two officers and 22 other ranks killed and four badly wounded and taken prisoner. Now Akyab really was clear of the enemy.

After over two years of fighting in the unpleasant mountainous and watery maze of the Arakan, Akyab, whose seizure had been the aim of the abortive Arakan campaign which had begun in November 1942, was now firmly in British hands.

Meanwhile the 81st West African Division had been driving the *Matsu Detachment* down the Kaladan valley towards their base at Myohaung. This detachment consisted of the equivalent of a regimental group commanded by Major General Tomotoki Koba, who as a colonel of a column had fought the 81st West African Division in the Kaladan in March 1944. Once Myohaung was taken, it was Christison's intention to relieve the 81st by the 82nd West African Division, which would press on to drive the Japanese into a trap which he intended to set at Kangaw. The fighting for Myohaung was fierce, with the Japanese repeatedly counterattacking to cover the withdrawal of their guns and transport. On 15 December, a Japanese battalion, supported by ten field guns and two 105mm guns, attacked a section of mountain guns supporting the 6th West African Brigade. Havildar Umrao Singh's gun section was overrun and his officer badly wounded. Umrao Singh and two men defended his gun with rifles, bayonets, and grenades. Seven Japanese rushed the gun, killing the two men, but he killed all seven. A second party rushed the gun. By now out of ammunition, but swinging a rammer, he killed two before he was borne down and bayoneted. Next day the West Africans counterattacked and retook the position, finding the gun intact and the gallant havildar lying under it still living, as was the officer who had seen the incident. Both recovered. Umrao Singh was awarded the VC.

The 82nd Division now took over from the 81st and continued the pursuit. This division was commanded by Major General Hugh Stockwell, whose predecessor had been sacked by Christison. Mountbatten had visited the division and expressed doubts about its commander, especially his drinking habits, and Christison decided to pay a visit.

> I was not at all happy with the Divisional commanders of African troops. Both had spent many happy years in West African conditions and had no experience of using Africans to fight the Japanese. I had had to remove the commander of 81 Division after the fiasco at Kyauktaw, and hoped 82 would be better commanded.* I took with me an American Major General who was attached to my HQ to learn about jungle warfare. Commander 82 Division met us and I noticed he had been drinking.

Together with the GOC of 82nd Division, a colourful character who wore a pair of pearl-handled revolvers, and an escort of African soldiers, Christison and the American set off in three jeeps to visit one of the rifle companies. After a while Christison queried the route being taken, as they were crossing a dry nullah, at which moment they came under fire:

> 'Out all', I shouted, and we dived for cover at the sides of the track. The escort jeep was still on the other side of the nala [nullah], and the second jeep managed to reverse into it. There we were, three generals and two ADCs in ditches on either side of the road on

---

* This is overly harsh, Kyauktaw was hardly a fiasco, and any blame for the situation in which the 81st West African Division found itself is Christison's. See Chapter 4.

which stood the now empty first jeep. We opened fire with our revolvers, though we couldn't see any Japs. Meanwhile the escort had crossed the nala and taken up fire positions. As we fired they followed suit, much to our dismay as their bullets whizzed past us. The driver of the second jeep crawled forward with a tow rope, attached it to the leading jeep, and pulled it into the nala where it could turn round. We crawled back to the nala and got into our jeeps. Suddenly I realised the American was not with us. The commander 82nd Division asked for covering fire and with his orderly crawled forward. The Japs opened fire, and I saw him replying with both his revolvers. We still had not seen a Jap, and I suspected they would be trying to get behind us and we must make a speedy get-away.

At that moment the GOC came in sight dragging the American along the ground with the help of his orderly. We lifted him into the escort jeep and drove him back to Divisional HQ. Africans came running from every direction shouting and cheering. The American uniform and cap, not unlike the peaked caps the Japs wore, plus the fact that he was unconscious and supported between two Africans, his face a whitish-yellow, seemed to indicate to the troops that we had brought back a Jap. The American had had a coronary, and died later.

Soon after, I was informed that the Commander 82nd Division was behaving in an extraordinary manner, and his Brigadiers no longer supported him. I sent for him. He sent a message that he could not come as he was ill. My DDMS [senior doctor] ordered him into hospital. I consulted Leese and he agreed he must be replaced. I sent my assistant military secretary [AMS] to the hospital with an adverse report for the Commander of 82nd Division to sign. The AMS arrived, and handed him the form. Drawing a revolver from under his pillow, the General shouted, 'Tear that up or you are a dead man'. Luckily a doctor was present, calmed him down, and he eventually signed.

Major General Stockwell was forty-two years old when he took command of the 82nd West African Division. He had spent three years with African troops in West Africa before the Second World War. During the Norwegian campaign in 1940 he had commanded one of the independent companies, the predecessors of the commandos. A spell as chief instructor at the Commando Training Centre at Lochailort followed on his return from Norway. He had commanded the 2nd Royal Welch Fusiliers in the Madagascar landings, before taking over the 29th Brigade and fighting with them as part of the 36th Division in their battle down the 'railway corridor' from Myitkyina. He was hard and experienced, and made some changes in the 82nd West African Division.

I found it rather a luxury organisation, the fighting soldiers were mixed up with 'carriers'. The first thing I did was to take them out of fighting units and put them in the 'tail', to avoid them getting involved with fighting. There were an enormous number of somewhat indifferent British NCOs in the Division. They were a hindrance. I took all of them out. I sent them back as first line reinforcement to British units in the Fourteenth Army. I made the Africans take over and the thing began to take shape.

I sacked some COs. They weren't battle-worthy. The colonial influence had softened their outlook. We were very tough and hard in 29 Brigade, this lot were soft, with carriers and 'chop boxes' [food boxes], gin etc. They hadn't got the stomach for the fight so away with them.

[As with most soldiers] Provided Africans are presented to the battle properly, with good orders, they know what they've got to do, and that they will be properly supported, they will fight marvellously and they 'saw the Japanese off'.

I had a free hand about how I presented the Africans to battle. It was my responsibility to win the battle with the 82nd Division. I picked out an RSM from the 3rd Nigeria Regiment, who had been awarded the Iron Cross fighting for the Germans in West Africa in the First World War. He stayed with me as a personal RSM for a year and a half. He advised me on the Africans and through him I could find out what they thought of their British officers. He was tremendous, I got him a DCM, and he must be about the only soldier to wear an Iron Cross and a DCM.

Christison had to tell Stockwell not to press too hard because he did not want the *Matsu Detachment* to join up with Sakurai's main body before the British could get behind them and cut their communications. He aimed to cut the road being used by the Japanese which ran close to the coast all the way to Taungup where it turned inland to Prome on the Irrawaddy. Christison:

The best place [to cut it], indeed the only possible one, was at Kangaw, where an approach by chaung could be made under the cover of mangrove swamps, and where there were a couple of breaks which could provide landing places. The Japs had fortified the Kangaw area. I flew over it and although I could see the defences they did not look very strong. Intelligence reports indicated that both beaches were mined, and I could see rows of stakes sticking out of the sea to defend against landing craft.

Christison decided that the first stage of the operation would be to land the 3rd Commando Brigade (Numbers 1 and 5 Army Commandos, and 42 and 44 Royal Marine Commandos) on the Myebon Peninsula, which dominates a network of chaungs, including the Daingbon Chaung, of which more later. On D −1, a Combined Operations Pilotage Party (COPP) crept in and fixed charges to a 600-yard line of anti-boat obstacles. These were blown just before H-hour creating a gap about twenty-five yards wide for the landing craft. The landing at Myebon took place on 12 January preceded by air strikes and a naval bombardment. 42 RM Commando was first ashore under cover of a smoke screen, followed by 5 Army Commando. There was little opposition, which was fortunate because the main enemy was the glutinous mud on the beach, which at low tide was 400 yards wide. Within half an hour of landing, the line of Pagoda Hill, about 400 yards from the beach, had been secured, and thereafter opposition firmed up considerably. By 14 January the attacking troops had reached a line about three miles inland, and repelled a spirited counterattack. Follow-up units from the 74th Indian Infantry Brigade landed, and by 16 January the whole peninsula up to the Kantha Chaung was in British hands, but not without some hard fighting.

The 3rd/2nd Goorkhas were ordered to take Point 262 on the northern bank of the Kantha Chaung which split the Myebon Peninsula from the mainland. A fighting patrol probing forward to Point 262 lost eleven men from mortar and machine-gun fire in a couple of minutes. By nightfall, most of the battalion was across the chaung and ready to attack 262 the next day. The enemy had transformed the brick stump of a pagoda into a strong bunker position sited on a knife-edge ridge covered with scrub and jungle which could not be bypassed on the narrow neck of land. A battalion gun was dug in on the position and fired over open sights on anyone approaching. After an air strike, D Company 3rd/2nd Goorkhas advanced to attack. Major Neill commanding B Company watched

first, Jemedar Dal Sing Thapa although severely wounded dragging his Bren gun up on to the top of the shattered red pagoda, directing his fire on a counter-attack force. When he collapsed from loss of blood, Havildar Bhopal Ale, could be seen scrambling up onto top of pagoda alternately firing and reloading his Tommy Gun and then hurling broken bricks from the pagoda on the advancing Jap counter-attackers. We could clearly see the Havildar laying about the enemy without any thought for his own safety. 262 was no more than 400 yards from where I was standing. Using my binos I could see every movement and it was much more exciting than watching Errol Flynn in the cinema. At 1530 the position won at low cost of nine wounded.

D Company dug in, and during the night three counterattacks as well as 'jitter parties' were beaten off. In daylight, D Company found the bodies of sixty-two Japanese, a spiked gun, and an undamaged 90mm mortar with large quantities of ammunition for both. A Japanese prisoner revealed that the position had been held by a reinforced company. A Gurkha rifleman who had been left for dead during the patrol action the previous day was found alive. He had been hit in the leg, and afterwards been bayoneted in the arms and hands.

Intelligence and reconnaissance now revealed very strong defensive positions from Kangaw village on the main road north-east of Myebon to the east side of the mountains on the opposite side of the Myebon Peninsula. These blocked the planned approach to Kangaw. Christison:

This presented a problem which had to be overcome immediately. It was essential to get a block across the road at Kangaw without any delay whatsoever, so I decided to make the approach from the south. This would be through the maze of chaungs in the mangrove swamps east of the Myebon river, aiming at outflanking the Japanese positions, which from our air photographs appeared to be sited facing north and north-west. The landing to be as close to Kangaw as possible. From there a bold advance could cut the road.

The overall commander for the Kangaw operation was Major General G. N. Wood, commanding the 25th Indian Division. He decided that a beachhead on the east bank of the Daingbon Chaung about two miles south-west of Kangaw should be seized by the 3rd Commando Brigade. The 51st Brigade should then pass through, capture Kangaw, and link up with the 74th Brigade which had crossed the Min Chaung from the Myebon Peninsula. The Japanese would be hemmed in between the two brigades and the 82nd West African Division coming down from the north. The route selected to the landing area at Kangaw was twenty-seven miles long, due south from Myebon, and up the Daingbon Chaung, the last leg of the approach being an eighteen-mile passage through a waterway whose banks might be held by the enemy. Brigadier Hardy, commanding the 3rd Commando Brigade, carried out a personal reconnaissance of the beaches; more mangrove-ridden swamps than beaches. As a deception to keep the Japanese eyes off the approach up the Daingbon Chaung, Christison sent the 7th/16th Punjab Regiment, who were Corps troops (directly under Corps command), to threaten Minbya, north of Myebon. The Japanese took the bait and put in a full-blooded attack at dawn, but in fierce fighting they were nearly wiped out. Lance Naik Sher Shah of the 7th/16th Punjabis was awarded the VC.

Hardy's plan was for 1 Commando to land first on 'Hove' Beach and seize Hill 170, and advance to take Kangaw village. 42 RM Commando would land next and establish a bridgehead between two smaller chaungs on their left and right which would include the main beach called 'Thames'. 5 Commando would land through 42 RM Commando and assist 1 Commando. 44 RM Commando, once ashore, would be brigade reserve. The landings went well, and by the evening of D +1, Hill 170 was secure, and two further hills, 'Milford' and 'Pinner', were in the brigade's hands. The Japanese reaction had as usual been swift, but counterattacks were beaten off. Efforts to infiltrate to Kangaw, moreover, met stiff opposition, so on 26 January the 51st Brigade was brought in with a troop of Sherman tanks of the 19th Lancers.

Eventually Kangaw village was captured and the road blocked. Christison:

At first light on 31 January he [the enemy] launched what was to prove the heaviest and most desperate attack of the whole campaign. As the sun rose, a battalion of the 154th Regiment, supported by a detachment of assault engineers, about 90 strong with 10 officers, broke into the centre of the perimeter and made an all-out assault on Hill 170 from the north. Defended by the Commando Brigade which had been concentrated there, the hill was also the harbour area for the troop of the 19th Lancers' tanks. It was obvious the enemy intended to establish himself on this position without any regard for the casualties it would cost him. Established here he would have cut off our troops from the beaches. Had this action been successful it would have been impossible for the 51st Indian Infantry Brigade to maintain their stronghold on the road at this critical time, and the whole success of the Kangaw operation would have been doomed to failure.

The first wave of the attack succeeded in reaching the hill where some engineers got amongst the vehicles in the tank harbour before they were eliminated. One tank was destroyed and one damaged by the engineer suicide squad armed with pole charges. Although they did not succeed in placing any charges on the tanks, the flames caused by a charge placed on a 15cwt truck ignited a tank's camouflage net, burning the whole crew to death. Twenty-six Japanese engineer dead were left on the position, and many who withdrew must have been wounded.

The engineer assault was followed by repeated waves of suicidal attacks on Hill 170 with heavy supporting fire. All attacks were repelled without any ground being given up, and with immense casualties to the Japanese, who persisted without regard to the carpet of their own dead which lay on the Hill and its approaches. The battle for Hill 170 continued well into the following day. The enemy left 340 bodies on the north corner of Hill 170 alone. The fighting had been at such close quarters that some live soldiers and marines, both British and Japanese, were extricated from beneath mounds of corpses, practically unhurt, but unable to move for the weight of bodies pinning them to the ground. For two further days the enemy persisted with a fresh battalion, but to no avail. By 3 February they had left a total of 700 dead on Hill 170.

By 4 February the battle was virtually over. The Japanese, realizing that they faced being cut off by the advancing 82nd West African Division, pulled out the remnants of their force and headed for the An Pass leading to the Irrawaddy Valley. By 18 February, they had been forced off their last toeholds north of Kangaw. Meanwhile heavy spring tides flooded the beaches at Kangaw, delaying the start of follow-up operations to chase them south to Kyweguseik on the road to the An Pass. But by 20 February the pursuit force consisting of the 7th/16th Punjabis and a troop of the 19th Lancers was on its way on their tails. The battle had lasted for twenty-two days, resulting in 1,008 enemy dead, collected, and buried.

Christison:

> The tenacity of both the 51st Indian Infantry Brigade and the Commando Brigade, and the great fighting qualities they showed throughout this fierce and decisive battle can not be too highly praised. They inflicted irreparable loss on the enemy in difficult circumstances and at a most vital stage in the campaign. These troops were now withdrawn from operations for a well-earned rest.

Two VCs were awarded for the fighting at Kangaw. Lieutenant Knowland of the Royal Norfolk Regiment attached to Number 1 Commando when his troop was overrun on Hill 170 inspired the remnants to hold on. As Private Ralph of 4 Troop Number 1 Commando relates:

> One of our officers in 4 Troop, Lt Knowland, walked about in the open, sometimes with a 2 inch mortar firing from the hip, sometimes with a Bren gun, or a Tommy Gun, anything he could lay a hand on. He took out a lot of Japs. He was killed and received a posthumous VC. It was 4 troop that took the brunt of the first attack, but we were helped by other troops, from 42 Commando and 5 Commando. It was a terrific battle. It was like Rorke's Drift. Some things stick in my mind. A Japanese Warrant Officer came charging waving his sword. Every man on the hill fired on him. Some idiot ran to get his sword, and was shot by the Japs. We dragged him back. There was a Japanese left by himself after an attack had been beaten off. He was likely to be taken prisoner, so he pulled a grenade and put it under his stomach, he was lying face down and blew himself to pieces. The enemy came within 20 yards of me. The Hill was overgrown so you couldn't see them until they got quite close. It was not frightening at the time. We were too busy. I don't think any of us expected to come out of it. But we had too much to do to think about it until afterwards. After the battle that was when the fear started.
>
> Lieutenant Knowland was a very recent member of the Commando, he joined at Myebon. He was a stranger to us. But he seemed a good, keen young officer. There was a private whose name I shall

not mention, who before we went into action was bragging he was going to win the VC. During the battle he hid behind a tree. There is no rhyme or reason for bravery. War is very peculiar. You get caught up in it, it is almost a game.

The other VC was awarded to Naik Jag Mal of the 8th/19th Hyderabad Regiment in the 51st Indian Infantry Brigade. Hutton (late of the 3rd/2nd Goorkhas), commanding the 51st Brigade, recommended two Indian majors, Thimaya and Sen, for promotion, and with Christison's approval, they became the first two Indians to command infantry battalions. Christison:

> I flew over the area from Myohaung to Kangaw following the river. At low tide I could see many lorries that had been driven in and abandoned, and the muzzles of a number of field and medium guns sticking up. We had deprived the enemy of much of his transport and guns which had been deployed north of Kangaw. All Japanese were now being hastily withdrawn to the south and I intended to make further landings from the sea to cut off as many as possible.

By this time the operation by the 26th Indian Division to secure airfields on Ramree Island had been mounted, on 21 January 1945. Christison:

> I had three operations, each widely different on hand: the Kangaw block, a landing on Ramree, and the capture of Myohaung by the West Africans; commanding all three from HMS *Phoebe*. All three assaults went in within three days of each other. The Ramree operation looked a copy-book piece with all the support the landings were to have. HMS *Phoebe* stood in about 2,000 yards off the beach with HM Ships *Queen Elizabeth*, *Rapid*, *Flamingo*, HMAS *Napier*, and HMIS *Kistna*. The minesweepers reported the area clear of mines.
>
> At zero hour, the great 15-inch guns of the *Queen Elizabeth* went off for the last time by any British Battleship. The Force Commanders on the bridge were watching through field-glasses. Some shells fell on a marsh behind the Jap defences, and I saw a number of duck spring up. 'Duck', I shouted.
>
> 'The Royal Navy never ducks', said the Admiral.
>
> We watched the leading assault craft going in led by an ML. All seemed going well and only a few Jap shells were coming back. Suddenly the ML was blown sky-high, and the other two leading

assault craft turned outwards and each was blown up at once. The remainder of the assault force swung back out of danger. For there was indeed a minefield, but closer to shore than had been swept by our minesweepers. Things looked bad and the Japs were now shelling the stationary landing craft, some of whom were picking up a few survivors.

'Only one thing for it', said the Admiral to me, 'you must lead them in. I'll lower a pinnace and send you through the gap in the minefield and they'll follow you. Should be quite safe – unless they have a second line'.

So a pinnace was quickly lowered, and off I set. I must admit I kept wondering if there was a second line of mines. There was not, and for the second time in less than three weeks, the Corps Commander was first to land. I jumped out, into waist deep water, splashed ashore, and lay down on the sand until the landing craft followed my lead and troops swarmed up the beaches. Presently Brigadier Cotterel-Hill commanding the landing brigade [71st Indian Infantry Brigade] arrived. He was furious. 'With respect, Sir', he said, 'I wish you would not come forward and command my troops for me'. I assured him they were all his.

We had quite heavy fighting on Ramree Island, the Lincolns [1st Battalion the Lincolnshire Regiment] particularly distinguishing themselves. Eventually we drove the Japs back into and around Ramree town, which they tried to hold until craft could be sent to evacuate them. But RN ships sunk all the craft and blockaded all the possible creeks. The Japs decided to fight it out, but were so reduced in numbers by this time that we soon drove them into the mangrove swamps, where they perished miserably, many being seized and eaten by crocodiles. One Jap doctor was picked up floating on a log in the sea, and even he tried to drown himself rather than be taken prisoner.

Christison was awarded an immediate DSO, which he commented was 'a rare award for a Lieutenant General'.[3] But he also had to cope with the wife of the Supremo:

Edwina Mountbatten paid another visit to my hospitals in Arakan, particularly to see the large numbers of the Commando Brigade who had been wounded in the Kangaw battle. She asked why so many had head wounds. I told her it was largely because they had refused to wear steel helmets. Brigadier Campbell Hardy (a splendid character) had told me his men must fight in their green berets as that was the distinctive sign of which they were so proud and on which morale rested.

Edwina said, 'this is nonsense, I'll tell Dickie and see he issues an order for them to wear steel hats in future'. The order duly arrived and coming from Mountbatten was readily accepted. So much of jungle fighting was at close quarters with sword, rifle butt, and small grenades which burst overhead in branches, that head protection was very important.

We now know that both the British and Japanese were mistaken about the aims of their respective opponents. We saw earlier that it was never the Japanese intention to hold their positions in the Arakan, the premise on which Operation ROMULUS was based. The tremendous efforts by the Japanese at Kangaw were not primarily in order to allow them to escape from Myohaung, but to prevent a British breakthrough to the Irrawaddy Valley through the Arakan Yomas. To begin with this was not the British plan, their priority was to seize airfields at Akyab and Ramree, which the Japanese had no intention of holding. However, after Ramree was taken, Leese thought that the 15th Corps could move east along the two routes Kywegu–An Pass–Pagan–Minbu on the Irrawaddy, and Taungup–Prome. This notion was reinforced when Christison visited Slim to be told by him, 'You must stop Sakurai getting his force over the pass [the An Pass]. You must destroy the lot.' But as Christison pointed out:

The Pass was so narrow that it would not take many to hold it. The sides reared up several thousand feet on either jungle-clad side. I now had no air supply. XIV Army had all available. Could I have some? No. 'If I drive too hard as far as I can supply by porters I may be doing just what you don't want'.

'All right', he said, 'use your judgment, but you know what I want'.

I flew back and issued instructions to General Stockwell, in command of 82nd West African Division. He pushed well up into the mountains, but was held some way west of An village. It was hard to know how much of Sakurai's force he was containing, how much had got through to Central Burma, and how much was still slowly, and with great stubbornness retreating down the road to Taungup.

The pursuit of the Japanese falling back from Kangaw had halted at the village of Kyweguseik, which had been converted into a formidable fortress on the coastal road. It was decided that while the 82nd West African Division battled south, the 25th Indian Division would carry out an outflanking landing at Ruwya thirty-three miles south-east of Myebon, and strike north for eight miles to seize Tamandu, an important staging post on the Japanese line of communications. From here Dalet would be seized as a jumping-off place for a final push to the An Pass, to bar the door to the escaping Japanese. The 2nd West African (Gold Coast) Brigade was put under command of 25th Division.

The assault at Ruwya went well, and by 28 February the advance north was progressing well when it became necessary to wind up the operation as quickly as possible as all aircraft were to be withdrawn from the Arakan to support Fourteenth Army's operations in Central Burma. Furthermore the Gold Coast Brigade, which was pushing on over a jungle track to the east, had suffered heavy casualties, and some 200 wounded Africans could not be evacuated until the road to Dalet had been opened. The 74th Brigade, which included 3rd/2nd Goorkhas, was given three days to complete this task, which necessitated the capture of all enemy blocks and bunkers in the area of Tamandu and the village itself.

The 3rd/2nd Goorkhas were given an objective nicknamed 'Snowdon', a wishbone-shaped ridge within easy striking distance of the road to Dalet and An, just east of Tamandu. In view of the urgency of the situation, the CO of the 3rd/2nd Goorkhas, Lieutenant Colonel Panton, emphasized in his orders that the position was to be taken regardless of casualties. Just before last light on 4 March, A and D Companies under Major Birtwhistle had occupied both arms of the wishbone, Snowdon West and Snowdon East, both of which for some unaccountable reason had been abandoned by the Japanese. Snowdon East was occupied by just one platoon commanded by Jemedar Gangabahadur Lama. Just north of the wishbone was another feature called 'Whistle', which a reconnaissance patrol sent by Birtwhistle found strongly held. The Gurkhas started to dig in, but having just their entrenching tools could construct only shallow pits.

After some probing attacks, a very determined assault by about seventy Japanese came in on Gangabahadur's platoon. It was beaten off, but further attacks on the remainder of the company on Snowdon West caused such heavy expenditure of ammunition that Birtwhistle ordered that stones and rocks were to be thrown instead of grenades in proportion four stones to one grenade. At about 0200 hours a formidable assault was mounted on Gangabahadur's platoon. Naik Bombahadur ran forward to one of his posts, cutting down five enemy with his Tommy gun before a grenade smashed the weapon and wounded him. Drawing his kukri, Bombahadur killed two more Japanese. The situation was now desperate: out of a platoon of thirty-four, Gangabahadur had eight dead and eleven wounded. Ammunition of all kinds was finished, so he decided to cut his way out and join Major Birtwhistle on Snowdon West. He ordered his men to fix 'swords' and charge the encircling enemy. His platoon, carrying their wounded with them, broke out bayoneting their way through the saddle between the two Snowdons, and joined Birtwhistle on Snowdon West. The enemy occupied Snowdon East and immediately began improving the position. They were not going to give up the feature easily twice.

Major Neill's B Company was in reserve, and at first light

The CO passed through my position and warned me to take Snowdon East. At 0800 I was called forward for orders, at Major Birtwhistle's HQ, and found the CO. There were two pimples on Snowdon East, one on the northern end, and another to the south. It was on the northern pimple that Gangabahadur's Platoon had fought and lost their battle. A thick early morning mist restricted visibility to 20 yards. The CO and I sat in one of the forward sections pits, but because of mist could see nothing. Through the mist we could hear the clink-clink of picks and shovels digging. The section commander told us that the enemy had been digging continually since retaking the position – some six hours.

The CO reminded me that the position was to be taken regardless of cost. The attack was to start at 1430 to allow the mist to clear, and men to have midday tea and biscuits. He was concerned about the state of the men's physique, resulting from inadequate rations and fighting for so long. He ended his orders by telling me that because of the shortage of ammunition, I could have only two minutes of bombardment from one troop of 25 pounders, and two medium guns. I was to take the FOO at present with Major Birtwhistle. Before leaving the CO, I asked the Adjutant for extra grenades.

I returned to my company, and the extra grenades arrived. Which brought the scale up to five per man. Our ammunition state was now 100 rounds per rifleman, 25 magazines per Bren, and 10 magazines per Tommy gun. At 1230, after tea and biscuits I led B Company forward between A and D Company's positions on Snowdon West. I took my O Group forward to point out the positions. Looking ahead we could see very little because of a thick screen of bamboo, although the mist was now clear. Above the tips of bamboo we could just see top of Snowdon East about 200 yards away, and that seemed to be covered with less dense primary jungle. From where we were we could not see how far the bamboo extended and up the slope of our objective.

Therefore despite the fact that there was not much time for recce, it was vital that I found out more about the ground. I ordered a section commander to patrol forward to get me information on terrain and enemy layout. He must draw the Japs fire to locate their automatic weapons. He took two scouts forward with his section following.

For ten minutes the digging continued, then there was silence. The Japs had obviously heard the patrol's approach. A grenade exploded, another, and another, followed by firing from the patrol's rifles, and to our relief the sound of the Jap machine guns firing. On his return the patrol commander reported that the bamboo extended for about 100 yards on both sides of the saddle and down into the saddle, stopping about 100 yards from the top of Snowdon East ridge. Beyond the bamboo and on the side of our objective was primary jungle, this was only in patches, but fallen trees brought down as a result of shelling presented obstacles. He had got to within 50 yards of the Jap positions. He had pinpointed five enemy machine-guns, and estimated that the position was held by about 2 platoons. Only the area of the pimple previously held by Gangabahadur was held by the Japs.

I gave my orders, we would attack two platoons up: 4 Platoon on the left would capture the northern part of the objective; 5 platoon on the right to capture the southern part of the objective. 6 platoon was in reserve. The Company R group* would go in between the two leading platoons. A and C Companies would support us with small

---

* The equivalent of tac HQ, the company main HQ under the second in command follows separately behind the rear platoon.

arms fire. The Battalion 3 inch mortars were in support, but had experienced problems registering targets because of the bad visibility. Communications from me to the CO were to be by line. The radios were unreliable.

At end of orders, platoon commanders left to brief their platoons. At this stage my FOO said he would not accompany my R Group as he had had enough. I realised that a frightened man would be no value, so I agreed to his remaining in A Company's position from where he assured me he would be able to give me support. I must be held responsible for the casualties inflicted on my company by inaccurate artillery fire. I should have taken this craven officer to the CO and asked for a replacement.

By 1415 with orders over, sections started moving forward. Rumours that 25 Div was about to be pulled out for retraining and refitting, were among the 1001 thoughts that range through an infantryman's mind as he prepares himself to cross a start line, glancing so frequently at the minute hand of his watch as it moves towards H Hour. There must have been many of us in B Company that hot afternoon that wondered if this was to be our last attack, and which of us would remain behind forever on the hill that rose in front of us. At 1428 the troop of 25 pounders and medium guns boomed out from gun island behind us and the shells whistled over our heads to burst on Snowdon East. For a moment we forgot our own thoughts as we watched the shells burst. Then the bombardment ceased it was H Hour. At 1430 both assault platoons fixed swords, and advanced. Three hours is not a very long time – the battle lasted exactly three hours. But the afternoon of 5 March 1945 was the longest of my life, I thought it would never end.

After crossing the Start Line all was quiet, except for the crackling of bamboo as the two platoons advanced. No sound came from Japs on Snowdon East. The assault platoons continued to filter through the bamboo thickets and on to the objective. Then the leading sections came through the bamboo and into the primary jungle. The trees had been splintered and shattered by our artillery fire. Many were felled in a criss-cross fashion making an obstacle to us that no Jap working party could have equalled had they toiled for days. On the right flank in the path of 5 Platoon the dry jungle had started to burn. It was while the assault platoons were struggling through this tangle of broken trees that the Japs first hit us hard with every weapon they possessed. Then they rolled grenades taped to mines down on us. The leading soldiers started to fall, tumbling over like shot rabbits. So far the assault did not falter, individual soldiers gave covering fire to others as groups leap frogged up the hill.

Then they hit us again, this time from Whistle, where the Japs had a rifle company dug in. They hit us with MMGs on fixed lines. The stream of bullets came at hip height, mowing like scythes through the timber, and 4 Platoon and the right flank of 5 Platoon. As the Jap fire started from our left flank so it intensified from the dug-in position ahead. With numbers of soldiers going down, we began to waver and finally halted, cover was sought, and the long fire fight which was to use up so much of our precious ammunition started. Lying on the ground among the tangle of trees, was relatively safe, but casualties mounted from the grenades and mines rolled down from above.

The guns on Whistle seemed to have unlimited ammunition as they never ceased firing until the very end of the battle. Apart from the dead our most seriously wounded casualties, were being caused by the mines: about 60 percent. The momentum of our attack was failing. I wondered then if the rumours about the Div coming out of the line were having a subconscious effect on our actions. No one in his right mind wishes to take risks that bring about his death or permanent injury. Sometimes in heat of battle, some soldiers take risks with little or no thought, and the effect of their action has results out of all proportion.

Content to remain where we were, I was doing no leading. I spoke to the CO on telephone, telling him we were held up. He said he could just see us. Neither A nor D Company could influence the battle because of the safety factor. [Could not see where they were firing?] I went forward to 4 Platoon, found the platoon commander was badly wounded, and told the Havildar to take command. I crawled to 5 platoon, and then asked for artillery fire on to Whistle. But because the gunner [FOO] was further back and couldn't see the target, all the ranging rounds for Whistle fell among my forward platoons, causing casualties, and effecting morale. A rifleman just in front of me was hit in the face by a large piece of shrapnel, reducing it to pulp and showering everybody in the vicinity with blood. If the FOO had been beside me at that moment I would probably have killed him. I crawled back and shouted at the gunner in 'Anglo-Saxon' and told him the result of his ranging. He shouted back his apologies and said the guns could not clear the crest and hit Whistle. There was nothing for it but to accept that the Jap machine gunners on Whistle, would continue to fire at us for as long as they pleased or ran out of ammunition. Our prospects looked bleak. How wrong I was to allow our FOO to be separate from me.

We were now absolutely on our own. It would be the infantrymen of the 2nd Goorkhas against the Japanese. Those who had the greatest pride in our regiment would win. It was terribly hot, and most of us had finished the water in our water bottles. A tree sniper now started to make a nuisance of himself. I decided I must try to break through with my reserve platoon.

Then the unexpected happened, one soldier gave us the true leadership we had lacked hitherto. 5 Platoon's left section commander Lance Naik Chamar Singh Gurung, rose to his feet and yelling obscenities to the Japs above him started clambering through the broken tree trunks and up the hill, in the face of showers of grenades and heavy rifle and machine gun fire. Urged on by the screams of encouragement from the men of his platoon, he ran on up spraying the hill with his Tommy Gun. Changing magazines as he ran, he was hit by goodness knows how many enemy bullets as he reached the first enemy trench. But he stumbled on squeezing the trigger of his Tommy Gun, falling dead across the lip of the Jap trench. He was the first man on Snowdon East that afternoon. His gallant conduct and inspiration turned what might have been defeat into victory. His action triggered off a series of other actions which resulted in the Japs being flung off Snowdon.

Rifleman Bhanbhagta Gurung, the second in command of a section, stood up and killed the tree sniper, and inspired by Naik Chamar Singh Gurung's bravery he yelled to those near him to follow, and started to run towards the top of the hill. Others rose and charged with a tremendous roar. The Japs met this attack with showers of grenades and rapid fire. The MMGs on Whistle cut down soldiers, and once again they wavered in the face of this murderous fire, and went to ground this time only 20 yards from Jap forward trenches. This however proved to be no repeat of the first time, without waiting for orders Bhanbhagta Gurung dashed forward alone attacked the nearest enemy foxhole just above him, throwing two grenades he killed the two occupants. Without hesitation, rushed to the next trench and bayonetted the Jap in it to death.

The leading platoons rose and fell upon the Jap defenders of Snowdon East, and the battle lasted until the last Jap soldier had been killed or run off. Bhanbhagta Gurung then attacked a lone machine-gun in a bunker, now out of grenades, he flung in two white phosphorous grenades, two Jap soldiers came out with their clothes on fire, to be cut down by Bhanbhagta Gurung with his kukri. A remaining Jap despite grievous wounds from burning phosphorous, continued to fire, thereupon Bhanbhagta Gurung crawled inside the bunker, where he beat out the Jap gunner's brains with a rock, capturing the machine gun.

Seven Japs with fixed bayonets counter-attacked, and were repulsed by a Naik with grenades, and a bayonet charge, killing two and putting the rest to flight. Enemy positions bypassed which started firing and holding up the reserve section were taken out by the section commander.

There were eleven men left in the right hand platoon. The left hand platoon, was still under fire when the platoon commander screaming with rage killed Japanese, his bayonet red with blood. He had six men left.

One NCO attacked the enemy using his Tommy Gun as a club, when out of ammo. Then drawing his kukri, charged the position hacking to death one enemy, two others fled.

The reserve platoon now came up as the assault platoons were pitching in to the enemy, and I told the platoon commander to take over the ground from the assault platoons. As they advanced they came under fire from the guns on Whistle, killing and wounding soldiers. As they reached the top, the machine-gun fire from Whistle stopped momentarily, and twelve Japs appeared with fixed bayonets and attacked the rear of 4 platoon. Seeing them the reserve platoon left hand section killed them.

It was chaos on the top of the objective. The first of the Japanese organised counter-attack Banzai charges, was beaten off with heavy losses. Snowdon East was now ours. My two assault platoons were smaller than one weak platoon. The part of Snowdon East held by enemy was 80 yards long by 30 yards wide. The whole area was pockmarked by trenches. All over the objective lay bodies.

I ordered the collection of water bottles from the dead of both sides, and to dig as fast as possible. I took a party to collect ammunition from A Company. While I was there I heard the sound of a second counter-attack. I grabbed a box of ammunition and returned. The attack was being beaten off and digging continued. One NCO killed four Japs with empty ammunition boxes.

A second counter attack beaten off. By now we had no grenades left, and no full Bren magazines, so ammunition was taken off each rifleman to fill some magazines. There were three more counter-attacks from enemy based on Whistle; all repulsed with heavy enemy losses. In the last three counter-attacks we used rocks instead of grenades, and to repel the final two used rocks, bayonets, kukris and the few rounds of Tommy Gun Ammunition which was all that was left.

I was in a forward slit with an NCO, when a Jap sniper fired holing the NCO's hat but not his head. I sprayed the bushes ahead with my Tommy Gun, and for a few seconds nothing happened, then as though in slow motion the Jap sharp shooter collapsed and came to rest lying on his back just outside the cover, his arms flapping very quickly for a second, just like a pheasant flaps its wings when it has been shot through the head. That was the last Jap to die on Snowdon East and the last we [3rd/2nd Goorkhas] shot in the war. Then there was silence. Looking round more than 60 percent of B Company had gone. I was very proud of them. They had captured Snowdon East regardless of cost.

I was relieved by C Coy. We crossed the Start Line 60 strong. Eleven men had been killed and 34 wounded, the majority very seriously. One died next day. Many never returned to duty. One lost the sight of both eyes. There were 35 Jap bodies on Snowdon East, and a further 80 in the vicinity. Rifleman Bhanbhagta Gurung was awarded the Victoria Cross.

Without air supply, all of which after 7 March 1945 was committed to Fourteenth Army or the NCAC, the 15th Corps was unable to follow up the Japanese into the Irrawaddy valley. Neither was Christison able to hinder the movement of the Japanese to join the main body of *Twenty-eighth Army* in the Irrawaddy Valley. The terrain was so suited to defence that most Japanese got away, only to meet their fate later. Christison's efforts in the Arakan did allow Operation DRACULA, the amphibious assault on Rangoon, to be mounted. However, the most important outcome was the securing of the forward airfields at Akyab and Ramree, without which the brilliant advance of Fourteenth Army to Rangoon would not have been possible. We left Slim in the last chapter 500 miles from his base at Dimapur. Despite all the imaginative use of river craft and homemade rafts, he would never have a chance in the race to beat the monsoon to Rangoon without airlift from Akyab, operational by 20 March, and Ramree, operational by 15 April.

10

Air War Burma

Air power was crucial to British success in Burma. Whether attacking Japanese bunkers in support of a rifle company, dropping sea mines to destroy enemy shipping bringing in reinforcements and supplies, or bombing ports and the bridges on the Thai–Burma Railway to interdict the line of communication, air power made its indispensable contribution to victory.

The fighting on land in Burma is complicated enough without shoehorning accounts by airmen in to the relevant chapters, while at the same time diverting the narrative to cover events in the air elsewhere in the theatre, hence the air war is contained in one stand-alone chapter. Accurately dovetailing accounts of actions by the airmen with what was happening on the ground is extremely difficult, and sometimes impossible in the conditions and terrain in Burma. So the aim of this chapter is to give the reader some idea of what it was like to fly and to fight over Burma as a young Allied aircrewman in the Second World War – and most were young, still in their late teens or early twenties.

Before allowing the airmen to speak for themselves, it may help if a little background is included to put what they say in context. During the British retreat from Burma the Japanese had complete air superiority, which they kept until well into 1943. The Allies meanwhile were expanding their air forces, and re-equipping with fighters capable of wresting control of the skies from the enemy and bombers with sufficient range and bomb load to mount a strategic offensive. The Japanese kept their aircraft back in the Moulmein and Rangoon area out of range of Allied fighters, only basing forward to strike Allied air bases in Assam and Bengal.

The Allies' first priority was to establish air superiority over their own bases. From the beginning they were partially successful thanks to the greater skill of their pilots and especially the ability to fly by instruments in bad weather, which offset the better performance of Japanese fighters.

But only when the British and American air forces were equipped with long-range fighters (Beaufighters and Lightning P-38s), in early 1944, were they able to wear down the Japanese air force, and capture air superiority from them completely. By this time the Japanese air force in Burma had been considerably depleted by sending air regiments to defend Japan and the Pacific islands. The ten air regiments in Burma under the Japanese *5th Air Division* consisted of about 220 aircraft (a Japanese air regiment contained anything from twelve to thirty aircraft). Allied Eastern Air Command at the same time had some 735 combat aircraft (not including the RAF and USAAF transport aircraft of Troop Carrier Command). Taking into account serviceability and other factors, this gave the Allies around 380 fighters and 200 bombers for operations, about three times as many as the Japanese. Nor did these Allied figures include aircraft allotted to the defence of Ceylon and southern India, and operations over the Indian Ocean and Bay of Bengal.

When the Japanese began their Imphal offensive, they moved all their air regiments to airfields in central Burma, which played right into the hands of the Allies, who mounted an unremitting interdiction campaign with long-range fighters and fighter-bombers. Between 10 March and 30 July 1944, the Japanese flew a total of around 1,750 sorties. During the same period the Allies flew 29,660 fighter sorties (18,860 RAF, and 10,800 USAAF), losing 170 aircraft in the process. By the end of July 1944, the *5th Air Division* had only 49 aircraft left (36 fighters, 11 light bombers, and 2 reconnaissance). From the opening of the Imphal offensive, the Allies were able to establish air superiority over any chosen area, and by mid-June absolute superiority over most of Burma. The Imphal battle brought about the destruction not only of the Japanese army, but their air force likewise.

Supply by air was the key to British success at Imphal and Kohima. By the time the road was open from Dimapur to Imphal, the RAF had flown in around 19,000 tons of supplies and over 12,000 men, and evacuated some 13,000 sick and wounded, as well as 43,000 non-combatants.

From early 1944 the Strategic Air Force, ten squadrons of Mitchells, Wellingtons, and Liberators (rising to fourteen squadrons by the end of the year), pounded Japanese communications mostly in southern Burma and Siam, including the major ports of Bangkok and Rangoon, as well as the other smaller enemy-held ports in the theatre. In addition sea mines were laid, and these, combined with air strikes on ports, caused the enemy to cease shipping movements in the Bay of Bengal and the approaches to Rangoon. The railways also received plenty of attention, especially the bridges. The Sittang Bridge had been blown by the 17th Indian Division in 1942. The progress of its subsequent repair by the Japanese was monitored by photo-reconnaissance Lightnings, Spitfires, and Mosquitos. No sooner had the first trains started to cross, than two of its main spans were destroyed by Liberators with 1,000lb bombs. It was kept out of use until the end of the war.

By the time the Fourteenth Army began its advance across the Chindwin in early December 1944, the Allies were able to muster some 827 combat aircraft, and around 500 transport aircraft. The Japanese *5th Air Division* in Burma, after receiving reinforcements, had a mere 66 aircraft, mainly fighters. The enemy did not use their meagre resources to best effect either. With characteristic rigidity, the Japanese air force persisted in mounting sorties in support of their ground troops, which despite inflicting casualties on Allied ground troops, had no effect whatsoever on the outcome of the fighting. They would have been used to better effect against transport aircraft, particularly those flying in the proximity of the battle area. The only time the Japanese tried this tactic, the Allies immediately switched their transports to night-flying, which diminished the supply sortie rate considerably.

Throughout the Battle of the Irrawaddy Shore and the advance down the Rangoon Road, the Allied Strategic Air Force struck Japanese communications, impeding the movement of supplies and isolating Mandalay and Meiktila. Without air supply EXTENDED CAPITAL would never have even begun. From 2 January to 21 May 1945, the Fourteenth Army received some 210,000 tons by air, and a mere 5,500 by road. In addition the 15th Corps in Arakan received 7,500 tons by air, dropped to units operating inland away from the sea communication system. Between 27 February and 26 March 1945, for example, Fourteenth Army and 15th Corps received 48,799 tons by air, an average of 1,743 per day.

As well as delivering forward, transport aircraft took back casualties and the sick. This was an enormous boost to morale, and saved many lives. From 2 January to 19 May 1945, some 40,000 sick and wounded were flown out, and around 31,000 reinforcements flown in.

Many airmen's accounts mention the hazards posed by weather and terrain in Burma. There were few beacons to aid navigation, and these were confined to the main airfields. All the aircraft of the time lacked equipment that was to become commonplace thirty or forty years later: weather-avoidance radar capable of detecting in darkness the dangerous cumulo-nimbus cloud (cu-nim to the aviators); radar altimeters to give a continuous readout of exact heights over the ground in all weathers; navigation systems that gave the aircraft's position to within a yard; and sophisticated traffic-control and blind-landing systems. The aircraft were unpressurized and lacked the power to climb over the cloud into calmer air. Even fighters could not do what a modern jet does when boxed in by weather and terrain, stand on its tail and pour on the power. Transports, such as Dakotas, gained height painfully slowly by today's standards and in bad turbulence were tossed about like a leaf in a gale. Aircraft that entered cu-nim cloud often crashed, after being borne up faster than an express lift, followed by hurtling earthwards, while the men inside were thrown about like peas in a pod. It might be completely inverted and have its wings torn off.

Sergeant Williams was a wireless operator/air gunner on Hudsons and later Dakotas on supply drops. Until specialist despatchers were carried, throwing out the stores was carried out by the wireless operator and the navigator. He described the flying conditions in Burma as

atrocious, there was always tremendous turbulence because of the heat. The bouncing up and down made it difficult moving supplies to the door to despatch them. We often flew through lightning. On a Hudson operation over the Chin Hills at 16,000 feet, we flew through a storm, the lightning flashed along the wing tips, lighting up the inside of the Hudson and the pilot's face white and tense with the strain of controlling the aircraft which bucked and dropped, thrown about like a ship in a boiling sea. The pilot was very strong and held it while we plummeted from 16,000 to 12,000 feet. But we got through, dropped our supplies, and returned to base pretty shaken.

Most navigation was a matter of good map reading and knowing the ground. Sergeant, later Warrant Officer, pilot Groocock flew Wellingtons, Blenheims, and Dakotas:

In the monsoon you had fantastic thunder storms, towering cu-nims, air currents, low cloud bases, and violent rain. We flew so many times to these places [jungle strips] we knew just about every valley in our area of Burma, so we knew which valleys we could fly up without coming to a dead end. Often there were clouds on the mountain tops, and you had to fly up a valley underneath. When trying to find a DZ, you hoped to find a hole in the cloud, find a valley leading in the right direction, drop, and climb back up through the hole.

The Americans played a key role throughout the air war in Burma from the very start. Without the American Volunteer Group (AVG), the Japanese air force would have had an almost completely free run in the early days of the campaign. The AVG, known as the Flying Tigers because of the fangs painted around the air intakes of their P-40 Tomahawk fighters, had been formed by Captain Chennault, a retired US Army Air Corps officer. He was an air adviser to the Chinese government and a colonel in their air force. He recruited about 100 air crew, many of them piratical characters, barn-stormers and air-circus pilots. By November 1941, one squadron was stationed at Toungoo by arrangement with the British, and two at Kunming in China. Their original task was to operate in China against the invading Japanese. When Japan invaded Burma, Chiang Kai-shek allowed the AVG to be employed for air defence there. In the first two raids on Rangoon the Japanese lost some thirty aircraft to the RAF, but mainly to the AVG, for far fewer Allied losses. Between 23 and 29 January 1942, the air battle over Rangoon cost the Japanese some fifty aircraft, and the fighting in February another thirty-four or so, of which the AVG accounted for the majority. By late February the Allied fighter strength was down to ten aircraft, and the surviving Tomahawks were pulled back to Magwe.

Corporal Jepson, an RAF radio mechanic, arrived at Mingaladon airfield just north of Rangoon in the middle of a Japanese air raid. His squadron had no aircraft, and he was called into the adjutant's office to be told

to go over to the AVG who were experiencing problems with their radios. They had nine fighters flying and only two had serviceable radios. I got seven out of the nine working. If something went wrong with American equipment, you pulled it out, chucked it away, and put in a new one. They couldn't do this in Burma at that time because there were no spares. They had good operators but no mechanics. I mucked in and helped whenever I could and really got involved with them. I had nothing to do in my own squadron so used to spend every day with the AVG and return back to my accommodation at night.

One evening I found my barrackroom empty in a state of chaos, and my kit bag sitting there. The squadron had all gone, to Rangoon docks to be evacuated on the last ship out, I later discovered, and left me behind. In the morning there was no one about, except a couple of RAF chaps destroying equipment who had been told that they might be flown out, and if this was not possible, they were to walk to India. I reported to the AVG squadron commander who said they would be responsible for me.

Eventually the aircraft were flown out to Magwe [south of Meiktila], some pilots flew with another sitting on their laps. I was in the radio truck and, with the other AVG ground crew, went by road via Prome. Eventually, there was a problem getting fuel at Magwe and, as the Japs were advancing, the AVG withdrew via Lashio, and eventually to Kunming. I went with them as a member of the AVG. I was the only RAF chap, and got teased a lot. They were a tough lot, but I liked them, they were very generous. The pilots were aged between twenty and thirty. Some of them were there for the money, some for adventure. They were marvellous pilots, some with 2,000 flying hours, they did not care about regulations, were very wild and drank a lot. Most of them had Chinese lady friends in Kunming. I was a bit isolated, and received no letters from home. My wife did not know where I was, or even if I was alive for six months until Chennault told me to send a cable via American Express in Kunming and charge it to the AVG.

Jepson made himself useful not only repairing radios, but also helping set up a system of beacons and early warning communications, mostly unsupervised:

It was very different from the RAF. All I got in the RAF was bored. In the RAF you spent a great deal of the time filling in forms and taking orders from corporals and sergeants, half of whom knew less than you did. When the Flying Tigers were taken over by the USAAF, Chennault asked me if I would accept a commission in the USAAF. He said he could arrange it. He could do most things but not that. So I was eventually returned to UK via India.

Flight Lieutenant Hughes's Blenheim squadron was stationed at Magwe alongside the AVG.

We suffered from the District Commissioner's paranoia about Japanese parachutists. He had covered the whole airfield except the runway with logs carried in by elephants, and sent the elephants away. So you only had room for aircraft on the runway and on each side. Before Rangoon fell, there was an elementary air raid warning system, and we operated for about four weeks, but this collapsed as the Japs advanced north. We had three raids in succession, each of around 27 aircraft, who came across and dropped their bombs in formation and wrote off most of the RAF aircraft. It was a bit of a shambles. The aircrew flew out in the remaining aircraft, which were just flyable, to Akyab and Dum-Dum [near Calcutta]. The ground crews arrived in India long after we got out of Burma.

I was sent back in to Burma to command a squadron, the plan being to fly Blenheims from eastern Burma, it never came off. I escaped [a second time] in the last Dakota out of Burma.

Pilot Officer Thirlwell was a photo-reconnaissance Hurricane pilot, who arrived at Magwe just after the last of his squadron's aircraft crashed. As he had no job, he was sent

to Lashio to investigate the possibility of flying out the squadron personnel by China Airways to India. I went to the orderly room Flight Sergeant for transport, and he said 'you can have this Wolseley Fourteen, but I want something in return'. So I swapped a typewriter I found in the house in which I was billeted for this car, and drove to Lashio. Having confirmed the availability of China Airways, I was flown to Calcutta, only to be sent back to Burma, where I spent most of my time rescuing the special cameras from crashed photo-recce aircraft. After getting out of Burma for a second time, I had an extraordinary period based at the Great Eastern in Calcutta, the most expensive hotel in town. I would get into my Hurricane at Dum-Dum, fly to Chittagong where I refuelled from petrol drums using a hand pump. Having spent the night with the British Consul, I would fly to photograph Rangoon, before returning for more fuel at Chittagong, and on to Dum-Dum to get the film processed as quickly as possible. After a shower in the Great Eastern I would sit down to dinner being served by bearers in white coats and gloves.

Flying Officer Braithwaite joined a reconstituted 60 Squadron RAF in Karachi in March 1942. Like many of the RAF squadrons in the theatre, it had Canadian, Australian, South African, and British aircrew. Braithwaite was to fight throughout the Burma campaign. In his first operational squadron,

> which had been decimated in Singapore, the CO had completed a tour of operations on Blenheims in the UK, as had one of the flight commanders. The other flight commander had flown a tour on Hampdens, also in the UK. Apart from them, there was very little operational experience in the squadron. We were equipped with Blenheims, which were old and rickety. We operated from Agartala and Dum-Dum near Calcutta, attacking troop concentrations and dock installations from about 10,000 feet. Our targets were mainly on the coast and along the Irrawaddy. We were escorted by Hurricanes and Mohawks.

Some found themselves in India and flying over Burma by chance. Sergeant Groocock was only nineteen with 300 hours' flying experience when he delivered a Wellington to Cairo from the UK via Gibraltar, down to West Africa and across to the Nile:

> we were very heavy taking off from Gib, with extra fuel tanks, and scraped over the sea wall at the end of the runway by inches. We had to fly a long dog-leg out into the Atlantic to avoid French Vichy fighters from Dakar who were paid $500 by the Germans for each British aircraft they shot down. Quite a few aircrew got lost flying over Africa on one of the legs to the Nile at Khartoum.
>
> We expected to join a squadron in the Middle-East, where aircrew were sent back to UK on completion of a six month tour. But we were stuck in a transit camp, and when I saw a notice asking for volunteers to ferry a Wellington to India, I and my crew volunteered for lack of anything better to do. We eventually arrived at 99 Squadron in Assam. I got out and said to the CO, 'here's your aircraft, how do we get back to Cairo?'
>
> 'Cairo! What makes you think you're going back to Cairo? You're in India now. Are you single or married?'
>
> 'Single', says I.
>
> 'Right, a tour in India for a single man is four years. Three years for a married man'

At the age of nineteen four years seems like a life-time. It was nearly four years before I got home. The squadron was just settling down to bombing ops over Burma. I had been the captain of a Wellington all the way from UK, but because of my inexperience of ops, I was made co-pilot, with the same crew, but with a more experienced captain. We bombed air fields, ports and railway mar-shalling yards, mainly at night for about six months in late 1942 early 1943, dropping 500 lb bombs from around 10,000 feet. Finding the target was not easy. There was not a lot of opposition. We were attacked by a night fighter once. We went low-level and corkscrewed, and lost him. We had flak over some targets, but nothing like the flak over Germany. I had taken part in one of the 1,000 bomber raids over Dusseldorf. Our main worry was ditching in the jungle. We were ill-prepared for survival. We had a silk scarf map of Burma, and a little compass. We had no money, just the Burmese version of the 'goolie chit'.*

At one stage I was sent to Bombay on a shipping recognition course, during that time my crew went missing. We had been together since forming up at the operational flying unit in UK.

Braithwaite also carried out numerous sorties between August 1942 and January 1943 in Blenheims, some in support of the first Arakan offensive.

We were often attacked by Jap fighters, they buzzed around but were distracted by the Hurricanes and Mohawks. We respected the Jap pilots, but their aircraft could not take damage, they were not armoured. If attacked, one ploy was to fly low, as close to the ground as possible. Some Jap fighters had telescopic sights, which required the pilot to put his eye to it to aim.† With his eye to the sight, the pilot could not fly low and fast without risking piling into the ground.

Although the Blenheim was slow, it was well armoured. A couple of Japanese pilots I met after the war said it was quite difficult to

---

* A 'goolie chit' was, and is, airman's slang for a document carried for use by downed aircrew to show to local tribes people guaranteeing a financial reward in return for the airman being handed over unharmed. Tribesmen on the North-West Frontier of India, where the practice of issuing 'goolie chits' originated, commonly castrated enemy dead.

† Unlike the gun-sight in most fighters, which allowed the pilot to fly 'head up'.

shoot down. Ours were well maintained by our peace-time trained and skilled ground crew.

All the same not many of us expected to live all that long. We were issued with rudimentary will forms, which few of us bothered to complete. At 20 or 22 years old you don't have much to leave anyway.

One of our crews had a lucky escape. Three crews were briefed to attack Japanese barges on the Mayu River. On take off, two of the aircraft went unserviceable, and turned back. One pressed on. We had been briefed to bomb at 10,000 feet, but because he was on his own, the one remaining aircraft attacked in a shallow dive. He was attacked by five fighters. On his return, he reported that his gunner had shot one down and damaged another; so he thought. The undercarriage on his Blenheim was damaged so he had to carry out a crash-landing at Dum-Dum. After the war the pilot made contact with the Japanese, and discovered that the chap they'd shot down was the local air-ace, and not only had they actually shot down another, but so damaged a third fighter that he crashed on landing.

Braithwaite's squadron moved to Bangalore in May 1943 to re-form as a Hurricane squadron, but in September 1943 he was posted to Number 62, a Dakota squadron, where he remained until January 1944. He spent much of his time supplying the 81st West African Division in the Arakan:

Clothing, rice and other non-breakable stores were dropped without parachutes from low level. Other kit was dropped from about 300 feet under parachutes. The people on the ground marked out the DZ with white crosses. Often it would be in a river valley. You would have to descend from 6 or 7,000 feet, drop, and climb out again. Often it took a dozen passes to get the whole load out, because of the short DZ and high ground all round. We carried around three and a half tons of supplies, and often did two or three trips a day. There was occasional interference from the Jap air force, but the main hazards were the terrain and the weather.

In February 1944 I had completed a 400 hour tour on Dakotas, and was sent to Number 1 Advanced Training Unit which trained bomb aimers and air gunners. From here I converted on to Liberators in May 1944. I spent the rest of my time in 99 Squadron on sorties to places like Martaban, Penang, and Moulmein, bombing railway yards and ports, and mining.

Pilot Officer Cobley, a Hurricane pilot, escaped from Singapore just before the surrender, in a river boat, and ended up in India joining 20 Squadron, which was re-equipping with the Mk IIC, fitted with two 40 mm cannon for anti-tank work.

They made the aircraft a bit unwieldy and you couldn't do aerobatics safely. We carried high explosive (HE) or armour-piercing (AP) shells. Each gun was loaded with only 16 rounds, which you had to fire singly, not in bursts like 20 mm cannons or machine-guns. You had to line up very accurately on the target, and attack one at a time.

We were supposed to have Spitfires as top cover, but didn't get it to start with. But operating very low as we did, with jungle trees below, it was difficult for Jap aircraft to see us, and in any case there weren't many about. I commanded a section – a pair of aircraft.

In the Arakan in late 1943, we started by operating from a jungle strip called 'Brighton', near the coast just behind our front line. After which we moved even nearer the front and flew from a strip on the beach, called 'Hove'. This was an agreeable place, living in bamboo huts. We swam, but had to look out for stingrays. We had a ration of drink dropped to us by parachute: four bottles of beer per month for the airmen, and one bottle of gin or whisky for the officers. We had a good mix of over half Commonwealth chaps

Our targets were bunkers, river boats, and occasionally trucks. We lost quite a few people, shot down by flak. During my time in the Arakan I took my flight up to Imphal where I was stationed for two months. At Palel airstrip, the Japs attacked one night, and some of them holed up around a hillock near the airfield, and come daylight the Gurkhas sorted them out. We had the RAF Regiment to defend us but they were not very effective when it came to counter-attacking

After Imphal we went back to the Arakan, where I was shot down. We had been sent to attack Akyab, where a Japanese General was supposed to be visiting. There was no aircraft there. I was leading, and was hit by flak. There was no target so the others peeled off. My engine kept stopping then picking up, and glycol smoke was coming out. I had 80 miles to go, and wasn't going to make it. I told the others to go home. I headed for the Kaladan Valley where I knew there were some relatively bare hillsides, and the West Africans were still about. I landed wheels up on a barer patch, and it was right by a West African forward patrol. The West Africans arranged for an L-5 to come in to a strip they had prepared and fly me out. I was back in the squadron before nightfall that day. I was very lucky, I didn't get a scratch.

On another occasion we were on a six aircraft sortie led by the CO. We never got to the target because the cloud was down on the deck. We could hardly see each other let alone the coast, when the CO ordered us back. We got separated, and I discovered I was over the sea with a cliff on my right wing tip, on the Naf Peninsula, behind our own lines. I discarded the idea of climbing over the cliff, thinking that there were plenty of Hurricanes in the pipeline, but only one of me. So I landed in the shallow sea by the beach near a village. The Headman and another fellow waded out and pulled me out. They sent a message, I don't know how, but I was picked up quite soon by truck.

Flight Lieutenant Parry carried out his first operations flying a Hurricane Mk IIC with 11 Squadron RAF at Imphal where there were six airstrips. Imphal and Palel were classified all-weather, but had narrow runways and little hard-standing space. The other four, Kangla, Tulihal, Wangjing, and Sapam, were fair-weather only, being constructed on paddy fields by flattening the bunds, and levelling the ground as much as possible. In the monsoon aircraft bogged in dispersal and while taxiing out. The weather was always a major hazard monsoon or no. Parry:

The Imphal plain was 2,500 feet high surrounded by mountains rising to around 7,000 feet. Clouds developed every afternoon, and cumulus especially fast. When returning from a sortie we sometimes found it difficult to out climb the cloud, as we did not have enough fuel left to keep climbing at full power for long enough. There was a tendency to try to find a way through the mountains below the cloud.

On one occasion we were on a squadron 'effort' south of Imphal, in two flights, not in the monsoon. The CO was leading the first flight of five aircraft, and I the second of six, spaced five minutes apart. We were returning from the strike along a narrow valley leading to Imphal. The clouds were across the top of the valley and over Imphal itself, like a lid on a basin. We were below cloud height, which was well down the slopes of the mountains on each side. Suddenly we ran into a severe rain shower, like a curtain ahead. The CO carried out the correct action, put his aircraft into line astern and climbed up through the cloud heading for the top of the cloud over Imphal, hoping to find a hole through which to descend. He gave me fair warning what he was doing over the radio. When I came to the rain barrier, I decided I wouldn't climb up through it, instead I gathered my aircraft into close formation and went through the rain below the cloud. I reckoned that it was only an isolated shower, and not very deep, and if I held my course between the the the two mountain walls, I would come out into a clear spot. I did after a couple of minutes. Unfortunately three of the aircraft in the COs flight were lost either because of excessive turbulence in the cloud, or the inexperience of the pilots. Only the CO and the most experienced pilot got through. Yet he had done the right thing, I hadn't.

Our Hurricanes were fitted with four 20 mm cannon, and our main tasks were ground strafing and escorting the Dakotas. Later the escort work diminished, and we were mainly used on strafing. At about the same time we were fitted with bomb racks and became Hurribombers for army support, carrying two 250 lb bombs.

As well as being on hand to support the army, we harassed the Japanese line of communication doing low-level 'Rhubarbs' by day and night. Strafing was dangerous at night. It was OK flying over the road with one's canopy open looking over the side for vehicles on the road, but once you closed the canopy to attack, and dived in at low level head-on, the thick bullet-proof windscreen reduced visibility considerably. As soon as you fired your cannon, your were temporarily blinded by the muzzle flashes. There was a grave danger of flying straight into the ground, and we lost a number of pilots on night operations.

Night operations were very fruitful, even when we didn't destroy trucks, because the presence of aircraft slowed down the progress of Japanese road convoys. When we came overhead they would usually park. Furthermore, once you spotted a road convoy and reported its location, the chaps going out at dawn would be able to work out where it had laid up for the day – they hardly ever risked moving by day.

On one occasion, I was out on an intruder raid armed with bombs, and saw a large Jap convoy on a road crossing an open plain

– a good place to attack. I dropped one bomb on the road ahead of the convoy, hoping this would be difficult to get round, and another behind them. I kept a patrol over the area, until another intruder pilot arrived. It was Squadron Leader Arjun Singh the CO of Number 1 Indian Squadron. I told him where I was, and he took over the standing patrol until dawn, when more aircraft appeared and dealt with the convoy. Some Japs got away, but most were caught.

The Japs were very good at camouflage. About an hour before dawn they would pull off the road under the trees on the sides. If there was insufficient cover, they would cover their vehicles with branches cut from further in. After a while we realised that the vegetation by the road was light coloured because of the covering of dust, whereas the branches brought from some way in was dark green. So we flew along the road looking for what looked like new growth, standing out fresh green against the khaki-coloured vegetation.

The Japs also took advantage of areas used by our army during the retreat of 1942, where we had set up refuelling points at intervals along the main road. Here vehicles had collected and been struck by the Japanese air force, or perhaps had been immobilised and abandoned. From time to time the Japs artfully parked some of their own vehicles among these trucks during the day. So we learned the pattern of the layout of these parks, and were able to spot when new trucks had been popped in. It used to annoy new pilots when they excitedly reported a concentration of vehicles, only to be told, 'don't bother with those, they are our own left behind in 1942'. Then perhaps a couple of days later, we would attack one or two of these parks where we had spotted some additional trucks, and the new pilots couldn't work out how we knew.

Sometimes smoke from cooking fires would betray the position of a parked-up Jap convoy. Even so, it could be frustrating, because although you could make out the vehicles from dead overhead, when you come in on an attack heading from say half a mile out, at an angle of dive, the trees covered the target and it was hard to spot exactly where they were. Just occasionally you would catch them in the open in daylight. Once I saw a Jap staff car on a winding road in the mountains. I strafed it, and saw it go over the edge down the hillside. I assume all the occupants were killed. On another occasion my flight was returning from a 'rhubarb', when we spotted a truck on a bare hillside. Only my tail-end-charlie had any ammo left and he asked permission to break off and attack. I said, 'yes', so in he went. I don't know whether he hit the truck or not, but the whole hillside behind it went up in an enormous ball of flame. I assume the truck was refuelling and he hit a fuel dump.

I took part in a great number of sorties in support of the army at Kohima and Imphal. We often came back not knowing whether we had hit the target or not. The army developed a system of sending us a 'strawberry', the opposite of a 'raspberry',* in the form of a signal telling us of the success of our strike, which was very heartening especially when we thought we had failed.

At Imphal we were aware of the Japs being around us in the mountains. They infiltrated at night to Kangla from which we did a lot of night-flying. We used to tell the new pilots, 'we are so close, we share orderly officer with them'. I was on one daytime sortie which was so close to the strip that our ground crew were able to watch the whole operation, lasting twenty minutes, from take-off to landing.

I did a lot of strafing at Kohima, which was the only bit of Burma that looked like a First World War battlefield from the air, with masses of shell holes, no trees, and artillery rounds and mortar bombs going off as we flew in. I was a bit worried I would get hit by our own artillery or mortars.

At Imphal, for example at the battle of Bishenpur, one could see the Japs from the air sometimes, especially tanks out in the open. We worked a 'cab rank' system of two aircraft permanently airborne during the day, which was called in on targets when identified by an RAF liaison officer with the forward troops. We were quite effective against tanks because they would have to close down. We carried mixed belts of ammo: ball, incendiary, high explosive, semi-armour piercing, and armour-piercing. Amour-piercing and incendiary was good against tanks. Our warrant officer armourer used to provide the right mix for whatever targets were about that day. When tanks appeared we were supposed to call in tank-busting Hurricanes Mk IIDs, with two 40mm guns. But we used to go for the tanks anyway hoping to hit fuel tanks and disable tracks.

We had very little opposition from enemy fighters, the Spitfires

---

* This was the slang at that time for expressing dissatisfaction.

dealt with them pretty easily. The majority of sorties by Jap fighters seemed to be sneak raids on airfields or ground targets, and they were a nuisance only. Flak was more of a problem for us. They would defend key points like bridges with bofors-type guns. Impossible to spot were their heavy machine-guns, you just saw the bullet holes when you returned, or an aircraft shot down.

You were always conscious that you might have to walk back if you were unlucky enough to be shot down. It was a bit worrying, but it helped that our CO, a New Zealander had done just this. During the retreat he had had to 'ditch' and walk until he found friendly forces. He had also been an RAF liaison officer on the first Chindit Expedition, so he knew what to do in the jungle, what to carry and so forth. He gave us the confidence to beat the jungle. In our squadron we flew in long trousers and long-sleeved shirts, wearing army boots and short puttees, so we were well equipped to walk if we had to. You tried not to think too much about what would happen if you fell into Jap hands, but concentrated on how you would get away into the jungle and survive. No one in our squadron had to do it. Others did.

There were many 'colonials' on our squadron: Canadians, Australians, New Zealanders, two Americans, South Africans, two from the West Indies, Indians, and Brits.

On the whole air crew in Burma carried out more sorties than their opposite numbers in Europe. For example, Squadron Leader Butler carried out 130 operations in Blenheims in 60 Squadron, which was later converted to Hurricanes, in which he completed a further thirty-four operations. After a spell on a communications flight, he asked to return to operational flying, and was sent to command 11 Squadron, equipped with Hurricane fighter-bombers. The squadron had an establishment of twenty aircraft which guaranteed twelve in the air on any one day, and enabled a good sortie rate to be maintained. In this squadron Butler regularly carried out three sorties a day, and sometimes four, clocking up 140 operations. With a total of 304 operations in Burma under his belt, and a DSO and a DFC, he was finally sent home for a rest.

Napalm had recently been introduced into the Burma theatre. Butler:

We carried napalm in the Hurricane's long-range tanks instead of fuel. It was very effective against the Japs especially close to our own troops. Napalm strikes were controlled by our own troops firing coloured smoke on to the enemy position. The colour was changed each day, to keep the Japs guessing. I as leader went in first followed by the other eleven. We would make three runs each, until we had expended our bombs and ammunition.

Among the most hazardous operations, supply dropping rated high on the list, especially in the monsoon, and at night. In November 1943, Groocock was posted to 194 Squadron, flying Dakotas, commanded by

A wonderful CO called 'Fatty' Pearson, who had been an airline pilot in East Africa. He said he would give me five hours familiarisation and if I passed I would be a Dakota captain, this was great, since I'd never flown a Dakota before. After dropping Gurkha para troops in training, the squadron went to Assam at Agartala to support the Fourteenth Army.

An operational tour was 500 hours. The Dakota was a marvellous aircraft, light on the controls, with very reliable engines, and you could land it on a 500 yard long strip at night. I flew into all the Chindit strips by night and day: White City, Broadway, Blackpool and Chowringhee. Aberdeen was the worst, especially at night, it was short with hills on three sides. You had to circle at 7,000 to 8,000 feet, waiting until you were called down by the controller. You circled down, and landed one way on the 500–600 yard long strip. You took off in the opposite direction. One night I came in too high, and knew I wasn't going to make it. So I opened up full throttle, found a little valley, and staggered along this at about 75 knots, managing to get away with it and come in for another approach.

One of our flight commanders Dinger Bell was attacked by a Jap night fighter while circling overhead Broadway. Both engines were knocked out, and four or five of the twenty or so soldiers in the back were killed. He managed to do a dead stick landing and get away with it – fantastic.

In early April 1944, we spent a lot of time supplying Imphal and Kohima. I took part in the fly-in of a whole division from the Arakan to Imphal. We had to creep in through the valleys, the mountains were covered by cloud.

My worst incident took place on a supply drop north of Kohima. We were flying at 8,500 feet, the mountain tops went up to 7,000 feet, but there was a layer of thick cloud between us and them.

Getting near where the DZ should have been we couldn't see anything. I thought with a bit of luck we'll find a hole and go down, so I told the two wireless operators to get the load ready to drop; it was bags of rice by free-fall that day. They started to pile the bags of rice by the door. All of a sudden, the air speed started to drop off. The natural reaction is to put on more power, but this makes the problems worse because it puts the centre of gravity back and pulls the nose up. I put on more power, and the speed dropped. Suddenly she flipped into a spin. I knew we had 1,500 feet to go before hitting the mountains. We dropped straight into the cloud, descending at 1,500 feet per minute. The altimeter unwound past 7,000 feet, and I thought any moment now. I took the correct recovery action, opposite rudder and nose down, and we came out of the spin below cloud at 4,600 feet, with two bloody great peaks on either side of us reaching up into the cloud. We collected our wits. The aircraft had been badly loaded to start with, and by stacking the rice by the door the aircraft's centre of gravity had been put out of limits. In the spin, it all fell forward putting the centre of gravity right, so the aircraft would fly OK. Fortunately no one had bailed out, because they couldn't get their parachutes on in time. We staggered along the valley, saw a column of smoke, it was the DZ – an absolute miracle. We dropped our load, the only aircraft out of twelve who made it that day. The others all turned back.

According to Pilot Officer Simpson, who was also in 'Fatty' Pearson's squadron, the technique for dealing with Japanese fighters in daylight was to

stay in cloud if you were flying at height. When below cloud, fly low right at tree-top level. If the fighter gets close, close one engine and do a steep turn. But most of the time we had RAF fighters to keep the Japs busy. Our biggest problem was the weather, particularly cu-nims stuffed into grey cloud so you couldn't see them, as well as poor maps and no navigational aids. We developed good techniques for overcoming these. You took the maximum possible fuel, and if the DZ was covered by cloud, you stooged around, until a hole appeared, and went in to drop. There were few aborted drops.

I crashed at Blackpool one night. As I was in the circuit, I could see a lot of people going round again. I thought, I won't do that. So I dragged it in at 68 knots, got to the end of the runway, over a huge tree, and plonked the aircraft down. The undercarriage on the port side cracked, and caught fire, while I belted down the runway holding it up on one wheel. At the end I swung it off to the left clear of the runway. As we came to a stop the aircraft was getting hot. We all got out of the hatch in the roof, because the load had shifted blocking the way to the door. I remembered we had the mail on board, right by the door, so I got a chap to give me a leg up so I could snatch the mail bags from outside.

After the war I met the chap who built the strip at Blackpool. He said they didn't clear the very end of the runway because the bulldozer broke down. I hit a mound of earth which they had left un-flattened.

On one occasion I flew a load of water including a small water trailer into Broadway. The Chindits didn't want the trailer, they just wanted me off quickly. So I just opened the taps to drain it, before lashing it well forward in the aircraft for takeoff. I must have been a bit flustered and disorientated, because I saw two lights on the runway and was opening up power, when a chap with a torch rushed out and waved and screamed 'those are the last two lights on the runway, you are facing the wrong way. I turned round and took off, and in the confusion forgot to make the 15 degree right turn immediately after take off. I heard trees bashing the bottom of the aircraft, did a stall turn to the right and the Dakota responded. On my return the fitter said, 'where have you been? The engine cowling is full of twigs and leaves'.

Sergeant Williams was also in 'Fatty' Pearson's 194 Squadron. He had previously been on Hudsons, also with Pearson, and had taken part in supplying Wingate's first Chindit expedition.

Wingate's columns lit bonfires on the DZ, and we signalled the code of the day with an Aldis lamp, and didn't drop till we got the right reply.* We could only drop 3,500 lbs from Hudsons, but twice that from Dakotas. On Hudson ops we had Mohawk escorts. On Dakota ops sometimes up to 20 Spitfires flying top cover.

After converting to Dakotas, 194 Squadron went to Agatala in February 1944 and supported 15th Corps in the Arakan, just as the Japanese mounted their offensive there. Sometimes the DZ would have

---

* This technique was used on other DZs as well as Chindit ones.

been overrun by the enemy, or so closely surrounded that aircraft running in to drop had to fly over Japanese positions. Williams:

> On our second sortie one night, we arrived over the DZ, and there was no reply to our light signal to the ground. We saw tracer coming up, so the Japs had got the DZ and we aborted the drop. The next sortie was in daylight, and we located the DZ, but as our aircraft flew over Jap positions near it, it came under fire and was hit in the port engine. The pilot closed it down to avoid a fire, meanwhile the navigator and second wireless operator were busily despatching loads.
>
> I noticed black smoke streaming past the door, and rushed up to tell the pilot. He told me to alert the crew to take up positions for a crash landing. By now we were down to about 300 feet above the ground, and had lots of supplies still on board. The pilot was having a problem maintaining even that height, we threw out the supplies as fast as we could. Slowly the pilot gained height, and the navigator gave him the course for home. We managed to get over the Chin Hills, and eventually made a good landing back at base.

Flying mules in could be troublesome. Bamboo stalls were constructed to keep them penned, but occasionally they would panic and the bamboo would snap, and the stability of the aircraft would be put at risk by a madly plunging mule threatening to kick a hole in the fuselage. In this situation the muleteers were under clear orders to shoot the mule, but sometimes in the heat of the moment they got carried away. This happened in Williams' Dakota: 'there were bullet holes in the ceiling, the floor and the fuselage. The fitters told us that some bullets had narrowly missed cutting the control wires'.

During the second Wingate expedition, the Dakota squadrons were also supplying Imphal and Kohima. On one of these trips Williams' crew flew a load of bombs into Palel for the Hurribombers, followed by evacuating the RAF ground crew of one of the Hurricane squadrons. Having loaded up and started a normal take-off

> and about to get airborne, a cross-wind gusted, the wing dipped dangerously, the pilot thumped the throttles back, but both oleo [shock-absorbing] legs collapsed. Every one got out OK, but sitting on the ground we were very shaken. Our beloved C Charlie was now a write-off – it was like losing our home. We felt insecure and lost.

Having to fly other Dakotas as and when they were available was not the same.

While waiting for his tour to end, Williams flew as spare crew with Groocock to drop urgent supplies at Jessami.

The weather was appalling, and over the dropping area it was ten/tenths cloud. I decided to use bad weather procedure which I had learned in training. I managed to contact ground control by wireless, despite the very severe atmospheric conditions, and asked if he could hear our engines and in what direction. Soon he told me. I gave the direction to Warrant Officer Groocock, suddenly we broke cloud and the DZ was right below us. We delivered a 7,500 lb load successfully.

Thirlwell, having started his photo-recce career in Hurricanes, was switched to B-25s in the same role. To give the B-25 the necessary range to fly to distant targets, as far as the Andaman Islands and beyond, all the armour and radios were removed. Thirlwell's first trip as captain was to the Andamans

to photograph the dock there. My photographer was LAC Fox. On the way back, suddenly a hard-boiled egg hit my instrument panel. It was Fox drawing my attention to the fact that he had seen two Navy Zeros coming up to attack us. I don't know how we got away with it, but instead of trying to climb, I put the nose down and ran for it, although they were faster than us, they obviously were short of fuel or something, because they gave up the chase.

The CO of the photo-recce squadron was 'Fatty' Pearson, who asked for me when he went to form 194. Which started as a Hudson squadron. I went to Cairo to collect one, having never flown a Hudson before. I had a half-hour check out on one, and was given a crew to fly it to India. As we landed at Bahrein on our route, the navigator said 'that's my 100th'.

'100th what?', says I.

'My 100th hour of flying', he replied.

I nearly had a fit. I had cheerfully taken his instructions all the way across the desert from Cairo to Basra and on to Bahrein.

After supporting the first Chindit expedition in Hudsons, Thirlwell along with the rest of 194 converted to Dakotas.

Even in monsoon storms when you had very little say in what happened to you, plunging down 3,000 feet and up again 2,000 in torrential rain and lightning, the Dakota was a wonderful aircraft. It had one snag, the cockpit leaked badly in heavy rain, and we used to put oilskins over our knees to keep the water off our laps.

Broadway was a difficult place to land at night because of mountains on either side, you approached downwind at 8,000 feet to clear the high ground, turned onto finals at 8,000 feet, and tried to pick up the light of the goose-neck flares marking the strip, there was no glide-path indicator, you went right in from 8,000 feet to touch down. My first landing there, the chap ahead of me with 24 soldiers on board made a nonsense, and tried to go round again, all I could see were his landing lights as he went straight into a hillside beyond the runway. I was at about 600 feet at that stage, and just held on, all I could see was a flaming aircraft ahead. I made it OK.

One of the most effective strike aircraft in Burma was the Beaufighter. It was originally designed as a fighter but came into its own as a fighter/bomber. It carried a crew of two, pilot and navigator. The Beaufighter crews were 'press-on' types. Pilot Officer Morrell joined 211 Squadron in late 1944:

The adjutant came out to greet me and fell flat on his back – he was drunk. We had a brilliant CO, Wing Commander Marr DSO and bar, DFC and bar, who had shot down six Japs. We had sixteen aircraft in our squadron, and in the year before I joined had lost 35 crews. I didn't know this at the time. I did my first op sortie on New Year's Eve 1944, as one of a pair attacking river craft on the Irrawaddy. We lost touch with the other aircraft in cloud, but got there OK. I had done lots of navigation using rivers, roads, railways etc. Pagodas were especially useful, you could see the Shwe Dagon's gold dome forty miles off in daytime.

We were highwaymen, anything that moved we hit. The big prize was a train. If there were no trains about, we attacked the stations, or the engine sheds. The Beaufighter was a formidable aircraft and had four 20 mm cannon, six machine-guns, eight 60 pounder HE rockets or eight 25 pounder AP rounds. We always used HE on river craft.

We normally flew alone, but on one occasion for example, we flew as part of an eight aircraft sortie to look for Jap MTBs up a chaung. We were to attack a position given over the radio by an Anglo-Burmese chap on the ground. We formed up in a taxi-rank, there was not much ground fire. We couldn't see the MTBs, or what damage had been done. The Burmese chap would say, 50 yards right, or add 50. He was killed by one of our rockets we were told later.

The other 'press-on' types could be found in Hurribomber squadrons, engaged on strafing in support of the army. Pilot Officer Bambridge was in 60 Squadron, equipped with Hurricane Mk IIDs:

Bombing and strafing fast and low was occasionally frightening, but as I was not very old, the fright did not last long. We went in in pairs. The bombs had an eleven second delay to give you time to get clear. I lost my number two on one strafe. He was hit and baled out OK, but he came across a Gurkha patrol who mistook him for a Jap and shot him dead. I flew with a survival kit consisting of a .38-inch revolver, a field dressing, a kukri, and some K rations.

The ultimate aircraft as far as some aircrew were concerned was the De Havilland Mosquito. Originally designed as a light bomber, and of wooden construction, it was faster than many fighters, but could carry 4,000lb of bombs, only 2,000lb less than the Flying Fortress. It could be fitted with rockets, and had four 20mm cannon and four machine-guns. Pilot Officer Hewes was a Mosquito pilot in 82 Squadron during the period when the Japanese were fighting to stave off disaster around Mandalay and Meiktila, and down the Rangoon Road.

We were after ground transport. Once we had cleared the Chin Hills, we descended to ground level and went on the hunt. We'd go deep into Jap territory at night. The flying conditions until the Monsoon came were good. Sometimes the Japs drove with lights on at night. We had a number of accidents on night ops, chaps flying into the ground. Once a water buffalo strolled across a forward strip at Kalewa as a Mosquito was taking off. They didn't see it, the aircraft caught fire, and as we had no fire or crash equipment we had to watch them burn to death.

The operating conditions were more dangerous than the Japs. If you landed in the jungle, the chances of getting out were remote. You were briefed on what to do, few made it.

Morrell's Beaufighter squadron was operating from a tarmac strip in the Chittagong area in what is now Bangladesh when the monsoon arrived early in 1945, as the Fourteenth Army was closing in on Rangoon.

We had to take off in the rain, sheets of spray flew up. You wouldn't do it nowadays. As you flew across the paddy fields, flocks of birds would fly up and hit the aircraft, hitting the windscreen and engines. The blood and feathers would soon blow off.

We covered the parachute landings at Rangoon, hitting targets of opportunity. Wing Commander Montague Brown our CO flew over Rangoon Jail and took the photo 'Japs Gone'. Our last crew was lost on 7 May, and on 8 May it was Victory in Europe day.

We went back to India to convert on to Mosquitos, *the* plane of all planes. We lost two crews on training. We were to have taken part in the invasion of Malaya, when some American dropped an atom bomb on Japan and it was all over.

11

The Rangoon Road and the Final Act

At the beginning of April, the monsoon was forty days away. By the shorter route alongside the railway from Meiktila, Rangoon was 320 miles south of where Slim's Fourteenth Army stood, or 370 miles down the Irrawaddy valley: 100 miles further than the march from the Rhine to the Baltic being covered by Monty's soldiers at that very moment. To get to Rangoon before the monsoon, Slim would have to average eight to ten miles a day. He had only two roads to his objective, and his supplies had to come from the base at Dimapur by air, boat, or truck, or via the newly won airfields in the Arakan. His line of communication stretched back to Calcutta; in European terms, a distance equivalent to supplying an army on the Bosphorus from a base in Rome via Trieste and Belgrade, but without a European, or even Balkan, road, rail, and river network; and the distance would increase daily as he advanced.

There was little to choose between the two routes for the first part of the advance. On either of them Slim's army would be operating off a single road, and leaving behind the open, good going of central Burma. But the further south one moved on the Irrawaddy axis, the more numerous the water channels encountered: and the Japanese could destroy the bridges, if they had not done so already. So Slim chose the railway axis for his main advance, with 4th Corps (5th and 17th Divisions), while continuing to push down the Irrawaddy route with 33rd Corps (7th and 20th Divisions). In this way, if seriously blocked on one axis, he could switch the effort to the other. To maintain momentum he would have to bypass or shoulder aside large numbers of enemy, and deal with them later.

Slim correctly assessed that General Kimura would try to hold him somewhere north of Rangoon until the monsoon arrived, to which end a Japanese army had been deployed on each route. Honda's *Thirty-third*

Army (*18th*, *49th*, and *53rd Divisions*) was ordered to hold at Pyawbwe, and the *56th Division* was to threaten the British flank from the Shan hills. Sakurai's *Twenty-eighth Army* was to prevent the advance down the Irrawaddy route.

On 2 April, Mountbatten decided that as an insurance against Slim being held up and failing to reach Rangoon before the monsoon broke, an amphibious and airborne assault would be mounted on Rangoon not later than 5 May; a scaled-down Operation DRACULA.

While Stopford's 33rd Corps mounted a series of attacks astride the Irrawaddy, Cowan's 17th Indian Division, leading the 4th Corps's advance on the railway route, moved off on 30 March, his objective Pyawbwe, held by about 7,000 Japanese with twenty-two guns. Cowan's plan involved a three-pronged pincer movement, a favourite Japanese ploy. His 99th Brigade advanced to the east of the road to come in to Pyabwe from the north-east, the 48th Brigade came down the main axis, the 63rd Brigade pushed south well to the west, to come in from that direction, while 'Claudcol' under Brigadier Claud Pert (two squadrons of Probyn's Horse, two armoured car squadrons of the 16th Light Cavalry, an SP battery, sappers, and two infantry battalions) pressed on beyond the 63rd Brigade to cut the road six miles south of Pyawbwe.

To allow Claudcol to carry out its swing to the south, it was necessary for the 63rd Brigade to take Point 900, which overlooked their route. Major Randle was commanding B Company of the 7th/10th Baluch:

> We had a squadron of tanks with us who reported the strong force of Japs on Point 900 were in the mood to surrender, so they said. The CO deployed the Battalion in attack formation, my company was on the left. It was a bare hill, we were engaged by Jap medium machine guns on our left, and dealt with that. The tanks [in support] had pushed off, they seemed to have a habit of doing this. Then as we went over a little crest, a soldier just in front of me, was shot by a Jap. On that my soldiers went mad, and we killed 124 Japs with bayonet, grenades and Tommy Guns, the men were screaming and had a wolfish look with bare teeth. I tried to take a few prisoners, but my Subedar said 'its no good, you're wasting your breath'. Unusually, we saw the Jap company commander running away; my boys put a burst in him. They gave me his sword which is on my wall now. We were on a high, adrenalin running all steamed up. My chaps were in a blood lust. Then about an hour later you

suddenly get a feeling of melancholy. My Subedar a hard Pathan said, 'its awful seeing the carnage. Even these Japanese were human beings'. The other company killed quite a few. We certainly sealed the fate of the Japs in that part of Pyawbwe. I think the Japs couldn't make up their minds. They saw us coming, and some Jap either out of fear fired at us, or thought I'll never have another chance like this. They never did. Once one of our chaps were shot, there was no holding them back. The enemy were well fed and equipped. But the position was not well prepared unlike the usual Jap positions. We had some casualties including a chap hit on a grenade on his belt which set it off.

The advance of Claudcol cut the road south of the town on the afternoon of 9 April, by which time Pyawbwe was surrounded, and the headquarters of the Japanese *Thirty-third Army* destroyed, while Honda and his staff escaped on foot. The next day, nine days behind the original schedule, Cowan closed in on Pyawbwe from all directions. When the town was entered, 1,110 Japanese dead and thirteen guns were found. The Pyawbwe battle was the biggest action of the Battle of the Rangoon Road, and according to Slim one of the most decisive of the Burma war; it shattered the Japanese *Thirty-third Army*.[1]

While the 17th Division mopped up, the 5th Division took over the lead, and the drive for Rangoon could really pick up momentum. 'They were off!' wrote Slim. 'I stood beside the road outside Pyawbwe and saw them go. Three hundred miles and, with luck, some thirty days before the monsoon to do it in.'[2] With Slim stood Rees, whose 19th Division had been brought forward to join 4th Corps, his GSO1, Lieutenant Colonel 'Jack' Masters, Messervy, the corps commander, and the other two divisional commanders. They

watched the leading division crash past the start point. The dust thickened under the trees lining the road until the column was motoring into a thunderous yellow tunnel, first the tanks, infantry all over them, then trucks filled with men, then more tanks, going fast, nose to tail, guns, more trucks, more guns – British, Sikhs, Gurkhas, Madrassis, Pathans . . . All these men knew their commanders and as the vehicles crashed past most of the soldiers were on their feet cheering and yelling. The Gurkhas of course went by sitting stiffly to attention bouncing four feet in the air without change of expression

... The romance of war – but only a fool would grudge us the excitement and sense of glory, for no one on that plain had wanted war, and all of us had known enough horror to last several lifetimes. (The 17th Indian Division had been in continuous contact with the enemy from January 1942 till now – three years and three months).

This was the old Indian Army going down to the attack, for the last time in its history, exactly two hundred and fifty years after the Honourable East India Company had enlisted its first ten sepoys on the Coromandel Coast.[3]

With the leading tanks were airfield engineers to reconnoitre the sites for airstrips, so that work could begin on them as soon as sappers and plant further back in the column arrived. By 16 April, the 5th Division had arrived just north of Shwemyo, where the road ran through a series of narrow defiles. Major General Robert Mansergh, commanding the division, pinned the Japanese frontally with one brigade, and swung another round through hills and jungle to take them in the rear at the point of the bayonet. The airfield was captured intact, as was the one at Lewe, south-west of Pyinmana. The town was strongly held, but out-flanked, nearly catching Honda for the second time in nine days. It was the story of the 1942 retreat in reverse: now it was the Japanese being hustled and dazzled out of their positions by quick thinking and fast footwork. Next stop Toungoo. Both the British and Japanese were racing to reach the town first. Kimura had also ordered the *56th Division* to move down the Mawchi Road to take the British in the flank. But Slim had a card up his sleeve. Karen guerrillas, armed by the British, rose up against the hated enemy, ambushed them, blew bridges, and cut their communications, while British officers called in air strikes by radio. At Mawchi the Japanese flank attack found the 19th Division waiting for them.

Covering fifty miles in three days, the 5th Division roared into Toungoo. Honda had just established his army headquarters and was forced to take to his heels, abandoning most of his equipment, and consequently took several weeks to re-establish control over the remnants of his army. The leading tank of the 5th Division encountered a Japanese military policeman still directing traffic at the main crossroads in town; disregarding his signals, it ran straight over him.

Two days later, the 5th Division reached Pyu, thirty miles south of

Toungoo. On the way they accepted the surrender of the 1st Division of the INA, just in time to put them to work on the captured airfields. The 17th Division, champing at the bit, was close behind, ready to take over the lead, and be the first in to Rangoon, sweet revenge for their disastrous defeat at the Sittang over three years before. However, the 5th Division swept on for another twenty miles, before handing over the baton in the Rangoon relay race. Messervy had already issued his orders for the capture of Rangoon. But in the way stood Pegu – fifty miles before Rangoon. Pegu is one of the biggest and most important towns in Burma, astride the Pegu River, crossed by two railway bridges and a road bridge. Major General Hideji Matsui, the infantry group commander of the *56th Division*, was in personal command, under orders to hold for as long as possible while all installations in Rangoon were destroyed.

Cowan's plan for capturing Pegu again involved a three-pronged attack, with the 48th Brigade crossing the rail bridges and advancing west of the river to seize the railway station, while the 63rd Brigade attacked the low hills at Shweban before pushing down the main road to take the road bridge in the town. The 255th Tank Brigade was to come in from the west, while the 99th Brigade were in reserve.

The 48th Brigade, having found both railway bridges blown, succeeded in getting a company across the wreckage of one, but could not make further progress for the rest of the day. The 255th Tank Brigade seized its initial objective but was stopped from penetrating the town by an anti-tank ditch. The attack on the main road bridge by the 63rd Brigade was also fiercely resisted. Randle:

> We ran into quite stiff opposition at Pegu. We put in an attack with A Company on my right. I had a bad day there. A Company didn't seem to have had such a bad time. We got on to a hill, in pretty thick stuff, but couldn't get on through, because the Japs had a medium machine gun and a 75 mm dug in in defilade. They also had quite a few mortars. My leading platoon commander was badly wounded and died of wounds. We had a stupid order that morphine could only be held by company commanders, so I had to administer the stuff instead of getting on with my own job. We were mortared badly in Company HQ, the FOO was killed, the Company officer was wounded, it was so steep, the 25 pounders couldn't get crest clearance and hit the Japs. The battalion mortars did quite a good job. I just couldn't get forward at all, it was a semi reverse slope

position, we couldn't get tanks up it was too thick. Every time we moved we got fired on from flank. Just over the crest the foliage was cleared so there was no cover. When we eventually captured the position we found the medium machine gun was dug in with logs overhead with a small slit allowing a critical arc of fire. At nightfall the Japs counter-attacked with a few tanks. I had the whole of the Corps artillery firing on my company front – about four field regiments, a medium regiment, and a troop of 9.2 [inch] heavies, on a front of about 200 yards.* My God it didn't half make a crump. It broke up the Japs' counter-attack. This convinced the Japs that they would never take the position back. The plan was that another company would push through me the next morning, and take the rest of the position. But at first light, my leading platoon patrolled forward and reported that the Japs had pushed off. That was that.

That was indeed that. The Japs had withdrawn. 17th Division cleared the rest of the town, and readied for the advance on Rangoon. The division had been driven out of Pegu just over three years before. Now, still commanded by Cowan, it was back, with the five battalions that had remained with it throughout the Burma campaign (7th/10th Baluch including John Randle, 4th/12th Frontier Force Rifles, and 1st/3rd, 1st/7th, and 1st/10th Gurkhas). The axis of 4th Corps's advance has been described as the longest and narrowest salient in the history of warfare. Pyawbwe to Pegu is 250 miles, so although perhaps no narrower than the sixty-mile-long corridor from Eindhoven to Arnhem in Holland along which Horrocks's British 30th Corps had driven the previous year in its failed attempt to relieve the British 1st Airborne Division, the 4th Corps' axis was over four times longer. The advance had been at a price: from the Irrawaddy to Pegu, the 17th Division alone had lost 719 all ranks killed, 2,767 wounded, and 71 missing. It had killed over 10,000 of the enemy, and captured 211 guns, and just 167 prisoners.

On the Irrawaddy axis, Stopford's 33rd Corps had cleared Allanmyo by 20 April, and on 1 May was about to advance on Prome and Rangoon. Suddenly, on 2 May, thirteen days early, the monsoon descended, and Fourteenth Army's drive for Rangoon bogged down:

---

* The battalion mortar officer, or gunner sergeant from the FOO party, in lieu of the dead FOO, would probably have coordinated the DFs in this position.

airfields were flooded, rivers rose, the terrain off-road was reduced to a stew of mud.

Fortunately the six assault convoys of Operation DRACULA had set off on 27 April from Akyab and Ramree Islands carrying the 26th Indian Division. Christison, whose 15th Corps was responsible for planning and executing the landing, had very little time to refine the plans:

> But having done so many ad hoc, I had no fears and told Mountbatten I could do it. Observers sent over from the European landings were horrified! Captured documents showed that the Japanese believed 12th April to be the latest date for us to attempt a sea-borne operation against Rangoon.
>
> There were three snags. Both the Japs and the RAF had heavily mined the Rangoon river, which would have to be swept. The sandy shoals meant that landing craft would have a 31 mile run-in; possibly in choppy water; and Elephant Point, at the mouth of the river, was defended by coast artillery and dual-purpose machine guns which would make minesweeping impossible.
>
> I therefore decided to drop Gurkha parachutists near Elephant Point and capture it on D minus one.

Early on 1 May a composite battalion of 50th Indian Parachute Brigade, made up from the survivors from the brigade's epic defence of Sangshak the year before, dropped from thirty-eight Dakotas five miles west of Elephant Point. Within two and a half miles of their objective, they were hit by bombs from Liberators, aiming at Elephant Point but dropping short. The battalion suffered some thirty casualties. The pouring rain which was so frustrating the 17th Division's efforts south of Pegu screened the Gurkha parachute soldiers' advance on the Japanese battery. Of the thirty-seven enemy gunners, only one survived.

Allied aircraft flying over Rangoon that same morning had seen two messages painted on the roof of the jail: 'Japs gone', and 'Extract digit'. The first could have been a ruse, but the second was an unmistakable RAF slang expression, so Wing Commander Saunders RAF landed his Mosquito on Mingaladon airfield. Although information about the painted messages had reached the British force off Rangoon, the landing went ahead as planned. Christison:

> Sweeping began at once, and before dawn on 2 May the fleet of landing craft left for their 31 mile run-in. It had become very choppy,

and the doctors issued sea-sick pills, which seemed to have very little effect, except to dehydrate the troops in the fierce sun. Luckily no opposition was met. The docks area was entered on 3 May. I stepped ashore at the docks.

Captain Knight was a Forward Observer Bombardment (FOB), whose job was to spot for naval guns in support of ground troops.

I was to land with the telegraphists [radio operators] in the first wave of infantry, and the 2 i/c plus Elliott [his driver] and the jeep and trailer would come in later in a larger landing craft.

The one thing that was not expected was the weather. The monsoon was expected at Rangoon in mid-May, but in 1945 it came ten days early. This meant a ten mile sea trip in a flat-bottomed LCA (Landing Craft Assault), not the most seaworthy of craft. Then followed sharing a boat with some twenty-five Pathans from the North-West frontier of India, all of whom were violently sea sick. At long last we got to the shore and the infantry staggered out, thankful to be on land at last. I was about to write 'dry land', but it was certainly not that. The torrential rain had turned the dust in to mud and the little paddy fields were two feet deep in water. The way forward was along the tops of the retaining walls of the paddy fields, about three feet wide, and exceedingly slippery. One false step and you were down in the mire.

So far there were no signs of the Japanese, and word came through that they had evacuated the city. Everything seemed too easy until we were going through a small village when we got our first casualty. A water buffalo, normally a most placid animal, kept by the locals for milk, no doubt frightened by the bombing and shelling, came down the village street at a full gallop. We all jumped out of the way with the exception of one unfortunate infantryman who took the full impact and was impaled on its horns killing him instantly. All we could do was lay him on a nearby veranda, cover him with a groundsheet and move on.

News came that one of the larger landing craft [an LCT] had struck a mine in the Rangoon river and had sunk, but no details were available. The next day we moved on a few more miles and it was confirmed that the Japanese had gone. Then came the worst possible news. The landing craft reported sunk had been carrying the rest of our party. Elliott had been below decks and the explosion of the mine had thrown him up smashing his head on the steel deck above, killing him. My 2i/c was thrown up in the air and landed on top of a lorry. The canvas cover took most of the fall, but the steel framework had broken one arm, several ribs, and he was badly shaken. A landing craft alongside had managed to get all the dead and wounded off before the LCT sank, but all the vehicles including all our worldly possessions had gone to the bottom.

So we arrived in Rangoon wet, weary, filthy and in a subdued frame of mind. I felt that the first essential was to get some fresh clothes for the party, and on making enquiries I learned that there was a Quartermaster's store of the Indian National Army not far away. We naturally looked upon them as traitors and the Indian troops treated them with the utmost disdain. There we found a clerk and I told him our requirements, two sets of everything for us. He said he could not supply us because we had not authority. I then committed an act of which I am not very proud, I put a magazine on my Sten and pointed it at him, saying, 'Do I get the goods, or do I pull the trigger?'. One of the RIN telegraphists interpreted in case he didn't get the idea, but the result was instantaneous. He darted over to the shelves and brought out shirts, socks, slacks, shorts, in fact all we could wish for.

It was wearing these borrowed garments that we went into Rangoon Jail to check whether there were any of our own prisoners of war there, and coming through the main gate, unknown to me, I had my photograph taken by a representative of the Times of India, who I think, assumed I was a POW.

On 3 May, the landing craft of follow-up waves on their way upriver were hailed by a sampan carrying Wing Commander Saunders. He had damaged his Mosquito on landing at Mingaladon airfield, and was unable to take off. So he and his navigator had made their way to the jail, where the POWs assured him that the Japanese had indeed gone. With considerable aplomb, he made his way to the docks, commandeered a sampan, and sailed down the Rangoon River to meet the 26th Division. Slim was rather pleased when he heard of the exploit. If Fourteenth Army could not get to Rangoon first, then a member of 221 Group RAF, which as far as Slim was concerned was part of his army in all but name, was the next best thing. Needless to say 15th Corps saw things in a different light, and regarded the capture of Rangoon as a proper reward for their two gruelling years in the Arakan, where they perceived themselves as even more forgotten than just about anyone else in Burma.

At 1630 hours on 6 May, the 1st/7th Gurkhas of 'Deadly' Hedley's 48th Indian Infantry Brigade, 17th Indian Division, advancing south, linked up with 1st Lincolns of the 71st Indian Infantry Brigade, 26th Indian Division, twenty-seven miles north of Rangoon. The meeting marked the end of one the greatest fighting advances in the history of the British and Indian armies. Throughout the Burma campaign Slim had met every challenge and risen above it. He had held the show together in the desperate days of the 1942 retreat, had proved to be a master of the grim defensive battles of 1944, and now had shown his quality in the offensive. As an ace of manoeuvre he was the equal of Manstein and Rommel, and logistically in a different league from the latter. His proficiency in *every* phase of war places him way ahead of Patton. On 7 May, Leese arrived at Slim's HQ to tell him that he was being transferred from command of Fourteenth Army to a newly designated Twelfth Army, a mopping-up force to wind down operations in Burma. Christison learned about this on returning to his headquarters at Akyab after the fall of Rangoon:

At my HQ I found Lieutenant General Sir Oliver Leese, Walsh his chief of staff, [and other staff officers]. I must set down word for word as I recorded it that morning what now occurred as it was a prelude to far-reaching changes, and a basis for uninformed comment by historians. After breakfast Oliver took me aside and said; 'Christie, Dickie has felt for some time that Slim has become a very tired man and I must say I agree. Now Dickie has suggested to me that I send Slim on indefinite leave, and I have done so. He has already left XIV Army. A new army is being formed for the invasion of Malaya and the eventual capture of Singapore. For prestige reasons it is being called XIV Army, and the present is to be called XII Army and clear up in Burma. Monty Stopford is to command it. You, with your many combined operations successes behind you are to take over XIV Army. You may have five day's leave and then proceed to GHQ in Delhi where you will prepare the plans for the invasion of Malaya. When you are ready, Dickie and I will come to Delhi and hear and approve your plan.'

I said to Leese, 'Did you sack Slim?'

'No' he replied, 'It was all very tricky. You know all this gup [nonsense] about Dickie being jealous of Slim, and I did not like the idea. I wanted Dickie to see him and do it himself, but he refused and said it was my job as his immediate superior. So I sent George Walsh to talk to Bill to see what his reaction would be. Bill flew into a rage and demanded to see me, and I had to tell him that both Dickie and I felt he needed a rest. He demanded to be flown to UK then and there'.

Walsh, whom I knew well, was not famed for tact and about the last person I should have employed on a delicate mission of this sort.

Although Christison's memoir, quoted on a number of occasions in this book, tends to be egocentric at times, and reveals a bent for stroking Mountbatten's ego, he recorded later, 'I went to see Oliver Leese at his home near Bridgenorth in 1977 and he agreed that my notes [above] were correct'.

As Leese told Christison, Slim refused the appointment to Twelfth Army, recognizing it as a demotion. A storm of protest greeted the news in Fourteenth Army, troops became near mutinous, and officers threatened to resign. When Slim arrived home, he was told that Leese had been sacked, and he was to take his place as CINCALFSEA; the second time Slim had stepped into the shoes of his would-be sacker – the first being Irwin's back in 1943.

The CIGS, General Sir Alan Brooke, who had no time for Mountbatten, wrote in his diary on 17 May: 'Leese is going quite wild and doing mad things, prepared a fair rap on the knuckles for him!'[4] On 18 June, he recorded, 'Drafted a letter to Mountbatten advising him to get rid of Leese who has proved to be a failure in South East Asia Command'.[5] On 29 June, he wrote: 'After lunch I had to go to the PM and tell him that we should have to withdraw Oliver Leese from South East Asia and replace him with Slim.'[6] It is hard to determine what part Mountbatten's jealousy of Slim played in the attempted sacking of this great general by the lesser men placed in authority over him. The account in Mountbatten's official biography is evasive, and reflects little credit on Mountbatten's loyalty to Slim who had won all his battles for him. Neither does it say much for Mountbatten's integrity as a commander.[7] Leese on the other hand, for all his faults, was straight, and readers must judge for themselves where the ultimate blame lies.

While Slim was on leave, the final act took place in Burma, the battle of the Japanese breakout. The Japanese were in four groups: the remnants of *Twenty-eighth Army* in the Irrawaddy Valley; the *56th Division* and parts of *15th*, *18th* and *53rd Divisions* in the Shan Hills east of Meiktila; the remnants of *Thirty-third Army* east of the Sittang between Toungoo and Nyaunglebin; and a hotch-potch of units under Kimura around Mokpalin–Moulmein. There were also numerous smaller groups of stragglers, bringing the total of enemy in Burma to around 60,000 – or so it was thought at the time: it proved to be an underestimate. All the Japanese wished to do by now was reach the Moulmein area and rendezvous with Kimura or make for Siam. The majority of the Japanese were in Sakurai's *Twenty-eighth Army* in the hills north of Pegu. The efforts of most of the remaining Japanese formations and units were directed towards getting Sakurai's men out.

The story of the finale is one of desperate efforts by the enemy to escape the trap, and of the British to eliminate them. It must be borne in mind that in May 1945 there was no expectation of the war with Japan ending before mid-1946, or even 1947. The intention for forthcoming operations in SEAC was the invasion of Malaya, Operation ZIPPER, in August 1945, culminating in the capture of Singapore by January 1946, and in the Pacific, the amphibious assault on the southern island of Japan, Kyushu, planned for November 1945, and on Honshu, near Tokyo, in spring 1946. Therefore large bodies of Japanese troops, however disorganized, could not be allowed to threaten the lines of communication in Burma, nor be given any respite during which they might reorganize, and resume operations. They might be starving, temporarily demoralized, and lacking warlike supplies, but they were as dangerous as a cornered African bull buffalo.

After formations had been withdrawn in preparation for the invasion of Malaya, forming a regrouped Fourteenth Army in India and Ceylon, troops remaining in Burma were redesignated Twelfth Army under Stopford, erstwhile GOC of 30th Corps. Both armies were under Slim's command. To begin with Christison was temporarily in command in Burma for the finale, which as he comments, rates little more than a footnote in many histories. However, an entire Japanese army was almost annihilated, in this, the last battle fought by the British against the Japanese. Under the new commander of the 4th Corps, Lieutenant

General Tuker, the 7th, 17th and 19th Indian Divisions formed the stop line along the Sittang. Christison:

> My plan was to try to keep the Japanese in the Pegu Yomas and let malaria, dysentery and the monsoon finish them off. Of course they would make every effort to break out across the main Rangoon–Mandalay road and this we could not entirely prevent. Our strong detachments with tanks, artillery, and spotter and strike aircraft could block the exits from the Yomas by day, but at night small parties could not be stopped from slipping through. But those that did would be faced by crossing paddy fields by day – often waist deep – and if they tried to enter villages would be spotted by aircraft and shelled. Finally they would be faced with crossing the Sittang in full flood. There was no food to be had in the Yomas, and soon troops were reduced to marching and fighting on bamboo shoots, grass and a handful of sodden rice if they were lucky.

The fall of Rangoon by no means marked the end of the fighting: mopping-up operations and fierce battles took place from the latter part of May to the first part of July. The Japanese were determined to prise open a corridor through which they could pass to safety and reorganization. To achieve this they attacked with characteristic ferocity, and courage. The accounts that follow give a flavour of the conditions and the type of fighting experienced by all formations involved.

On the west bank of the Irrawaddy the leading battalion of the 89th Brigade in the 7th Indian Division, the 1st/11th Sikhs, clashed with parties of enemy before moving to a blocking position to ambush a group thought to be some 2,000 strong, with about seventy three-ton trucks, several bullock carts, and guns. In the early hours of 9 May, the enemy ran into the main body of the Sikhs, and spent the day trying to break through. The Sikhs outflanked the Japanese and attacked their transport column. Eventually the Japanese managed to break contact and head away to the west whence they had come. The 4th/8th Gurkhas immediately followed up and sat astride the only motorable track in the vicinity, and by 12 May they were surrounded by an enemy group desperately fighting to break the ring. They concentrated their attack on one company of the 4th/8th, and during the ensuing battle, the fourth VC awarded to the 7th Indian Division was won by Rifleman Lachhiman Gurung. His citation reads:

At 0120 hours at least 200 enemy assaulted the company position. The brunt of the attack was born by Lachhiman Gurung's section and his own post in particular. This post dominated a jungle path leading into the platoon locality and before assaulting it, the enemy hurled innumerable grenades at it from close range. One grenade fell on the lip of Rifleman Lachhiman Gurung's trench. He at once hurled it back at the enemy. Almost immediately another grenade fell directly inside the trench, and again he snatched it up and threw it back. A third then fell just in front of the trench. He attempted to throw it back, but it exploded in his hand, blowing off his fingers, shattering his right arm and severely wounding him in the face, body and right leg. His two comrades were also badly wounded and lay helpless at the bottom of the trench. The enemy, screaming and shouting, now formed up shoulder to shoulder and attempted to rush the position by sheer weight of numbers. Rifleman Lachhiman Gurung, regardless of his wounds, loaded and fired his rifle with his left hand. For four hours after being wounded he remained alone at his post, waiting for each attack, meeting it with fire at point-blank range from his rifle. Of 87 enemy dead counted in the immediate vicinity of the company position, 31 lay in front of this rifleman's section, the key to the whole positon. Had the enemy succeeded in overrunning and occupying the trench, the whole of the reverse slope position would have been dominated and turned. By his magnificent example he so inspired his comrades to resist the enemy to the last, that although surrounded and cut off for three days and two nights, they held and smashed every attack.

The enemy, harried by Hurribombers, and artillery with the aid of flying OPs, finally dispersed into the jungle. They left over 300 dead, and all their trucks. Their guns were never found. At this stage troops in Burma heard of the cessation of hostilities in Europe.

Gunner Harding was with Fox Troop, 503 Battery, 139th Field Regiment Royal Artillery (25pdrs), part of the 7th Indian Division advancing down the Irrawaddy route.

There was little rejoicing as far as we were concerned. There was nothing to celebrate with anyway for as usual, the promised beer ration had not materialised, and we had to be content with the small rum ration. Our war was still grinding on against a stubborn enemy to whom surrender was unthinkable and Victory Day in Burma seemed a long way off. The rain teemed down, the hot sun broke through low, grey clouds, the vegetation steamed, we pespired, then down came the torrents once more.

To everyone's intense disappointment and disgust, our eagerly awaited return to monsoon billets in Yenangyaung was cancelled and we were informed the Regiment was to move south on May 21st to an area halfway between Allanmyo and Prome in support of 33 Brigade. The prospect of more rain sodden gun positions filled us with misery. We cursed the bloody copulating Japs as we climbed into trucks and took the road south, but our existance was as nothing compared with that of our long-suffering infantry for whom we had the greatest respect. While we travelled in dry, relative comfort, they, weighed down with mortars, Bren guns, and entrenching tools, slogged through dripping jungle, splashed thigh-deep across swollen chaungs or swamps, pushed their way through tall spear grass, and manned muddy holes throughout long tense nights.

The move was caused by the enemy having established a bridgehead on the east bank of the Irrawaddy opposite Kama about twenty-five miles north of Prome, and aimed to use this as an escape route to the Pegu Yomas. The 7th Indian Division moved in to trap the Japanese on both banks of the river. Gunner Harding:

We reached the bridgehead area on the morning of the 22nd May. Turning right off the main road along a rough track running through dense jungle, we travelled about ten miles before taking up position. It was enclosed by forests and to our front a rutted track, which led to the enemy's bridgehead and the river, disappeared into a gloomy tunnel formed by arched, dripping boughs and thick vegitation. The Japanese, consisting mainly of the remnants of the 54th Division from the Arakan and what was left of their forces retreating from the north, had chosen an ideal spot to carry out their infiltration tactics, but once out of the jungle, they had to cross the Prome road and the fairly open country to the east.

The Japanese were subjected to artillery fire by day and night, and air attacks by day. Inevitably, under cover of darkness large numbers of enemy managed to infiltrate, and cross the main road, although there were fierce little actions when they bumped the waiting infantry. As a result there was a constant trickle of wounded British and Indian soldiers being ferried to the main road in jeeps. By the end of May, the enemy opposition on the west bank of the Irrawaddy had almost ceased, so the positions on the Prome Road were thickened up. Here, on one occasion, the 2nd King's Own Scottish Borderers were attacked by about 300 Japanese striving to force their way through to the east. After three hours of fighting, 138 enemy lay in front of the Borderers' positions, and eight prisoners were taken. To the south of the Borderers, another large enemy group tried to break through the 2nd/8th Punjabis of the 20th Division, who in the ensuing battle accounted for over eighty Japanese. By the end of May the battle of the Kama bridgehead was virtually over, with a body-count of 1,396 enemy, and many more undiscovered in the thick jungle. Altogether seventy-four prisoners were taken – an unusually high number. 'Although disorganised, lacking in equipment and without supplies, they could be depended upon to turn at bay and fight fanatically if cornered. For all our loathing of the Japanese Army for the foul deeds it had perpetrated', wrote Gunner Harding, 'we could not but grudgingly acknowledge the courage and sheer tenacity of its soldiers'.

From operating in the Irrawaddy valley, the 7th Indian Division was moved at the end of June to the Sittang. Here the *Thirty-third Army* was deployed in two groups on the general line of the Sittang River, south of Toungoo, on both banks. One group was east of the river about thirty miles south of Toungoo, and the other on Nyaungkashe (pronounced Nyongkashay) on the Sittang bend near the mouth of the river. The task of the *Thirty-third Army* was to keep open escape routes for the *Twenty-eighth Army*.

The 7th Division was ordered to block the southern escape route. Its 89th Indian Infantry Brigade was ordered to hold a sector along the west bank of the Sittang River, including the Rangoon–Moulmein railway (the bridge carrying this line over the Sittang had been destroyed in the retreat in 1942). The brigade was astride a vital escape gap, and here the 4th/8th Gurkhas and 1st/11th Sikhs endured the brunt of the Battle of the Sittang Bend. Lieutenant Farrow, the Intelligence Officer of the 1st/11th Sikhs, whose account is interspersed with official reports, noted:

Never, perhaps has the term 'fluid' been more aptly applied to operations. The fluidity was not only tactical, but physical as much of the fighting was carried out in an area which is waist-deep in water from early July to the end of the monsoon.

The whole area was submerged, with the exception of villages, railways and canal banks. The railway was the only supply line and was easily threatened by the Japanese using boats to move up the old Sittang River channel, which swung in towards the railway from the west. The British artillery had to be sited on the railway, whereas the Japanese guns could be placed on the east bank, with a secure line of supply and excellent observation. Farrow quotes an account from the 4th/8th Gurkhas' newsletter of the time:

In broad daylight the rain, at its heaviest, reduced visibility to under a hundred yards, whilst at night one could scarcely see at all. From the lower Sittang, westwards for twenty five miles, stretches an area as flat as a table, raised almost imperceptibly a few feet above sea level. All its chaungs are tidal. The surface of this low lying area is chequered with paddy-fields in some of which ploughing was being done, but in the majority no work had been carried out, and the coarse Kaing grass was allowed to grow rampant usually waist high though in some areas it grew to six feet or more. To complete the picture, you must imagine, superimposed over all this, one to two feet of water, over ploughed mud, through long grass, often over paddy bunds. Villages stood in this area of grass and water, a mile or two apart, dense little areas of trees and houses, water-logged and muddy. In a defensive position in a village one felt fairly secure, with a mile or so of flat treeless water all around for the Japs to splash through. And, conversely, one felt equally conspicuous when advancing towards a Jap-held village. The water had several other effects. Ambushes had to be very carefully laid in the rare patches of firm ground, through which the few permanent tracks usually ran, for no man can find cover or comfort in water. Boots were permanently wet, and many feet rotted painfully. And, most important of all, no trenches could be dug down. Instead, little pill-boxes had to be erected of wood and earth, roofed over to form bunkers. These were awkward to conceal, and were consider-ably less proof to shell fire than dug down defences, an important factor in view of coming events. Wild life in the area consisted of masses of leeches an increasing quantity of Japs, mosquitoes and, oddly enough, rats. Leeches came in all sizes and boots being for the most time under water, they had an undisturbed feast. Cigarettes became popular with many people as the only practical means to get the leeches to drop off. Sikhs being non smokers were not so fortunate.

One more feature of the area must be mentioned – the railway line. Ten feet or so above the surrounding water ran a single-line railway track, the main Pegu–Martaban line. This formed our only line of communication to the Sikhs at Abya and brigade headquarters at Waw, and little jeep trains with a jeep at either end of three or four trucks (conventional railway box and open wagons) trundled up and down at about ten miles an hour between Nyaungkashe and the road head at Waw. (The jeeps had iron-flanged wheels and these trains became terribly vulnerable later on to Japanese artillery east of the river). The line provided us with bridges to defend, with gravel to surface the little built up paths around headquarters, with the only dry ground into which to dig latrines and graves; and, not the least of its features, it provided the Japs with a first class and a very vulnerable objective.

The Japanese held posts on the west bank of the river at several places, all accessible by boat from the east bank. The 4th/8th Gurkhas were grouped round Nyangkashe, the 1st/11th Sikhs were based on Abya railway station, Satthwagyon and Laya, while the 3rd/6th Gurkhas were well to the north. After some fighting to clear themselves some elbow room, the battalions settled down to their tasks. With so many key points to guard (bridges, railway stations, and the line itself), the brigade's striking force consisted of just battalion headquarters and two understrength rifle companies of the 1st/11th Sikhs. Furthermore, it must always be borne in mind that everyone thought that months if not years of fighting lay ahead, so leave parties from the brigade had been sent away in order that as many men could be rested ready for the start of another campaign in October. Farrow:

Tuesday 3rd July 1945
The expected Japanese offensive materialized, aimed at the Gurkha's main position at Nyaungkashe, the Sikh's at Satthwagyon, and the bridge on the railway embankment at Laya. At the same time an enemy party dug themselves in on the railway embankment between the Sikhs and the Gurkhas.

All the positions held firm, though the attacks were pressed with utmost fury, that on Nyaungkashe alone costing the enemy nearly

100 dead. Assault having failed to capture the positions, there began
a close investment of them, combined with an endeavour to soften
them up with artillery fire from the east bank and heavy mortars
from the near bank of the river. The enemy disposed four 150 mm
or 105 mm guns and at least four 75 mm guns, and the fire of these,
thickened up by a considerable number of heavy mortars, was very
accurate and particularly trying in positions such as those in the
villages, where all defences had had to be built up as digging down
was impossible, and a shell anywhere 'on the island', which was
'unmissable', was either a direct hit or a near miss.

Soon the 4th/8th Gurkhas were surrounded and being heavily
attacked. The Sikhs were also under heavy enemy pressure, and isolated
platoons surrounded with all communications, radio and telephone, cut.
Jemedar Bagh Singh and the twenty-two men of his platoon on the
outskirts of Satthewagon village held off a determined attack by 150
enemy for over eight hours, finally forcing them to withdraw to the far
end of the village. On the wire round the platoon position were thirty-
three enemy bodies. During the battle

> Sepoy Babu Singh arrived from Jemedar Bhag Singh and reported
> that the platoon was surrounded, had been very badly attacked all
> night and was running short of ammunition. He had divested himself
> of his clothing, donned a loin-cloth and crawled along a flooded
> stream; he then mingled with some villagers whom the Japanese were
> clearing from the village, and passed within a yard of a Japanese
> sentry to get to the Battalion.

He later received the Military Medal for his gallantry. The next day,
Major Webster's A Company of the 1st/11th Sikhs was ordered to clear
Satthewagon village, establish contact with Jemedar Bhag Singh, and
after clearing enemy from the pagoda just beyond, take up a position in
the village. It was 1100 hours before the village was cleared.

> A Company then proceeded to reconnoitre the pagoda position in
> strength and drew very heavy automatic and mortar fire. The enemy
> were located on an isolated mound around the pagoda and sur-
> rounded by flooded rice fields often waist-deep in water. Sepoy
> Gurdial Singh was the leading man of the section detailed to discover
> the strength of the enemy. He succeeded in reaching a point thirty

yards from the enemy position when he was wounded. He signalled to the remainder of the section to give him covering fire and crawled nearer the enemy. Although Sepoy Gurdial Singh was again wounded, he continued to crawl forward to within a few feet of an enemy machine gun post and then lobbed grenades into the post, killing three Japanese and silencing the machine gun. It was now obvious that this position could not be taken without adequate artillery or air support.

At this stage the brigade commander decided to withdraw the Gurkha company from the Sittang bridge position into the main defences at Nyaungkashe. The next day the 1st/11th Sikhs were ordered to extricate an isolated Gurkha company from east of Satthewagon, so further attacks on the pagoda position were called off. Meanwhile casualties to 4th/8th Gurkhas mounted. The RAP, sited in the only solidly built house, received a direct hit from three 105mm shells, killing or burying almost everyone in it, including the adjutant. Later, over a period of fifteen minutes, 143 shells fell within the perimeter, most unpleasant for troops in flimsy above-ground defences. The situation might have been worse had it not been for the RAF, whose aircraft were over the enemy gun areas by day whenever the appalling weather allowed.

For two days and nights the 1st/11th Sikhs attacked to relieve the Gurkha company. The planned air strikes did not materialize, and the artillery support, already meagre, was cut for lack of ammunition. One of A Company's platoon commanders, Lieutenant Jogindar Singh, was killed, and Major Webster seriously wounded.

Sepoy Ujagar Singh volunteered to bring in the body of Lieutenant Jogindar Singh. This involved crossing two hundred yards of flooded rice fields swept by enemy artillery and small arms fire. Sepoy Ujagar Singh reached Lieutenant Jogindar Singh and hoisted him on his shoulder but he himself was almost immediately wounded. Although his leg was broken and he could not walk, he dragged himself and the body back to cover, where he fell unconscious through exhaustion and pain.

Subedar Gurbachan Singh, took over A Company when Major Webster was wounded when the company came under very heavy fire a few yards from the enemy's position and suffered very heavy casualties. He was always to be seen where the fire was hottest and the situation most critical, cheering and encouraging his men. It was chiefly due to his initiative and able leadership that all the wounded were evacuated and his company successfully withdrawn from its precarious position in close contact with the enemy. Company Havildar Major Jaswant Singh dragged two wounded men to cover from a very exposed position a few yards from the enemy. He then swam with one man across a flooded stream to a place of safety and then returned to accomplish this hazardous undertaking under heavy enemy fire a second time. Lance-Naik Bakshi Singh found himself the only non commissioned officer in his platoon. He set a fine example of courage and devotion to duty in leading his men against impossible odds time and time again until he was ordered to withdraw. It was due to the courage and initiative of this young non-commissioned officer that the platoon, together with all the wounded, was successfully withdrawn. Sepoy Ralla Singh was the sole survivor of a section pinned to the ground close up to the enemy's position. He immediately manned the Bren gun and covered the other two sections of his platoon which had been ordered to withdraw. He then saw his platoon commander lying wounded close by and went to his aid. He dragged the platoon commander back bound by bound, stopping only to engage the enemy with his Bren gun. He successfully brought back his platoon commander and the Bren gun through two hundred and fifty yards of flooded fields under continuous enemy fire to safety.

By the early hours of 7 July the battalion was reduced to two weak composite companies. Two officers and five VCOs had been killed or wounded and the proportion of non-commissioned officer casualties was heavy. The CO told the brigade commander that until air support was available in sufficient strength to neutralize the various strongpoints he was unable to put in any further attacks. The brigade commander decided to withdraw the 4th/8th Gurkhas from Nyaungkashe on the night 7/8 July, and hold Abya as the forward position. The plan involved the 1st/11th Sikhs holding Satthewagon as a layback for the 4th/8th Gurkhas, while the 4th/15th Punjabis from another brigade held Abya.

On the morning of 7 July, the enemy attacked the Gurkhas in strength, overrunning a platoon which had been reduced to a total of seven of whom five were wounded. In one of a series of attacks on this platoon, the enemy left twenty-five dead in and around this small post. That night:

> The withdrawal commenced at 9.45p.m. and was carried out by the whole force moving in a hollow square with the wounded in the middle. In that waste of water, with a large number of stretcher cases to be man-handled as well as mortars and wireless sets, any idea of an orthodox thinning-out withdrawal was abandoned.* The three guns of the 136th Field Regiment could not possibly be got away, so they were rendered unserviceable and what ammunition there was destroyed.
>
> The effort involved in the all-night carry of the wounded was formidable. It was not possible ever to put stretchers down as the occupants would have been drowned.

Nearly all the Sikhs and 4th/15th Punjabis holding the route saw Japanese on the move, but the withdrawing force met no enemy, nor were they shelled. On 7 July the weather cleared and the RAF could operate, and this and the heavy casualties inflicted on the enemy caused them to withdraw in their turn. When the Japanese discovered that the 89th Brigade had pulled back, they returned, only to be thrown back from the railway at Laya with heavy losses. Their objective had been Waw, which they hoped to open as a corridor for the southern group of *Twenty-eighth Army*. Here they failed, although Farrow learned on 9 July that 'the Japanese have at last forced a corridor further north to assist the escape of their troops. Pleasing to know they could not force a corridor in our sector.' The 89th Brigade was pulled out to the Pegu area.

Attacks in the southern sector by the Japanese continued to mid-July, when the enemy shifted their attention to the sectors held by the 17th and 19th Indian Divisions. Intelligence reports indicated that 20 July would be their D-Day for the breakout of *Twenty-eighth Army*. Parties of Japanese, each about 500 strong, debouched from their forming-up areas in the Yomas, and attempted to cross the Rangoon–Mandalay road. Using the same routes time and again, the attempt lasted two weeks. Equipped with armoured vehicles and well supported from the

---

* That is, thinning out forward troops, and moving back in stages through a series of laybacks.

air, the 17th and 19th Divisions, well sited in depth, exacted a merciless toll on the Japanese. Running the gauntlet of the Sittang proved especially dangerous for the enemy, not least because they insisted on repeatedly using the same crossing points. The 'Battle of the Breakout' was a disaster for the Japanese. By 4 August most of those who were going to gain the eastern bank of the Sittang had made it, although they still had to face in-depth positions manned by Force 136, using the Sittang's tributary rivers as additional stop lines. Sakurai's breakout cost his army 16,920, of which about 4,000 were missing and 11,000 killed. Cowan's 17th Indian Division slaughtered the Japanese *55th Division* on the banks of the Sittang, upstream from where they themselves had been subjected to the agony and humiliation of leaving so many of their number behind after the bridge had been blown in their faces in the early hours of 23 February 1942. Cowan had been the deputy divisional commander then. The revenge exacted on the Sittang in July and August 1945 was only the tailpiece. For in the preceding year or so, the 17th Division had also smashed the Japanese *33rd* and *18th Divisions*, who had caused it such affliction in the long 1942 retreat.

On 6 August 1945, the first nuclear weapon in history was dropped on Hiroshima, followed on 9 August by a second on Nagasaki. Raids on Japanese cities continued until 14 August, when, following the personal intervention of the Emperor Hirohito, the Japanese government accepted the Allied terms of unconditional surrender. The war against Japan was at an end.

In Burma the fighting went on until the very last minute. The entry for 14 August in the War History of the 4th/14th Punjab Regiment reads:

Information received that the air strike which we had called for on Jap concentrations at Kalagyaunggyi had been successful. Greater part of village in flames

Warning received that no relaxation of offensive action must be allowed despite what may have been heard on broadcasting service, as enemy patrols in any case could not be expected to have received any 'Cease Fire' orders.

On 15 August the War History records:

Orders issued that all troops will take DEFENSIVE action only following the report of successful termination of SURRENDER negotiations with TOKIO [sic].

The 4th/14th Punjabis was a typical Indian Army battalion, with one company of Sikhs, one of Dogras, one of Punjabi Mussalmans, and one of Pathans. By August 1945, Major Gadsdon was the only surviving company commander of a total of seven who had served in the battalion since November 1944. 'I was lucky never to receive a scratch from the enemy although I had bullets that passed very close on several occasions.'

The unexpectedly early Japanese surrender was greeted with profound relief. John Randle of the 7th/10th Baluch:

We thought it [the war] would go on and on. We were wearing a bit thin by then. I had been in Burma from the beginning. If my CO had said you have earned a rest, even before we went back in in early 1945, I would have taken it. But I would never have asked for it. Couldn't put your hand up and say I've had enough. Till the bomb was dropped the prospect of fighting on across Burma, Siam and China didn't appeal.

When I heard rumours about the bomb, my Company was defending a gunner gun box [base for guns]. I went into the gunner mess and heard about it there. The full significance did not sink in at once. We were on the banks of the Sittang with the rain pissing down. We had some captured Jap MGs and fired a terrific *feu de joie*. The gunners fired star shell. Brigade HQ asked what we were firing at.

We were ordered to arrange the surrender of the Japanese *18th Division*. The CO was on leave and I was the acting second-in-command. The CO, Adjutant and I sent in a message to the camp where Japs were, and when we arrived a whole crowd with fixed bayonets rushed up, and I thought we were going to be killed. It turned out to be a quarter guard. Only one chap could speak English, a Chicago University-trained fellow. We took the view that this was not the time for arrogant behaviour, and we would teach them how to treat defeated people.

We told them all to hand in their weapons at the railway station. They agreed, and asked about their swords. They wanted to hand them in personally and not be dumped with the rest of the weapons. We told them that at the end each officer would hand his sword in individually to officers. The Divisional Commander would hand his in to our Brigade Commander.

Each Jap officer came up, saluted, unsheathed his sword, and handed it over. We had six or seven crack Tommy Gunners standing by with one up the spout and safety catch off in case some Jap officer decided to go to his death hacking off the head of a British officer.

The Japs did fatigues for us. We had a cricket match and they rolled the pitch. I have to admit I came to admire the Japs, for the way they behaved, they were neither obsequious nor arrogant; just well disciplined.

In Burma the British fought their longest land campaign of the war. 'British' is, however, an incorrect description because, as we remarked earlier, considerably more Indian troops fought in Burma than all the other Allies added together. There were 340,000 Indian to 100,000 British, 90,000 Africans, and around 65,000 Chinese. Some 10,000 Americans took part, including forty-seven USAAF squadrons (there were fifty-one British and Commonwealth). But to the Indian Army, albeit under British leadership, unquestionably belongs the victor's wreath for inflicting on the Japanese army in Burma the greatest defeat in their history. The Japanese lost 190,000 killed in Burma, three-fifths of the men they sent there, or thirteen times the number of British and Commonwealth dead.

Joining the 7th/10th Baluch

John Randle

John Randle's account of joining the Indian Army is typical of the experiences of many young men recruited straight from school or commissioned from the ranks of British regiments in the Second World War, when the Indian Army expanded eight-fold. The composition of Indian units varied from regiment to regiment, some being of all one race, Sikhs or Gurkhas for example, others, like the 7/10th Baluch which Randle joined, with heterogeneous companies. His account also conveys some of the problems of equipment shortages, lack of training, and also the ethos that in *general* terms would have applied to all Indian Army units who suddenly found themselves fighting the Japanese in Burma.

> When war broke out I was at school at Berkhamstead and in the Officers' Training Corps [the predecessor of the present Combined Cadet Force (CCF)] and headed for the Indian Political service via the Indian Army, hoping to serve in the Baluch Regiment. I had passed into The Royal Military College [RMC] Sandhurst, but at the outbreak of war the War Office decided to close the RMC and cease recruiting regular officers for the duration. So I enlisted as an other rank in a British regiment and gained a wartime commission into the Indian Army.

> With his fellow cadets bound for India he was sent out in a trooper.

> We had been living like animals on board the trooper, but at the Officer Cadet Training Unit at Bangalore we became Gentlemen Cadets. We had bearers and were waited on at table, and could call for a drink. The syllabus was not much help in preparing to fight the Japs in Burma, not surprisingly – there was a tremendous lack of training in all-arms tactics and use of support weapons, tanks etc.

But this was 1941 and the Army had a lot to learn. The quality of instructors was not high. Many of them were passed over majors, unlike the specially selected people at the RMC they were a bit of a second eleven. At Bangalore we also had British NCO instructors of the old school who were hard men. The Indian army was being expanded to fight in the Middle East, and the Japanese invasion was unexpected. People forget that the North West Frontier was a problem throughout the war, and quite a lot of Indian battalions were deployed there.

Colonel 'Boomer' Barrett a friend of my Father, persuaded me to join the Baluchis. They had a fine record. I didn't join the battalion I wanted, the 2nd, thank heavens, they went to Malaya and I would have gone into the bag. The Regiment had Pathans, Punjabi Mussalmans [Muslims], and Dogra Brahmins from the foothills, all fine fighting men. I joined 7/10th Baluch in Madras, a war-raised Battalion. We joined the 17th Indian Division, then a very second line formation, which was due to relieve the 10th Indian Division in Iraq and release them for service in the Western Desert. The Battalion was up to strength in numbers but pitifully short of experienced officers. I was 19 and was made a company commander. I wouldn't have made a good section commander. One of the other companies was commanded by a chap even greener than me. I don't understand quite why this happened. It was disgraceful. We didn't know we were going to War. In Burma there was I a boy in command of 120 men. I made mistakes. I don't think anyone's life was lost because of this. But no British soldier would have served under what would appear to him to be an incompetent officer. It says a lot about the Indian soldiers that they were prepared to give their loyalty to us.

The backbone of the Indian Army was the Viceroy's Commissioned Officer [VCO]. Many of them had a lot of service, and though they had no experience of modern war, they had led men under fire on the Frontier. They held the Battalion together. My grizzled old Subedar could have commanded a company a hundred times better than me. But in the system of the time, a green second lieutenant was considered a better soldier. In military terms it is all cock. But I learned very fast, I was young and tough. I didn't speak very good Urdu. Even if the VCOs spoke English it was very bad form for a VCO to speak to a British officer in English. The vast majority of soldiers couldn't even read or write. It was a delightful

Army, there was no 'bumf'. Every evening, in peacetime, the Havildar Major read out the orders for the next day to the company.

The Indian soldier wasn't fighting for the defence of India against Hitler. He fought because in northern India, especially, there was a strong tradition of serving the British; and because of the culture of honour, *Izzat* [meaning honour, glory, reputation, including respect for one's personal integrity].[1] Because of the land system, a small property was able to support only one son, so there was a culture of younger sons joining government service, the army or police. They got two square meals a day, pay, pensions, and were honoured and respected members of their community. Their whole history was one of service, for Moguls and so forth, and was not anything to be ashamed of. The regiment was the thing. The soldiers became your men in a way that the British soldier didn't. They identified themselves with their leaders rather than any politics. We were told, 'keep out of politics'. This was important in the mess where there were Indian Commissioned officers (not VCOs).

There were also religious taboos. Although it was a very tolerant society. We had Muslims, Hindus and in some regiments, Sikhs, all in same regiment. My first company were all Punjabi Mussalmans. I knew nothing about the Muslim religion. We had no lectures on Indian religions at Bangalore. I made mistakes at first. To a Mohammedan the next most unclean animal after a pig is a dog. One day having tea with my Subedar I put some milk into a saucer for my little puppy. The Subedar picked up the saucer and smashed it. This was bad manners and uncharacteristic, but it was an object lesson. Later on in the war commanding a Pathan company, I became a sort of honorary Muslim, and was allowed to go to the burial of my dead. Muslims, especially Pathans, don't like infidels attending funerals. Every year there was *Ramazan* [Ramadan]. Unless you were fighting you were allowed no intake of liquids and food between dawn and dusk. They didn't expect you to fast, but you couldn't stand outside your tent knocking back a glass of lemonade. Tempers got very short, you had to be very tactful.

We officers had our own mess and cook. Officers even ate bacon and ham. This wasn't mentioned. Later in war I ate Indian food. As the only British officer in a company, my ration was a couple of biscuits and half a tin of warm bully beef. I decided this was ludicrous. Fighting in Burma the rations were mostly dhal, very lightly curried with ghee, and japattis (unleavened bread). Lentils are very good value food. We lived on that all through Burma and were well sustained. Occasionally we liberated a chicken or goat. But we didn't get a lot of meat. We drank an enormous amount of tea, very strongly brewed, with condensed milk, and lots of sugar, which gave you plenty of energy. I have never been so fit in my life.

The VCOs, havildars, and naiks were trained, but the sepoys had done only the basic training at the regimental depot. We had the Vickers Berthier, bought by the Indian Govenment before the war, which was like a Bren. We got the Bren later. We had 2 inch mortars with smoke and HE bombs. Just before going to Burma we were issued with Tommy Guns, a formidable weapon, which the soldiers liked. It had the old drum magazine, weighed a 'bomb', but got 50 rounds off and for close-quarter fighting [with its large .45in bullet, a real man-stopper] it was terrific. In 1944 when sten guns were about to be issued and Tommy Guns withdrawn, the Division said they wouldn't soldier without Tommy Guns.

The Division was all poised to go to Paiforce in January 1942, and all our preparations were aimed at serving in the the Middle East. There were three brigades, 44th, 45th, and 46th. When the Japanese invaded Malaya, the leading brigade was on its way to embark in Bombay when they turned the train round and sent it to Calcutta: 44th and 45th Brigades went to Malaya. We in 46th Brigade also left from Calcutta and thought we were off to Singapore, but went into Rangoon. With the innocence of youth, we thought, oh God we are going to a backwater and shan't see any war.

Everything about our attitude and clothing was Middle East orientated. We were still dressed in Khaki Drill shirts and shorts, and the soldiers wore puggarees [a long slip of muslin bound round the helmet]. For communications we still had heliographs, flags, and telephone line. We did have some very elementary radios which were hopeless. At six o'clock in the evenings the troposphere came down and the sets wouldn't work all night. We had sets down to company HQ so I was on the battalion net. The radios weren't soldier proof. In the retreat from Burma we didn't use line, although we did in Imphal when we were static. A lot of the time we used our runners.

The Division had very lavish transport scales [for mobility in the desert], including American Chevrolet 15 and 30 cwt trucks. In Burma we picked up mountain batteries, but we had no armour or recce elements. The transport was not sufficient to lift all the marching troops in the division. But we could move stores etc in our own transport. This required a very high driver training commitment, and also training in maintenance. We had some Bren gun carriers. The Battalion was numbered right through platoons 1 to 6 in HQ Company (machine gun platoon, carrier platoon, signal platoon etc), A Company started with number 7 platoon.

APPENDIX B

Organization of a Column

Strength

Officers	19
Other ranks	396
Ponies	12
Mules	60
Bullocks	15

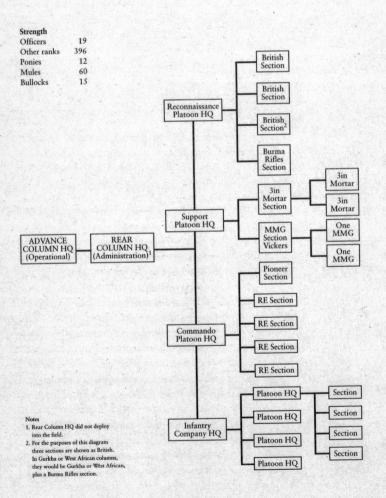

Notes

1. Rear Column HQ did not deploy into the field.

2. For the purposes of this diagram three sections are shown as British. In Gurkha or West African columns, they would be Gurkha or West African, plus a Burma Rifles section.

Chindit Loads and Rations

Typical load carried by a marching Chindit

As listed by Lieutenant Colonel C. P. Vaughan DSO, 7th Battalion The
Nigeria Regiment

Personal weapon and ammunition
Two type 36 grenades
One filled Bren magazine
One spare shirt or bush jacket
One spare pair jungle green trousers
One pair of gym shoes
Mess tin
Knife, fork and spoon
Drinking mug
Filled Waterbottle
First Field Dressing
Water-proof wallet for personal letters etc
Four pairs of socks
Chagul (canvas water bag, carried empty on the march, and filled
    when approaching camp)
One small towel, soap, toothbrush and nailclippers
One bottle mepachrine tablets (anti-malaria)
One water sterilising outfit
One gas cape
One groundsheet
One lightweight blanket
1–5 day's K rations (depending on when supply drop last carried out)
Orange handkerchief (a Wingate invention on which was printed a
    map of Burma on both sides, and could be worn on the head as
    a recognition signal to friendly aircraft)

Matchet [machete] and sheath
Toggle rope
Entrenching tool
Clasp knife

In addition officers and British NCOs (in West African battalions) carried:

Wristwatch [in 1944 a privately owned wristwatch even by NCOs
    was by no means common, and they were issued]
Prismatic compass
Torch
Maps, pencils, notebooks, etc
Lightweight Jungle hammock

Wingate disapproved of both carrying anything not absolutely necessary and of every man wasting ten minutes a day shaving. So we all grew beards.

K Rations

At this time, in SEAC, there were no equivalents of the one-man ration pack familiar to generations of British soldiers since the Second World War. Several days' worth of standard army rations, such as Compo designed for ten men, or rice and dhal in the case of Indian troops, is difficult to split up satisfactorily among marching troops without a transport backup. There is a considerable difference between the feeding arrangements of troops on a regular line of supply, and operating in conditions that allow for food to be cooked centrally (perhaps by companies as in John Randle's description in Appendix A), and a group of men behind enemy lines whose culinary arrangements may be hurried, and where it is often a case of every man for himself. In these circumstances Wingate resorted to K Rations, for lack of anything better. The K Ration was designed to sustain assault troops for the first few days until a proper supply chain came into operation, and allowance should have been made for the fact that they were so deficient of calories and other nutrients that troops would suffer great hardship if kept on them for any length of time. The K Ration consisted of three meal packs in one box, as follows:

Breakfast pack

Fruit bar
A 4oz tin of bacon and hash
A small packet of biscuits
A packet of coffee powder (replaced in British packs by packet of
    tea, sugar and powdered milk)

Dinner or lunch pack

4oz tin of processed cheese
A packet of biscuits
A small pack of Dextrose tablets (so revolting that even the mules
    refused them, wrote one Chindit)
One packet of lemonade powder

Supper pack

4oz tin of meat loaf
Packet of biscuits
Chocolate bar
Packet of soap powder
Packet of cigarettes
Toilet paper

K Rations were very unappetizing, and remained so for well after the Second World War. In the author's experience K Rations were so loathed even by Americans that a British one-man ration pack could be bartered for almost any item of United States personal kit one could name.

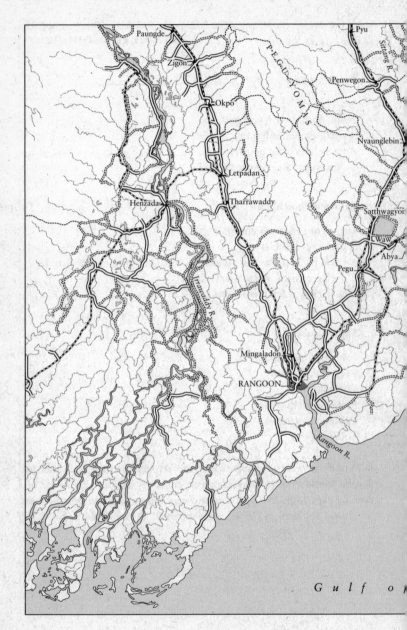

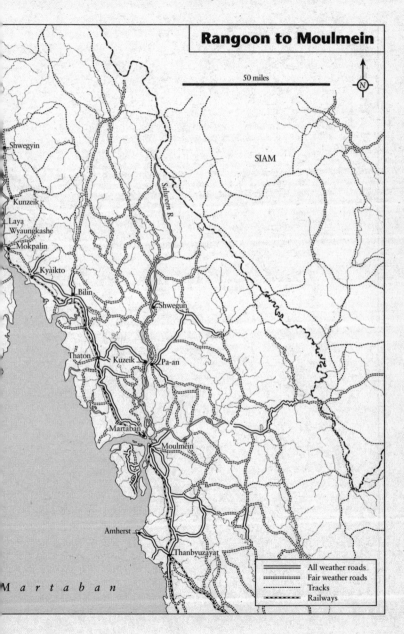

Rangoon to Moulmein

50 miles

N

SIAM

Shwegyin

Kunzeik

Laya
Wyaungkashe

Mokpalin

Kyaikto

Bilin

Shwegun

Salween R.

Thaton

Kuzeik

Pa-an

Martaban

Moulmein

Amherst

Thanbyuzayat

M a r t a b a n

All weather roads
Fair weather roads
Tracks
Railways

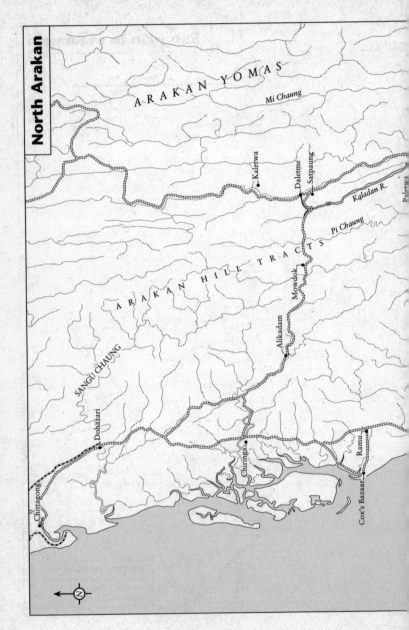

North Arakan

ARAKAN YOMAS

Mi Chaung

Kaletwa

Daletme

Satpaung

Kaladan R.

Paletwa

Pi Chaung

ARAKAN HILL TRACTS

Mowdok

Alikadam

SANGU CHAUNG

Dohazari

Chittagong

Chiringa

Ramu

Cox's Bazaar

N

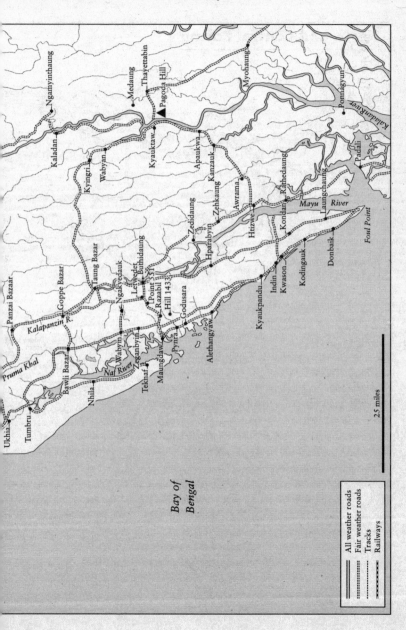

Ngamyinthaung

Medaung Thayetabin Pagoda Hill

Myohaung

Ponnagyun

Kaladan River

Kaladan

Kyingri Wabyan

Kyauktaw

Apaukwa

Kanzauk

Rathedaung

Padli

Awrama

Laungchaung

Mayu River

Foul Point

Zedidaung Zehkaung

Hparabyn

Htizwe

Kondan

Panzai Bazaar

Taung Bazaar

Ngakyedauk

Buthidaung

Letwedet

Point 552

Razabil

Hill 1433

Godusara

Indin

Kwason

Kodingauk

Donbaik

Goppe Bazar

Kalapanzin R.

Maungdaw

Wabyin

Zeganbyin

Pyinma

Alethangyaw

Kyaukpandu

Pruma Khal

Naf River

Teknaf

Bawli Bazar

Nhila

Tumbru

Ukhia

*Bay of
Bengal*

25 miles

All weather roads
Fair weather roads
Tracks
Railways

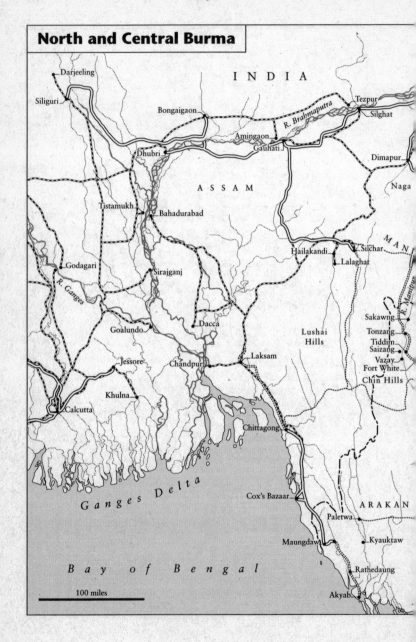

North and Central Burma

I N D I A

Darjeeling

Siliguri

Bongaigaon

Tezpur

R. Brahmaputra

Silghat

Amingaon

Dhubri

Gauhati

Dimapur

A S S A M

Naga

Tistamukh

Bahadurabad

Hailakandi

Silchar

M A N

Lalaghat

Godagari

R. Ganges

Sirajganj

R. Manipur

Sakawng

Dacca

Lushai
Hills

Tonzang
Tiddim
Saizang
Vazay
Fort White

Goalundo

Laksam

Jessore

Chandpur

Chin Hills

Khulna

Calcutta

Chittagong

G a n g e s   D e l t a

Cox's Bazaar

A R A K A N

Paletwa

Kyauktaw

Maungdaw

Rathedaung

B a y   o f   B e n g a l

Akyab

100 miles

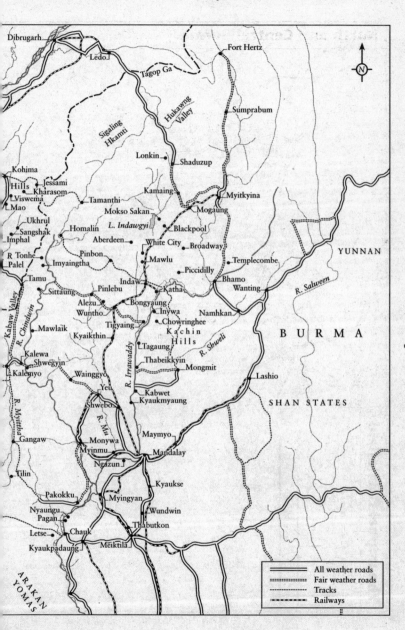

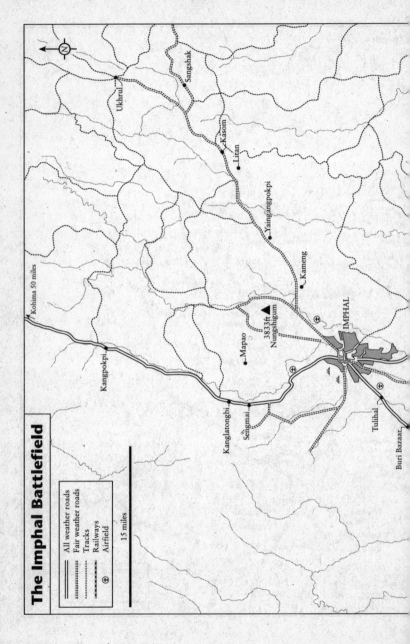

The Imphal Battlefield

All weather roads
Fair weather roads
Tracks
Railways
Airfield

15 miles

Kohima 50 miles

Ukhrul
Sangshak
Kasom
Litan
Yaingangpokpi
Kameng
Kangpokpi
Mapao
3833 ft
Nungshigum
Kanglatongbi
Sengmai
IMPHAL
Tulihal
Buri Bazaar

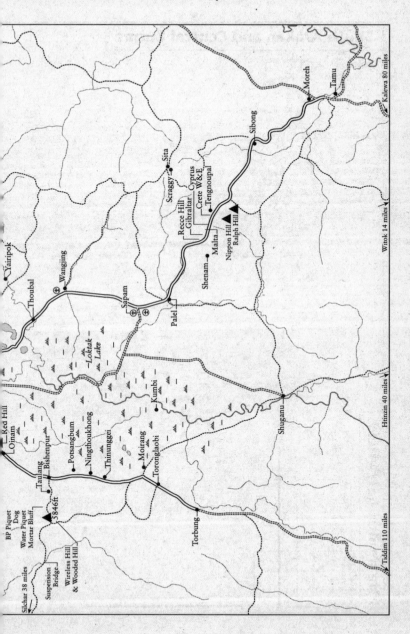

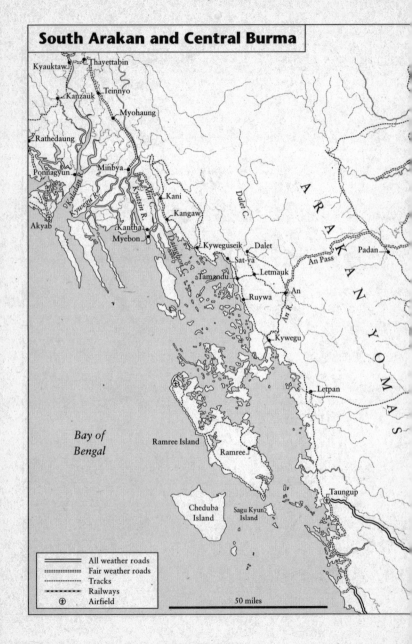

South Arakan and Central Burma

Kyauktaw
Thayettabin
Kanzauk
Teinnyo
Myohaung
Rathedaung
Ponnagyun
Minbya
Kani
Kangaw
Akyab
Kantha
Myebon
Kyweguseik
Dalet C.
Dalet
Sat-ya
Tamandu
Letmauk
An Pass
Padan
Ruywa
An
Kywegu

Kaladan R.
Kywegu R.
Kyatsin R.
Min R.
Daingbon
An R.

A R A K A N   Y O M A S

Bay of
Bengal

Letpan

Ramree Island
Ramree

Cheduba
Island
Sagu Kyun
Island

Taungup

All weather roads
Fair weather roads
Tracks
Railways
Airfield

50 miles

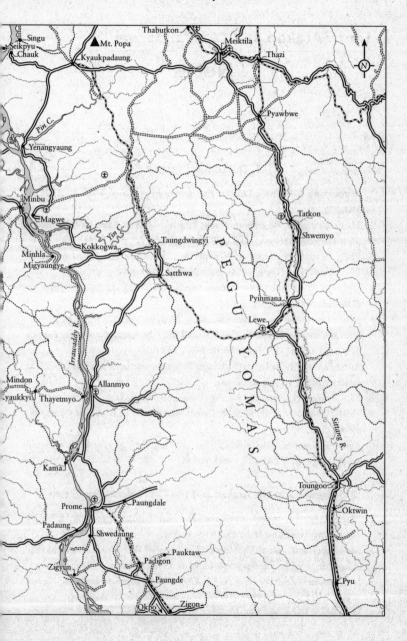

Notes

1. The Longest Retreat

1. James Lunt, *A Hell of a Licking: The Retreat from Burma 1941–42* (Collins, 1986), p. 30.
2. Major General S. Woodburn Kirby, *The War Against Japan*, vol. II, *India's Most Dangerous Hour* (HMSO, 1958), Appendix 2, pp. 440–41.
3. Philip Mason, *A Matter of Honour: An Account of the Indian Army, its Officers and Men* (Cape, 1974), pp. 490–91.
4. Ian Lyall Grant and Kazuo Tamayama, *Burma 1942: The Japanese Invasion* (The Zampi Press, 1999), p. 334.
5. John Masters, *The Road Past Mandalay* (Michael Joseph, 1963), pp. 157–8.
6. Slim at Chatham House in 1948. Quoted in Louis Allen, *Burma: The Longest War 1941–45* (J. M. Dent & Sons, 1984), p. 611.
7. Aung San was the father of Sun Aung San, who was until recently a political prisoner of the regime in Burma.
8. Pat Carmichael, *Mountain Battery* (Devin Books, 1983), p. 168.
9. Field Marshal Sir William Slim, *Defeat into Victory* (Cassell and Company, 1956), p. 110.
10. Julian Thompson, *The Imperial War Museum Book of War Behind Enemy Lines* (Sidgwick & Jackson, 1998), p. 141.

2. Striking back: The Arakan and the First Chindit Expedition

1. Major General S. Woodburn Kirby, *The War Against Japan*, vol. II, *India's Most Dangerous Hour* (HMSO, 1958), p. 351.
2. See for example, Julian Thompson, *The Imperial War Museum Book of War Behind Enemy Lines* (Sidgwick & Jackson, 1998), chapters 6, 7, and 8.
3. David Fraser, *And We Shall Shock Them: The British Army in the Second World War* (Sceptre, 1988), p. 299.
4. Woodburn Kirby, pp. 309–10.

5. Thompson, p. 253.
6. Field Marshal Sir William Slim, *Defeat into Victory* (Cassell and Company, 1956), p. 163.

3. The Arakan: Both Sides Take the Offensive

1. Anon., *History of the 5th Royal Gurkha Rifles (Frontier Force)*, vol. II, 1929–1947 (Gale & Polden, 1956), p. 364.
2. Field Marshal Sir William Slim, *Defeat into Victory* (Cassell and Company, 1956), p. 215.
3. Ronald Lewin, *Slim: The Standard Bearer* (Leo Cooper, 1976), p. 126.
4. John Masters, *The Road Past Mandalay* (Michael Joseph, 1963), p. 157.
5. George Macdonald Fraser, *Quartered Safe Out Here: A Recollection of the War In Burma* (HarperCollins, 1992), p. xiv.
6. Fraser, pp. 36–7.
7. This statement is my own conclusion, based on my reading of the Japanese thinking that had they been successful in the Arakan they would not have been held back. I believe the British also feared an invasion of India at the time.
8. Slim, p. 240.
9. Major General S. Woodburn Kirby, *The War Against Japan*, vol. III, *The Decisive Battles* (HMSO, 1961), p. 150.

4. The Arakan: Kaladan Valley and Victory on the Maungdaw–Buthidaung Road

1. Field Marshal Sir William Slim, *Defeat into Victory* (Cassell and Company, 1956), p. 245.
2. Slim, pp. 246–7.

5. The Japanese Main Assault: Kohima

1. O. G. W. White, *Straight on to Tokyo: The War History of The 2nd Battalion The Dorsetshire Regiment (54th Foot)* (Gale and Polden, 1948), p. 77.
2. This discrimination included Indian King's Commissioned officers not being invited to social events in Malaya and being banned from travelling in compartments reserved for Europeans in trains.
3. Tony Gould, *Imperial Warriors: Britain and the Gurkhas* (Granta Books, 1999), pp. 269–71. Hari Chand Badhwar later became a major general in the Indian army after Independence, and Dhargalkar a lieutenant general.

4. Major General S. Woodburn Kirby, *The War Against Japan*, vol. III, *The Decisive Battles* (HMSO, 1961), pp. 191–2.

5. Field Marshal Sir William Slim, *Defeat into Victory* (Cassell and Company, 1956), p. 311.

6. White, pp. 92–5.

7. White, p. 98.

8. White, p. 115.

6. The Japanese Main Assault: Imphal

1. W. J. P. Aggett, *The Bloody Eleventh: History of the Devonshire Regiment*, vol. III, *1915–1969* (The Devonshire and Dorset Regiment, 1995), pp. 341–3.

2. Aggett, p. 343.

3. Aggett, p. 347.

4. Aggett, p. 341.

5. C. J. N. Mackay, *A History of the 4th Prince of Wales's Own Gurkha Rifles*, vol. III, *1938–1948* (William Blackwood & Sons, 1952), p. 189.

6. Field Marshal Sir William Slim, *Defeat into Victory* (Cassell and Company, 1956), p. 337.

7. Slim, p. 334.

8. Winston S. Churchill, *The Second World War*, vol. III, *The Grand Alliance* (Cassell and Company), p. 539.

7. The Second Chindit Expedition

1. 'Gurkas are not subject to mass suggestion, but require careful training, familiar leadership, and love'. John Masters, *The Road Past Mandalay* (Michael Joseph, 1963), p. 151.

2. Stevens, G. R., *History of the 2nd King Edward VII's Own Goorkha Rifles*, vol. II, *1938–1948*, p. 199.

3. Stevens, pp. 231–2.

4. The C-47 Dakota, the great workhorse of the Second World War and for years after, had one door, and could carry twenty paratroopers or a few more troops in the air-landing role, and had a radius of action of 450 miles (350 miles towing the US glider). The C-46 Commando had two doors, carried forty paratroopers, and had a radius of action of 500 miles. Twenty C-46s carried a lift equivalent to thirty C-47s.

5. Julian Thompson, *The Imperial War Museum Book of War Behind Enemy Lines* (Sidgwick & Jackson, 1998), pp. 186–7.

6. Field Marshal Sir William Slim, *Defeat into Victory* (Cassell and Company, 1956), p. 261.

7. Slim, pp. 269–70.

8. Charlton Ogburn, *The Marauders* (Harper, New York, 1959), p. 279.

9. Slim, p. 384.

10. Alex Danchev and Daniel Todman (eds), *War Diaries: 1939–1945, Field Marshal Lord Alanbrooke* (Weidenfeld & Nicolson, 2001), p. 404.

11. Ronald Lewin, *Slim: The Standard Bearer* (Leo Cooper, 1976), p. 161.

12. Letter from Slim to General Sir Geoffrey Scoones dated 20 May 1956, in Scoones papers, Department of Documents, Imperial War Museum, Accession Number 96/43/1, quoted in Thompson, p. 418.

13. Masters, p. 211.

14. See Thompson, p. 256.

15. See Thompson, p. 253.

16. Thompson, Appendix B, p. 430.

8. The Battle of the Irrawaddy Shore: Mandalay and Meiktila

1. Field Marshal Sir William Slim, *Defeat into Victory* (Cassell and Company, 1956), p. 374.

2. Slim, p. 384.

3. Alex Danchev and Daniel Todman (eds), *War Diaries: 1939–1945, Field Marshal Lord Alanbrooke* (Weidenfeld & Nicolson, 2001), p. 613.

4. Slim, p. 413.

5. Slim. p. 429.

6. John Masters, *The Road Past Mandalay* (Michael Joseph, 1963), p. 303.

7. Major General S. Woodburn Kirby, *The War Against Japan*, vol. IV, *The Reconquest of Burma* (HMSO, 1965), p. 313.

9. The Arakan – A Watery Maze

1. G. R. Stevens, *History of the 2nd King Edward VII's Own Goorkha Rifles*, vol. II, *1921–1948* (Gale & Polden, 1952), p. 255.

2. Stevens, p. 240.

3. Then yes, but not since 1994. See the Glossary.

11. The Rangoon Road and the Final Act

1. Field Marshal Sir William Slim, *Defeat into Victory* (Cassell and Company, 1956), p. 496.
2. Slim, p. 496.
3. John Masters, *The Road Past Mandalay* (Michael Joseph, 1963), p. 303.
4. Alex Danchev and Daniel Todman (eds), *War Diaries: 1939–1945, Field Marshal Lord Alanbrooke* (Weidenfeld & Nicholson, 2001), p. 692.
5. Danchev and Todman, *War Diaries*, p. 698.
6. Danchev and Todman, *War Diaries*, p. 700.
7. Philip Ziegler, *Mountbatten: The Official Biography* (Collins, 1985).

Appendix A

1. Philip Mason, *A Matter of Honour: An Account of the Indian Army, its Officers and Men* (Jonathan Cape, 1974), p. 127.

Illustrations

Number 14. The author is grateful to Lieutenant Colonel Murray, Queen's Own Cameron Highlanders, for information about this picture. The 1st Camerons played a significant part in the Kohima battle, especially breaking through the roadblock at milestone 37½ on 14 April, and capturing the Naga Village on the night 4/5 May 1944.

The bathing facilities were provided by the 2nd Division Mobile Bath Unit, an ad hoc unit formed by the 2nd Division without any support from 33rd Corps or Fourteenth Army. The men in the unit were found from those too old or infirm to serve in infantry battalions. After the bather had finished soaping himself in the half oil drum, each named after a film star, he was hosed down with hot water, dried himself, and was ready for the fray. When the Bath Unit was in operation during the Battle of Kohima, a complete change of clothing was issued regardelss of rank. Later during the advance into Burma, the length of the line of communication precluded the issue of fresh clothing.

This picture was probably taken at Wetlet, south-east of Shwebo, and about thirty miles west of the Irrawaddy, in late January 1945, during the events described in Chapter 8.

Bibliography

Aggett, W. J. P, *The Bloody Eleventh: History of the Devonshire Regiment*, Vol. III, *1915–1969* (The Devonshire and Dorset Regiment, 1995)

Allen, Louis, *Burma: The Longest War 1941–45* (J. M. Dent & Sons Ltd, 1984)

Anderson, Duncan, *Slim*, in *Churchills' Generals*, edited by John Keegan, (Warner Books, 1993)

Anon., *History of the 5th Royal Gurkha Rifles (Frontier Force)*, Vol. II, *1929–1947* (Gale & Polden, 1956)

Barclay, Brigadier C. N., *The Regimental History of the 3rd Queen Alexandria's Own Gurkha Rifles*, Vol. II (William Clowes and Sons Limited, 1953)

Bidwell, Shelford, *The Chindit War: The Campaign in Burma 1944* (Hodder & Stoughton, 1979)

Carmichael, Pat, *Mountain Battery* (Devin Books, 1983)

Colvin, John, *Not Ordinary Men: The Story of the Battle of Kohima* (Leo Cooper, 1994)

Fergusson, Bernard, *The Trumpet in the Hall* (Collins, 1970)

Fraser, David, *And We Shall Shock Them: The British Army in the Second World War* (Sceptre, 1988)

Gould, Tony, *Imperial Warriors: Britain and the Gurkhas* (Granta Books, 1999)

Hickey, Michael, *The Unforgettable Army: Slim's XIVth Army in Burma* (Spellmount, 1992)

Lewin, Ronald, *Slim: The Standard bearer* (Leo Cooper, 1976)

Lunt, James, *A Hell of a Licking: The Retreat from Burma 1941–2* (Collins, 1986)

Lyall Grant, Ian, *Burma: The Turning Point* (The Zampi Press, 1993)

Lyall Grant, Ian, and Kazuo Tamayama, *Burma 1942: The Japanese Invasion* (The Zampi Press, 1999)

Mackay, C. J. N., *A History of the 4th Prince of Wales's Own Gurkha Rifles*, Vol. III, *1938–1948* (William Blackwood & Sons, 1952)

Mackay, C. J. N., *History of 7th Duke of Edinburgh's Own Gurkha Rifles* (William Blackwood & Sons, 1962)

Mason, Philip, *A Matter of Honour: An Account of the Indian Army, its Officers and Men* (Jonathan Cape, 1974)

Masters, John, *The Road Past Mandalay: A Personal Narrative* (Michael Joseph, 1963)

Mountbatten, Vice-Admiral Earl, *Report to the Combined Chiefs of Staff by the Supreme Allied Commander South-East Asia, 1943–1945* (HMSO, 1951)

Seaman, Harry, *The Battle at Sangshak: Burma 1944* (Leo Cooper, 1989)

Slim, Field Marshal Sir William, *Defeat into Victory* (Cassell and Company, 1956)

Smurthwaite, David (ed), *The Forgotten War: The British Army in the Far East 1941–1945* (National Army Museum, 1992)

Stevens, G. R., *History of the 2nd King Edward VII's Own Goorkha Rifles*, Vol. II, *1921–1948* (Gale and Polden, 1952).

Swinson, Arthur, *Kohima* (Cassell, 1966)

Thompson, Julian, *The Imperial War Museum Book of War Behind Enemy Lines* (Sidgwick & Jackson, 1998)

White, O. G. W., *Straight on to Tokyo: The War History of the 2nd Battalion The Dorsetshire Regiment (54th Foot)* (Gale & Polden, 1948).

Woodburn Kirby, S., *The War Against Japan*, Vol. II, *India's Most Dangerous Hour* (HMSO, 1958)

——, *The War Against Japan*, Vol. III, *The Decisive Battles* (HMSO, 1961)

——, *The War Against Japan*, Vol. IV, *The Reconquest of Burma* (HMSO, 1965)

Ziegler, Philip, *Mountbatten: The Official Biography* (Collins, 1985)

Index of Contributors

This index serves two purposes: it lists those whose writings or recordings are here quoted and gives due acknowledgement to the copyright holders who have kindly allowed the publication of material held in the Museum's collections. If the copyright owner is not the contributor, their name appears in round brackets after the contributor with whom they are associated. Where the papers quoted are not contained in a collection under the contributor's name, but form part of another collection, this is indicated in round brackets. Every effort has been made to trace copyright owners; the Museum would be grateful for any information which might help trace those whose indentities or addresses are not known. The number in square brackets is the accession number in the collection.

Ranks are as they were at the time of the experiences described. Decorations are not shown.

Department of Documents

Sound Archive

Index

(Note: page numbers in **bold** refer to maps)